MW01030896

Praise for *Crossing Broadway*—

"Far too many people still view Washington Heights through the prism of
the recent past. Crime, drugs, and rampant lawlessness—all of which scarred
the neighborhood in the late '80s and early '90s—are the first things that come
to mind. In fact, Washington Heights has emerged phoenix-like from the
ashes of the crack years and is experiencing a renaissance that is reshaping and
redefining the community. *Crossing Broadway* tells the complete and true story
of this much-maligned neighborhood with erudition, élan, and the soft touch
of personal attachment. Robert W. Snyder's book is a testament to the tenac-
ity, dynamism, and vitality of the people who have made Washington Heights
their home. If you want to truly understand Washington Heights, then *Crossing
Broadway* is an absolute must-read."
—**Led Black, writer, filmmaker, and editor-in-chief of
www.UptownCollective.com**

"*Crossing Broadway* gives an immediate sense of the transformation of urban
life since World War II, especially the 'urban crisis' of the 1960s and 1970s and
its aftermath. A skillful writer, Robert W. Snyder has constructed a strong, engaging narrative that covers a long sweep of history, balancing big themes with
closely told stories of everyday life."
—**Joshua B. Freeman, Distinguished Professor of History, CUNY Graduate
Center, author of *American Empire, 1945–2000: The Rise of a Global
Power, the Democratic Revolution at Home***

"*Crossing Broadway* is a terrific book that successfully links the story of immigrant communities and ethnic succession in Washington Heights to the larger
history of the city of New York and the nation at large. Robert W. Snyder shows
how the topography of northern Manhattan reinforced boundaries of race,
class, and ethnicity and made efforts to unite the community around common
interests more difficult. He usefully reminds us that history is made, not by
impersonal forces such as deindustrialization or market revitalization, but by
the actions of individuals who, in the case of Washington Heights, remade their
city in the face of capital flight, crime, and community abandonment."
—**Eric C. Schneider, University of Pennsylvania, author of
*Smack: Heroin and the American City***

CROSSING BROADWAY

CROSSING BROADWAY

WASHINGTON HEIGHTS AND THE PROMISE OF NEW YORK CITY

ROBERT W. SNYDER

CORNELL UNIVERSITY PRESS
Ithaca and London

Copyright © 2015 by Cornell University

All rights reserved. Except for brief quotations in a review, this
book, or parts thereof, must not be reproduced in any form without
permission in writing from the publisher. For information, address
Cornell University Press, Sage House, 512 East State Street, Ithaca,
New York 14850. Visit our website at cornellpress.cornell.edu.

First published 2015 by Cornell University Press

First paperback printing 2019

Library of Congress Cataloging-in-Publication Data

Snyder, Robert W., 1955– author.
   Crossing Broadway : Washington Heights and the promise of New
York City / Robert W. Snyder.
      pages cm
   Includes bibliographical references and index.
   ISBN 978-0-8014-4961-1 (cloth)
   ISBN 978-1-5017-4684-0 (pbk.)
   1. Washington Heights (New York, N.Y.)—Social conditions—20th
century. I. Title.
   F128.68.W2S69   2015
   974.7'1—dc23   2014016070

For Clara, Max, and Allison

and

in memory of Max and Mildred Snyder

CONTENTS

CROSSING BROADWAY

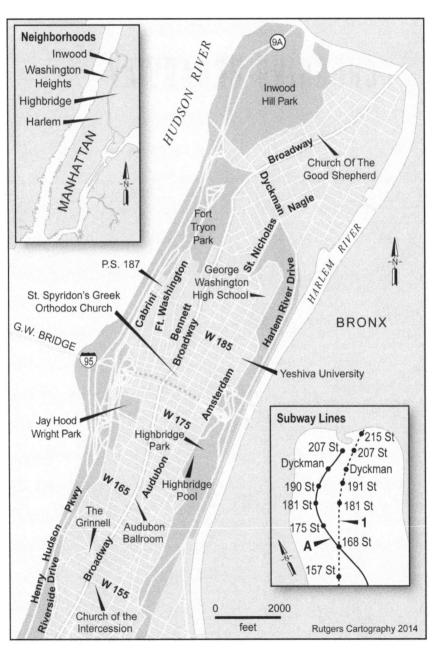

Figure 1: Washington Heights in the New York Metropolitan Area. Map by Michael Siegel, Rutgers Cartography, 2014.

PROLOGUE
A PLACE I THOUGHT I KNEW

WHEN CRACK DEALERS TOOK OVER blocks in the northern Manhattan neighborhood of Washington Heights in the 1980s, one of the first things to go was places for kids to play. Dealers set up shop in apartments, seized upper floors for their lookouts, and made sure that no street games interfered with customers who drove into the neighborhood. Sidewalks became dangerous. Parents kept their children indoors. The drug trade cast a shadow over the entire neighborhood, and certain blocks looked as though they would become close to uninhabitable.

Two neighborhood activists set to work reclaiming the streets. Dave Crenshaw, an African American, and Al Kurland, whose mother was a Jewish refugee from Nazi-occupied France, knew that there were good kids and concerned parents on blocks dominated by drug dealers. Together, the two men organized local teens to clean up a grimy playground at 165th Street and Edgecombe Avenue so the public could use it again. By day, African American, Dominican, and Puerto Rican kids played basketball. At night, families watched movies while Explorer Scouts grilled and sold hot dogs.[1] Danger was never far away, though, so they taught their kids what to do if they were caught in a shootout: dive to the sidewalk and lie flat until the shooting stops. More than once, gunshots forced kids to put the drill into practice.[2]

Crenshaw, Kurland, and their neighbors struggled through the crack years, when soaring murder rates in New York City raised the specter of a city that would expire in spasms of gang violence. From the northern Bronx to the Rockaways in Queens, people wondered if their neighborhood would collapse and if their city was condemned to endless blight. Nowhere did such fears loom larger than in Washington Heights.

I took the neighborhood's problems personally and professionally. I was born in 1955 and lived the first year of my life in Washington Heights. In 1956 my parents moved to the New Jersey suburbs, but I grew up on their stories of our old neighborhood. They affectionately described Washington Heights as a great place for working people, with cheap rents, beautiful parks, and good subway connections. To my parents, life in the New York of the 1950s—a city of strong public institutions shaped by the New Deal—was confirmation that a city life was a good life. Although my early years were strongly influenced by suburban life—during a return visit to the neighborhood at the age of three I was badly rattled by the sound of sirens and was sure that walking into the lobby of our old apartment building was tantamount to burglary—my parents' tales eventually won me over, and I came to consider Washington Heights part of my family geography.

As a teenager in the 1960s and 1970s, my occasional walks through the western Heights on visits to the Cloisters convinced me that the neighborhood was still a fairly happy place. In 1980, however, when I interviewed elderly Irish Americans in northern Manhattan for a graduate school course in oral history, many of their recent stories revolved around fear of crime and the unease they felt at sharing their streets with Spanish-speaking neighbors. My sense of Washington Heights' serenity was further shaken in 1983, when I served as an alternate juror in a trial for the murder of an elderly woman at 712 W. 175th Street, about ten blocks south of where my parents had lived. Then, in July 1986, I read in the *New York Times* how U.S. Attorney Rudolph W. Giuliani and U.S. Senator Alfonse D'Amato, in disguise, had ventured to Washington Heights to demonstrate the ease of buying crack in northern Manhattan. From that point on, it seemed to me, lurid news stories depicted Washington Heights as the crack capital of New York City.[3] From afar, I asked myself: How did a good neighborhood get so bad? And how had fear of crime come to dominate politics, journalism, and everyday life in New York City? My parents' stories, still filed in my memory, came to look more like nostalgia than a depiction of the possibilities of contemporary urban life.

If Washington Heights had come to seem somewhat alien, and parts of it had become frankly dangerous, somehow there was always something that drew me back to its streets. In September 1989, at the height of the crack epidemic, I returned to northern Manhattan on a fellowship from the Gannett

Center for Media Studies at Columbia University to study how crime reporting depicted Washington Heights. Over nine months I patrolled with the police, read community newspapers, interviewed residents, and discovered much more about life in northern Manhattan. I also learned that there was more to the Heights than crime. Although the whole neighborhood had a bad reputation, and fear was indeed widespread, I found out that the drug dealers were concentrated in limited areas. The dangers were real, but so too was the vigor of the neighborhood and the doggedness of its residents who held tight and made lives for themselves. Still, the police warned me to wear a bulletproof vest if I accompanied them east of Broadway, the avenue that has long been the neighborhood's sharpest dividing line, into drug dealers' turf.[4]

For several years I became active in Beth Am, The People's Temple—a small but dynamic Reform synagogue in Washington Heights whose social action committee tried to bring together Jews and Dominicans to improve local public schools. Around that time, after talking to so many people and doing massive amounts of research in police and city data, I began to think of writing a book that would tell the story of the neighborhood and its people. There were fantastic stories to tell and numerous citizens who deserved to take place in the history of twentieth-century New York City. But I set aside the idea of writing at length about the neighborhood for a good long while. Convinced that Washington Heights would never escape the shadows of crime, poverty, and ethnic tensions, I didn't want to write a story about my parents' old home with a sad ending. And in the early 1990s I just couldn't imagine a good future for Washington Heights.

It turned out that I was wrong about what would become of Washington Heights. And while I didn't know it, the people who would help make the Heights a better place—like Dave Crenshaw and Al Kurland—were already living and working there even as I formed and stuck to my negative impressions.

My change of mind began in 2003, when Regina Gradess, a friend from Beth Am, encouraged me to check out all the changes in northern Manhattan. I took a long walk around Washington Heights, thumbed through an optimistic local newspaper called the *Manhattan Times*, and finished my short visit intrigued by the sense of ease on streets once dominated by the crack trade. Seeking to blend exercise and research, in 2004 I entered a foot race called Salsa, Blues and Shamrocks sponsored by Coogan's, a local bar and restaurant. On race day, we ran up avenues lined by musicians playing Jewish klezmer music, rhythm and blues, salsa, and Irish ballads. On one block after another, I was struck by how the ethnic groups that once seemed to be at war with each other were getting along—at least for the day.

Convinced that what was happening in Washington Heights was important and worth explaining, I dug into books, municipal reports, and newspaper clippings. I spent hours walking up and down the sidewalks of northern
Manhattan. I unearthed my old notes from days in squad cars and nights
in meetings at Beth Am. My parents' stories of their years in Washington
Heights were never far from my mind.

New York has plenty of neighborhoods that stand for things larger than themselves: Harlem and the African American experience, the Lower East Side and
immigration, Greenwich Village and the bohemian life, Times Square and
popular culture. Such levels of fame have so far eluded Washington Heights.[5]
Indeed, it is not hard to see why. New York is so big and complicated that no
neighborhood is a perfect microcosm of the entire city. Nevertheless, if you
want to understand how New York City weathered the passage from the New
Deal to the urban crisis to twenty-first-century globalization, there is no better vantage point than Washington Heights.

In the decades after World War II, an industrial seaport dominated by
European immigrants and their children became a multiracial metropolis
renewed by African Americans from the South, by Puerto Ricans, and from
the 1960s on by immigrants from Latin America, Asia, and the Caribbean.
A city of dynamic capitalism, ethnic tribalism, and ever-wider gaps between
rich and poor, New York passed from the New Deal to the new Gilded Age.[6]
These trends were already brewing in the 1950s when my parents lived at 550
Fort Washington Avenue, just north of West 185th Street. On street corners
and in subway cars, in apartment hallways and in public meetings, people in
Washington Heights asked themselves the kinds of questions that concerned
all New Yorkers. What are crime and fear doing to the city? What will happen
to kids who grow up here? In a neighborhood of many ethnic groups and
many formal and informal boundaries, people wondered about how to place
themselves in Washington Heights, in New York City, and in the wider world.
Digging into their history helps us understand not only the past—crowded
as it is with nostalgia, false lessons, and hidden heroes—but also the best and
worst possibilities of our urban future.

The radical geographer David Harvey, drawing on the American sociologist Robert Park and the French urban theorist Henri Lefebvre, has influ-
entially argued that "the right to the city" is "one of the most precious yet
most neglected of human rights." It is more than a property right, Harvey
argues, and more than a right to resources. Indeed, it is nothing less than a
collective "right to change ourselves while changing the city."[7] Like Park and

Lefebvre, Harvey recognizes that the desire to remake the city and ourselves can founder on the worst aspects of human behavior. Cities can be wracked by social segregation, and they can easily become places that do not foster our best selves. As Harvey acknowledges, "the right to the city is an empty signifier. Everything depends on who gets to fill it with meaning."[8]

The Washington Heights residents I interviewed never uttered the phrase "the right to the city," but it captures the passions and complexities of their lives from the New Deal to the present. By experience, they knew that the right to the city is never won easily. The first step—escaping from a murderous dictator (like Jews or Dominicans) or rejecting a life of rural poverty (like the Irish and African Americans) was hard enough. Once settled into New York City, poor and working-class residents of Washington Heights grappled with jobs that could leave calluses on their hands and bruises on their souls. For most of them, however, the effort was worth it because the promise of New York—a chance at changing your life with hard work and a little luck—came true often enough that it seemed like a worthwhile effort.

Only intermittently did residents of Washington Heights think of anything like the right to the city as a collective right to be exercised by the majority for the good of all. Far more often, they were inclined to think of their city in narrower ways shaped by the logics of race and ethnicity. Although they didn't phrase it this way, in essence they asked themselves: What does the right to the city mean? Is the neighborhood turf to be defended against outsiders? A market or an asset to be cultivated for financial gain? Or a community to be enjoyed in common by all? In confronting these questions, residents of Washington Heights wrestled with the vast social and economic forces that remade their neighborhood and New York City in the second half of the twentieth century. They also faced an inner struggle with their own cosmopolitanism and their own loyalties to turf and tribe.

In a neighborhood of immigrants and migrants, there were bound to be differences over what it meant to have a better future. Some people defined it modestly: a move from the simple apartment on the east side of Broadway to a fancier one on the west side of Broadway. Others had grander visions: a move to a single-family home in the New Jersey suburbs. Others defined a good future, in ugly and exclusive ways, as a neighborhood with no African Americans or Jews or Dominicans. (All of these attempts at exclusion failed.)

Whatever their many differences, Washington Heights residents were roused to action when they saw a threat to the future of their neighborhood. They awakened from their everyday lives—sometimes for better, sometimes for worse—when they sensed the possibility that they, or their children, might have a lesser future than they had imagined.

In its perch atop Manhattan, Washington Heights is set between Harlem to the south and Inwood to the north, and bounded by the Hudson River to the west and the Harlem River to the east. The neighborhood has long been home to migrants, immigrants, and their children. Since the early twentieth century, the Heights has been a neighborhood of ethnic enclaves. In the 1930s and 1940s, it was noted for its German Jewish population. Today, it is the home of the largest Dominican community in the United States. The combination of diverse ethnic communities and the rough topography of Washington Heights—with its great ridges and hillside streets—encourages sharp and territorial visions of community and identity. Depending on the era, Broadway has been a boundary between white and black, Irish and Jewish, affluent and poor, Dominican-born and American-born.

Listening to my parents, it seemed like Washington Heights was a place where everyone got along. But of course there were divisions and their memories were partial. A global neighborhood before the word "globalization" was in vogue, Washington Heights took shape at the intersection of streams of migration that stretched from Germany, Greece, Ireland, Russia, Poland, Cuba, Puerto Rico, the American South, and the Dominican Republic. Its sidewalks echoed the accents of Frankfurt shopkeepers, African American farmers, Greek florists, Irish transit workers, Russian artists, and Dominican revolutionaries. On opposite sides of Broadway, Jewish refugees from Hitler found new homes three blocks from an apartment building that housed Paul Robeson and Thurgood Marshall. Over time, one building, the Audubon Theatre and Ballroom on Broadway at 165th Street, was the setting of vaudeville shows, a Jewish synagogue, transit workers' union meetings, the Spanish-language San Juan Theater, and the assassination of Malcolm X.

Whatever their differences and whenever they lived there, the Irish, Jews, Greeks, Cubans, African Americans, Puerto Ricans, and Dominicans from Washington Heights tell virtually the same story: it was a neighborhood where your life was defined by the little world of your block and its immediate surroundings. At its best, a local life—with people who spoke your language, with a church or synagogue around the corner, with a bar or bakery down the street, in a neighborhood gilded with river views and green parks—was intimate and nourishing. Yet most inhabitants of Washington Heights lived with highly defined boundaries and with limited knowledge of other groups. At their worst, enclaves bred exclusion and compounded the problems that in time tore the neighborhood apart. Living in almost self-contained two- or three-square-block cantons blinded residents to concerns that they shared with people who lived ten blocks away. Isolated from one another, these enclaves could not command the power or the resources to change neighborhood conditions.

New York has long been invigorated by the tension between the parochial desire to stick with your own kind and the cosmopolitan street smarts that come from learning to navigate the changes you can see on a ten-block walk through Manhattan. Washington Heights was unique not in its parochial tendencies (which appear in all New York neighborhoods) but in the ways that its topography—which could be beautiful—reinforced ethnic isolation. Washington Heights today also stands out for overcoming—or at least outlasting—urban problems.

In the great changes that swept the Heights from the 1940s onward, the neighborhood's ethnic mix changed, its economic health declined, and its crime rate increased. Then came the horror of the crack years. As crime rose, people who couldn't escape to the suburbs hunkered down and prayed for the storm to pass. Fear turned neighbors into threatening strangers. Isolation made it hard to recognize shared interests. Residents had limited collective leverage to shape the circumstances that diminished their lives. Street life and public culture, the sources of New York's vitality, became tense and precarious.

The heroes of Washington Heights stepped out of their familiar worlds to work in new ways with new people and unfamiliar communities. In a neighborhood where so many people lived "parallel lives," only ten blocks apart yet oblivious to one another, those who made a better future possible were the bridge builders who had the imagination to understand that others shared their hopes and fears.[9] In actions big and small, they fought for a generous and inclusive right to the city. Indeed, in all their struggles to get anything done about crime, decaying parks, poor housing, and inadequate schools, people had to expand their allegiances, commitment, and visions. First they had to find allies in their neighborhood; then they had to find resources outside the neighborhood to improve conditions. Both were difficult to achieve. New York politics, after all, emphasizes tribe and turf. And, beginning in the fiscal crisis of the 1970s, the city's formerly expansive liberal vision shrank into a cramped and crabbed version of its older self. Shattered political horizons discouraged thinking about any kind of larger good. Federal policies turned away from cities, leaving them to struggle with problems far too large to address on their own.

In Washington Heights, beleaguered residents fought back. Inspired by everything from anger at deteriorating local conditions to the advice of radical elders, Crenshaw, Kurland, and others built coalitions across racial boundaries to fight for better schools and housing, to reduce crime, and to reclaim public space. As the streets became safer, people could walk the sidewalks and visit their parks. There, they could encounter each other not as threatening strangers but as New Yorkers with whom they might have something in common—even if it was nothing more than a desire for fresh air on a sunny day.

People in Washington Heights in the 1980s and 1990s developed what the sociologist Robert J. Sampson calls "collective efficacy"—a sense of "social cohesion" that meshed with a well-grounded expectation that when things went wrong, they could count on people in the neighborhood to help set them right. (Figuring out the difference between wrong and right was no easy thing in a heterogeneous neighborhood. People who over the years tried to keep religious, racial, or ethnic groups out of Washington Heights thought they were in fact doing something good for their neighborhood.) The collective efficacy of Washington Heights was less regimented than anything that could be called unity and more impersonal than anything that could be called warm-hearted neighborliness. It was manifested in things like helping a stranger in distress, calling the police to report a crime, or going to public meetings. It was not achieved consistently across the neighborhood, and, in order to be effective, it often needed to be matched by larger civic or governmental powers. But it was attained in enough places to revive the neighborhood in difficult times and to sustain it long enough to enjoy the better times that came to New York City in the late 1990s and early 2000s.[10]

Indeed, forging collective efficacy in Washington Heights involved turning one of its foremost characteristics—its density—into an asset. Unlike residents of the suburbs or of city neighborhoods made of single-family homes, people in Washington Heights found the raw materials of collective efficacy close at hand. It was the density and diversity of life in Washington Heights that made a short walk a journey into another world. People who recoiled from that lived in isolation. People who embraced the neighborhood's fragmentary geography with the goal of finding allies could find partners in neighbors, nonprofit organizations, religious institutions, and elected officials. Together, they sustained Washington Heights during the economic decay of the 1970s and the violence of the crack years. This book is, at its heart, the story of how that sense of collective efficacy was formed, endured trials, and helped Washington Heights recover. Today, the neighborhood is a symbol, in New York City and beyond, of bustling energy, cultural vitality, and the transforming power of immigration.

In its close brushes with disaster, the history of Washington Heights shows how human action can avert terrible possibilities; the story that follows has its share of people who can stake a reasonable claim to being heroes. Yet neighborhood activists alone could not revive a neighborhood. In decades of struggles against crime, poverty, housing decay, and inadequate schools, improvements in Washington Heights usually rested on support from larger entities of local, state, and federal government. In an age when federal support for cities has declined, and a global economy creates international forms of inequality and interdependence, Washington Heights—indeed, New York City—often wrestled with problems that were well beyond residents' control. Those larger trends are critical features of any history of the Heights that does not devolve into nostalgia or fodder for neighborhood boosters and real estate developers.

Since the 1970s, some of the strongest ideas in politics and government treat society as a marketplace and human beings as narrowly economic creatures who seek only to increase individual gain. Yet the liberals, radicals, Democrats, and public-spirited residents who sustained Washington Heights through its hardest years fought for a richer vision.[11] Part of that vision was a sense that the neighborhood, indeed the city, was something to be shared by its citizens. The political and intellectual foundation for their struggles was a mixed inheritance that dated to the era of the New Deal. As contemporary historians have noted, the problems of postwar American cities—and Washington Heights—can be traced to patterns of racial and economic inequality that emerged during the Depression and World War II. Yet the era of the New Deal also produced some good ideas and institutions—like Social Security—that sustained people in Washington Heights and helped them recover from the years of the urban crisis. As unfettered markets increased the gap between rich and poor, other institutions, policies, and organizations worked to support common standards of living. As the New Deal order receded ever further into the past, residents of Washington Heights worked in their own ways to sustain a vision of New York City where government, public institutions, and communal efforts nourished the best of the human spirit and protected people from social and economic forces far beyond individual control. They did not preserve the neighborhood of La Guardia and the New Deal in amber. Sometimes, they had to overcome racial inequalities from those years. Sometimes, they worked to restore amenities like parks that were opened during the New Deal. More often, they toiled to create new institutions and new alliances—in everything from community organizations to housing cooperatives to new public schools—to meet the demands of difficult times.

In their labors, the peoples of Washington Heights took the neighborhood as far as they could from crisis into recovery. In the end, however, they achieved an incomplete victory. As Heights residents often observe, the recovery that they started has brought a gentrification that threatens to price out the people who sustained the neighborhood through its most difficult years. Whether that transforms the neighborhood, or instead fosters a new but recognizable middle-class community that includes the children of Dominican immigrants, is not yet clear. Washington Heights, like the rest of New York City, is a place that confounds simple predictions.

Still, as the years of crack and high crime become a distant memory, some things are clear. My intuitions that began to take shape in 2004 have proven true: Washington Heights has survived and the sad tale that I had once believed was the unavoidable story of the neighborhood turned out to be only a chapter, albeit a terrible one, in the larger account. In preparing this book, across hours of interviews and days spent in the New York City archives, I learned that the neighborhood my parents recalled so fondly had more problems than they remembered. More important, I also learned that the people in Washington Heights have long had greater strengths than I ever imagined.

CHAPTER 1

AN ORDINARY NEIGHBORHOOD
IN AN EXTRAORDINARY CITY

AT THE NORTHERN END OF MANHATTAN ISLAND, the landscape has always been more than a physical setting. For centuries, it has been something that people worked with and against to define their identities, their possibilities, and their ways of life in changing times.

Upper Manhattan is long and narrow. Two great ridges run south to north, leaving a valley between them. The western ridge overlooks the Hudson River; the eastern ridge looks down on the Harlem River. Both ridges end at Dyckman Street. The land north of Dyckman remains relatively flat on the east side of the island. On the west side, however, it rises to form Inwood Hill.

Long before Europeans arrived, native peoples lived around the eastern edge of Inwood Hill in a settlement widely referred to as Shorokapok. Archaeological investigations show that they hunted, farmed, fished, and gathered shellfish. As the archaeologists Anne-Marie Cantwell and Diana diZerega Wall note, it was not a wilderness when Europeans arrived—the indigenous people had already lived in the region for millennia—but an area dotted with small communities connected by paths. The inhabitants, the Munsee (sometimes called the Lenape), were a coastal people, skillfully taking advantage of the opportunities offered by a meeting of land and water in a fertile estuary. When Henry Hudson sailed into their domain in 1609, their territory was known as Lenapehoking, the Land of the People. The incoming Europeans, as the historian Gregory Dowd puts it, were "new people in an old world."[1]

Figure 2: Washington Heights, framed by parks and rivers. Courtesy NYC Municipal Archives.

The earliest visitors to Lenapehoking were a mixed cast of explorers, adventurers, and traders drawn from an ocean world that washed against Europe, Africa, the Caribbean islands, and North America. Henry Hudson, an Englishman working under a contract with the Dutch East India Company, sailed past upper Manhattan in 1609, seeking a passage to China. He was soon followed by mariners with trade on their minds, but most of them were sojourners who did not linger long. The first of the newcomers to winter over was Juan Rodriguez, a man of African or mixed-race ancestry from the island of Hispaniola, which would one day harbor the Dominican Republic. Rodriguez sailed in on a ship captained by a Dutchman and set himself up as a trader in 1613. The European presence expanded, and by 1625 the Dutch West India Company had established the settlement of New Amsterdam, at the southern tip of Manhattan Island.[2]

Encounters between natives and strangers were shadowed by fatal incomprehensions and inescapable inequalities. Europeans and Munsee bargained and fought over the land under their feet. Although a folk tale suggests that Peter Minuit purchased Manhattan Island from the natives at a meeting place by Inwood Hill, no single deal sealed the fate of the Munsee. Instead, in negotiations framed by Dutch and English desires for acquisition and Munsee efforts to maintain a presence in the face of increasing numbers of Europeans, the natives tried "to buy time and protection." In the end they failed. By the eighteenth century, the lands that make up modern New York had all been sold to settlers. The Munsee, as Cantwell and Wall put it, became "strangers in their own land." It would not be the last time that comfortable residents of northern Manhattan found their world turned upside down by the arrival of new people.[3]

In 1776, when General George Washington and his officers drew up plans to defend Manhattan from British forces, a hill on the northwest end of the island was an obvious site for a fort. It was the highest point in Manhattan, with steep sides on all but its southern slope, and some 230 feet above a narrow spot in the Hudson River. The Americans built there a five-sided earthwork, Fort Washington, along with a riverside battery and outer works to the north, south, and east. Paired with another American fortification on the Jersey side of the river—Fort Lee—they could put British ships in the Hudson in a crossfire. Yet for all its geographic strengths, Fort Washington had a sad destiny.[4]

In August, British troops routed American forces from Brooklyn. In September, they landed on Manhattan Island and drove the Americans northward. Washington set up his headquarters in Mount Morris, the country mansion of a British colonel and departed Loyalist, near what is today the eastern end of West 161st Street. In October, however, Washington left Manhattan under the press of British forces. Troops at Fort Washington stayed behind. The garrison grew to 2,800: too many for the fort and too few to hold upper Manhattan.[5]

On November 15, 1776, British and Hessian forces attacked and captured Fort Washington. As the defeated American troops marched out of the fort, the victors laughed at them; some of the Americans were beaten and robbed. The captured fortress was renamed Fort Knyphausen, after a Hessian officer. An American outpost, where Margaret Corbin stepped in to replace her slain husband at his artillery piece during the fighting, was renamed Fort Tryon after the royal governor, Sir William Tryon. The Americans learned a lesson that would be repeated in northern Manhattan, especially in the section that came to be known as Washington Heights: geography is important, but it is not destiny.[6]

The area was largely rural into the middle of the nineteenth century, when wealthy New Yorkers bought the old farms and built suburban estates that looked and felt far from the crowded streets of downtown Manhattan. By the 1870s, the name Washington Heights was widely in use. The names of the landowners linger on the landscape. Audubon Avenue is named for John

James Audubon, the artist, naturalist, and ornithologist whose wooded estate stood above the Hudson near what is now West 155th Street. Bennett Park in the Heights, on the site of Fort Washington, recalls James Gordon Bennett, publisher and editor of the *New York Herald* and a landowner in northern Manhattan.[7] In rare locations, elements of the old patrician landscape remain—like the soaring entrance to the old Billings estate, Tryon Hall, which winds up toward Fort Tryon Park from the Henry Hudson Parkway.[8]

The Washington Heights of estates with river views began to change dramatically in the early twentieth century, when subways reached the neighborhood. In hilly northern Manhattan, contractors kept the subway on an even grade by laying tracks in deep underground tunnels. And that meant digging a tunnel more than two miles long northward from 158th Street beneath the ridge that defines the eastern Heights. On the night of October 24, 1903, when workmen tunneled through difficult rock north of St. Nicholas Avenue and 193rd Street, a three-hundred-ton boulder fell on a crew. Ten workers died; it was the worst disaster in the construction of the subway system.[9]

Still, in 1904, the Broadway line opened service to 157th Street; in 1906, it pushed on north to serve Inwood and Kingsbridge in the Bronx. The stage was set for massive real estate development in northern Manhattan. In the Heights, neighborhood boosters and real estate developers had hoped to create neighborhoods of "high-class residence property." An article in the

Figure 3: The country in the city: the Billings estate atop Washington Heights. Collection of the New-York Historical Society.

New York Times in 1908 noted the quickening pace of real estate development along Broadway between 133rd and 163rd streets. The next stretch of Broadway to see "high-class" growth would be between Broadway and the Hudson from 155th to 165th streets.[10]

Some of these predictions came true. In the early twentieth century, particularly in the southern end of the Heights, churches, cultural centers, and residential buildings suggested genteel aspirations for the neighborhood. The gothic revival Church of the Intercession at 155th and Broadway, consecrated in 1915 and set on a bluff amid the gently rolling lawns of Trinity Church Cemetery, seemed more like an Anglican country cathedral than an Episcopal church in Manhattan. Diagonally across from it on Broadway, at Audubon Terrace, there emerged a complex of educational and cultural institutions in ornate Italianate style. Advertisements for nearby apartment buildings touted their amenities, their views, their reasonable rents, and their proximity to the subway. The thirteen-story Riviera advertised suites of five to ten rooms; the nine-story Grinnell offered nine-room apartments and three duplexes.[11]

Both Washington Heights and Inwood had enclaves of affluence. But, overall, housing in the neighborhood was best suited to people of moderate income looking for an escape from crowded downtown neighborhoods like

Figure 4: The city arrives: Broadway at 156th Street, 1920. Photograph by Arthur Hosking. Courtesy of the Museum of the City of New York.

the Lower East Side, where densities topped 700 people per acre in 1910, compared to 161 people over the rest of the borough. Indeed, in 1910, one-sixth of all New Yorkers lived in Manhattan south of 14th Street.[12]

On the eve of the subway's arrival, as the historian Clifton Hood points out, there was more available land in northern Manhattan and the Bronx than there was farther downtown. Developers had every incentive to build housing that could be put up fast at a low cost to provide rental income for landlords. In Washington Heights and Inwood, as in the Bronx, many developers built new-law tenements—exactly the kind of housing that would appeal to people jammed into older tenements further downtown.[13]

New-law tenements in northern Manhattan were particularly common east of Broadway. Erected under the Tenement House Act of 1901, these were an improvement over the old dumbbell tenement, with its awkward railroad-flat layout, limited airshaft ventilation, and shared toilets in the hallway. Each new apartment had to have running water, a water closet, and an exterior window. The narrow airshaft of the old dumbbell tenements was expanded to become more of a courtyard. Buildings aimed at more middle-class tenants boasted six stories and elevators.

The apartments east of Broadway often had ornate decorations on their facades but more modest interiors. They were a significant improvement for tenants over the congested streets downtown. The new apartments to be found in the Heights, as one resident, Leo Shanley, put it, were "grim, but comfortable."[14]

A state law that granted tax breaks for residential housing construction fueled another housing boom in the 1920s. As vacancy rates climbed, tenants gained bargaining power against landlords: some bargained for a paint job, a new appliance, or a break on rent in exchange for signing a lease.[15]

With the completion of the IND subway line to the west of Broadway in 1932, the Heights and Inwood became even more accessible. By the end of the 1930s, the Heights had much of the face it would wear into the twenty-first century: simpler housing to the east of Broadway and more elaborate housing (like the art deco apartment buildings of upper Fort Washington Avenue) to the west. The George Washington Bridge opened in 1931, spanning the Hudson River between 179th Street and Fort Lee, New Jersey. Heading across the bridge toward New York in the late 1930s, you would have seen northern Manhattan's defining landmarks: the Henry Hudson Parkway coursing along the river (albeit at the cost of ramming a highway through the hillside forests of Inwood Hill Park); the Cloisters, the Metropolitan Museum of Art's museum of medieval art, tall above the river on the ground that once held the Billings estate; and the ramparts of the Columbia Presbyterian Medical Center.[16]

Figure 5: Fort Tryon Park on the site of the old Billings estate. Courtesy NYC Municipal Archives.

The Jewish, Irish, and Greek New Yorkers who moved into Washington Heights were immigrants and the children of immigrants, drawn to the neighborhood by its affordable housing, good transit connections, and parks. New York is often described as a city of ambition, a place where big dreams propel ordinary people to the summits of riches and fame. The truth is both more complicated and more prosaic. While some New Yorkers harbor visions of wealth and power, far more define their hopes for a better life in more modest ways: a better job, a comfortable apartment, good schools for the children, and the prospect that life in New York City would be better than it might have been in a place left behind.

Consider Maria Anna Sofia Cecilia Kalogeropalos, who was born in New York in 1923 to recently arrived Greek immigrants. She grew up on 192nd Street in Washington Heights, where her father ran a drugstore. Until the Depression, her family enjoyed a modest prosperity. Despite some unhappiness in her family life, Maria went to neighborhood public schools, performed in school productions, and took trips downtown with her mother to Central Park and the New York Public Library. She sang in contests and on the radio. The highlights of her week, however, were entirely in Washington Heights: a regular Tuesday night dinner at a local Chinese restaurant and Sunday mornings singing in Saint Spyridon, the Greek Orthodox church that anchored northern Manhattan's Hellenic community. Her eventual fame as the opera singer Maria Callas, won after her family left the Heights, was unusual. The pleasures she derived from everyday life in Washington Heights were typical.[17]

Despite its immigrant character, the neighborhood's early history was not a story of easy racial or ethnic integration. In many ways, Washington Heights was born with a nasty tendency to keep others out. As early as the 1920s, when the modern neighborhood began to take visible form, there were tensions over inclusion. Blacks were the clear-cut victims of exclusionary practices, while Jews could be found among both victims and perpetrators.

In the 1920s Dr. Charles Paterno, a physician and real estate developer, noticed the quickening pace of real estate opportunities in the Heights. At 182nd Street and what is today Cabrini Boulevard, Paterno owned a mansion, built in 1907 and designed to look like a castle, with white marble interiors and an indoor swimming pool. Paterno wanted to preserve the value of his estate while developing his holdings in the Heights. His ultimate goal was to attract middle-class people who were already leaving the city for suburbs, where mock-Tudor homes were highly fashionable. Paterno's solution was Hudson View Gardens, an elegant, carefully landscaped cooperative apartment complex designed in a Tudor style that offered suburban amenities in Manhattan.[18]

Dr. Paterno touted Hudson View Gardens with lavish advertisements, some of which were designed to be virtually indistinguishable from news stories. In his vision, Hudson View Gardens' financing was a sure investment. Its landscaping was elegant. Its tastefully appointed apartments were perfect for the modern woman who wanted to be emancipated from household drudgery. He also borrowed another selling point from the elite suburbs of the time: he made it plain that no Jews would live there. This last detail was never set forth with the clarity that Paterno reserved for describing his onsite steam laundry, but in the language of the 1920s, he was perfectly clear. Hudson View Gardens was a "restricted community," an "exclusive" community, open only to "desirable" families that had to be "approved" before they could move in. "In Hudson View Gardens," an ad that ran in 1925 concluded, "you live among the kind of people you like, and have a say about new neighbors."[19]

Despite efforts by Paterno and others to keep them out, a substantial number of Jews found homes in Washington Heights. For blacks, it was another matter.

Washington Heights was a natural destination for African Americans moving up out of Harlem. Beyond the western avenues of Broadway and Riverside

Drive, the most convenient routes up into Washington Heights from Harlem were Edgecombe and St. Nicholas avenues.

On December 10, 1927, a letter went out to property owners in the southern Heights:[20]

> As an owner in the section North of 155th Street, South of 162nd Street, West of Edgecombe Avenue, and East of Amsterdam Avenue, your properties are vitally affected by certain conditions, namely the occupancy by colored tenants of two houses on St. Nicholas Avenue, between 158th and 159th Sts.
>
> The owners within this area are organizing the Neighborhood Protective Association of Washington Heights, with the objective of maintaining the private houses and apartments in the section for occupancy exclusively by white tenants.

The letter listed twenty-eight contributors—a few of them businesses but mostly individuals—who had pledged financial support to the Association. Judging from their last names, they came from a mixture of backgrounds: Jewish, Irish, Italian, German, and British. "The completion of the subway line along St. Nicholas Avenue will greatly increase the value of all property along the Avenue and adjacent thereto and it is important that you co-operate with us in keeping the neighborhood a high class one as it has been up to date," the letter stated. The letter, signed by N. Roth of 478 W. 159th Street, temporary secretary of the Association, stressed that "this is not an effort at race discrimination but a matter of preserving present values and making possible the enjoyment of increased value when the new subway is completed. Your property will greatly deteriorate should this condition be allowed to spread and you will also have many vacancies in your apartments and will suffer great loss thereby."

Word of the plan reached the National Association for the Advancement of Colored People at its headquarters in New York City. James Weldon Johnson, the author, poet, songwriter, and diplomat who served as general secretary of the NAACP, feared that a public campaign against the Association would only advertise the NAACP's inability to prevent segregation in its own backyard. Instead, the NAACP wrote directly to Association members. In a letter dated February 20, 1928, the NAACP described a pending case that could overturn the validity of restrictive covenants and vowed to fight them "by every possible legal means."[21]

The letter-writing campaign failed. A memo circulated within the NAACP dated April 4, 1928, noted that a municipal court judge in New York City had ruled against the black tenants at 966–968 St. Nicholas Avenue and awarded the possession of the premises to its owners. Still, the Association could not entirely prevent blacks from moving into other buildings in the southern part of Washington Heights. By the late 1930s there was an African American presence in the southern part of the neighborhood.[22]

Indeed, in 1938 it was substantial enough to frighten real estate analysts who interpreted integration as a sign of a neighborhood in decline. When the appraisers for the federal Home Owners' Loan Corporation (HOLC) looked at northern Manhattan to gauge its suitability for housing loans, they rated the area that the Neighborhood Protective Association of Washington Heights "defended" as an area in decay. Its appraisers color-coded their maps, and in northern Manhattan the results were striking. The white and affluent area north of 181st Street along Fort Washington was coded green—most desirable for investment. Inwood, the eastern Heights above 181st Street, and the western Heights south of 181st were all coded blue—stable but unlikely to appreciate in value. The racially and ethnically mixed eastern Heights from 181st Street south to 155th Street was coded yellow—declining. Harlem south of 155th Street and east of Convent Avenue was colored red for deteriorated—and therefore a poor choice for loans. (Out of this practice came the expression "redlining.")[23]

The NAACP's unsuccessful fight against housing discrimination in the southern Heights illuminated both the organization's caution and the hostile legal climate that confronted blacks in New York City. The HOLC appraisal system, which codified discriminatory lending practices at work in the private sector, revealed some of the worst tendencies to come out of the federal government in the 1930s. Nevertheless, other policies radiating from Washington in the 1930s would change the political culture and landscape of New York and Washington Heights for the better.

For most of the Depression and all of World War II, New York City was governed by Mayor Fiorello La Guardia. "The Little Flower," son of an agnostic Italian father and an Austrian Jewish mother, served in Congress during the 1920s. He distinguished himself as an independent Republican, a radical even, who opposed immigration quotas, defended dissent and freedom of speech in a conservative time, and spoke up forcefully for rent controls. In 1932, he lost his seat in the Democratic landslide that sent Franklin D. Roosevelt to the White House. One year later, in 1933, voters disgusted by Tammany Hall incompetence and corruption in the face of the Depression elected La Guardia mayor.[24]

La Guardia defined urban New Deal liberalism with energetic city government and vigorous public works. He extolled New York as a city where, in the words of the municipal radio station, WNYC, "more than seven million people live in peace and enjoy the benefits of democracy."[25] He was a critic of machine politics who also understood the passions of ethnic politics. With energy, outrage, and pungent humor he mobilized reformers, radicals, and New Yorkers of immigrant stock—especially Jews and Italians. He worked effectively with Edward J. Flynn, leader of the Bronx County Democrats and a New Deal supporter, but despised the old Democratic Tammany organization, an Irish stronghold, as corrupt and ineffective. Winners in this process, especially Jews, embraced La Guardia. Losers, especially the Irish, felt displaced. La Guardia was also sensitive to the plight of the city's growing African American population. Like FDR, La Guardia won votes from African Americans who appreciated the relief, public works jobs, and housing opened up to them by the mayor and the New Deal. Nevertheless, La Guardia and Roosevelt's efforts could not overcome the deep inequalities that burdened black New Yorkers. The consequences of all of this would be played out on the streets of Washington Heights and Harlem to its south.[26]

New York in the 1930s was a city grappling with the Great Depression and the international crisis that culminated in World War II. The Crash of 1929 staggered the frothy optimism of the 1920s and left Gotham with crippling unemployment among not only working-class people, who could be bitterly familiar with uneven patterns of work, but also among middle-class residents whom social workers dubbed "the new poor." ("I've never had to ask for food before," says a man in a coat and tie at a Salvation Army food pantry in a newspaper cartoon by Denys Wortman. "I don't quite know how to begin.") In newsreel images of Japanese troops marauding in China, in magazine photos of the Spanish Civil War, and in the haunted words of newly arrived refugees from Nazi Germany, New Yorkers became uncomfortably familiar with the prospect of a second world war.[27]

The mayor brought to a city in crisis a transforming vision to city government. In his opposition to Tammany Hall, La Guardia centralized and modernized city government and municipal agencies. More visibly, he remade the city with dramatic public-works projects. Alternately encouraging and benefiting from new forms of federal aid, La Guardia helped usher in a new era of federal urban policies. New York City benefited handsomely.[28] New Yorkers enjoyed the fruits of the La Guardia administration when they visited one of the sixty new playgrounds opened during his first year in office; when they moved into the First Houses on the Lower East Side (the first public housing project built by a city in the United States); or when they drove across the Triborough Bridge and down the East River Drive. Their bodies, minds, and spirits were nourished in schools, libraries, hospitals, and colleges built or enhanced under the La Guardia administration.

A broad front of Democratic New Dealers, Republican reformers like La Guardia, labor union members, and radicals who belonged to the Communist Party, its allies, and the Socialist Party invigorated New York City politics in the La Guardia years. For all the real differences between them, all saw fundamental flaws in the city and in the nation's economic and political practices. In their response to the crisis, they dreamed big and fought hard. "'No one shall starve' is a medieval slogan," said La Guardia in 1933. "The community owes a greater responsibility today. 'Everyone shall live' is a more fitting principle upon which our unemployment relief and our public works relief must be based."[29]

The era's fusion of liberalism and radicalism—based in part on Communists' embrace of the New Deal during their effort to become part of a broad alliance in the Popular Front (which they disastrously abandoned when Moscow deemed it no longer useful)—found musical expression in the cantata "Ballad for Americans." Written in a short form for a WPA Federal Theater Project revue, the piece gained enormous fame when Paul Robeson, the great African American artist and activist aligned with the Communist Party, performed it on a CBS radio show in 1939. "Ballad for Americans" offered a racially and ethnically inclusive vision of American history. Expansively egalitarian, the piece affirmed the importance of ordinary people in sustaining democracy. ("Nobody who was anybody believed it. Ev'rybody who was anybody they doubted it.") The song quickly became an anthem for leftists and liberals. In a gesture that reflected how much ideas from the left of center influenced cultural politics at the time, "Ballad for Americans" was performed at the Republican presidential convention of 1940. (Some critics said this was proof that the fundamental vision behind "Ballad for Americans" was kitschy and insufficiently radical to prevent the song's co-option.)[30]

Together, liberals, New Dealers, and radicals made the city a place where great changes and a better future seemed possible. In swing jazz, in the Coney Island crowds drawn by Reginald Marsh, and in the blare of tabloid headlines, New Deal New York had energy and exuberance. The tenor of the times could be heard in the 1936 Broadway musical *Babes in Arms*, about the teenage children of unemployed vaudevillians who put on a show to avoid being sent to work on a farm. The show used memorable songs by Richard Rodgers and Lorenz Hart to lampoon racists and suggest the benefits of a collective economy. One of the best numbers, "The Lady Is a Tramp," celebrates the inclusive, egalitarian spirit of New York. The heroine of the song gets "too hungry for dinner at eight." Her pleasures are ordinary ("I go to Coney—the beach is divine") and loves her baseball ("the bleachers are fine.") She disdains society circles and concludes, "I like La Guardia and think he's a champ. / That's why the lady is a tramp."[31]

President Roosevelt, whose federal spending made New Deal New York possible, told his secretary of labor, Frances Perkins, "We're going to make a country in which no one is left out." In Washington Heights, the promise and challenge of that vow took physical form on June 14, 1936, with the opening of the Highbridge Pool on Amsterdam Avenue between 172nd and 174th streets, a location with a commanding view of the Harlem River and the Bronx. The site took its name from the High Bridge just below it, opened in 1848, which carried the Croton Aqueduct over the Harlem River. The pool measured 228 by 166 feet. Its bathhouse—built to hold 4,880 people and designed in the style that Lewis Mumford called "sound vernacular modern architecture"—greeted Amsterdam Avenue with a great bowed portico.[32]

Highbridge, a modern, spacious swimming pool built by laborers from the New Deal's Works Progress Administration, was one of eleven pools unveiled in New York that year out of Roosevelt and La Guardia's commitment to expanded public recreation facilities. La Guardia, ever a political showman, inaugurated Highbridge Pool with his powerful parks commissioner, Robert Moses, in a nighttime ceremony. Four thousand people, the *Times* reported, crowded into the complex; another thousand peered through a fence around its perimeter. La Guardia threw a switch to illuminate the pool and a show put on by trained swimmers and divers.[33]

The opening of Highbridge Pool eased the sting of hard times in northern Manhattan, but it could not by itself endure the hardships of the Depression. And just south of Washington Heights, in streets dominated by African Americans, conditions were worse. There, African Americans endured a discriminatory job market, high rates of unemployment, poverty, and overcrowded, expensive housing. In New York's segregated housing market African Americans paid high rents for second-rate housing because landlords could jack up their rents (and scrimp on maintenance), secure in the knowledge that black tenants had few alternatives. A Health Department study of 1935 found that the average monthly rent in Central Harlem was $52. In the rest of Manhattan, it was $44. In one case, on Amsterdam Avenue, January 1935 found white families renting apartments for $60. Black families moved in during July. Afterward, the landlord reduced the building's staff from seven to four. He also raised the rent to $75. The pattern, as historian Cheryl Greenberg observed, is clear: "Blacks, poorer than whites, had to pay more for rent, thus spending a higher proportion of their income for housing."[34]

The hardships wrought in Harlem by poor living and working conditions were compounded by crime. As black residents struggled through the Depression, many reached a conclusion that would be repeated in their neighborhood in later years: in Harlem, both crime and the cops were major problems. Crime figures for black neighborhoods should be interpreted with care because they can reflect poor record keeping, policing that is aggressive to the point of being unfair, and police corruption that permits crimes of vice to flourish. By the 1930s there was also a tendency among social scientists and policymakers to think of African American men as somehow innately criminal while ignoring, as the historian Khalil Gibran Muhammad has shown, the racism and structural inequalities that directed some black men into crime. With all these limitations, the statistics still suggest a grim state of affairs. During the Depression, homicide rates fell in New York City as a whole. In Harlem, under the pressure of hard times, they rose from nineteen per 100,000 in 1925 to twenty-four per 100,000 in 1937. Moreover, relations between Harlemites and the police were famously bad. Policing in the neighborhood was corrupt, ineffectual, and brutal.[35]

In March 1935, longstanding grievances in Harlem—including white storeowners' discrimination against black job seekers on 125th Street—erupted in rioting. The immediate event that sparked the uprising was a false rumor that Lino Rivera, a sixteen-year-old youth caught stealing a penknife from a Kress Store on 125th Street, had been killed while in custody. Rioters moved along 125th Street between Fifth and Eighth avenues, smashing windows and looting stores. The initial targets were white-owned stores, but as events progressed the target was property in general. By the night's end three people were dead and 626 windows were broken.[36]

The outbreak prompted efforts by the La Guardia administration and the federal government that eventually improved life in Harlem. African American migration to New York continued, driven by the desire to leave violence and Jim Crow in the South and the lure of jobs and a better chance at freedom in the North. By 1940, the black presence in upper Manhattan had expanded into the southern part of Washington Heights.[37]

Yet the defining tension in the Heights during the 1930s and 1940s would not be racial so much as religious and ethnic as Washington Heights—the discriminatory policies of Hudson View Gardens notwithstanding—became the home of many Jews. At first the neighborhood drew the wealthy (who eventually decamped for Central Park West). In the 1920s, people moved in from Jewish sections of Harlem, to be followed in the 1930s by Jewish refugees from Germany. By one rough calculation, in 1930 three-eighths of the people in Washington Heights were Jewish. Like other Jewish neighborhoods in the Bronx and in Brooklyn that emerged in the 1920s, Washington Heights was a neighborhood dominated by immigrants and their children. There, Jews emerged from the immigrant experience and became "at home in America," as the title of Deborah Dash Moore's book put it, in a distinctly Jewish context.[38] By 1940, the Jewish population of Washington Heights included a visible number of German Jews who arrived after the Nazis rose to power.[39]

While most Jews lived in the middle-class areas west of Broadway, such as Fort Washington Avenue, there were also some working-class Jews, most of them skilled workers. My grandfather and grandmother, Russian Jewish immigrants, moved from Brooklyn to Washington Heights around 1928 with my father, his brothers Lou and Tom, and his sister Helen. Using a survival strategy common to working-class families, they moved repeatedly— sometimes exchanging work for a few months' rent (my grandfather was a painter and one-man contractor) and sometimes exploiting the housing surplus to negotiate breaks on rent from landlords eager to attract tenants. At different points they had apartments on Audubon Avenue, St. Nicholas Avenue, and 178th Street. If the practice sounds like a tenant's paradise, the reality was something less. Frequent moves were disruptive and tiring. When I asked my father where he had lived, he responded in one word that echoed with exhaustion: "Everywhere."

My father found pleasures in Washington Heights. He learned to swim in the Harlem River with a distinctive stroke: one hand moving overhead in a conventional crawl, the other moving sideways to clear away floating debris. He also started to hang out at boathouses on the Hudson near the foot of Dyckman Street, where he discovered the canoeing that was to be one of the great joys of his life. Overall, however, he remembered the 1930s as a hard time: want at home, fascism abroad, and, by the end of the decade, a looming threat of war. During the depths of the Depression, when my grandfather was repeatedly unemployed, the family got by on credit. When storeowners tired of my grandmother's inability to pay up on time, she walked farther from home to find merchants who would lend to her. Shopping trips became ever longer and ever more wearying. One of my father's most vivid memories was watching his mother go door to door in their apartment building, begging pennies from fellow tenants, so she could get money to buy potatoes to boil up and feed the family. Such memories, experienced alongside the Roosevelt administration's efforts to forge just prosperity, made my father a lifelong New Deal Democrat.

Less numerous than the Jews, but also present in northern Manhattan, were the Irish—who tended to live east of Broadway. During the 1930s and 1940s, the Irish of Washington Heights and Inwood were working-class people. In a time when some joked that the IRT subway line stood for Irish Rapid Transit, northern Manhattan had a reputation for being the home of many transit workers. Nevertheless, the Irish were a minority in the neighborhood: about 12 percent of the population in 1940, concentrated in Roman Catholic parishes that sprawled like an archipelago from the southern end of the Heights to Inwood. By the era of the New Deal, the Irish of northern Manhattan had left behind the deep poverty that their ancestors had experienced in the Five Points in the middle of the nineteenth century. Politically, however, they often felt a sense of ebbing power. The Democrat Al Smith, who was strongly associated with Irish New York, was defeated in the 1928 presidential race in a campaign marked by vicious anti-Catholicism. In New York City, under La Guardia, the Irish leaders of Tammany Hall lost power. During the Depression, fewer Irish immigrated to the United States and the remittances once sent back to Ireland by immigrants declined as earnings in America dried up. For those Irish who did leave the United States for Ireland, there was a stigma of failure.[40]

The living costs of families in Washington Heights and Inwood were close to the city's median in the 1940s—with about half of Gotham's families spending more on rent and family expenses and half spending less. On average the rents in northern Manhattan were higher than in the rest of the borough, but the apartments people rented were relatively new and even spacious. In 1943, a group of newspapers that included the *New York Times* published the *New York City Market Analysis*, a study of the city's social and economic characteristics based on 1940 federal census data. The report called New York a "city of a hundred cities." (Washington Heights alone, it noted, was larger than Fort Wayne, Indiana.) Color coding identified neighborhoods and sections of neighborhoods by rent and "family expenditures." Across the city, the most common color on the map was green, denoting families whose rent was $30–$49 per month and had annual expenditures of $1,800 to $2,999. Sections dominated by families with higher rents and expenditures climbed up from orange to red to purple. Neighborhoods dominated by people with less to spend—under $30 a month in rent, and under $1,800 in expenditures—appeared in blue. Washington Heights in this map was largely green—with pockets of orange, purple, and red west of Broadway. Inwood was similarly green, with patches of orange west of Broadway and an enclave colored red in northwest Inwood.[41]

The green hue of the Heights and Inwood put it on the same level as neighborhoods such as Highbridge in the Bronx, Astoria and Long Island City in Queens, and Brownsville in Brooklyn. Blue neighborhoods, where people spent less, included East Harlem and the Lower East Side in Manhattan, and Williamsburg in Brooklyn. Unlike the HOLC appraisers, who placed significant emphasis on race and ethnicity when they interpreted neighborhoods, the newspapers that funded the *New York City Market Analysis* were interested in counting consumers who would be of interest to advertisers. By that measure, the residents of Washington Heights were doing well.

The tendencies toward a broad but modest prosperity in northern Manhattan were matched by a general preference for elected officials who supported the New Deal at city and national levels. (A bit of an irony, since the Roosevelt administration's HOLC rated about one-quarter of the Heights a declining area.) During the 1930s and 1940s, majorities of New York City voters backed Fiorello La Guardia for mayor and Franklin D. Roosevelt for president. Roosevelt, however, always ran better in northern Manhattan than La Guardia. The discrepancy suggests that some voters who preferred the Democratic Roosevelt for White House also voted for Democratic candidates for city hall, reducing but not overturning La Guardia's pluralities in northern Manhattan. One possible explanation for this is different levels of support for La Guardia among Irish Catholics and Jews.[42]

The Jews and Irish of Washington Heights and Inwood, like so many city dwellers, lived in urban villages organized around their own ethnic group. For the Irish, life was defined by the Roman Catholic parishes that stretched from Saint Rose of Lima in the southern Heights to Good Shepherd in Inwood. (You didn't live on 174th Street near St. Nicholas Avenue, but in "Incarnation Parish.") Jewish life, lacking the firm institutional structures of Roman Catholicism, was more decentralized. Nevertheless, there were still specific buildings, streets, and sections of the Heights identified with Jews.

By living near other Jewish or Irish families, attending specific houses of worship, and belonging to specific social organizations, members of both communities established environments where people they dealt with on a day-to-day basis were mostly just like them. Life in such enclaves seemed safe and secure. Historian Steven Lowenstein's comments on the neighborhoods' German Jews also apply to other Jews and to the Irish: "While living physically near the rest of the population, they could still, with little feeling of internal contradiction, live lives that revolved around their own ethnic community. Like many other ethnic New Yorkers they could live near people different from themselves and remain separate from them."[43]

By the second half of the 1930s, German Jewish refugees were clustered around the intersection of Broadway and Fort Washington Avenue near 158th Street. Although never a majority of the neighborhood's Jews, the German arrivals stood out for their language, their specialty shops, and their formality. Contrary to stereotypes that they were either the Berlin elite or Weimar intellectuals, many of them were country people from southern Germany, particularly Hesse and Bavaria. When they thought of cities left behind they were more likely to think of Frankfurt and Wurzburg than Berlin. "Their model," Lowenstein wrote, "was not the cosmopolitan and bustling German capital but rather the sleepy provincial towns and villages of southern and central Germany with their half-timbered houses and traditionalist ways of thinking."[44]

The refugees' arrivals in Washington Heights were the product of desperate flight. Rosalyn Manowitz, the American-born member of a refugee family in Washington Heights, had friends and relatives who had escaped to England, Canada, the United States, Shanghai, and Palestine. She also counted relatives and family friends who could not escape the Nazis and perished.[45] Another refugee, Michael Cohn, who arrived from Berlin in 1935 and settled into 103 Thayer Street, recalls that the German Jews were not always welcomed into the neighborhood. Money was tight for some of the newcomers. When they brought extra relatives or boarders into their apartments to better cover the rent, they were accused of creating overcrowding. For some neighborhood residents, the appearance of a German Jewish peddler at their apartment door—laden with food and household items—was nothing more than a nuisance.[46]

Indeed, some of the people who were uncomfortable with the German Jewish presence were themselves Jews. The newcomers confounded eastern European Jews in the neighborhood. The German Jews' conception of Judaism was strongly religious, even Orthodox, so they could think of themselves as German in nationality and Jewish in religion. This bewildered eastern European Jews, whose identity was more ethnic and who found the Germans totally assimilated. If the eastern European Jews were baffled at the German Jews' loyalty to the German language, the German Jews looked down on Yiddish. To eastern European Jews who recalled hardships in Poland or Russia, the old country was a place to be left behind. But for German Jews, who had lived good lives in Germany until the rise of Hitler, immigration meant the loss of a beloved home and sometimes a loss in status. One man, a banker in Germany, kept up his old habit of a daily shave from a barber even when he worked as a dishwasher in New York. As they themselves knew, they were not above exaggerating the comforts of their former lives. In a joke widely circulated among German Jewish refugees, two dachshunds are talking. One says, "In Germany I ate white bread every day." His companion replies, "That's nothing, in Germany I was a Saint Bernard."[47]

German Jews tended to be lower middle class, with a significant number of skilled working-class people among them; few of them showed signs of abject poverty. To Jews who had experienced or heard about the poverty of the Lower East Side, the newcomers seemed to have skipped a stage of suffering in a way that was somehow unfair. To anti-Semites, who were present in the Heights in the 1930s, the relative comfort of the German Jewish immigrants was a sign that they were somehow the beneficiaries of a favoritism that was not extended to native-born Americans.[48]

Despite these difficulties, the German Jews settled into the Heights. By 1940 they had set up their own clubs, synagogues, and communal organizations. They could read the *Aufbau* or the *Jewish Way*, both newspapers for German Jewish refugees. Without leaving the Heights they could visit a

German cabaret at Lublo's Palm Garden or buy kosher wurst at Bloch and Falk. One of the largest Jewish organizations in the neighborhood was the Immigrant Jewish War Veterans, composed of Jewish veterans who served in the German army during World War I.[49]

While the elegance of the Grinnell and other majestic buildings on Riverside Drive was only a block away, most of the German Jews found homes on the cross streets running between upper Riverside Drive and Fort Washington Avenue, on modest blocks of modest six-story apartment buildings with fire escapes. These were not the buildings with grand courtyards and names such as The Plymouth, Dayton Court, and Chateau D'Armes that could be found just to the east on Fort Washington Avenue. Rather, they were solid apartment buildings on narrow streets where immigrant and native-born kids could play stickball. For socializing there was "the wall" that formed the western edge of Upper Riverside Drive as it wound uphill from 158th Street to the 160s. Flat-topped and a perfect height for sitting, the wall became a popular spot for gathering and hanging out, especially for teenagers.[50]

Former residents of the Heights recall hanging out at the wall with great fondness. But the conviviality of the neighborhood was delicately balanced against ethnic friction. Indeed, over time, the neighborhood around Broadway and Fort Washington Avenue became known as the Fourth Reich. The name does not sound entirely friendly. It speaks of an alien presence, a domineering presence, and that appears to have been the intent. The phrase was clearly directed at German Jews, but the expression anticipated a growing strain of hostility against all Jews in northern Manhattan in the late 1930s. In this respect, the neighborhood was not unique. Other parts of New York City where Jews and Irish shared the same neighborhood—the South Bronx, the Fordham and Highbridge sections of the Bronx, and Flatbush in Brooklyn—saw similar tensions. In the same years Boston also saw Irish Catholics attack Jews. If the causes for this conflict were metropolitan and even international in their dimensions, they were played out on the intimate terrain of parks and sidewalks in northern Manhattan.[51]

By the late 1930s, relations between the Irish and the Jews in northern Manhattan moved from distant to hostile. Beyond simple anti-Semitism, hostility stemmed from competition for housing as more Jews—including German refugees—moved into the neighborhood. Working-class Irish resented the relative affluence of the Jews who lived west of Broadway. Political rivalries mattered as well. The decline of Tammany Hall and the rise of Mayor Fiorello La Guardia's local New Deal coalition, which prominently included Jews, made some Irish feel politically threatened. Looking abroad during the Spanish Civil War, many Jews supported the Loyalists and many Catholics supported Franco. As Hitler consolidated power, Jews—especially German

Jews—supported Britain as a counterweight to Nazi Germany. To the Irish, however, Britain was still the oppressor of Erin.[52]

From the late 1930s through World War II, Washington Heights and Inwood were scarred by violent acts of anti-Semitism. The main perpetrators were Irish youth gangs, particularly the Amsterdams and the Shamrocks, inspired partly by the Christian Front and Christian Mobilizers, two ultrarightist groups influenced by the ideas of Father Charles E. Coughlin of Michigan. Coughlin, a right-wing populist who regularly broadcast over the radio, laced his writing and speeches with anti-Semitism. As belligerence increased in Europe and Asia, violent tensions were fanned on the streets of American cities.

The Front and Mobilizers, as the historian Ronald H. Bayor has shown, appeared in the Heights and Inwood in 1939. During the war years, their rallies were succeeded by vandalism of synagogues, insults blaming Jews for the war, and gang attacks on Jewish youths. A report issued in December 1943 by the Anti-Defamation League of B'Nai B'Rith chronicled what it called "a serious condition of anti-Semitic hoodlumism in the Washington Heights area."[53] A ten-year-old boy's statement was typical of many collected.

> About two months ago, on a Sunday afternoon, at 174th or 175th Street, between Fort Washington Avenue and Broadway, I was coming home from the theatre, when about eight or nine kids, about 11 or 12, came over. They asked me if I was a Jew, I said 'yes', and they called me names like 'dirty Jew,' 'Jew boy' and a lot of things about Jews. They got me against the wall—two big ones—and they started hitting me in the stomach and I broke away. I started running and they threw rocks at me. One hit me in the back.[54]

The report also documented lackadaisical responses from the police (along with examples of adults driving off the attackers), and the anguish of the Catholic neighbors of a Protestant minister who expressed "shame and regret for the fact that the young hoodlums are young boys and girls of the Catholic faith."

A Jewish boy who was accosted while playing with his Catholic friend near J. Hood Wright Park (for generations "Jew Park" in the local slang) testified to both Jewish-Catholic friendship and his would-be assailants' inability to imagine it.

> A group of five boys came over to me and my friend and asked us if we were Jewish. I kept still throughout the entire conversation, cause

I knew if I talked I would give myself away that I was Jewish. My friend said, truthfully, that he was a Catholic and what church he came from. Then the boys said, "Well, if you see any Jewish kids you tell us. We don't want to hurt any kids of our kind, we just want to get the Jewish kids." One of the boys said, "We caught a kid down the street who is Protestant, but he got tough and we messed him up. So if you see any Jewish kids you tell us." Then they walked away.[55]

Among the Jews who faced such threats was Max Frankel, who fled with his mother from Germany to Poland, then back to Germany and finally to the United States. While his father survived the war in a labor camp in Siberia, mother and son settled into an apartment at 645 W. 160th Street that he recalled as "the southern, poorest section of the Jewish ridge" that stretched down western Washington Heights. Life inside his section of the Heights was comfortable. He joined a Boy Scout troop, went for Hebrew lessons at Hebrew Tabernacle, and hung out at "the wall" overlooking Riverside Drive.[56]

While Frankel knew the derision of more established Jews, he also knew the fear that came from crossing neighborhood boundaries. To walk from the western side of Broadway, with its kosher delicatessens and Jewish bakeries, to the eastern side was to enter another world. There, "two taverns, a shellfish market, and a photo studio featuring freckled faces signaled an abrupt demographic shift." The far side of Broadway, in these years, was Irish territory. To pass through it was to risk a punch, the sting of a fist clutching a metal ashcan handle, or a shot from a rubber-band zip gun. Frankel accumulated fines at his public library because he was afraid to walk through Irish streets to return his borrowed books. Sometimes, Irish raiders ventured into his neighborhood. "Every Halloween," he recalls, "they would invade our turf, swinging cotton stockings filled with pebbles and powdered chalk; each white or pink spot on our clothing signified a painful hit."[57]

It would be wrong, however, to conclude that all Catholics were the enemies of all Jews. Noreen Walck, née Lane, was born to Irish immigrants in 1934 and grew up in the Heights in Incarnation Parish. All of her friends on her block were Jewish. Although she started out in Catholic schools, she hated the uniforms and the presence of the nuns so she "tormented" her mother until she let her go to George Washington High School. There she found a life-changing teacher and memorable courses in art and journalism. She thrived. "I think the best thing that ever happened to me was growing up with Jewish people," she said years later. From a Jewish family, Sophie Heymann, a refugee from Germany who moved to the Heights in 1938, found her best friend in St. Rose of Lima Parish: Marion Heaney, an Irish girl. She recalls no troubles as a Jew walking the streets of Washington Heights in those years.[58]

Jewish and Irish boys made friends, too. (My Uncle Tom's best friend in the Heights was Irish; any hint of an ethnic rivalry between them went no further than my uncle rooting for Jewish boxers and his buddy rooting for Irish boxers.) But the experiences of Walck and Heaney suggest a point that would be confirmed again and again in the history of Washington Heights: when the streets are under the control of edgy, angry young men, the streets are in a bad way. And mothers' networks of order, which were themselves embedded in the politics of turf, had limits. Moms' authority did not reach from one side of Broadway to the other. It is also difficult to avoid the conclusion that some of the bigots in Washington Heights were acting out attitudes they had picked up from their parents.

Individual friendships testify to the best possibilities of life in Washington Heights in these years, but the hostilities in the neighborhood were too deeply entrenched to be remedied by individual friendships alone. And the two institutions that should have moved more forcefully to address the tensions in Washington Heights—city hall and the police department—did not take vigorous action. Mayor La Guardia was reluctant to exercise the kind of bold leadership needed to define the problem of violent anti-Semitism as something more than a series of random individual acts. La Guardia did order the police department to investigate the Christian Front—an organization with sympathizers in both the Boston and New York police departments—after the Federal Bureau of Investigation arrested members of a conspiracy to bomb Jews and Jewish institutions in 1940. Otherwise, he moved cautiously. In December 1943, the Anti-Defamation League documented attacks on fifty Jewish children ages six to thirteen and acts of vandalism against nearly every synagogue and two Protestant churches in Washington Heights. In January 1944, a municipal investigation accused the police of inaction in the face of anti-Semitic violence and vandalism. The Anti-Defamation League and other groups strongly endorsed the report. Mike Quill, an Irish city councilman and president of the Transport Workers Union, a man of the Left and an opponent of anti-Semitism, called for a mass meeting in the Bronx. (Bronx Borough president James J. Lyons responded that it would be better to deal with the issues identified in the report quietly.)[59]

As the year 1944 wore on, however, a solution began to emerge through aggressive policing, the organization of Jewish defense units and school escorts, and concerted efforts by Catholic, Protestant, and Jewish religious leaders to condemn prejudice. Larger national currents helped, too. With the end of the war, virulent anti-Semitism was discredited as the poisonous ideology of the defeated Nazis. The domestic animosities of the war years were also diminished by a recognition of Jewish wartime service, postwar prosperity, and the actions of civic groups organized to counter bigotry. A growing

political consensus against anti-Semitism made any association with it a lia-
bility. In the 1945 motion picture short *The House I Live In*, the singer Frank
Sinatra persuades a gang of Christian kids to lay off a Jewish boy by ridiculing
religious prejudice as a Nazi way of thinking and reminding them of Jewish
military service in the war. (His rendition of the title song omits the original
version's reference to "neighbors white and black," but extols America as a
country of "all races and religions.") A 1945 report to the American Jewish
Committee on a "Christian Front" meeting in Queens said that the assem-
bled crowd responded to the speakers with "some amount of righteously in-
dignant heckling" and more. "Be it said to the eternal credit of our Christian
neighbors in Queens County," the author of the document wrote, "that one
obviously Gentile young man kept yelling, 'what about our Jewish buddies
who died on Iwo Jima.'" The author also noted the actions of "a 16-year-old
kid (whose face was a map of Ireland) who repeatedly shouted 'Nazi! Nazi!'
When a cop dragged him to the outskirts of the crowd, the kid grabbed his
nightstick, threw it to the ground, ran like hell and was never caught."[60]

Ethnic divisions in the neighborhood were one thing. Racial divides were another. There is an old saying that Washington Heights begins where Harlem
ends. The implication is clear: Washington Heights is a white neighborhood.
If African Americans dominate the streets, the neighborhood is Harlem. Precisely where this happens has varied over time.

In 1939, *The WPA Guide to New York City* defined Washington Heights as
the area from 135th Street to Dyckman Street. The southern part of the neighborhood, the guide added, was "often called Hamilton Heights." The prospect
of an integrated Washington Heights first emerged there. As the same guide
noted a few pages later, "The lower Washington Heights section overlooking
Harlem, particularly between 145th and 155th streets and Edgecombe and
Amsterdam avenues, has in recent years been populated largely by well-to-do
Negroes, who live in costly private homes and in apartment buildings such as
the thirteen-story Colonial Parkway Apartments at 409 Edgecombe Avenue,
which has eighteen penthouses."[61]

The boundary between Harlem and Washington Heights was one of perception. The artist Faith Ringgold, born in 1930, grew up in Sugar Hill—
by one definition the area stretching north of central Harlem from 145th to
155th streets between Amsterdam and Edgecombe avenues. Sugar Hill had
a reputation as an enclave of the black middle class, but the term middle
class should not be interpreted narrowly. For African Americans, middle
class identity has long been defined less by white collars and elite status than
by steady and often manual labor coupled with values of respectability and

responsibility. Ringgold's painting *Tar Beach*, which captures an imaginary scene from the life of an African American girl and her family in Harlem in the 1930s, is ordinary in its setting. On their rooftop, "tar beach," the resort of working-class families of all races and ethnic backgrounds before air conditioning, a family relaxes with a card game while two children lie on a mattress. Above them on the horizon, sparkling against the night sky, is the George Washington Bridge. The painting is about dreams and aspirations, about transcending the boundaries of circumstance and neighborhood. The bridge might be in Washington Heights, but in a Harlem girl's mind it is a part of her world. On the ground, however, realities could be more limited.[62]

In the early 1940s, after his father died, Roger Wilkins moved from Kansas City to 160th Street with his grandmother and mother, a social worker and graduate of the University of Minnesota. Wilkins thought himself a resident of Harlem, but others called his area Sugar Hill. He attended a "de facto semisegregated" PS 46 in a "ragged" building with white teachers and administrators, a largely black student body, and a "thin trickle" of refugee students. His family was short on cash but had middle-class values. Outside, the world of the streets prevailed. Sharp men from gambling rings conveyed the notion that "criminal enterprise was one way out of the box we were in." By the time he was ten or eleven, Wilkins was pilfering from stores and talking street talk—much to his mother's distress. Still, he wasn't a genuine tough guy and he didn't join a gang. Indeed, he was scared of a gang on 163rd Street, and he knew that the gangs from deeper in Harlem were tougher than any that he would face nearby. So he found protection by letting a boy from the 163rd Street gang copy his homework. By the time Wilkins was twelve his widowed mother had remarried and moved them to Grand Rapids, Michigan. There, as the one black pupil in a junior-senior high school with a student body of twelve hundred, he was initially "shunned and isolated." Over time, however, he found friends and success as a student and an athlete. Other African Americans who remained on the border of the Heights and Harlem found troubles.[63]

Living around 145th Street and Seventh Avenue, Harry Belafonte—born in 1927 to West Indian parents—grew up in poverty that did not dim his mother's aspirations for a better life. Walking to PS 148 between Amsterdam and Broadway was a daily gauntlet at the hands of local Irish and Italian kids. At school, he recalled in his memoir, "I walked the halls ready to explode if another student so much as bumped me accidentally as he went by. And that happened a lot." For a time, he "passed" as white so his mother, who presented herself as a Spaniard by way of the Caribbean, could live in an all-white building at 114th Street and Manhattan Avenue. When he enrolled at George Washington High School at the age of fourteen, he began an "inexorable drift toward kinship with black students" and noticed the fights of black, white, and Hispanic gangs. "The constant awareness of race—and the daily challenges to fight based on race—only left me more alienated than ever," he wrote later. In the middle of his freshman year, angry and struggling with what he would later recognize as dyslexia, he dropped out. After a period of odd jobs, he enlisted in the U.S. Navy.[64]

During World War II, African American migrants to New York increased the population and size of Harlem. If African Americans previously lived in the area between 110th and 155th streets from Third Avenue to Amsterdam Avenue, the newcomers pushed west past Amsterdam Avenue and north of 155th Street. Conflict followed. Historian Dominic J. Capeci Jr. described Washington Heights as "a continual battleground during the war," one where "apartment houses opened to black tenants were vandalized by white youths." Mayor La Guardia ordered greater security efforts in the neighborhood, but the incidents continued. "Buildings that housed black residents were disfigured by red paint and crude swastikas," Capeci noted. "In fact, white parents encouraged their children to commit these acts."[65]

The day-to-day ebb and flow of such conflict was heightened by the Harlem Riot of 1943, which erupted from black anger over racial discrimination, overcrowded housing, and police violence. The riot was ignited when a white policeman shot and wounded an African American soldier on leave in a dispute that began as a disorderly conduct incident and escalated into a struggle over the officer's nightstick. False rumors that the soldier was killed sparked outrage. Mobs fought with police, looted stores, and overturned cars. Six people died, according to police—all of them African Americans. In its northern reaches—along Eighth Avenue to 145th Street and Seventh Avenue to 140th Street, the uprising lapped against the southern borders of Washington Heights.[66]

Growing up in the 1940s at 1061 St. Nicholas Avenue at 163rd Street, Jacques d'Amboise experienced his neighborhood as a tightly defined place touched by a sense of menace. Born Joseph Ahearn in Massachusetts in 1937 (his French Canadian mother eventually concluded that her name would serve her children better in ballet), he lived on a block with Irish, Jewish, German, Italian, Dutch, Polish, and Hispanic kids. To the east was Amsterdam Avenue—a street that marked the boundary of his familiar world and the beginning of a black area. Moving in the junior divisions of gangs, he heard street talk filled with warnings against crossing Amsterdam ("if you do *they'll* get you") and vows that "we'll get them" if they came to the white side. Once, when he did cross over Amsterdam to help a neighbor to a hospital, he was confronted by a gang of black youths and frightened—but was helped by a black girl who told the boys to let him pass.[67]

Young d'Amboise's best friends were Jimmy Comiskey, a young Irish intellectual, and Abie Grossfeld, a Jewish athlete. Yet for all the fun of handball and hanging out at Dave's Candy Store on 163rd Street, he did not find his neighborhood entirely warm and nurturing. He fought with a nasty white guy named Farel who taunted him about his dancing. He found the gang scene mean and alienating. In 1951, he left the life of the block to embrace the world of ballet. He kept up with some friends from the neighborhood, but later described his departure as being like an "amputation."[68]

Other white residents found different ways and reasons to leave. In the aftermath of the 1943 Harlem Riot, both Irish and Jewish residents began to move north from the streets of the southern Heights, bound for areas with white majorities.[69] For many of them, it was the first of a series of moves that made them feel like displaced persons. At the same time, African Americans who moved to the Heights found an intricate geography of blocks dominated by black or white families, with acknowledged boundaries that could be risky to cross.

In 1945, Celedonia "Cal" Jones, grandson of a World War I veteran of the 369th Infantry, better known as the Harlem Hellfighters, moved from Harlem to 525 W. 151st Street. As far as he was concerned, he was in the Heights: he was north of Harlem and west of St. Nicholas Avenue in Sugar Hill. Jones, born in 1930, had moved frequently with his family in Harlem in pursuit of good deals on rent. He even resided briefly in Brooklyn while his father, a handyman who was often out of work, labored as a longshoreman. But his frame of reference for understanding the Heights was West 143rd Street in Harlem, between Lenox and Seventh avenues—a tough, crowded block, where order was provided by siblings who looked out for each other and mothers who kept an eye on things. (Despite the street rivalries of young black and Irish men on the streets of upper Manhattan, both describe how their home blocks were patrolled by mothers who kept watch and preserved order.)[70]

For Jones, the streets provided work and play; they were the place where he played box ball and collected soda and beer bottles to return for the deposits. By the time he was nine, he could walk to baseball games in the Polo Grounds at 157th Street. When he reached the age of fourteen, he could also get downtown to work in the garment district, pushing racks of clothing up and down between 10th Street and 38th Street. (More than once, he lied about his age to get work.) But the streets were also where he experienced exclusion. When he moved north to 151st Street in 1945, his block was mostly black. West 152nd Street was mixed, and 153rd Street was white. But the main dividing line was Broadway: west of it was white territory, patrolled by a gang called the Irish Dukes. To the north were the Graveyard Boys, again whites, who taunted black kids and waged acorn fights with them in Trinity Church Cemetery.

Compared to what he remembered of crowded 143rd Street, 151st Street was "a better neighborhood, in many ways." But 151st Street would not be home like 143rd Street. Like other young black men who moved to lower Washington Heights in the 1940s, Jones found a less-than-welcoming neighborhood. With few friends in his neighborhood, and no prospect of making friends farther north, he looked downtown for company. Even though he lived in Washington Heights, he kept up with his old friends from around 143rd Street in Harlem. In high school, under the influence of a teacher, he became active in the 1948 presidential campaign of Henry Wallace. He ventured north occasionally to an event at the Audubon Ballroom on Broadway between 165th and 166th streets, but the focus of his life was not in the Heights.

John Culpepper, who moved to the lower Heights in the same years, learned similar lessons. He remembers crossing 155th Street only to be asked by a white man on the corner, "What are you doing here, boy?" Culpepper explained that he was on his way to the library. He was allowed to pass, but the boundary had been asserted. Such encounters could make for a tight existence. "You stayed mostly secured to where you lived," said Culpepper.[71]

Although the experiences of Jones and Culpepper anticipated the resistance that African Americans would face when they tried to move into white neighborhoods after the war, the end of the war also summoned up moments of solidarity. Dorothy Goddard, who grew up on 186th Street east of Audubon Avenue, recalls that VJ-Day turned the street into a carnival. She and her girlfriends marched around the neighborhood singing patriotic songs until they were hoarse. At a block party, she remembers, "the adults were busy sampling the Italian wine, the Irish whiskey and the Jewish pastries that appeared on tables everywhere."[72]

Such festivities recall the ideal platoon of World War II films such as *A Walk in the Sun*, with one Irishman, one Italian, and one Jew (but no African American). Such inclusions and exclusions, with their high ideals and compromised realities, echoed in New York. At its most idealistic, the La Guardia administration anticipated a better city that would emerge from wartime. "New York of tomorrow, as envisioned by Mayor La Guardia is to be a new kind of city—more beautiful, healthful and convenient; a more comfortable place in which to live, work and play; a more interesting city to visit," asserted the "victory edition" of *New York Advancing*, a report issued by the municipal reference library. "It is to be more efficient, a great democratic community where, in keeping with its history and the new era opening before the world, millions of people may enjoy larger measures of freedom."[73]

The optimism of *New York Advancing* looked past the looming challenges of converting to a peacetime economy, finding housing for veterans and their families, and meeting the changing expectations of men and women who had glimpsed new ways of working and living during wartime. Some of this surfaced in concern over young people, such as the latchkey children of defense-plant workers or teenagers old enough to break free from parental restraint but too young for the constructive constraints that might have come from participation in the war effort. "In spite of optimism, philanthropy, and youth conferences," the famed sociologist Robert S. Lynd said in a 1945 conference at New York's city hall, "this is one hell of a world for kids to be trying to grow up in." La Guardia, at the same conference, expressed a fear that demobilized servicemen would take the jobs of high school students training for work in vocational trades, thereby sinking teenagers into unemployment.[74]

The problems of demobilization were daunting enough. It was even harder to confront social problems that contradicted La Guardia's notion of New York as "a great democratic community." Newspaper and magazine reports identified violent and criminal youth in New York and other cities as "delinquents"; they also sensationally covered crimes committed by African Americans and the Harlem Riot of 1943. But the news media, and the La Guardia administration, were slow to recognize the growth of gangs and clashes among white, black, and Hispanic youths in changing neighborhoods. In northern Manhattan one early observer of the problem was the journalist Bradford Chambers, who was educated in sociology and wrote for the *New York Times* and the *American Mercury*. As early as 1944, Chambers chronicled black and white gangs fighting at Amsterdam Avenue and 122nd Street. After the war he reported on fighting that broke out near City College at 138th Street and Convent Avenue when black and Puerto Rican gangs from Harlem moved west across Amsterdam Avenue into white turf claimed by gangs such as the Hancocks and the Irish Dukes.[75]

Yet city hall did not put these animosities in a spotlight. The La Guardia administration was reluctant to recognize racial and ethnic gang conflict in New York City partly out of desire to avoid demonizing black New Yorkers and partly out of blindness to a new and contentious reality emerging on the city's streets. While La Guardia had a grand vision for New York's future, he also glossed over the unsolved problems in his own administration. The gulf between his rhetoric and reality was widest for African Americans. When it came to racial issues, his biographer Thomas Kessner has observed, La Guardia preferred a safe lie that all would be well to a dangerous truth.[76]

The ten years after World War II were a turbulent but generally optimistic time in New York City. The city's seaport industrial economy remained strong. La Guardia was gone, but the spirit of the New Deal still dominated New Yorkers' visions of the future. The total population of the city—7,891,957, according to the 1950 census—was higher than it had ever been. Manhattan north of 155th Street had a robust population of 214,099 residents. African Americans from the South and Puerto Ricans came to the city looking for freer and more productive lives, while white families began to trek to single-family homes in suburbia. Eventually these arrivals and departures, along with deteriorating economic possibilities for black and Hispanic newcomers, transformed the city. But for much of the 1950s, few anticipated the wrenching changes to come.[77]

The interracial gang fights that Bradford Chambers found twenty blocks south of Washington Heights in the late 1940s suggested looming problems for northern Manhattan. But none of this made an impression on my parents in 1952, when they made their way to upper Fort Washington Avenue to enjoy four good years.

During World War II, while my father was a U.S. Army sergeant in Europe, his parents had moved to the Highbridge section of the Bronx, just across the Harlem River from the Heights. After he was discharged, he lived with them, worked for a while as an offset printer, and then became a mechanic for the Mosler Safe Company. He also resumed canoeing on the Hudson River, which is how he met my mother.

My mom, a Bronx native and Hunter College graduate, worked as a secretary. On her mother's side her genealogy stretched back to the Van Alsytnes, seventeenth-century Dutch settlers in the Hudson Valley; her two grandmothers were immigrants from England and Germany. Her father worked on the IRT subway line. Growing up my mother moved in a heterogeneous crowd that included Jews, Italians, and Swedes. Her boyfriend, a Swedish American fellow, was part of the Hudson River boathouse scene. When he died in a scaffolding collapse while he was at work building a smokestack, my father and his boathouse buddies took my mom out to cheer her up. Eventually the other fellows faded from the picture and my parents married.

The rental market was tight in 1952, but one day their friend who worked in a real estate office called: she had an apartment open in Washington Heights at 550 Fort Washington Avenue, but demand was so fierce they would have to take it immediately. They took it, moved in during May of 1952, and never regretted it.

For both of my parents, Washington Heights was a step up. My dad said good-bye to sharing a room with his brother. My mom, who endured long commutes from Morris Park in the Bronx to college and jobs in Manhattan, delighted in the swift ride on the A train from 181st Street to midtown that put work and window shopping within easy reach.

Their two-bedroom apartment was on the top floor of a five-floor walkup. When they moved in the lobbies and halls badly needed a paint job, so my father circulated a petition with other tenants to get the landlord to paint. His own father painted and wallpapered their apartment. A short walk down Fort Washington Avenue brought them to 181st Street, with plenty of stores and a great Jewish bakery. A short walk up Fort Washington Avenue brought them to Fort Tryon Park, with its winding pathways, benches, and broad views of the Hudson River. They were pleased to have an affordable place in a nice neighborhood.

For my parents, the biggest municipal issue of the day was the tight housing market. When they solved that problem by renting at 550 Fort Washington Avenue, there was little that troubled them. The issues that would wrack the city by the mid-1960s—particularly battles over integration and fear of crime—did not define their lives. Both had seen anti-Semitism at work in the job market in the 1930s and 1940s, and my mother recognized that some of the offices where she worked as a secretary refused to hire blacks. My father knew of boathouses that accepted no Jews, but he made a point of canoeing at ones that accepted people of all faiths.

The realities of segregation and discrimination in residential housing did not figure significantly in my parents' understanding of northern Manhattan. Tensions between white residents and black and Hispanic people moving into the southern Heights had been a source of friction since the 1940s. But my parents lived in the northern Heights in a section that was overwhelmingly white. Like most New Yorkers, their sense of their neighborhood was limited to a few blocks. They lived out their uptown lives on Fort Washington Avenue between 181st Street and Fort Tryon Park and made an occasional trip east to the stores on Broadway. When I asked my mother if there were areas in the neighborhood that she avoided, she answered that she wouldn't venture south of 175th Street. It was a more crowded and "mixed" neighborhood, she explained. Nothing in the daily routines of her life would have brought her there. If she had walked south, she might have glimpsed signs of a more conflicted future for Washington Heights.[78]

In the summer of 1955, the *New York Times* published a series, "Our Changing City," on New York and its suburbs. Washington Heights was included in an article on the West Side of Manhattan that covered everything from 14th Street to Marble Hill in the Bronx. The chief demographic reality of the West Side, the article pointed out, was the growth in the black and Puerto Rican population. The piece described Washington Heights as the "chief habitat" of the middle class, but also noted heavy overcrowding and high rents in Morningside Heights and Manhattanville to the south of the Heights. "A characteristic of West Side life," it argued, "is the mixture of races and nationalities in run-down neighborhoods with antiquated housing in close proximity to modern houses and apartments with all the comforts and conveniences. These contrasts of squalor living next door to luxury have created frictions, resentments, and fears."[79]

The *Times* found a mixture of changes, opportunities, and problems in the neighborhoods near Washington Heights. But even where the *Times* saw problems, it generally saw problems that could be solved. In Harlem, a neighborhood of growing black and Hispanic communities, it recognized crime, a housing shortage, narcotics addiction, tuberculosis, and a high rate of infant mortality. But it also focused attention on improvements in employment, construction of new housing, schools and youth centers, and growing black political power in the Democratic Party. "In short," the article argued, "the community is riding a wave of optimism, attributable in part to the general business and industrial prosperity of the city, state and nation, and in part to the gradual curtailment of the two root causes of many, if not most, of Harlem's problems—the twin evils of racial segregation and discrimination."[80]

In articles on the lower and upper Bronx, the *Times* acknowledged white resistance to integration and white people leaving neighborhoods to avoid living alongside black and Puerto Rican newcomers. "The Irish," an article noted, "have concentrated in the Highbridge section, in the region of Yankee Stadium, and the Jews near there and along the Concourse." Highbridge in 1955, just across the Harlem River from Washington Heights, was where my grandparents and aunt, uncles, and cousins lived on University Avenue.[81]

The series "Our Changing City" offered equal parts of analysis and optimism. But its optimism was grounded in something more than simple boosterism. The New York of the mid-1950s was still an economic powerhouse with a strong manufacturing sector, a vigorous port, and a heavily unionized workforce. From housing to hospitals to recreation facilities to schools, New York offered an array of social services—delivered by unions, city government and service organizations—that made the city, in the historian Joshua B. Freeman's words, "a hybrid form of municipal social democracy." (The postwar face of this could be readily seen in northern Manhattan: in 1951, in Inwood on eastern Dyckman Street, the New York City Housing Authority opened Dyckman Houses—a high-rise project of 1,167 apartments.) New York was a center of liberalism with a strong labor movement. And while the Communists who had been a vigorous force in the years of the New Deal and Popular Front were waning by 1955, a leavening of socialists and ex-Communists continued their activism in ways that tilted the city's political culture to the left. Unquestionably, the city's housing market and job market treated whites better than blacks and Puerto Ricans. Without doubt, new public-housing construction disproportionately displaced blacks and Puerto Ricans. In retrospect, it is clear that the city's economic base in the 1950s as a seaport manufacturing city was vulnerable.[82]

Yet there was still, in 1955, a sense that New York had great years ahead of it and great prospects for its newest arrivals. This optimism, with all its accompanying blindness and paternalism, echoed in the pages of the *New York Times*: "The West Side says it assimilated the Dutch and the English and the Irish and the Germans and the Italians and the Jews and all the others, and it can assimilate the Negroes and the Puerto Ricans. Aren't we Americans all?"[83]

Such boosterism could not put a halt to trends, some economic and some cultural, that would drive further demographic changes on Manhattan. In 1956, my parents left Washington Heights for New Jersey. Mosler was sending my father on more and more calls in North Jersey. A move to the suburbs would shorten his commute, give me a yard to play in, and give him a quiet place to relax at the end of the day. After a wearying search, my parents found a Cape Cod house in Dumont, a New Jersey town on a direct bus line to the city. Having banked my mother's salary for years, they put down $5,000 of the $13,000 price for their new home.[84]

Long after they left the city, my parents voiced their love for its crowds, its many peoples, and its vitality. They respected its public institutions, especially the schools. And my father always said that it was a better place than the suburbs for a working man looking for a job because you didn't need a car to get around and you could easily fit a job interview into a lunch break. In Dumont, my parents settled into a neighborhood of new houses, spindly trees, and little conviviality. When she first visited the town, my mother recalled later, she noticed the absence of high walls and wondered where all the guys went to play handball. The short answer was that they didn't. In Washington Heights, a short walk with me in a baby carriage brought her to Fort Tryon Park and an easy conversation with another adult. In Dumont, it just brought endless walks around suburban blocks, heavy with wondering about when one of the local women might finally talk to her.

My parents cherished the happy family life that they built in Dumont, lovingly recorded with snapshots and home movies, but they always felt a greater identification with New York City. Their departure for Dumont— and the stories they told about the metropolis they left behind—had none of the anger, bewilderment, or fear of suburbanites who left the city under the shadow of crime or racial and ethnic conflict. But for those who remained behind in the Heights, there would be other stories to be told.

By 1950, the population of southern Washington Heights was almost one-third people of color. Black real estate dealers bought up private homes and ran them as rooming houses for black and Puerto Rican tenants. A Puerto Rican minister received many requests for information on apartments in the Heights because, as he put it, "This is one of the few nice places where relatively poor people can live."[85] No one set out a welcome mat for the newcomers. A report on Washington Heights released by the Protestant Council of the City of New York in 1954 noted: "With the population mobility and the inroads of Puerto Ricans and Negroes, human relations problems have mounted. Several incidents were reported, such as the throwing of an incendiary bomb into an apartment house occupied by Puerto Ricans at 182nd Street and Audubon Avenue. Although the offenders were never apprehended, community sentiment attributes this incident as arising from the tensions between the Irish and Puerto Rican groups in the community."[86]

In the churning of old-timers' departures and newcomers' arrivals, the mothers' networks that had once helped to keep order in the neighborhood broke down. Rifts among whites, blacks, and Latinos meant that they would not be rebuilt. In 1954, a municipal study noted that delinquency rates in southern and eastern portions of the Heights were exceeded only by those of the city's most dangerous neighborhoods.[87]

The changes in southern Washington Heights did not proceed at a uniform pace. The southwest Heights, the center of the German Jewish community, remained overwhelmingly white but with some ethnic variations. Frank Hess, born in 1941 and the son of a German Jewish man who spent three months in Dachau, lived at 652 W. 160th Street and recalls it as mixed—Jews, Irish, Italians, Argentines, Mexicans. One block away, as he recalls it, West 160th Street was entirely Jewish. Maurice Murad, born in the United States to Iraqi Jews in 1938, grew up at 611 W. 158th Street. He played baseball for the Paiutes, alongside black, Puerto Rican, and German Jewish refugee teammates. On the streets, his friends were comfortable enough with their differences to tease each other about them. While he occasionally saw guys get in fights over girls, the Irish and Hispanic gangs on the east side of Broadway were a distant presence in his life.[88]

Murad remembers his neighborhood in the fifties as a place with little conflict. Hess remembers some awareness of racial and ethnic tension in the same period, but that this could be defused at an individual level. In music class at George Washington High School, the big public high school in the Heights, he sat next to Charles Horton, a black kid up from Alabama whom he remembers as both "a sweet guy" and a gang member. One afternoon, he was sitting with a friend at 160th Street and Riverside when he saw a substantial gang heading toward them. Running would be futile, Hess thought, so he sat tight. The gang prowled around Hess and his friend until a familiar face loomed up: "Hess, what are you doing here?" asked Horton. The tension dissolved.

Not all encounters ended so amicably. As far back as the 1940s, when Joseph Ahearn feared walking east of Amsterdam Avenue into black turf, young men of color faced harassment if they ventured into western parts of the Heights. By the 1950s, the combination of turf consciousness, a growing black and Latino population in northern Manhattan, and the lure of Highbridge Pool, the New Deal's local gem, set the stage for increased confrontations.

As Ira Katznelson has observed, "From start to finish, the New Deal flourished with ethical compromise." In Washington, DC, that meant compromises with conservative southern Democrats who limited the New Deal in ways that harmed women and African Americans. In Washington Heights, the compromises were fought out on city streets. Highbridge Pool in Washington Heights was officially integrated, but on the streets outside it white kids tried to bar young people of color from going inside to swim. One African American man, a teenager at the time, recalled that he loved the pool—with its grand size, its superior maintenance, and the old men there who sold great french fries. But the trip to Highbridge Pool was a problem. There were no black families near the pool, he said, so white gangs could act with impunity. Sometimes, the gangs threw bottles at him and his friends inside the pool. The broken glass left behind was the only mess he recalled seeing at Highbridge Pool.[89]

CHAPTER 2

A USELESS AND TERRIBLE DEATH

IN THE HOUR BEFORE 11 P.M., on the hot night of July 30 in 1957, two groups of young men converged on Highbridge Park. Before the night was over one boy would be dead and one would be wounded. The assailants eventually faced reform school, prison, and the electric chair. And the city around them glimpsed, through the tangled narratives of a murder trial and sensational news coverage, profound questions about New York's neighborhoods, crime, youth gangs, and race and ethnic relations.[1]

From downtown, from Harlem, and from the lower fringes of the Heights, traveling in twos and threes in order to be inconspicuous, came some eighteen members of the Dragons and the Egyptian Kings: allied gangs of young Latinos and African Americans with a few Irish members. Ten of them were under fifteen. They carried knives, chains, baseball bats, a machete, and garrison belts with big brass buckles that could be filed sharp at the corners and swung in a fight. Some were there to confront the Jesters, a gang from the Heights that one of them described as "Irish boys" (even though it counted a few blacks and Latinos among its members and allies). The Jesters had chased black and Hispanic boys from the Highbridge Park pool, and taunted them as "spics" and "niggers." Some of the Dragons and Egyptian Kings were there to uphold reputations as fighters, to maintain the honor of their gang. Others were there because they feared retribution if they failed to show up for a raid on the Jesters. Some were nervous. Some had been drinking. Some were angry.[2]

From the north, from a more Irish section of the Heights, came Michael Farmer, fifteen, and Roger McShane, sixteen. While their status as gang members was the subject of speculation at the time, it seems that McShane was a Jester. Farmer was at the very least a friend of the gang. Farmer and McShane were residents of a neighborhood once largely Irish, Jewish, and Greek that was uneasy at the prospect of racial integration. They had spent the evening listening to rock-and-roll records in Farmer's apartment. Then they went outside to sneak through a hole in the park's fence and swim in the pool. Once they entered the park, boys from the Dragons and Egyptian Kings spotted them. Farmer and McShane had walked into trouble.[3]

Looking up a staircase in the park, McShane later recalled, they saw two boys with garrison belts wrapped around their fists. They climbed the stairs anyway. McShane saw the other gang members in the shadows. Accounts differ over whether the two groups exchanged words or physically confronted each other. From then on, the actions seem relatively clear: McShane bolted and told Farmer to run.[4]

But Farmer, who walked with a slight limp from a bout of polio, was not quick. The gangs surrounded him and attacked. Farmer collapsed under a barrage of kicks, blows, and stab wounds. Bruises and cuts found on his hands suggested his futile attempts to defend himself. Other attackers ran down McShane and stabbed him. Then they all scattered into the night. A bleeding McShane staggered from the park, hailed a taxi, and told the driver about Farmer. The taxi driver took McShane to a nearby hospital.[5] Police were summoned. Officer John Collich found the mortally wounded boy lying in a clump of bushes. Farmer's attackers were African Americans, Latinos, and a few Irish, but the dying boy saw only black skin. According to the notes of the policeman who found him, he said, "The niggers got me, the Egyptian Kings, please help me, I can't breathe."[6] An hour later, he was dead. McShane survived.

In April 1958, four of Farmer's assailants were found guilty after a long and sensational trial. Eleven more participants in the attack, too young to be treated as adult criminals, were sent to juvenile facilities. Newspaper stories, magazine articles, a radio broadcast, and books told the story to New York and the nation.

Three times—in the early news reports on the slaying, in a municipal psychiatrist's research on reactions to the killing, and in the trial of the defendants accused of killing Farmer—city officials and journalists dismissed the possibility that racial or ethnic conflict had anything to do with the case. In doing so, they ignored years of racial and ethnic conflict over the use of municipal pools in New York City as well as the words of the participants in the Farmer tragedy—then and since. Of course, psychological factors, the dynamics of youth gang culture, and a tendency toward violence among young males all figured in the case. But when the mayor, journalists, and courts refused to see the racial and ethnic factors in the case, they blinded themselves to conflicts and inequalities among blacks, whites, and Hispanics that would soon redefine the city and shatter the optimism of the urban New Deal order.[7]

Journalists, and elected officials, rarely tell stories that people are not ready to hear. And in New York City in the Farmer case, both the press and Mayor Robert Wagner were reluctant to recognize resistance to integrated swimming in a city with a reputation for political liberalism, a city where public pools were officially open to all but in practice subject to segregationist pressures.[8] Indeed it is no surprise that Highbridge Pool was the setting of a confrontation. Pools, like amusement parks, were places of freedom, autonomy, and expression for urban youth, as Victoria W. Wolcott has written. Black and white young people both valued them, but for blacks to enjoy them they frequently had to overcome white resistance to integrated swimming. As Jeff Wiltse has observed of northern cities in the 1940s and 1950s, public swimming pools were uniquely volatile scenes for racial conflict. Bodies in swimsuits suggested new levels of public intimacy, and whites—inspired by racism, fear of black men, and fears of interracial sex—violently assaulted blacks who sought to swim alongside them. In the face of such rejection, the integration of swimming pools became a cause of the civil rights movement. Indeed, as Martha Biondi has recounted, during the late 1940s and early 1950s civil rights activists fought heroically to integrate the pool at Palisades Park, an amusement park just across the Hudson River from Washington Heights in Fort Lee, New Jersey.[9]

Yet in its day the Farmer case was portrayed in the news media neither as a civil rights case nor as a harbinger of racial and ethnic conflict. The authorities who framed public discussions of the Farmer episode repeatedly looked away from the racial and ethnic dimensions of the killing. This turned the crime into an example of what Arnold R. Hirsch has called "hidden violence"—hidden not because it was invisible, but because it was not fully recognized in its time for all that it was.[10]

Part of what obscured the Farmer case was the time and place of its happening. The killing occurred in the waning days of the idealistic but sometimes blind liberalism of the 1950s, under which many New Yorkers failed to appreciate the wrenching racial conflicts and inequalities brewing in the city. Activist groups such as the NAACP recognized and fought segregation in housing and education in New York, but they lacked the political influence to consistently propel their concerns to the heights of government attention and media visibility. For their part, all the major actors in the case had different reasons for playing down the significance of race and ethnicity in the killing. Mayor Wagner, a New Deal Democrat, did not embrace the kind of backlash politics that would push race to the forefront of political debate in New York during the 1960s and 1970s. In the courts, Judge Irwin D. Davidson sought a trial without mention of race precisely because he thought that mention of race would make it easier to convict the defendants, the majority of whom were black and Hispanic. And the city's press, while not in lockstep in its coverage of the killing and trial, frequently deferred to government authority in coverage of the case in ways that amplified Mayor Wagner's less-than-searching discussion of the episode. To look back on the Farmer case is to see a New York torn between bigotry and denial of bigotry, between liberal ideals of inclusion and emerging recognition of exclusion, between fear of violence and a belief that city government could guarantee order and justice. It was also a city poised on the edge of a massive demographic shift.

Thus, while the context of Farmer case recalls the turmoil of other cities in the years after World War II, when conflicts over race and housing moved to the center of local political debate, there are important differences. In Detroit, as Thomas Sugrue has written, where working-class home ownership was relatively common, racist fears of integration combined with fear of losing the value of hard-earned houses. In such situations, white resistance to integration took the form of attacks orchestrated by entire communities. Similar actions occurred in Boston, Baltimore, and Chicago.[11] In Manhattan, by contrast, where renters vastly outnumbered property owners and the lure of the suburbs beckoned, most white people had no economic incentive to resist integration in the name of preserving property values. Instead, they moved. But before they left, tensions and gang fights in neighborhoods such as Washington Heights contradicted the city's reputation as a liberal, well-governed city that would escape battles over integration. The raid planned by the Dragons and Egyptian Kings, and the subsequent murder of Farmer, represented a violent and anguished cry just before the beginning of a new racial and ethnic regime in northern Manhattan.

Michael Farmer lived at 575 W. 175th Street, a short walk from Highbridge Park.[12] In the summer of 1957, with increasing African American and Latino migration into Manhattan, Highbridge Pool was an oasis to be enjoyed and a prize to be fought over. Parks department film footage from the 1930s shows whites and African Americans swimming together there peacefully, as Marta Gutman has noted. But the streets outside, of course, were another matter.[13]

Figure 6: Highbridge Pool and water tower during the La Guardia administration. Courtesy NYC Municipal Archives.

Highbridge Pool was not unique in this regard. In East Harlem in the 1930s, Robert Moses noted, local Italian Americans barred Puerto Ricans from the Thomas Jefferson Pool. The worst fights took place not at the pool itself, he said, but on nearby streets that were difficult to police. Such white resistance to integration contributed to the Harlem Riot of 1943, which lapped against southern Washington Heights.[14] For the African Americans, the riot expressed the anger, frustration, and disappointed hopes that followed migration to northern cities. For Irish and Jewish residents, the riot sparked moves north to areas with white majorities.[15]

From 1940 to 1970 the population of New York City grew from 7.5 to 7.9 million. But this modest increase masked a dramatic change in the city's ethnic and racial composition. The city's white population, not counting Puerto Ricans, fell from seven million to five million. As the city's white population diminished, the number of New York's African American residents grew from 458,000 to 1,668,000 and the city's Puerto Rican population grew from under 100,000 to almost 1,000,000.[16] Amid these demographic shifts, the African Americans and Latinos, just like the Jews and Irish before them, were moving in search of better housing. Washington Heights was one of the places with the solid housing stock and neighborhood amenities that people sought. Tensions were climbing by the summer of 1957 as more black and Puerto Rican families were moving onto previously white streets—often under the pressure of blockbusting realtors.[17]

Not all ethnic interactions were combustible; much depended on the settings of encounters. Robert Greenfield, an Irish American from West 157th Street, an integrated area on the borderlands of the Heights and Harlem, played basketball on multiracial Catholic Youth Organization teams organized by his father. Unlike the pool, with its increasingly tense atmosphere, adult-supervised sports allowed young men from different ethnic and racial groups to build teams with a shared sense of interest. Sports provided an outlet for aggressive feelings that might lead to fighting in other contexts, and gave young men an arena for interaction without the challenges of competition over girls. (Off the courts, Greenfield himself knew members of the Egyptian Kings and dated a Puerto Rican girl.)[18]

Living on 182nd Street between Amsterdam and Audubon avenues, Maureen Murphy—the daughter of Irish immigrants—went to school at Saint Elizabeth's and played stoopball, stick ball, and hopscotch with Jewish, Irish, Greek, and Polish kids. She remembers some ethnic and religious rivalries, and how many whites fled after Puerto Ricans and African Americans arrived in the early 1950s. Her parents stayed. Her father was a bus driver and a union man with a strong sense of "faith, family and social justice"; her mother was a former live-in maid who worked with a priest at the Church of the Incarnation to establish a community center in the basement of her building that served Puerto Ricans and African Americans. In the process Maureen picked up "street Spanish" and learned about "living with poverty, hunger, neglect, and marginalization."[19]

The music scene in the Heights also saw a degree of integration that illuminated the neighborhood's best possibilities. Jim Clarke, born in 1944 to immigrant parents from Ireland, was raised at 371 Wadsworth Avenue between 191st and 192nd streets. He knew about gangs, but he thought it was smart to stay out of them. By the time he was fourteen, he was hanging out on street corners in his neighborhood singing in the style of music that would later be called doo-wop. His first singing partner was Sam Garcia, a Puerto Rican. Over the years he also sang with black, Irish, and half Jewish/half Puerto Rican partners. On the corner of 192nd and Wadsworth, at the Audubon Theater, in record stores, listening to the radio, going to the Paramount to see the Alan Freed show, and watching *American Bandstand* on television, Clarke absorbed the musical influences of everything from the Mills Brothers to rock and roll to jazz.[20]

In the scene that Clarke was part of, young men went into the streets not to seek fights but to find singing partners. They sang in what Clarke thought of as a New York sound, with a hard edge. They sought not turf to defend but places with great echoes and acoustics, like the tunnel leading into the IRT subway station at 191st Street or the great open space under the overpass in Fort Tryon Park.

The musical scene in the Heights was not in a universe entirely apart from racial and ethnic conflict. Stitt Junior High School in the Heights had its share of tensions, but it also produced Frankie Lymon, whose singing with the Teenagers, a group with African American and Puerto Rican members, produced the hit recorded in 1955, "Why Do Fools Fall in Love?" Yet the co-operation and musical mixing that fueled the Heights musical scene, driven by a shared desire for expression that could be best realized only by working with the best and most companionable singers you could find, was one element in a neighborhood that was alive to both youth culture and ethnic change.[21]

Far more dangerous, and far more prominent in the media, were the fighting gangs that emerged from the same streets. The 1950s were distinguished by widespread concern with the issue of juvenile delinquency rooted in middle-class anxiety over working-class youth culture and the emergence of a youth culture grounded in popular music and the mass media. At the time of the Farmer case, the American media were in the middle of a crucial shift in the depiction of delinquency. In the early 1950s, as the historian Michael Flamm writes, analysts stressed "the universality of the problem, which affected every community and all teens regardless of race, class, and locale." By the end of the decade, and with even greater force in the 1960s, race was invoked to explain crimes committed by young people. The shift in perspective damaged the prospects of the black struggles for justice, sharpened racial conflict, and split the multiracial coalition that formed the bedrock of Wagner's New Deal mayoralty.[22] The murder of Michael Farmer occurred in the middle of this transition. From the vantage point of the Farmer case in Washington Heights, it is possible to look back to the relative confidence of New York liberalism in the 1950s and forward to the racialized concern with crime of the 1960s.

To be sure, the gangs were not the only reality for young people in Washington Heights. There were lots of kids (like Clarke) who stayed away from the world of fighting gangs. Gary Zaboly, born in 1950, who grew up at 501 W. 169th Street at the corner of Amsterdam Avenue with Hungarian, Italian, and Spanish ancestry, was attacked by both black and white gang members. He vividly remembers looking out his apartment window to see two Latino boys fighting with garbage can lids as weapons. Fights occurred both within and between ethnic groups. In Zaboly's mind, Highbridge Park was both a place to play and a place that could turn scary and dangerous if one were unlucky enough to encounter the wrong person or group. When he looked at gangs like the Jesters, he didn't see defenders of his neighborhood. He saw mean, nasty guys who were as likely to hurt him as an interloper with dark skin.[23]

In earlier decades in Washington Heights, networks of watchful mothers had kept an eye out and maintained order on individual blocks. Their capacity to do this should not be idealized: after all, it didn't seem to do much to control the anti-Semitic violence of the World War II years. Nevertheless, into the 1950s, sharp-eyed moms could keep violence and disorder within limits. But as the demography of neighborhoods changed, and youth culture grew more autonomous, the communal ties that gave mothers their authority frayed. Equally important, the rise of fighting gangs brought to the streets hard young men well beyond the reach of maternal oversight and chastisement.

According to a municipal study of 1954, delinquency rates in southern and eastern portions of the Heights were exceeded only by those of the city's most dangerous neighborhoods, such as Harlem. In June 1955 the city's Youth Board—created in 1948 to fight juvenile delinquency and already active in Harlem, and the Upper West Side—extended its activities into the Heights as far as Dyckman Street. Clearly, this was an effort to keep a problem from getting worse. But in Washington Heights, tensions were brewing.[24]

In the summer of 1957, the atmosphere around Highbridge Pool grew tense. Although security at the pool generally kept conflict to sharp words or a scuffle, there were rarely police on the streets outside the pool where gangs, mostly organized on ethnic lines, would gather.[25]

Jack Boucher, captain of the Jesters, explained in a 2007 interview that he saw the purpose of his gang as defending his part of Washington Heights against the people whom neighborhood parents described as riffraff—black and Hispanic youths. Keeping them out of the pool was part of keeping them out of the neighborhood. The members of the Jesters were mostly Irish and Catholic; they gathered, Boucher recalled, on their "gang block": West 167th Street between Amsterdam and Audubon avenues. In pursuit of their goals, the Jesters might ally with a gang from farther north, the Fanwoods, who had some black and Hispanic members. But they would not seek an alliance with the Kings—a gang of largely black and Hispanic membership—whom he saw as his confirmed adversaries. (At the same time, Boucher's first girlfriend in this neighborhood was Puerto Rican; he once shared a mitt with a black youth playing baseball; and he had a passing acquaintance with Leoncio De Leon, who was in the group that attacked Farmer and McShane.) The warring factions of northern Manhattan were both neighbors and enemies.[26]

The lines of conflict in northern Manhattan could be navigated on individual terms. Irish kids left behind in a changing neighborhood could join a black or Puerto Rican gang for protection; similarly, the first black or Latino youth on a white block might seek to join an otherwise Irish gang. But these were alliances of necessity and interest, born of isolated youths' attempts to ingratiate themselves with the racial or ethnic majority on a block, or of gang leaders' efforts to fortify their ranks before a fight. Protection was always the goal. For individuals, boundaries could be porous. But good feelings about an individual did not necessarily mean warmth for an entire group.[27] Race could be negotiated, but it could not be negotiated away.

The police department's statements about the killing were contradictory. At first, an anonymous police source told reporters the case had a racial dimension. Later, a named, high-ranking police source, acting chief of detectives Edward W. Byrnes, told the *Times* and the *News* that race had nothing to do with it.[28] In the politics of journalism, sources that disclose information that is likely to disturb their superiors can insist on anonymity, which makes possible their candor. At the same time, an institution that wants to place its authority behind an announcement will use a high-ranking member who speaks openly for attribution. In the aftermath of the Farmer case, the contrast between an anonymous police source saying that the killing was part of a racial conflict and a high-ranking officer saying the opposite for public attribution suggests a department that was actively working to stamp the story with the nonracial interpretation—something municipal officials had done previously in comparable instances in New York and elsewhere. The sources' contrasting responses to the killing reflect a tendency that would be seen later in the Wagner administration's actions: a desire to describe the case in the least inflammatory way possible.[29]

The Farmer murder raised the specter of racial violence; it put the police in the position of being asked to prevent a racial conflict at the very time that patterns of urban migration were making the boundaries of neighborhoods more contested. An early article in the *Post* quoted an anonymous source on the Youth Board saying that the Wadsworth Avenue police precinct in Washington Heights had "a record of ineptness and crudity in dealing with racial disturbances in the area, which has a 15-year history of racial friction." Indeed, as a municipal investigation would later discover, there was dissatisfaction with the police in the Heights; there was also concern with racial and ethnic conflict. Nevertheless, in dismissing the racial dimension of the crime,

Byrnes diminished the gravity of the incident, reduced expectations of the police, and guarded them against criticism. He also undermined the analysis of the killing.[30]

Like the *Times* and the *Daily News*, the *Post* repeated Acting Chief of Detectives Byrnes's claim that racial tensions were not a factor in the killing, but followed with another paragraph: "Many residents in the area, including some boys who belong to street gangs, disagreed with police and blamed the tragedy on racial friction which, they said, has recently been increasing in the area." A similar pairing of perspectives appeared in the *Herald Tribune*.[31] By contrast, *El Diario de Nueva York*, a Spanish-language daily tabloid, combined sympathy for the victim with acknowledgement of the conflicts that led to his death. With a large Puerto Rican readership and with Latinos prominent among the defendants (two of the seven who eventually stood trial were from Puerto Rico, and a third was from the Dominican Republic), *El Diario*—a paper with a reputation as "the champion of Puerto Ricans"— devoted sustained attention to the story. *El Diario* published photographs of Farmer's grieving parents and McShane in his first communion suit. At the same time, a prominent story said, "Motivos raciales fueron la causa aparente de la tragedia, segun las autoridades," or "Racial motives were the apparent cause of the tragedy, according to the authorities."[32]

The most tormented coverage of the case appeared in the *Amsterdam News*. The paper covered sensational crimes in Harlem for its black readership, but it seemed uncomfortable reporting an interracial murder that could fuel racist reactions. To recognize race as a factor in the killing would expose the harassment of black youths trying to use Highbridge Pool, but it could also result in the depiction of young black men as perpetrators of racial violence. (The paper's stance had a precedent: in 1943, both Mayor La Guardia and Adam Clayton Powell Jr., the first black member of the New York City Council, said publicly that the Harlem Riot was not a race riot. Their motives were complex, but they sought to uphold a politics of interracial unity and deflect charges of black hooliganism.) The *Amsterdam News*' "No Racial Bias in Teen Warfare" article began, "Contrary to race-baiting reports, the Upper Manhattan gang killing of one boy and stabbing of another early last week had no specific racial overtones, although teenage friction has been rampant in the area, an *Amsterdam News* study showed this week." This lead was immediately followed by recognition of a Bronx gang slaying that involved "Negro youths only" and a stabbing of a white youth in Brooklyn by two black boys in an incident that the article called an "exception to the non racial element of the current violence wave."[33] The story then jumped to page twenty-four, where—in a less prominent section of the paper—it delivered a uniquely insightful discussion of southern Washington Heights, the neighborhood's demography, the mixed composition of the gangs, and the increase in violence as more black youths used the pool. "Reliable sources say that racial incidents have occurred frequently between individuals," the article concluded, adding, "the chance of white gang versus colored gang warfare is reduced due to integration. But, it is not completely out of the question."

In photojournalism, questions of race and ethnicity were hard to avoid. "Teen-age Burst of Brutality," a two-page spread in the August 12, 1957, edition of *Life* magazine, ran photos of the "Grim Egyptian Kings" that depicted nine defendants looking grim and sullen, with eyes downcast. They overwhelmingly appeared as young men of color, with the two white defendants among them barely visible. In contrast, the photo of the "Laughing Jesters" leaves the impression of white youths who are spirited but hardly menacing (even though one youth in the photo is black and three might be Latinos).[34]

Overall, *Life* depicted New York as a city where gang violence might break out anywhere. This sweeping statement belied the clear fact that Farmer's murder occurred in a park and a neighborhood that were hotbeds of racial and ethnic tension. *Life*'s description also meshed uneasily with the optimism of the city's tradition of New Deal liberalism. New York City government in 1957 was dominated by a liberal ethos that assumed that the city could be integrated peacefully. Despite the conservative weight of McCarthyism in the 1950s, Mayor Wagner—son of a U.S. senator who sponsored some of the most important legislation of the New Deal, including the Wagner Act that established collective bargaining rights for unions—presided over a city whose politics was defined by liberals, New Deal Democrats, socialists, and ex-Communists. Mayor Wagner aligned himself with liberals, the labor movement, and regular Democrats. His Catholicism endeared him to Catholic Democrats, his liberalism recommended him to Jews, and he wooed African American voters with a formal commitment to civil rights. Temperamentally, Wagner was a cautious executive. The *Nation* reported that "a bit of the father's wisdom that the Mayor frequently cites is to the effect that often the best way to handle a problem is to do nothing; you'd be surprised, he says, how frequently today's crisis fades away tomorrow. 'When in doubt, don't,' the Mayor often quotes his father as having said."[35]

Mayor Wagner, a principled and cautious man whose base of support was so broad that it was open to splintering, faced many problems that could not be solved with benign neglect. He was, in fact, most vulnerable at the points exposed by the Farmer case: crime, policing, and the struggles over racial integration. Irish Catholics in Washington Heights who resisted integration and African Americans who wanted to exercise their right to swim at

Highbridge Pool were all part of Wagner's political base. At the same time, Wagner's Republican opponent in the 1957 mayoral race, Robert K. Christenberry (whom Wagner would soundly defeat), hammered at Wagner and called New York "sick with crime." Wagner called his critics "irresponsible" and vowed to approach crime with both the "hard" response of law enforcement and the "soft" response of counseling.[36]

Wagner also worked to conceal perceptions of racial conflict and dissatisfaction with the police that surfaced in the Heights after the Farmer killing. He suppressed a report by Dr. Maurice Greenhill, a psychiatrist and director of the New York City Community Mental Health Board, who directed an investigation of 125 people's reactions to the killing in the southern Heights. Greenfield's study was executed despite concern in the police commissioner's office that it would "'stir up' hysteria" and "reveal that the police had been remiss." Indeed, Greenhill did uncover residents' strong conviction that the incident was due to a "lack of police." Less frequently expressed, but still prominent, was the belief that the killing was due to "racial issues," to "newcomers" in the city or neighborhood, and to parents' "inability to control their children." A municipal researcher found, in one Puerto Rican family, a victim of the Jesters, a friend of Michael Farmer, and a mother frightened that gangs would now attack Puerto Ricans.[37]

Greenhill's researchers found widespread attitudes of "hopelessness, helplessness and fear," with few expectations that the underlying problems of crime and gang violence would change. Parents now kept their children indoors under supervision, or directed them to stay away from Highbridge Pool. Moreover, fear and anxiety crossed ethnic divides: one section of Greenhill's report quoted Irish, black, Jewish, and Puerto Rican families all talking about their deep sense of fear. Yet the Wagner administration did not use this information to affirm a multiracial response to the Farmer slaying. Instead, city hall muffled the voices of black, white, and Hispanic families in Washington Heights.

When Greenhill distributed a press release on his research without first showing it to city hall, Mayor Wagner summoned him and told him to clear any statements on juvenile delinquency with the mayoral executive secretary, William R. Peer. After further conversations between Greenhill and a *Times* reporter, city hall narrowed Greenhill's domain: he could answer only questions that were not related to his research on Washington Heights. A *Times* article published August 17 summed up the clash of perspectives.

> Dr. Greenhill was asked for his views about the effects of publicity on juvenile delinquency. Mr. Peer had said that he had a strong feeling

that publicity was bad because it suggested crime to susceptible youths. Dr. Greenhill had expressed an opposite view.

The doctor again hesitated for a time before answering. Then, speaking slowly, and measuring each word, he said:

"When people are anxious about a problem it is much better to talk about it or read about it than bottle it up. Also when people in delinquency areas have the opportunity to express anxiety, corrective measures inherently begin moving within families and groups of families.

"Where one family is not able to cope with a problem alone, they can receive support from the families around them, from the whole block."

Dr. Greenhill's report was locked up. When a Republican state senator running for city comptroller sued to see the field reports from the investigation, a judge denied the suit.[38]

A public meeting on juvenile delinquency called by the mayor at city hall was no more illuminating. At the gathering, held on August 20, thirty speakers from city government, charities, settlement houses, and the courts proposed everything from expanded social work to changes in the comics to more foster homes. The meeting gave many stakeholders the sense that they were being heard, but the wide range of proposals committed the mayor to no clear course of action that might alienate anyone.[39]

A short walk north of city hall in the Criminal Courts Building, on the same day as the mayor's meeting on juvenile delinquency, indictments were announced for first-degree murder in the death of Michael Farmer. In the *Times*, with its emphasis on policy and government, the stories were covered together under the headline, "14 Boys Indicted in Two Killings; City Parley Held." The *Post*, with a different emphasis, covered the indictment with this headline: "Park Knifing Murder Rap May Send 7 Youths to Chair." Two months later, the New York *Mirror* of October 3, 1957, kept the pathos of the killing alive with a story about young people from Farmer's neighborhood who pooled their money to buy a gold chalice in his memory. The *Mirror* reprinted a poem by Farmer's mother that began, "A chalice for Michael, my first-born boy, / A chalice for Michael, my pride and my joy."[40]

At a pretrial hearing on January 13, 1958, the courtroom of Judge Irwin D. Davidson in the Criminal Courts Building at 100 Centre Street was jammed with spectators and seven teenage defendants: Louis Alvarez, sixteen; George Melendez, sixteen; John McCarthy, fifteen; Charles Horton, eighteen; Richard

Hills, fifteen; Leroy Birch, eighteen; and Leoncio De Leon, fifteen. The court appointed all the defense attorneys save one because the defendants were too poor to afford their own counsel. It was, the *Times* reported, "the largest first-degree murder trial in the history of New York County in terms of numbers of defendants and lawyers." Judge Davidson, who presided over the trial, was a former state assemblyman and congressman who put himself through law school by working as a Borscht Belt entertainer. In the assembly he had worked on legislation related to slum clearance, workers' compensation, and civil rights. He served one term as a U.S. congressman from the West Side of Manhattan, elected on the Democratic and Liberal lines, before becoming a judge.[41]

After a panel of 250 potential jurors was exhausted, seventy-five more were brought in. Eventually, an all-male jury, including two African Americans, was chosen. Two alternate jurors, also men, were selected.[42]

The prosecutor, Robert R. Reynolds, made his opening statement to the jury on February 5. The charge was first-degree murder. Reynolds argued, according to the *Times*, that the seven accused boys had gone to Highbridge Park "'to punch out, fight and kill' any member of 'the so-called uptown gangs.'" In general, press coverage at the start of the trial expressed revulsion at the murder and a lack of sympathy for the defendants. The *Post* noted, as the *Times* did not, that conviction for first-degree murder carried a penalty of death.[43]

Two days later, Murray Kempton, columnist for the *Post*, published "The Evidence." Kempton combined dogged reporting, sharp but complex prose, and an egalitarian conscience. Born and educated in Baltimore, he had been active in the Young People's Socialist League and the American Labor Party. He joined the *Post* in 1942, left the newspaper to serve in World War II, and returned to the *Post* after the war. In the 1950s he covered subjects as varied as jazz, baseball, McCarthyism, unions, and the emerging civil rights movement.[44]

In "The Evidence," Kempton meditated on what might be learned from this trial. He described Patrolman John Collich's discovery of the mortally wounded Farmer, and how his dying words were ruled "inadmissible under the rules of evidence." Judge Davidson's ban on the mention of Farmer's words, "The niggers got me," removed from consideration a phrase that could have established a motive for a killing. This omission, Kempton suggested, would powerfully shape the case. Farmer's words—which never appeared in the press or in the trial—suggested a racial conflict that would make it easier to convict the defendants. Without those words, the trial would say little about how tensions in the neighborhood had fostered a killing. (In his book published after the trial, Judge Davidson prominently reprinted Farmer's words, recognized the racial and ethnic elements in the gangs' hostilities, and offered this thought: "Although there was little doubt that the antagonism between the Jesters and the downtown gangs had led to the death of Michael Farmer, legally that information was not relevant.")[45]

Kempton—writing during the trial and without actually reprinting Farmer's words—said this: "The reality, or the closest approximation, is that Michael Farmer was a victim of a war between an Irish gang, the Jesters, and a mainly Negro-Puerto Rican gang, the Egyptian Kings. It would certainly not justify murder if we could be told that some of the Egyptian Kings could not swim in the Washington Heights pool because the Jesters drove them away. But it would teach us something about the reality; unless we learn about the reality, can anyone hope that Michael Farmer's death was not as useless as it was terrible?"[46] However, Kempton continued, "any defense attorney who discusses that reality is in danger of harming his client. He could be establishing a motive that would only add to the weight of evidence against his client. And so there is no set for this play; it is presented in air."

The race-sensitive perspective found in Kempton's coverage appeared in only one other newspaper, the *Amsterdam News*, which, even while naming race as an issue, moved with caution. A front-page headline of February 22 announced Judge Davidson's forbidding any discussion of prior events around the pool: "Race Issue Ruled Out in Trial of 7." Deep within the story by Al Nall, a fuller perspective appeared: "This ruling was expected to blot out the question of race, which may be the basis for the whole ruckus."[47]

Given the stakes of a first-degree murder indictment and how race had been ruled out of the proceedings, the case was destined to be complex. Defense attorneys clashed repeatedly with the prosecution and charged that confessions had been extracted with beatings and coercion, a contention that one of the defendants maintains to this day.[48] And the courtroom was not isolated from the tension on the streets. In his book on the case, *The Jury Is Still Out*, published in 1959, Judge Davidson recalled the "grim phalanx of black-jacketed, greasy-haired boys and young men" who attended the trial. A minister from rural Phillipsburg, Pennsylvania, David Wilkerson, was so disturbed by the case that he traveled to New York and interrupted the trial to preach to gang members. He later wrote a much-reprinted book about his experiences, *The Cross and the Switchblade*. Roger McShane, a witness for the prosecution, received a letter that said, "if them guys get the chair we'll kill you." Allegations of police brutality prompted a letter to *El Diario*; its author, who claimed to represent nine gangs, vowed, "We will slowly but surely finish off all the cops." Judge Davidson received letters calling him "Pontius Pilate," "sentimental idiot," and, often, "Jew Bastard." "When they ran out of names they fell back on Communist," he wrote.[49]

Despite the limitations placed on presentable evidence, the trial illuminated the hostilities that fostered the crime. Lawyers for Charles Horton feared that his conduct left him vulnerable to a first-degree murder conviction and the electric chair. But if the boys had been goaded over time, had gone to Highbridge Park looking for a peace conference or a fight, and then had attacked Farmer in a hysterical outburst, then their crime was manslaughter and not first-degree murder. And they would be saved from the electric chair.[50] Any likely defense for Horton had to address some of the racial and ethnic aspects of the crime and, when called to the stand, Horton's testimony illuminated the racial politics of the Heights. Prosecutor Reynolds asked him why, on the night of the killing, he took a secluded park path to Highbridge Pool that avoided city streets. "Because the colored boys are recognized when they go up in this all Irish neighborhood," Horton replied. "You had white Irish boys with you too," observed the prosecutor. "That still didn't change my color," answered Horton.[51]

Larger portraits of the Dragons and Egyptian Kings were uncertain and disturbing. Testimony suggested that both sides had access to firearms, but ultimately the night's worst wounds were inflicted with blades. Alvarez's attempts to get reinforcements from the Bronx for the raid on the Jesters suggested a gang world of citywide dimensions, but his failure to produce allies for the foray spoke to the limits of the Dragons' and Egyptian Kings' power. And the Dragons and Egyptian Kings were not uniformly bellicose. Hills, one of the accused, had trooped uptown, Kempton reported, because he "had been put through a gauntlet of belts swung by bigger boys for failing to show up at a previous gang muster." Out of a crowd of as many as seventy-five boys gathered in front of a candy store at 152nd Street and Broadway, only about eighteen headed off to Highbridge Park. Some went home early because their parents held them to a firm curfew.[52]

Summaries in the case began on April 7. Defense attorneys repeated the charge of police brutality, argued that there was no intention to kill anyone that night, and reminded the jurors that they would be judging defendants who were more children than adults. Prosecutor Reynolds rejected the charge of police brutality. He alluded to the conditions that fostered the crime and dismissed them, saying, "If those in the Highbridge Park area were doing wrong, the defendants cannot resort to homicide to solve the problem."[53]

Judge Davidson's charge to the jury on April 14 ruled out the possibility of the death penalty for five of the seven boys. In his view, as he explained later, the charge of murder in the first degree—defined by premeditation, deliberation, and the intent to kill and punished by execution in the electric chair—applied to only two of the defendants: Alvarez, who went to High-bridge Park with a knife, and Horton, who carried a machete. And even Alvarez and Horton, he reminded the jury, could be convicted of a lesser count of murder—which did not carry the death penalty—if jurors saw fit. Moreover, under the same doctrine—when in doubt over which degree of a crime best fits the evidence, the lesser degree should prevail—the remaining five youths would face lesser charges of first or second-degree manslaughter. Neither carried the death penalty.[54]

Late in the day the case went to the jury. Jurors failed to settle that night and resumed deliberations the next day. Just after 6:30 p.m., they delivered a verdict: Luis Alvarez and Charles Horton (whose machete was not likely to have inflicted the deep stab wound that killed Farmer) were found guilty of second-degree murder, which carried a penalty of twenty years to life. They were not going to the electric chair. Leroy Birch and Leoncio DeLeon were convicted of second-degree manslaughter, which carried a sentence of up to fifteen years in prison. Richard Hills, George Melendez, and John McCarthy were acquitted. A juror, Saul Siegel, said afterward that jurors acquitted Hills and Melendez because they concluded that they had been forced to join the raid. McCarthy, he said, was acquitted because jurors agreed with his lawyer's claim that he was mentally incompetent. Courtroom reactions were subdued. Among parents in the hallway, prayers of thanks and screams of anguish broke out.[55]

On April 16, 1958, the news was a front-page story across New York City. The *World-Telegram* and *Daily News* focused on the pain of Farmer's family, while *El Diario* and the *Post* seemed concerned with the defendants and their families. The *New York Times* emphasized the size and intricacy of the trial, but ignored the complex hostilities that swirled around the case. In the *Times*, Farmer was simply "a 15-year-old polio victim" slain in a park by gang members. (This was an oversimplification: while Farmer was the victim of a terrible crime, he was no stranger to the world of gangs and fights that rose up to claim his life.)[56] In an editorial, the *World-Telegram* wondered "whether the jury made the most of its opportunity to set an example." An editorial in the *News* expressed a preference for first-degree murder convictions for all of the "punks" (which would have meant electrocution) but recognized that such a verdict was unlikely to withstand an appeal. "The jury," the editorial concluded, "handled the defendants as it would have handled adults, flatly rejecting the 'these poor kids never had a chance' hooey."[57]

For its part, the weekly *Amsterdam News* announced the verdict with a brief front-page bulletin on April 19. Its next edition returned to the story with an article by Al Nall, who quoted defense attorneys casting doubt on the justice of the verdict. He added, "Viewers of the trial contend that the case went according to Mississippi justice, in that the race issue was not permitted, even though the all-white rival gang, 'The Jesters,' had said they didn't want 'niggers and spics' swimming in the Highbridge Park pool." Nall's trenchant article ran on page twenty-six, where it was less than likely to gain wide attention.[58]

Kempton, in his April 17 column "The Verdict," saw shades of gray.[59] With the jury's judgment, he wrote, "we are left with most of the regrets, doubts, and confusions that we had at its beginning so long ago." Unlike the *News*, whose editorial argued for treating the defendants as adults, Kempton referred to the defendants as "boys" or "children." He stressed not the accountability that would be demanded of adults, but the vulnerability of children who should be protected from their environment. Nevertheless, he added, "I had thought all along that there were two things that society could do which would represent abandonment of these children. One would be to electrocute any one of them. The other would have been to acquit any one of them." Kempton concluded, "what Michael Farmer deserved was not vengeance but the risen conscience. His death was not as useless as it was horrible because no one will go to the electric chair for killing him. It is useless, not because no one will die for it, but because no one will be the better for it."

Judge Davidson sentenced the convicted defendants on May 28. Horton and Alvarez, convicted of second-degree murder, received the mandatory twenty years to life. Birch, convicted of second-degree manslaughter, received seven and a half to fifteen years. DeLeon, convicted of second-degree manslaughter, received a sentence of five to fifteen years. At the sentencing, the *Times* reported, "Davidson said he was imposing sentence 'with a sense of frustration and a heavy heart' because the trial had done nothing toward ending juvenile delinquency."[60]

With the trial over, efforts to analyze it began. Edward R. Murrow narrated an award-winning CBS Radio Network report, "Who Killed Michael Farmer?," written and produced by Jay L. McMullen, that used the voices of parents, gang members, educators, social workers, criminologists, and psychiatrists to explore the case. The report recognized rivalries over the pool and neighborhood instability. While the report stressed psychological explanations for delinquency, it also showed that antidelinquency programs were understaffed. In a telling omission, it quoted a police officer's expurgated version of Farmer's dying words that wiped away the racial dimension of the murder. Nevertheless, the Murrow broadcast maintained a faith in the effectiveness of public institutions that was a hallmark of liberal New York. New York, Murrow suggested, need only find the will and adequate funding to prevent future tragedies like the Farmer killing. "The problem of juvenile crime continues," said Murrow at the end of his broadcast. "The experts may list all sorts of causes. But they agree on one answer to why these conditions continue to exist: We permit them to."[61]

Lewis Yablonsky, a sociologist who ran an anticrime project on the Upper West Side of Manhattan and interviewed gang members involved in the Farmer killing, was interviewed for Murrow's broadcast. His book on delinquency and the Farmer case, *The Violent Gang*, argued, "Not only the racial mixture of the gangs but also the individual members' social and psychological dynamics demand assessment if the forces at work in the disorganized slum that produce violent gangs are to be properly evaluated."[62] Judge Davidson also published a book on the trial, *The Jury Is Still Out*. In it, he hammered at juvenile delinquency and endorsed government programs for violent youths. He concluded with a proposal to identify "incipient juvenile delinquents" and house them in self-governing communities where they would be productively socialized.[63]

Such explanations reflect a tendency in the 1950s to explain juvenile delinquency through references to youth culture and individual psychology. In this analysis, larger social forces and the urban environment received diminished attention. In 1958, for example, Harrison Salisbury published a series on juvenile delinquency in the *New York Times* that spawned his book *The Shook-Up Generation*. He argued, "Geography and propinquity—not racial differences—lie at the heart of street combat." Salisbury blamed delinquency on a "shook up generation" and anticipated the next wave of violence in the suburbs. Unfortunately, this analysis directed attention away from the ways that city neighborhoods bred racial and ethnic youth violence just when citizens and elected officials needed to understand the problem.[64]

The multiracial dynamics of the gangs that warred over Highbridge Park lent superficial support to the idea that race had nothing to do with the Farmer slaying. And black, white, and Hispanic parents all had reasons to embrace the delinquency explanation because it reduced the opprobrium directed at their children. But to recognize the more frightening and complex reality of the case—that deeply embedded patterns of discrimination and conflict were breeding violence among young people, largely along racial and ethnic lines—was difficult for many New Yorkers to accept. Little in the media or politics prepared them to see otherwise.[65]

Motion pictures at the time of the Farmer case depicted delinquents as emotionally disturbed people, products of broken homes or poor neighborhoods. The play *West Side Story*, which opened in September 1957, barely weeks after Farmer was killed, was more explicit in addressing the racial, ethnic, and neighborhood dimensions of juvenile delinquency. The New

York-born Jets and the Puerto Rican-born Sharks battle over a small piece of West Side turf and truly hate each other. The danced prologue to the play makes it clear that from the start the Jets are intent on keeping Puerto Ricans out of "their" neighborhood. Yet reviewers in New York City, and for newspapers in Washington, DC, where the play premiered, were more likely to discuss the show as a brilliantly tragic musical about a war between two gangs of juvenile delinquents—one Puerto Rican, the other composed of ethnic whites. The strongest recognition of the play's relationship to the city appeared not in a New York City newspaper but in a British publication. Marya Mannes, an American journalist writing in the BBC's *The Listener*, opened a piece on *West Side Story* with the comment that "the people of this great city are turning dark while the buildings are turning light—a complete reversal of values from the days when I was a child and New York was a town of white faces and brown buildings." Later she added that the play showed how "race hatred is not only criminal stupidity, but proof of profound inadequacies in the hater." Mannes's coarse and humane observations suggest the range of New Yorkers' reactions to the transformation of the city.[66]

At the more particular level of Washington Heights, the encounters between black, white, and Hispanic youth that prefigured the Farmer case were all too local, and too small, to gain the attention of public officials or newspapers with the power to prompt citywide recognition of growing problems. All fell beneath the radar of either journalistic newsworthiness or mayoral crisis management. Ironically, both the neighborhood's troubling aspects (discrimination around the pool, young men massing for violence) and its better side (Greenfield's integrated basketball team, the common concerns of parents) failed to receive public recognition of a kind that might have made a difference in people's understanding of the issues facing northern Manhattan.

And just as there were many routes to the belief that race and ethnicity were not central to the case, there were also many reasons for accepting the outcome of the killing and the trial that followed. For readers of the *Daily News*, which took a tough attitude toward the defendants, there was enough punishment—four of seven defendants sent to prison—to satisfy the paper's demand for a stern response to a killing. For readers of the *Post* and *El Diario*, the same sentence brought relief at the fact that teenagers were not going to the electric chair. *Amsterdam News* readers found assurance that young black men were not becoming part of a new strain of racial and ethnic conflict. Readers of the *New York Times* learned that the city's institutions of justice could cope with a large and complex case, and that justice had been done in the slaying of a polio victim.

Indeed, it is striking to see how many different New Yorkers, faced with a crime that suggested deep problems in their city, sought reassurance over understanding. To look further and deeper was simply beyond the categories of thought and action that dominated New York City in the 1950s. Black and Hispanic families with hopes for integration, white parents who wanted their city to continue in its familiar ways, parents of all races who feared violence and did not want to lose control over their children, a mayor who presided over a large and divergent coalition grounded in a belief that city government could meet the challenges of its time—all of them could see, in the Farmer case, the outlines of a grim future. Most, and particularly those in authority and with some access to the media, tended to look away from that prospect.

In 1957 and 1958, those closest to the streets—as gang members or as residents of changing neighborhoods—were most likely to see these transformations in racial or ethnic terms. But political leaders who dominated the city were unable or unwilling to see the racial and ethnic conflicts that framed the Farmer case. Fearful of discussing the racial dimensions of such cases because they did not want to give ammunition to bigots or reactionaries, and optimistic that ameliorative social welfare institutions could solve the worst problems, they looked at neighborhoods like the Heights and stressed delinquency.[67] For all their differences, the reporters of the *Amsterdam News* and Mayor Wagner faced the same issue: the challenge of talking about race, crime, and discrimination in ways that fairly comprehended causes and consequences, along with innocence and guilt, without using race alone to explain why an individual young man might commit a crime. As the pages of the *Amsterdam News* suggest, exploring the place of race in the Farmer murder could illuminate the crime and also contribute to the demonization of young black men. The difficulty of addressing this dilemma speaks loudly about New York City's inequalities, the limits of its political leadership, and its inability to incorporate blacks and Hispanics into the city's civic fabric alongside whites on a basis of equity and shared interests.

In the thinking of the 1950s social problems might exist and they might breed crime, but the city's and state's leaders, as Schneider has observed, "thought they could be ameliorated painlessly by an expanding economy and traditional liberal programs." Neither Mayor Wagner nor Governor Nelson Rockefeller wanted to face the volatile issue of racial and ethnic conflict. "Instead," Schneider concludes, "they created a narrative based on the violence of aberrant individuals." Black and Latino leaders often bought into that idea, even if they came to that political and social understanding on very different premises. Thus, unable or unwilling to grasp the significance of racial and ethnic conflict in turbulent neighborhoods, New York's elected leadership clung to a vision of their city as a place that was not divided into hostile camps—even as it became just that.[68]

In his final column on the Farmer case, Murray Kempton acknowledged that the ordeal emerged from conflicts embedded in the city's fabric. "When will we ever be tired of such things happening to children and ourselves unchanged by their happening?" he wrote. "It is not the end. It is just the middle. Highbridge Pool was not just last July 30; it is tomorrow. It is, I'm very much afraid, as long as we live. We will be back there very soon, unchanged."

As if just to prove Kempton's point, six weeks later, in Jefferson Park in East Harlem, a gang of Italian American teenagers roused by the cry of "spic in the park" attacked a Cuban man, Julio Ramos, and beat him to death. In May 1959, five teenagers were convicted in this case; sentences ranged from five to fifteen years to seven and a half to twenty years.[69]

The New York that produced the deaths of Michael Farmer and Julio Ramos took enduring form in the film *West Side Story*, released in 1961. The flaw of the film, like its predecessor on Broadway, was that it depicted Puerto Ricans without having seriously asked them how they themselves felt about life in New York. Compounded by a limited Puerto Rican presence in the cast and the absence of subtle or significant depictions of Puerto Ricans in other media, *West Side Story* has been criticized ever since for stereotyping Puerto Ricans as knife-wielding thugs.[70]

The point is important, but there is also much that *West Side Story* gets right about the New York City of the gang years. In the film's opening sequence, the camera moves in an aerial shot across the Manhattan skyline, passing the Battery, the George Washington Bridge, and Columbia University before descending to the level of tenement rooftops. Finally, it comes to rest on Riff, the leader of the Jets, on a playground. *West Side Story*, as the scene suggests, will not be about a city of soaring skyscrapers and exalted visions. Instead, it will be about the world of streets, blocks, and turf—the basic elements of the Farmer case. As the danced remainder of the opening makes clear, the Jets are local tough guys, lords of the block. Yet they are not universally beloved defenders of the neighborhood. On the playground, they intimidate kids. When they find the first Puerto Rican arrival in the neighborhood, they sneer menacingly—until he comes back with friends and protection. At that point, a gang war is on.

Adult authorities are powerless to stop the fighting. The police officers in the film are represented by a buffoon (Officer Krupke) and a thug in plainclothes (Lt. Schrank). The social worker that tries to get the two gangs to make nice at a dance is clueless and ineffectual. Although the Jets instigated the fighting, by the time their rumble is approaching both sides are convinced the other "began it."[71]

The romance between Tony and Maria that defines *West Side Story* had counterparts in real life. One member of the Jesters, who warred against the Dragons and the Egyptian Kings, once had a Puerto Rican girlfriend. But the power of groups and boundaries could overcome individual devotions. In *West Side Story*, when the Puerto Rican Anita goes into Jet territory on a peaceful mission after a deadly rumble, she is brutally assaulted.

The only adult in the film who talks candidly about the madness of hate and violence is Doc, the owner of the candy store where the Jets gather. Work-worn and pained, speaking with what sounds like the accent of an immigrant Jew, Doc says to Action of the Jets, "When I was your age . . ." Action shoots back, "You was never my age, none of ya."

The exchange grasps something that New Yorkers in Washington Heights and other neighborhoods glimpsed as the late 1950s gave way to the early 1960s. In the churn of arrivals and departures, New York was becoming a different kind of city—one defined by new peoples and new questions. In the Farmer case, New Yorkers were shown to be reluctant to face the challenges and implications of integration in a public pool. What would happen if integration came next to public schools?

CHAPTER 3

APARTNESS RULES OUR ROOST

BY 1964, anxiety about integration was running high in Washington Heights. A modest number of black children were being bused into PS 187 in the western Heights under a program that allowed minority children to claim seats in underutilized white-majority schools. Some white parents feared that more strenuous efforts were coming. In February, Ellen Lurie, a parent activist who favored integration, told a television interviewer that her son's classmates at PS 187 were saving their allowances to go to private school if integration came to their neighborhood. She called the thinking behind such behavior as a sickness, setting off a firestorm in the playgrounds and corridors at PS 187. A letter came: "Mrs. Lurie: You better keep your dirty mouth shut about the integration. This is only a warning. If we are forced to send our children to harlem schools—we will take care of you and your kids fast.—You dirty Jew:::"[1]

Crank telephone calls followed. Her son, Leib, recalls a rock thrown through one of their windows. Wrapped around it was a three-by-five-inch piece of notebook paper; on it were written the words "nigger lover."[2]

Events moved quickly. Leib remembers his father gathering the family for what he called his "Jews in Poland" speech about how the failure to confront hatred had led to the Holocaust. Equally important, Ellen Lurie believed that integration should be a two-way street where whites traveled as much as blacks. Overriding the concerns of her own mother, Lurie withdrew her son Leib and daughter Sara and transferred them to PS 161 in Harlem, at 133rd

Street and Amsterdam Avenue. In her diary, she noted that she and her husband chose PS 161 because, with its many Puerto Rican students, her kids'
"skin color wouldn't stand out." She also liked that PS 161 was "a new building so they'd get the lift of newness" and "not the stereotype of ugly Harlem."
The morning pattern of a city bus ride to 137th and Broadway followed by a
walk up to Amsterdam soon grew routine for Leib and Sara. The rest of the
experience was filled with surprises—most of them good.[3]

Ellen Lurie's actions were part of a larger struggle over school integration
that shook Washington Heights and New York City in the 1960s. In picket
lines, municipal hearings, classroom arguments, and inflamed headlines,
New Yorkers took the issues of hostility and exclusion that surfaced in the
Farmer case to a higher level. Schools were the gateways to prosperity in a
time when education, and not brawn, was becoming the requisite for a decent
job. Good schools also introduced students to the shared knowledge and experiences that were vital to democratic citizenship. These were close to universally held beliefs. No one doubted that a good education mattered.

Yet it was also true that schools defined neighborhoods. School attendance zones (which could be arbitrarily drawn) dictated who went to which
school—who was an insider and who was an outsider. When parents talked
about defending the neighborhood school, they were really talking about defending their neighborhood. In this vision, newcomers were invaders. Just
as mothers watched over blocks in Washington Heights to maintain order
in earlier years, they now began to organize in the western Heights to maintain the boundaries of their neighborhood. Many of Lurie's neighbors in the
western Heights saw school integration as a new and disturbing issue. The
newest arrivals in northern Manhattan were cast as invaders who unsettled
a desirable status quo on the streets and, now critically, in the schools. But
fifty blocks downtown, in Harlem, the inequalities between black and white
schools were an old and bitter concern.

Lurie lived in the Castle Village apartments at 180 Cabrini Boulevard, one of
the most beautiful and affluent sections of Washington Heights. She was best
known in the neighborhood for her work at the Fort Tryon Jewish Center and
at the Young Men's and Young Women's Hebrew Association (YM-YWHA)
of Washington Heights and Inwood, where she volunteered to get the Y to
move from mostly Jewish concerns to a wider embrace of "community problems." Lurie's work in the Heights embraced big issues like ethnic change
and small projects like getting trees planted (she was an avid gardener). Her
specific words about "apartness" in Washington Heights were prompted by
her work at the Fort Tryon Jewish Center, but her thinking on inclusion and

exclusion was shaped in the 1950s by her efforts as a social worker in East Harlem.[4]

Although Lurie called herself an "untrained social worker," she took up the vocation out of her desire to live a life that shaped the issues of her time. An NYU graduate who married her high school sweetheart at the age of nineteen, her work as a volunteer on the presidential campaign of Senator Estes Kefauver in 1952 confirmed her passion for politics; in the same year, she started work at the James Weldon Johnson Community Center and Union Settlement House in East Harlem. There, she joined a circle of activists, social workers, and urbanists (among them Jane Jacobs) who explored the neighborhood's public housing. Soon she was in the thick of wrenching struggles over integration, public education, and urban renewal. By 1962, she was a skilled organizer with a knack for cultivating newspaper reporters, a probing researcher, and a sharp analyst of the political currents that coursed through city neighborhoods and city hall.[5]

Within the western Heights, where Lurie lived, there seems to have been a general sense of satisfaction with the neighborhood public school, PS 187, and the public school system in general. And no wonder: in middle-class Jewish neighborhoods like Lurie's, where the children of immigrants found unprecedented prosperity, comfort, and belonging, the public school system had been a tremendous success.

The public school system that Lurie and her neighbors knew emerged over the decades between the consolidation of New York as a five-borough city with a centralized public school system in 1898 and the Great Depression in the 1930s. Teachers became part of the civil service, and a Board of Examiners created tests to ensure that measurable qualifications, not political connections, would determine who was hired. At the same time, the economic uncertainty of the Depression made a career in teaching especially attractive for intelligent, well-educated college graduates. By 1940, as Diane Ravitch has observed, the strength of the New York City public school system was formidable. Promotion rates and levels of student achievement were high.[6] New York City's public schools also benefited from striking increases in government spending. From 1948 to 1965, annual city spending on public schools went from $250 million to $1.1 billion, even though actual student enrollment increased only slightly. By the middle of the 1960s, expenditures per pupil in the city's public schools outstripped those in almost every major city in the country and most suburbs.[7]

For Jewish New Yorkers in the middle of the twentieth century, enthusiasm for the public schools reflected cumulative changes. In the late nineteenth and early twentieth centuries, as the historian Deborah Dash Moore has observed, public schools offered immigrant families "social mobility as a reward for school success." Over time, however, reform efforts and the work of Jewish students, parents, and teachers changed the professional place of Jews in the public school system. While the Irish had prospered under the old Tammany-dominated system of hiring, civil service reforms created new professional pathways to teaching that Jews sought to fill. By 1940, 56 percent of new teachers were Jewish. From 1940 to 1960 in New York City, six out of ten newly hired public school teachers was Jewish, typically graduates of one of the city's tuition-free public colleges or veterans who were beneficiaries of the GI Bill.[8]

Thanks in part to the efforts of Jewish teachers and parents, public schools became less the centers of a crabbed process of Americanization and more the strongholds of a democratic ethnic pluralism that was—for Jews, at least—both welcoming and affirming. Public schools could be at once public and distinctly Jewish. In heavily Jewish neighborhoods like the western Heights, where Catholic children often went to parochial schools, Jews could numerically dominate the student body in ways they could find comforting. At the same time, as postwar prosperity beckoned, public schools pointed the American-born children and grandchildren of immigrant Jews toward higher education and the middle class.[9]

Figure 7: George Washington High School. Courtesy NYC Municipal Archives.

In Washington Heights, there was no better representative of the school system that had evolved since the 1930s than George Washington High School, perched atop Fort George Hill in the eastern Heights overlooking the Harlem River. Students approached the school on a long, curved driveway that led them from Audubon Avenue up to an entrance defined by Ionic columns. Nicknamed "the country club on the hill," the building had two swimming pools and a cupola with a commanding view of the city. A music classroom was decorated with a 1938 WPA mural, *The Evolution of Music*, executed by Lucien Bloch, a Swiss-born fresco muralist who was a close associate of Frida Kahlo and Diego Rivera. The mural depicted scenes that were consistent with the promise of the New Deal and Popular Front: six panels evoked sound waves, instruments from many continents, and a multiracial chorus. Stuyvesant and Bronx Science high schools may have been more elite academically, but over time George Washington High School would produce its share of famous graduates, including U.S. Senator Jacob Javits, the novelist Howard Fast, the diplomat Henry Kissinger, and New York City College psychology professor Kenneth Clark.[10]

From Lurie's Washington Heights, the public schools looked welcoming and meritocratic. In Harlem and in other black sections of New York, the public school system had a different history. By the early 1960s, as the historian Jerald E. Podair has argued, New York City effectively had two school systems. One, which largely served white students, had seasoned teachers, students whose reading abilities matched or exceeded national standards, and a disproportionate number of winners in national science projects such as the Westinghouse competition. The other system, which largely served black students, had crowded schools, undertrained teachers, students with reading levels an average of two years behind those of their white counterparts, and a dropout rate twice that of the rest of the city.[11]

Although the two systems could seem to be worlds apart, in northern Manhattan they rubbed against each other. The border between upper Harlem and the lower Heights was ethnically, racially, and geographically ragged. Moreover, for administrative purposes, in the early 1960s the public schools of Washington Heights were part of a larger district that covered the area stretching from upper Harlem (District 12) through Washington Heights (District 13) to Inwood (District 14).

As early as the 1930s, it was obvious that Harlem's public schools were a poor match for black aspirations. The Mayor's Commission on Conditions in Harlem, appointed by La Guardia in response to rioting there in 1935, described Harlem schools as "shabby," unsanitary, and marked by "fire hazards." The commission found a school that served lunch for one thousand children when it had seats for only 175. Backing up the findings of the commission, Teachers Union Local 5 of the American Federation of Teachers said that Harlem schools suffered from "overcrowded classes, dangerous lack of adequate recreational facilities, antiquated and unsanitary school plant, 'horrifying' moral conditions, inadequate handling of the over-age child, and shortage of teaching staff." Although Harlem activists from churches and the Communist Party won some improvements—appropriations for new schools, repairs at most existing Harlem schools, and changes in discriminatory patterns of school zoning—overcrowding remained a problem. Nonetheless, Harlem schools had a strong number of strivers, one of whom confronted segregation in both Washington Heights and the nation.[12]

Kenneth Bancroft Clark, born in 1914 in the Panama Canal Zone to Jamaican parents, moved to the northern edge of Harlem with his mother and sister when he was four. Clark's schoolmates at PS 5 at 140th Street and Edgecombe Avenue included Irish kids from the neighborhood, Jewish students from the West Side, and a small number of African American children. Clark spoke English and Spanish, so the Irish and African American kids nicknamed him "Spanie." One of his best friends was an Irish boy, Henry Moore. Clark ate lunch at his house.[13]

Looking back on his youth, Clark recalled that he had a sense of his own racial identity—he was thrilled to see a black teacher at his school—but generally he remembered his instructors as teachers who expected the same of all their students, black and white. By the time Clark entered Junior High School 139, on 139th Street between Seventh and Lenox Avenues, the growth of Harlem's black population had given the school a black majority. Still, his teachers insisted on high educational standards.[14]

Yet when it came time for Clark to go to high school, his white guidance counselor told him to go to a vocational school. Clark's mother—an active member of Marcus Garvey's Universal Negro Improvement Association and an organizer and shop steward for the International Ladies' Garment Workers' Union—would have none of that. She herself had taken night classes at George Washington High School. She wanted her son to go there, too, and study in an academic program.[15] To Clark's embarrassment, his mother had him pulled out of class and accompanied him to the guidance counselor's office. As Clark recalled it, she said, "I don't care where you send your child. You can send him to a vocational school if you want to, but my son is going to George Washington High School." Clark enrolled in George Washington, in the same class that included the future novelist Howard Fast, and proved himself an excellent student with a knack for economics. He graduated (devastated when a teacher he admired did not give him an award for excellence in economics) in 1931.[16]

Clark pursued his undergraduate education at the historically black Howard University in Washington, DC. He thrived there in the company of academics, intellectuals, and activists. He went on to become the first African American student to enter the graduate program in psychology at Columbia University, earn his doctorate, and win an appointment as an instructor in psychology at New York City College in October 1942. In 1946, he and his wife, Mamie, also a Columbia PhD in psychology, founded what became known as the Northside Center for Child Development, an integrated center for the psychological evaluation and counseling of Harlem's young people.[17]

Kenneth and Mamie Clark both fought discrimination at the national level. When a lawyer asked Kenneth Clark why he did so much work on southern segregation when New York City's schools were also segregated, he answered with action. In February 1954, at an Urban League dinner at the Hotel Theresa in Harlem, with Mayor Robert Wagner in the audience, Clark called on the city's leaders to recognize their own role in maintaining a segregated school system. In the name of "a more democratic education," he called on the Board of Education to study school segregation in Harlem. After the dinner, Mayor Wagner called the superintendent of schools, William Jansen. The mayor asked him if there was anything to Clark's claims. Jansen replied—as would be said many times—that school segregation was simply the result of segregated housing patterns that were beyond the board's control.[18]

At Northside, the Clarks brought together the NAACP, B'Nai B'Rith, unions, Harlem groups, schools, social welfare agencies, and religious institutions to study school segregation in New York City. Participants in meetings there made plans to push for an end to school segregation and the improvement of Harlem schools. Then the U.S. Supreme Court announced its decision in *Brown v. Board of Education*.[19]

Word of the decision reached the Northside Center when a radio in Mamie Clark's office broadcast the news: the Supreme Court had ruled unanimously in *Brown v. Board of Education of Topeka, Kansas*, that racial segregation in public schools was unconstitutional. (To sweeten the victory, the decision had even cited Kenneth Clark's work.) Immediately, a party erupted. Staff members and children celebrated. After the euphoria died down, a feeling endured: from now on, things would be different.[20]

After the *Brown* decision, Kenneth Clark redoubled his efforts in New York. In a forum at Hunter College he described a case of racial gerrymandering in lower Washington Heights, where white students were sent to a school almost a mile to the north of their neighborhood, even though PS 46 on West 156th Street, in a more black and Hispanic part of the Heights, was the nearest school. In a meeting of the Urban League attended by Arthur

Leavitt, president of the New York City Board of Education, Clark criticized Board of Education policies and called for a study of Harlem's schools. Leavitt agreed. The Public Education Association, an education reform organization founded in 1895, carried out the research.[21]

In November of 1955, the Public Education Association released a report comparing conditions in elementary and junior high schools with student populations that were 90 percent or more white with schools where the population was 85 percent or more black and Puerto Rican. Washington Heights, the report showed, had two of Manhattan's five minority-majority junior high schools and six of its twenty-three minority-majority elementary schools.[22] The report did not break down its findings on a school-by-school basis, but its revelations were still damning. Typically, the black and Puerto Rican majority schools were older, more crowded, not as well maintained, and staffed by less experienced teachers. Their students' scores on reading and arithmetic tests were lower.

The report was ambiguous about what these statistics meant. On the one hand, it condemned segregation and encouraged school superintendents to design school zones that would promote integration whenever possible. On the other hand, it acknowledged the ethnic checkerboard of New York's neighborhoods and absolved the Board of Education of deliberately pursuing segregation. In any case, the city's official response was tepid and evasive. Proposals for action were followed by reports that justified inaction. In the face of white parents' opposition, Superintendent of Schools William Jansen backed away from changes in school zoning and teacher assignments. As relations between Clark and the superintendent hardened, parents from the border of Harlem and Washington Heights took action.[23]

Bernice and Stanley Skipwith, expressing impatience with the status quo and an assertiveness about school integration that was increasingly common among black New Yorkers, in 1958 joined with other parents in Harlem and Brooklyn to boycott segregated schools. Initially, their plan involved 21 children.[24]

The Brooklyn side of the dispute ended quickly when six children there were quietly reassigned, but in Harlem the boycotters hung on. The boycotting students were tutored, the *Amsterdam News* reported, in "English, mathematics, social studies, world events, music, French and art appreciation" at the Mid-Harlem Community Parish, then under the leadership of Rev. Eugene S. Callender—a rising activist minister. Their instructors were a mix of licensed teachers and graduate students from Columbia University and New York University. Children also watched the educational shows that could be found on television. When instructors missed sessions, the boycotters' attorney, Paul Zuber—who had studied at Brown University and

Brooklyn Law School and was on his way to becoming a bold legal advocate for integration—took over.[25]

The Board of Education accused the parents of educational neglect and pressed charges against them in Domestic Relations Court. Justice Nathaniel Kaplan found four of the mothers guilty. Less than two weeks later, however, the boycotters' fortunes turned when Bernice Skipwith and Shirley Rector, another parent, came before Justice Justine Wise Polier—a La Guardia appointee with a reputation as a fighter on integration and juvenile justice. She was also the daughter of the renowned Reform rabbi Stephen Wise and a former Northside board member.[26] After lengthy hearings, Justice Polier dismissed the charges against the parents. In her judgment, the Board of Education had no right to ask them to send their children to inferior schools—and the schools in question were, she concluded, inferior "by reason of racial discrimination." Although Justice Polier allowed that Board of Education polices could not be blamed for the de facto segregation, she refused to let the matter rest there. Using teacher preferences to explain inequalities between schools was no excuse, she argued: such practices were no more defensible than allowing police officers to reject difficult assignments. For Justice Polier, the situation was clear: "The Constitution requires equality, not mere palliatives." She did not specify how the Board of Education should remedy this problem, but said "determination, resourcefulness and leadership can bring the situation in the New York City school system into line with the constitutional guarantee of equal protection of the laws."[27]

The board moved to appeal Justice Polier's decision, much to the anger of black parents and integrationists, and then dropped the matter. The Skipwith case looked like a breakthrough. James L. Hicks, columnist for the *Amsterdam News*, acclaimed the decision for establishing what his paper had been saying for years: that "Negro children" were being sent to "segregated, inferior schools." Kenneth Clark concluded (mistakenly) that the Skipwith case would open the way for challenges to de facto segregation in the North in the way that the *Brown* decision opened up assaults on de jure segregation in the South.[28]

The euphoria that Justice Polier's decision inspired among supporters of integrated schools was not universally shared in northern Manhattan. In March 1959, when a Board of Education appeal seemed to be making headway, the *Amsterdam News* surveyed local school boards from Harlem through Washington Heights to Inwood. The mix of responses suggests a degree of opposition to integration and wariness toward taking a public stand on the issue. The results were discouraging for integrationists. Three local school board chairs (two from Harlem, one from Washington Heights) supported an appeal: in effect, they wanted to challenge Polier's ruling. Two (one from

Inwood, one from Hamilton Heights) declined to comment. The *Amsterdam News*, which vigorously fought discrimination against black children in the schools, ran its story about the upper Manhattan boards under the headline, "Local School Board Clams Up on Issue." Above it, a shorter headline read, "Are These Our Enemies?"[29]

Ellen Lurie was an early supporter of integration. In a 1956 study of the George Washington Houses in East Harlem, she wrote: "Social, economic and racial segregation can all be deadly to community life. It is apparent that integration, even when it is accepted policy, cannot take place without consistent effort." But she also knew how deep currents of fear and bigotry undermined efforts at inclusion. In 1959 she described tensions within the multiethnic student body of Benjamin Franklin High School in East Harlem: "All our research and studying has led down one main alley—students do not want to attend this school because they are afraid of the neighborhood. In East Harlem and Harlem Negroes and Puerto Ricans are afraid of the Italians; below 96th Street Whites are afraid of Harlem. If Benjamin Franklin is closed for such reasons then surely it appears as though East Harlem is being sacrificed to the forces of fear." Part of the solution, she thought, was to reform public housing so that the projects contributed to a vigorous community life with a healthy degree of order that flowed from the bottom up. She also thought that "Planned Integration" must be explored "fearlessly" because its impact "could be highly desirable."[30]

Vital city neighborhoods had room for both the individuals and the collective, Lurie argued in a letter written in 1963. Schools were "the corker" in this equation, she added, and required "the greatest thinking, stress, etc., and the greatest decentralization."[31] In neighborhoods and schools that permit a person to "rub elbows with all sorts and conditions of people," she continued, people could develop a "respect for one's neighbors" that could be a foundation for "political responsibility." "Without it," she stated, "social life, in its largest sense, amounts to little more than a cat and dog fight."

Contemplating her city, with its growing struggles over school integration, she wrote: "We are now in the middle of the worst such cat and dog fight our city has seen. Only if we permit a significant degree of change will democracy, as we know it, survive."[32] Lurie wanted intimacy without homogeneity and social change from the bottom up, not as a result of orders from a top-down bureaucracy. But the recent history of Washington Heights showed how difficult it would be to reconcile these objectives.

The prospect of working in her own neighborhood made Lurie uneasy. As early as 1961, when she became a member of the executive board of the

Parents Association at PS 187, she noted in her diary that her "sudden presence" in Washington Heights, after years of living in northern Manhattan but "interfering" in East Harlem, seemed to rattle people. She added, "I complicate it by seeming too efficient and I'm instantly asked, 'How do you do it with 4 kids?' What can I learn to do so I won't be suspect?"[33] The anxiety that Lurie sensed was partly about the prospect of the integration in neighborhood public schools. PS 187—the Lurie children's school—was part of local districts 12, 13, and 14, which reached from 125th Street in Harlem to the northern tip of Inwood. Although PS 187 drew most of its students from the heavily Jewish western Heights, it was part of an administrative structure that encompassed more black and Hispanic areas to the south. As much as families might try to deny it, the future of public education in the western Heights was bound up with neighborhoods to the south with the kinds of schools that parents boycotted in the Skipwith case.

From 1951 to 1958, community organizations, schools, and the Board of Education tried to address what they called "the problems of interracial acceptance" in school districts 12, 13, and 14. Their efforts were recorded and lauded in *Community in Action: A Report on a Social Integration Project in School Districts 12, 13 and 14, Manhattan, 1951–1958* by Assistant Superintendent Truda T. Weill. The report noted that in northern Manhattan economic status ran from "extreme poverty to wealth" and housing ranged "from elegant mansions reminiscent of Victorian splendor to squalid tenements bursting at the seams." The races, religions, nationalities, and languages of northern Manhattan made a visit there "a tour of the world." Yet the area, the report said, was an uneasy place. A "Negro and Spanish-speaking influx" had left the area's whites fearful and anxious. "Negroes" were angry at whites "because of actual and historical discrimination." "Spanish-speaking" children (in these years, mostly Puerto Rican and Cuban) needed to be taught both English and "new cultural patterns."[34]

Weill's report charted a progression from a community art show to an "intervisitation" program that paired schools from Washington Heights and Harlem to study topics such as "People From Many Lands Build Our Nation." Brotherhood Week observances followed, along with the creation of a community newspaper. Educators, clergy, and leaders of neighborhood organizations formed committees to fight delinquency and vandalism and "promote good citizenship." In 1957, participants held an overnight interracial conference at the Hudson Guild Farm in Netcong, New Jersey. The report noted that the conference benediction used the language of the Psalms to affirm the spirit of the gathering: "How good, and how joyful, for brothers to dwell together in unity."

For all its idealism and optimism, the report made no mention of deliberate efforts to create integrated schools in northern Manhattan. Moreover, in his foreword to the report, Superintendent of Schools Jansen wrote that "the schools and the educators" would not be able to "correct the situations created by segregated housing" or "remedy situations created by employment practices." He added, "They cannot coerce social situations nor social institutions over which they have no control but they can do many positive things to eliminate the ignorance and the hostilities which result in segregation."[35]

The Board of Education's claim that it could do nothing to remedy the segregated housing patterns that skewed school populations become a justification for inaction. By the early 1960s, however, the appearance of black and Hispanic students in the public schools of Washington Heights and Inwood would spark both new demands for changes in the schools and hostility toward integration in Lurie's own backyard. She would confront them as a parent and as a member of her local school board.

Lurie brought to her board high hopes and an acute knowledge of Washington Heights. Sitting in Fort Tryon Park on a warm June day a few months before she assumed her seat, she saw dense blocks of rent-controlled apartment buildings that were worn but not wrecked and solid but not handsome.[36] "I know so many of the people who live in those buildings," she wrote. "I know of their warmth and friendliness to each other; I know, too, that so many of them grew up here, went to the same school their children now attend." Some were driven to Washington Heights by Nazi persecution, others by racism and oppressive living conditions in Harlem.[37]

In Washington Heights, she observed, they inhabited a fragmented neighborhood with "no communication between groups about common concerns or common needs." People commonly complained about the "changing neighborhood" but rarely took action.[38]

South of 181st Street, where black and Puerto Rican families were moving into the Heights from Harlem, residents could see how their neighborhood was changing. Yet change did not have to lead to "panic and decay" if people learned to work together: "If only this community could be awakened to its needs—and its potential—how fast and how far it could move!"[39]

For all the energy and idealism that Lurie brought to her local school board, the school system was on shaky ground. Debates over integration, falling test scores, and a scandal in the use of school construction funds all reduced public confidence in the system. In response, New York City in 1962 reduced the number of school districts from fifty-four to twenty-five and increased the

number of board members in each district from five to nine. It also stripped
borough presidents of their power to appoint local board members. (Reformers presumed that the appointments were politically motivated.) In the new
system, the Board of Education selected local board members from lists of
names proposed by members of parent, community, and business groups in
each district. The new local school boards were expected to be more representative than their predecessors. They were also supposed to advise the board,
bring community views to the attention of the school system, and communicate the system's perspective to communities. Lurie was one of the nine
appointed to the new local school board for districts 12, 13, and 14.[40]

In the minutes of an open meeting of the local board for districts 12, 13,
and 14, held October, 30, 1962, at PS 28, at 155th and Amsterdam, Lurie,
serving as secretary, set down the range of people and educational concerns
to be found in northern Manhattan. Community representatives came from
areas as different as Harlem and Inwood, and from the Riverside-Edgecombe
Neighborhood Association, which worked to bridge northern Harlem and
southern Washington Heights. From PS 186, Mrs. Ruth Singer asked for better access to play space during lunch hours and floodlights on the schoolyard
at night to deter drug dealing. Isaiah Robinson Jr., president of the Parents
Association of Junior High School 139, pushed for "more integration in the
schools" and immediate attention to overcrowding. Leslie Foster, the president of the Parents Association at PS 187, wanted to get parking privileges in
front of the school for teachers and clarification on how to handle communications with parent groups. The range of concerns, from the mundane matters of administration to demands for integration, suggested the disparities
among schools in northern Manhattan.[41]

It was possible—but difficult—to create integration in northern Manhattan, where the school population was growing in black and Latino areas
and shrinking in white areas. Busing could take students from an area of
one racial majority to another, but whites resisted this and blacks took this
opportunity in only modest numbers when it was offered. In mixed areas, it
was possible to build schools that drew from both sides of racial and ethnic
boundaries. Another option was to pair schools from adjacent communities
so that students of all races attended one school for the early years of their
elementary education and another in later years.

In a time of rapid change, however, familiar boundaries were unstable.
And even when demographic trends aligned to produce racially and ethnically mixed communities, they rarely received the municipal services that
they needed to make integration succeed. As the New York University sociology professor Dan Dodson observed as early as 1946, "At the point where
contact is made between Negroes and whites, where community services

should function at their best in order to facilitate the integration process, and relieve as many sources of friction as possible, there is too frequently such a deterioration of services that the deterioration itself aggravates or obstructs the integration process."[42]

Neighborhood activists, even when they wanted to promote integration, lacked the support they needed to turn their ideas into action. Lurie and her colleagues, the sociologist David Rogers observed in *110 Livingston Street: Politics and Bureaucracy in the New York City Schools,* constituted a local school board that was "perhaps more committed to desegregation than any other local board in the city." They had no power, however, to make sweeping policy changes that would bring about their visions. The Board of Education, at the summit of the system, was in a better position to engineer citywide efforts on behalf of integration. It was acutely sensitive, however, to signs of opposition from the bottom up. And in northern Manhattan, grassroots opposition to integration was building.[43]

In August 1963, the Board of Education received some forty letters from Washington Heights and Inwood on the subject of busing to achieve integration. Letters from Inwood tended to come from the western part of the neighborhood, notably from the white and relatively affluent area around Park Terrace. The majority of Heights letter writers were from the economically comfortable western Heights along Cabrini Boulevard and Pinehurst Avenue—in effect, Lurie's neighbors. All were strongly opposed to any busing of white students out of their own neighborhoods.[44]

Here, in a new guise, were mothers standing as defenders of the neighborhood. Women wrote the majority of the letters from the Heights and half the letters from Inwood. Many writers seemed to have Jewish names. They did not present themselves as part of an organized movement. A few wrote as representatives of Parent Associations, but the vast majority simply wrote as parents. Their tone ranged from angry to earnest to utterly serious. All of them praised the idea of the "neighborhood school" and categorically rejected any plan to bus their children outside their neighborhood. In the Heights and Inwood, a notable minority of writers combined their opposition to busing their own children with an acceptance of the open enrollment plan that bused black children into their neighborhood. Some recognized that black families suffered from unequal educational opportunities. Others recognized that segregated schooling was related to segregated housing, but proposed that the city integrate housing first and let integrated schooling follow. (No one, however, offered concrete suggestions on how to do this.)[45]

The residents of northern Manhattan who wrote the board to praise "neighborhood schools" were part of a growing and determined citywide opposition to integrationists like Lurie. Resisters emerged first and strongest in western Queens, specifically Jackson Heights, where they gathered in the fall of 1963 under the banner of an organization called Parents and Taxpayers (PAT) to oppose pairing schools with black and white majorities to achieve integration. (Such pairings were called "Princeton plans" because they had been put into effect in the New Jersey municipality of the same name.) A Princeton plan in Jackson Heights, Parents and Taxpayers argued, would disrupt families and communities, cost lots of money, undermine property values in Queens neighborhoods of single-family homes, and reduce children to "chattels of the state." Bernard Kessler, counselor to Parents and Taxpayers, said he represented a citywide organization with affiliates that were pledged to mutual support in legal challenges, picket lines, strikes, and boycotts. The allies of Parents and Taxpayers were mostly in Queens and Brooklyn, Kessler told a *New York Times* reporter, but they could also be found in an organization called Washington Heights Parents and Teachers.[46]

The day after the *Times* introduced PAT, another story, deep inside the paper, announced the formation of a citywide integrationist organization, the Interracial Parents Committee. The Committee claimed members in Washington Heights, Inwood, and Harlem. Its coordinating committee included Ellen Lurie.[47] More significantly, in March 1964, another integrationist organization emerged—EQUAL—which sought to counter Parents and Taxpayers. Although EQUAL defined itself as "a primarily grass-roots organization, organized with the avowed purpose of helping parents living in predominantly white communities to exert as much influence as possible in the fight to secure quality-integrated schools," its membership included black activists and white leftists. Its core principle was "quality education for all children in integrated public schools." From 1964 to 1966, EQUAL's foremost public representative was Lurie: passionate yet deeply informed; militant yet precise in her analysis of the politics and demography of public education; and radical in her commitment to the concerns of ghetto communities. The radicalism of Lurie and EQUAL could alienate both moderates and school officials.[48]

The year of EQUAL's founding, 1964, was one of the most tumultuous in the history of New York City. In marches, meetings, and headlines, New Yorkers wrestled with questions about schools and urban order that would define the city for years to come. Integrationists moved first in a public school boycott led by Reverend Milton Galamison with help from Bayard Rustin, a master of the theater of protest fresh from the March on Washington for Jobs and Freedom that witnessed Martin Luther King Jr.'s "I Have a Dream Speech." On February 3, 45 percent of New York City's 1,037,757 public school students stayed home—roughly four times the usual percentage of absences—in support of civil rights.[49] Boycotts were strongest in African American and Puerto

Rican neighborhoods, weaker in white areas such as northwest Manhattan. Despite freezing temperatures, there were demonstrations at three hundred schools. At George Washington High School, some fifty students and teachers picketed outside. (A few counterdemonstrators chanted "two, four six, eight—we don't want to integrate" before police told them to leave.) From inside, Principal Henry T. Hillson called the pickets "terribly misguided" but sent them coffee. "We're not going to let them freeze to death," he said. As would be expected, Ellen Lurie was in the thick of things—working the phones in the basement of the Lenox Terrace apartments in Harlem, deploying demonstrators, and bucking up morale before heading off to city hall to demonstrate. At the end of the day, the president of the Board of Education, James Donovan, dismissed the boycott as a "fizzle." Rustin, however, said, "I think we are on the threshold of a new political movement."[50]

PAT responded with a march against busing. On March 12, in a wet snowstorm, some ten to fifteen demonstrators gathered at the Board of Education headquarters in Brooklyn, then marched across the Brooklyn Bridge to rally at city hall. The crowd, which was estimated to be 70 percent women (with virtually no African Americans) carried signs such as "Can a bus bring a sick child home?" and "Have child—won't travel." Angry and exultant, smiling and waving at the television cameras, the protestors marched around city hall six abreast for more than an hour. Organizers called it a total success.[51]

Three days later Galamison responded with a second boycott and a demonstration at the Board of Education. It was significantly smaller than the February event, and only 287,459 students—about 28 percent of all pupils—were absent. The coalition behind the second boycott was also smaller, reflecting disagreements over tactics and goals. CORE and the NAACP did not support the second march and Puerto Ricans were not much in evidence among boycotting students. While Malcolm X supported the second boycott, Rustin did not. Over time, it became clear that Rustin thought the movement needed to address not just schools but social and economic conditions in a broad alliance that would not be knit together by ever more militant acts.[52]

The debate sharpened in May with the release of the Allen Report, named for state commissioner of education James Allen; its authors included Kenneth Clark. The document evaluated the Board's progress toward integrating public schools (which was limited) and offered a plan to come closer to the goal (which was becoming ever harder to attain). Recognizing both the value of integration and opposition to busing young children, the Allen Report proposed a reorganization of New York's school system. Young children would go to neighborhood schools through the fourth grade, then travel to intermediate schools for grades five through eight, and then move on to high school. The construction of "educational parks" to house intermediate schools and high schools in accessible and integrated locations would bring students together in new and superior facilities. The relative boldness of the Allen plan heartened integration activists. It frightened the members of Parents and Taxpayers.

Less than a week after the release of the Allen plan, Rustin organized a march for the NAACP and CORE to mark the tenth anniversary of the Supreme Court's *Brown* decision on segregation. The protest, called the March for Democratic Schools, also expressed support for the Allen plan. Rustin, aware that PAT had drawn fifteen thousand protestors in March, said he sought fifteen thousand plus one. Instead, he drew some five thousand marchers. Rosemary Gunning of Parents and Taxpayers said the differences in turnout "should eliminate any doubts about how the parents of all races feel about the neighborhood school."[53]

After the march, at the Four Square Bar near Pennsylvania Station, a favored haunt of African American postal workers, Murray Kempton caught up with Rustin. Kempton, observing black men staring deep into their drinks, spoke with Rustin and concluded that a span of history that had begun with the *Brown* decision had come to an end with the Allen Report. Later, in the *New Republic*, Kempton wrote that the year's demonstrations formed a pattern of fragments and defeats: "A chapter is over; all the energy, the imagination, the courage, and the hope which wrote that chapter could hardly not, before long, be revived again. But whatever chapter comes will be something new. We asked too much of the Negro when we expected him to carry almost by himself the burden of America as Eden, and endure and never get weary."[54] Before the summer of 1964 was over, Harlem would erupt in rioting after a police officer killed a black teenager in a confrontation on the east side of Manhattan.

In Washington Heights, the Lurie family lived miles from the Harlem rioting but in the middle of anxiety over school integration. While African American children were bused into the Lurie children's school, PS 187, most white parents in the western Heights showed little to no enthusiasm for sending their children away from their neighborhood school for the sake of integration. The Luries were among the few who had other ideas.

In 1964, the two oldest Lurie children, Leib and Sara, were settled in to PS 187. Both kids were thoroughly at home in the little world of western Washington Heights. They lived in Castle Village at 180 Cabrini Boulevard. Nearby were Bennett Park, Fort Tryon Park, and the little commercial strip around Gideon's Bakery on West 187th Street. Leib found work as a delivery boy for a dry cleaner; Sara and her friends developed crushes on a young man who worked at a pizza parlor. Like most New Yorkers, their definition of their neighborhood was a small one. When Leib met people from Saint Elizabeth's Parish, on Wadsworth Avenue just below 187th Street on the east side of Broadway, they seemed to him to be from far away.[55]

Ellen Lurie's sudden decision to withdraw Sara and Leib from PS 187 shocked the children's classmates and placed both children in a situation that most white parents viewed with dread. Yet both Sara and Leib recall their time at PS 161 as one of the best things that ever happened to them. Sara remembers that she was treated "like royalty" at PS 161. She made friends there easily, sometimes visiting them at their homes in housing projects and sometimes bringing them back to Washington Heights. Her one experience of fear in these years took place in Castle Village, when she brought home a friend from PS 161, a black girl named Sharon Long. A woman in Sara's building kicked Sharon and said, "We don't want any niggers here." For Sara, the contrast between the welcome she received at PS 161 and the rejection of her friend at Castle Village spoke volumes.[56]

Leib's time at PS 161 started slightly rougher. At first, mutual playground taunts got him a bloody nose from the fast fists of George Gaines. By the following year they were good friends and part of a crowd that included Jorge Mendez and Richard Santiago. Together the four boys played dodgeball, did homework together, and visited each other's homes. Leib found a great teacher in Mrs. Lehrer and a taste for the Cuban sandwiches that he could buy near his school. He also got a job delivering envelopes for a merchant near PS 161 for a rate of $1 per delivery; only later did he figure out that he was working for a numbers runner.[57]

In her diary, Ellen had more complex and conflicted views. "At first homework shockingly easier," wrote Lurie of the differences between 187 and 161. She worried that Sara was copying one of her classmates' "sloppy speech." Economic inequality diminished the range of offerings at 161: "At 187 recorders for 3rd paid for by PA [Parents Association]—here no music." (To compensate, she noted in her diary, she arranged library and theater trips for her children.) Parents also had a different approach to school, she noted: "Parents who wait in front of 161 immediately kiss their children & often & hard. At 187 they say Let me see your work." She also saw intense rivalries at 161 between black and Puerto Rican parents: "everyone cuts & bites each other so—such suspicion & distrust is sickening—yet we made them this way by never trusting them."[58]

Leib and Sara attended PS 161 for two years. Leib went on to JHS 152 in Inwood, then Stuyvesant High School. Sara returned to PS 187 with no great fanfare, and then went on to JHS 152 and then to George Washington High School. Leib looks back on his time at 161 as an experience that made him more open to different people and different ways of living. At JHS 52, Sara started moving more into an adolescent world—hanging out with her friends and going to dances at the YM-YWHA on Nagle Avenue. She did not always find it easy to be the daughter of Ellen Lurie, whose activism sometimes took her away from the family. It was awkward to read in the newspaper that her mother bit a policeman who grabbed her at a demonstration. After the assassination of Martin Luther King Jr., Sara even feared that someone might want to kill her mother.

For all the memories that Leib and Sara carried from PS 161, their family also intersected with the life of a PS 161 student who headed north—Daryl West, a resident of the Manhattanville Projects. Daryl started out at PS 161 but was then bused north to PS 187, where he met Leib and Sara's younger sister, Rebecca. He encountered no hostility in Washington Heights, and met Rebecca when they were both in a "gifted" class at 187. "In my neighborhood, it wasn't cool to speak properly or be in the gifted class," he recalled. Friends in Harlem teased him for going to a "smarty school."[59] After school at 187, Daryl went to Rebecca's house to play board games like Monopoly. There were no board games in his home neighborhood; kids played street games like "kick the can." Daryl found Ellen Lurie a welcoming host who offered him a choice of sandwiches (at home for him it was only peanut butter and jelly) and "made you feel okay." "I just remember the warmth and openness of the lady," he recalled.

Years later, West said that going to PS 187, in a mostly Jewish neighborhood, made him more open to other cultures when he served in the military. He also believes that he got a better education than if he had stayed in Harlem. The Luries showed "love and respect" to him. Becky and her family, he recalls, were "genuine." He knew other kids at PS 187, but remembers being invited only to visit the Luries.

On a sunny Saturday afternoon in October 1965, a *New York Times Magazine* writer observed mayoral candidate John V. Lindsay on a crowded corner in Washington Heights, standing tall in a gray suit atop a blue station wagon. In a hoarse voice, speaking into a handheld microphone, the Republican congressman explained why he wanted to go to city hall. "I want to be Mayor of our city so I can give it a new start," he said. "I want to see a restoration of the greatness of our city."[60]

Lindsay's campaign, which included a television ad calling New York's schools one of the major sources of the city's distress, resonated with integrationists like Ellen Lurie. She became one of his supporters, drawn to his campaign by her frustrations with the Wagner administration and Lindsay's sense of energy and idealism.[61] Lindsay's candidacy was driven by his own ambitions as a Republican liberal and a growing sense that New York—beset by rising crime, battles over schools, racial tensions, and the growth of the suburbs—was a city in decline. Tall, fit, broad-shouldered, and handsome, with an amiable smile, Lindsay served seven years in Congress representing Manhattan's Upper East Side. While he endorsed Great Society initiatives including Medicare, federal aid to education, and immigration reform, as an urban Republican he shared his faction's passion for "good government." His disdain for the fading Tammany tradition made him hostile to the Wagner administration. When he declared his candidacy, Lindsay argued that New York City suffered from "long years of one-party rule" and a domination by "power brokers" who left its inhabitants "beset with hopelessness and despair."[62]

For Lindsay, the political tendencies of Washington Heights were promising but complicated. U.S. Senator Jacob Javits, a liberal Republican, was elected to Congress in 1946 to represent Washington Heights and the rest of the West Side above 114th Street. Lindsay also had a congressional ally in Rep. William F. Ryan, a Reform Democrat whose district, starting in 1962, included Washington Heights and Inwood.[63] Yet Lindsay's desire for change was not universally shared in Washington Heights. Northern Manhattan was also the home of Democrats who identified with the moderate and slow-moving Wagner administration. The dominant local Democratic club was the Washington Heights Progressive Democrats, an organization of Democratic regulars (as opposed to the more liberal reformers). The club's leaders were city councilman David Friedland and state senator Joseph Zaretsky, a Wagner ally and perennial minority leader in the Republican-dominated state senate. In northern Manhattan moderate Democrats in the Wagner mold, not liberal Republican reformers like Lindsay, were dominant.[64]

There were also conservatives uptown. By 1965 the Conservative Party, founded in 1961 to combat liberal tendencies in the Republican Party, was making inroads in Irish Catholic sections of Inwood that once would have been expected to vote Democratic. The Conservative candidate in 1965 was William F. Buckley, a well-off Irish Catholic with an estate in Connecticut and an apartment in Manhattan who edited the conservative journal of opinion *National Review* with wit, scorn, and an occasional step into the gutter. All conservatives could warm to Buckley's pledges to cut taxes, slash government spending, and transform the welfare system. In Irish Inwood, Buckley's support for the police was sure to resonate. Most important for the issue of schools and integration, Buckley's running mate for city council president on the Conservative ticket was Rosemary Gunning of Queens, the executive secretary of Parents and Taxpayers. Backers of PAT in northern Manhattan could see explicit support in the Buckley team.[65]

Lindsay won the election with 45 percent of the vote citywide. He carried Manhattan, but returns in northern Manhattan told a different story. In the 80th and 81st Assembly districts, which stretched from the southern Heights through Inwood, Democrat Abraham Beame defeated Lindsay. (Beame had strong ties with African American regulars, which would have helped him in the southern Heights. He could also draw on Jewish supporters and moderate or party-loyal Democrats who could not bring themselves to vote for a Republican.) Moreover, in the 81st Assembly District, which reached from the northern Heights through Inwood, Buckley received 14 percent of the vote—a bit better than his 13 percent citywide.[66]

In his inaugural speech, Lindsay vowed to "build what must be built," "preserve what must be preserved," and "change what must be changed." Recent history suggested that efforts to change the public schools in older, whiter sections of the Heights would meet resistance. Equally significant, the attitudes of African American activists were hardening. In the fall of 1966, the spirit of the Allen Report was put into action to create an integrated school in Harlem that would draw students of all races, Intermediate School 201. The effort collapsed because whites refused to send their children to school in Harlem and blacks rejected the white, liberal, integrationist principal who was assigned to the school. It was, in the words of the historian Jerald Podair, the "last gasp of the integrationist impulse."[67]

In December 1966, four of nine board members in districts 12, 13, and 14 resigned over their frustration with the central board's rejection of their integration proposals. In that same year, Lurie was up for a five-year reappointment as a local board member. For all her activism and protests, Lurie could honestly argue that she was working to help the board achieve its stated goal of integration. Moreover, her district's screening panel, her colleagues on her local board, and her district superintendent all agreed that she deserved a five-year term. Nevertheless, the central board reappointed her for only one year. Lurie was livid. In her personal papers, she kept a clipping from a Heights-Inwood newspaper headlined "Mrs. Lurie Reappointed to School Board." The story contained a quote from Lurie herself: "I shall not keep my eyes closed or my ears covered or my mouth shut. I have only one year, but you know and I know that others will take my place. The twentieth century will not be kept waiting much longer."[68]

Lurie's frustration was matched by an eagerness for action in city hall. By the spring of 1967, after more than a year in office, Mayor Lindsay was troubled by the slow pace of change in his city's schools, skeptical of the value of the public school bureaucracy, and eager to win better funding for the city's

school system. When he asked the state legislature to treat the city's five bor-
oughs as five separate entities when it came to school funding (which would
raise the amount of money allocated to the city as a whole), the legislature
responded by asking the mayor to decentralize the city's public school system
down to the borough level. Lindsay then went a step further and proposed
decentralization that reached to a community level. He also appointed a task
force led by McGeorge Bundy, president of the Ford Foundation, to study how
New York City communities might control their own schools. In May of 1967,
the Ford Foundation announced that it would fund community-control ex-
periments in demonstration districts located in Harlem, lower Manhattan,
and the Ocean Hill–Brownsville section of Brooklyn.[69]

In May of 1968, the board in Ocean Hill–Brownsville dismissed thirteen
teachers and six supervisors, claiming that they were undermining community control. The United Federation of Teachers (UFT) opposed the dismissal
and the Board of Education reinstated them. The Ocean Hill–Brownsville
board, however, refused to take them back. In response, 350 of the 556 teachers in Ocean Hill–Brownsville went on strike in support of their ousted colleagues and supervisors. The local board dismissed them, too. Negotiations
over the summer failed to settle the dispute. When school resumed in the fall,
the UFT turned the battle of Ocean Hill–Brownsville into a citywide war.[70]

All parties brought to the ensuing struggle their deepest hopes, fears, and
convictions. Black parents came with anger over inferior schools and the
Board of Education's resistance to their demands for change. UFT members
recalled their hard-won unionization that gave them a ladder into the middle
class. Black radicals saw their worst expectations of whites played out in UFT
president Albert Shanker's efforts to win the strike by making it the biggest
confrontation possible. White radicals saw a struggle to liberate education
from the dead weight of bureaucracy. Jews heard anti-Semitic taunts and concluded that they were witnessing the death of interracial cooperation. Jews
and blacks could both bring rising assertions of ethnic pride—Jews from
Israel's victory in the 1967 Six-Day War, blacks from the black power movement. At the same time, many Jews and blacks brought clashing resolves to
the fall of 1968: for Jews, a refusal to give up hard-won gains; for blacks, an
insistence that they would not be turned back on the threshold of change.[71]

From September 9 through 11, 98 percent of the city's teachers walked
out in protest over the Ocean Hill–Brownsville dismissals. The Board of Education again promised to reinstate the dismissed teachers, but the Ocean
Hill–Brownsville board rejected the idea and recruited new teachers, most
of them young supporters of community control. (While the local board was
accused of anti-Semitism, 70 percent of the new teachers were white and half
were Jewish.)[72] The UFT responded with another walkout, from September

13 to September 30. Classes resumed for the first half of October. Then, from October 14 to November 19, the UFT waged its final strike.[73]

For the most part, Washington Heights and Inwood staggered through the strike far from the glare of publicity. In northern Manhattan, as elsewhere, custodians who supported the striking teachers locked up schools and opponents of the strike opened them.[74] Erwin Haas, acting superintendent in northern Manhattan, tried to keep the schools open—an effort that put him at odds with the UFT and its supporters. Leonard Strauss, president of the parents' association at PS 187, worked to organize a committee of parent associations from throughout the district that would give local parents a significant say in any decentralization plan. From the start, there were divisions: district schools from upper Harlem declined to join in the effort, possibly because they felt their interests would clash with those of their more white, affluent neighbors in the western Heights. Within the committee, Strauss and most whites backed the UFT, while African Americans and Latinos supported Haas's attempt to keep the schools open. George Washington High School opened with fifteen of 225 teachers and fifty of five thousand students in attendance—all signs that the faculty supported the strike and the students respected their picket line. The *Times* reported a brief takeover of the district office. It also noted that five hundred students attended classes at the YM-YWHA.[75]

There were particularly sharp divisions at PS 187. First the school was closed and the PTA supported striking teachers. Then it opened with the approval of the district office. Reports came in that the American flag had been burned. A parent wrote to protest the opening of the school with a "group of guitar playing, non-staff hippie teachers."

The strike ended on November 19. In April 1969, the New York Legislature adopted a school decentralization plan that divided New York City's elementary and middle schools into what eventually became thirty-two districts, each with about twenty thousand students. Although the UFT supported the plan, advocates of community control opposed it because it preserved much of the power of the Board of Education and the UFT.[76]

Black and white New Yorkers looked at each other over a devastated landscape with new eyes. At worst, individuals on each side could now believe that their opponents were capable of worse than they had imagined. Friendships were severed, alliances broken, lives changed. The irony of this was that for all the racial polarization wrought by the strike, there were real examples of people defying the call for racial loyalty: white teachers went to work in Ocean Hill–Brownsville; Bayard Rustin supported the UFT out of loyalty to labor union principles. In a dispute that was often defined by its extremes, such actions were lost in clouds of anger. The clash of values and loyalties that suffused the strike also obscured that it was probably more about power—above all black parents seeking the power to ensure that their children would be educated well—than it was about the unbridgeable cultural differences that were articulated by the extreme partisans of both the UFT position and community control. "What gave the 1968 teachers' strike its terrible significance," the historian Peter Eisenstadt has concluded, "was its ability to magnify real, but in the end relatively small, differences into unbridgeable chasms."[77]

The ugliest struggle in postwar New York did not end with the UFT's return to work. In Washington Heights, as elsewhere, the disputes that animated the strike emerged in the decentralized boards (which controlled elementary and junior high schools) and the high schools that stayed under the control of the central Board of Education. In northern Manhattan, where the old alignment of districts 12, 13, and 14 reached from Inwood down to 125th Street in Harlem, the new southern border for the district followed a rough line that stretched from 132nd Street on the Harlem River west to 135th on the Hudson River and north through Inwood. The new, somewhat smaller, boundaries seemed to offer better opportunities for the allocation of funding, improvements, and services. They also locked into one administrative unit, now called District 6, supporters and opponents of change in local public schools.[78]

The new local boards had limited but significant powers. They had virtually a free hand in choosing a district superintendent and they could distribute "specially targeted federal funds." In schools with reading test results in the bottom 45 percent of citywide performance, they could hire teachers outside the competitive Board of Examiners list—with the hope that instructors so hired could work more effectively with needy students. Most important for defining public life and politics, local boards were required to hold regular public meetings. In northern Manhattan, these would become forums for debates between defenders of the old order and those who wanted change.[79]

The central Board of Education retained control of budgets, school construction, and school maintenance. Teacher's wages, work rules, hiring, firing, and promotions would still be negotiated by the central administration and the UFT. Finally, the Board of Education would appoint a chancellor for the entire system who could suspend or dismiss an entire community board or any of its members who violated the central rules or instructions.[80]

Nonetheless, the modest but undeniable powers of the local school boards gave both new residents seeking a share of power and longtime residents trying to preserve the old ways substantial reasons to enter into school board politics. They would bring to these contests real divisions: the 1969 mayoral election showed a gap between mostly African American and Latino sections of northern Manhattan, which gave Lindsay 65 percent of the vote, and mostly Irish and Jewish areas, which gave him only 45 percent.[81] Washington Heights became a battleground between the old New York that was wary of Lindsay and newer residents who supported him.

In the 1960s, radical movements of blacks, leftists and Latinos had demanded sweeping changes in economics, politics, and structures of power. By the early 1970s, however, political adversaries in northern Manhattan—representatives of old and new Washington Heights, defenders of the status quo and their opponents—shared a venerable definition of urban politics that emphasized turf, ethnic and racial factions, and the delivery of services. This development and its larger implications caught the attention of the political scientist and historian Ira Katznelson, who studied the Lindsay administration's neighborhood government programs in northern Manhattan out of the Columbia University Bureau of Applied Social Research under a grant from the National Science Foundation. Why had broad struggles for social change given way to narrow debates over patronage jobs in the local schools?[82]

To find the answer, Katznelson and a team of researchers looked at everything from history to survey data to political theory. The result was *City Trenches: Urban Politics and the Patterning of Class in the United States*, published in 1981. The book remains a rich mixture of data and analysis that can launch debates on the absence of socialism in America and the fate of 1960s radicalism. Central to the book is a passage from the Italian Marxist theorist Antonio Gramsci: "The superstructures of civil society are like the trench systems of modern warfare." By this, Katznelson explained, customary political ideas and practices are like military trenches: they define the battlefield and what the battle will be fought over. In American urban politics, Katznelson concluded, the most important trench system is the one that separates "the politics of work from the politics of community."[83]

According to conventions of urban American politics established before the Civil War, he argued, workplace politics was about class and economic power. Politics in residential neighborhoods was about turf, tribe, and wringing gains from city government. Unlike European countries, where deeply entrenched historical factors pushed people to think of themselves as workers both on the job and at home (and made them more prone to socialist ideas), in the United States "most members of the working class thought of themselves as workers at work but as ethnics (and residents of this or that residential community) at home." The incendiary labor questions that roiled American factories rarely produced a sustained level of conflict in workers' neighborhoods or sustained a radical consciousness among workers off the job.[84]

Lindsay's local initiatives were intended to integrate African American and Latino residents into government and politics in the ways that political machines once introduced European immigrants to American ways of voting and governing. The ironies and misperceptions in this were many. Lindsay, as a Republican, had disdained the urban machine tradition associated with the Democratic Party. Moreover, machine Democrats had an uneven record at incorporating blacks and Latinos into the urban polity. Finally, there was the question of power. Machine politics thrived when it connected local needs to larger pools of money and patronage jobs. But as Katznelson observed, the structure of the boards directed the radical demands of black activists (Dominicans were not yet a powerful presence) into local forums that could not address sweeping demands for justice.[85]

In census data research, surveys, firsthand observations, and interviews, Katznelson and his research staff noted how the old school wars of northern Manhattan, and the great school strike, were refought in the confines of the local school board. Elections to the school board were distinguished by low turnouts and a style of campaigning that made it difficult for voters to discern substantive issues. Neighborhood solidarity was strong at the ballot box. Residents of the western Heights, which had long been resistant to change in the public school system and generally aligned with the UFT, voted regularly and in large numbers. Board meetings could be angry, rambling, and punctuated by protests and ethnic slurs. Nevertheless, they were a public forum for airing important concerns that might otherwise have been ignored.[86]

This was not a story of co-option or sellouts, but a story of pressing needs inadequately met on a landscape defined by real differences and bitter competition. Calls for a redistribution of wealth and power were pushed not on class terms but on ethnic terms. African Americans may have had bigger goals than could be accommodated in the trench system, but once they entered it their representatives had no choice but to fight within the limits of logic.[87]

Decentralization set up fierce political contests over relatively modest prizes. Community school districts, even when they worked in concert with central authorities, could not overcome the larger inequalities that shaped the lives of students, teachers, and parents. Nevertheless, decentralization directed neighborhood residents' attention toward local inequities and away from the larger economic gulfs between cities and suburbs. Struggles for scarce resources were fought out at the local level—where resources for redistribution were most limited. The grinding realities of the new system were expressed in a letter that Home R. Wade, business administrator of District 6, wrote to the Board of Education in 1971. His letter was a plea for better telephone service in schools where communications systems had reached an "almost unbearable state." Guidance counselors and assistant principals had no working telephones, and a principal had to leave her office entirely to make or receive calls. To make matters worse, local residents assumed that the District 6 office had the wherewithal to solve the problem. "You see," he wrote, "the term 'decentralization' has led the public to believe that the District Superintendent and his staff" were at "the focal point" of "every situation and that he is the 'mountain' that stands in the way of progress—this is a pitiful state of affairs for a man who must conform to bureaucratic procedures before he can make any improvement."[88]

In Washington Heights, battles over scarce seats in good schools reached a crescendo in arguments about PS 187. In 1968, half of the fourteen schools in the northern Manhattan district had white majorities. By 1971, all of the schools in the district had African American and Latino majorities. Two schools, however, had student bodies that were roughly 40 percent white. One of them was PS 187, located in the western Heights and widely recognized as one of the best schools in Washington Heights. It was also integrated. In April 1974, a *Times* report described PS 187 as a school of 826 students—44 percent white, 40 percent Spanish-speaking, and 16 percent black.[89]

The neighborhood around PS 187 had a reputation for political liberalism. On school matters, however, residents of the western Heights generally tried to fend off the kind of population changes that had transformed other schools in the Heights. Still, by the 1970s, demographic changes suggested that some kind of reckoning was coming for PS 187. Thanks to white departures and an aging white population, the number of students at PS 187 was shrinking. It was at 87 percent of its capacity, while the average school in the district was at 113 percent. Black and Latino parents pleaded that their children be allowed to take the school's empty seats. To the PS 187 parents who wanted to preserve the school as it was, this raised the issue of the school "tipping" into an all black or Latino school. To complicate matters, students who graduated from PS 187 normally went on to JHS 143 at 182nd Street and Audubon Avenue, a mile from PS 187. By 1974, JHS 143 was an overcrowded school with some two thousand students: 64 percent Latino, 21 percent black, and 15 percent white or Asian. It was also in a rapidly changing neighborhood scarred by drug dealing and street violence. Many parents at PS 187 saw JHS 143 as a rough school with a largely Latino population. If ethnic bias figured in their thoughts, so did safety.[90]

In JHS 143, the thought of losing students from PS 187 was troubling. Integration was threatened: if the white and more affluent students from PS

187 ceased to arrive, the junior high school was likely to become an entirely black and Latino school. Race and ethnicity aside, with fewer students JHS 143 would receive less funding from the city. If PS 187 had empty seats, why not let them be filled by children from any of the area's crowded elementary schools? Administrators and members of the Parents Association alike at JHS 143 thought their school was being maligned.[91]

JHS 143 did have some strengths in music and science. Laura Altschuler, who had arrived in New York as a refugee from Nazi Germany, gave her son a choice: stay on at PS 187 or go to JHS 143. He chose JHS 143, largely because it offered musical instruction and science labs that could not be matched in PS 187. He was hit over the head with book bags at JHS 143, she recalls, but he survived and learned more about science and music. Other parents at PS 187 saw the situation differently.

In 1972, the local board voted 5–4 to change PS 187 from an elementary school serving grades K-6 into one that educated children from kindergarten through eighth grade. Under this plan, the school would fill more of its seats and its students wouldn't have to leave to attend JHS 143, a middle school many PS 187 parents saw as problematic. If parents at PS 187 breathed a sigh of relief, parents from other schools in the district were outraged. The Board of Education also condemned the plan.[92]

The K-8 policy at PS 187, to parents and local board members who supported it, was consistent with decentralization: they were shaping the school in their community, an integrated one at that. The Board of Education thought otherwise. Without students from PS 187, JHS 143 was ever more likely to become an entirely black and Latino school. Moreover, the Board argued, enrollment procedures were at issue: keeping students at PS 187 longer would upset the pace at which students moved from elementary school to junior high school to high school. Pickets at PS 187 and an angry meeting of the local school board failed to settle the dispute.[93]

On a June morning in 1974, the last day of the school year, the chancellor's representatives went to PS 187 to seize the records of upper-level students. In the view of the chancellor's office, these students did not belong at PS 187 and instead should have been at JHS 143. With the students' records in hand, the chancellor's staff could direct the students where they wished. Outside the school was a picket line of some one hundred angry parents. Three times they blocked the chancellor's men from entering the school. At noon, students left the school; their year was over. At 1:30 p.m., one of the chancellor's men again attempted to enter. Blocked by children chanting "Go Home," he tried a side door, pounded on a locked door, and then tried again. Some thirty-five protestors blocked the way. Eventually, with the help of police, women were pushed aside and children carried off. Amid cries and shouts, the chancellor's aides entered the school, seized the records of two hundred students, and carried them away.[94]

In July, seeking to avoid a confrontation at the start of the school year, the chancellor offered to negotiate and, only three days before school started, an agreement emerged. Students in PS 187 could stay there through eighth grade, but the seventh and eighth graders among them would for administrative purposes be part of a junior high school in the neighborhood.[95]

PS 187 would remain a K-8 school, an integrated school, and one of the best schools in northern Manhattan for decades to come. When Marielys Divanne immigrated to New York City in 1988 from the Dominican Republic with her mother, a schoolteacher in their native country and then a factory worker in Manhattan, they lived at 600 W. 142nd Street. Her mother did not like their neighborhood schools, and asked around about which was the best in her district. The answer was clear: PS 187. Thanks to her mother's lobbying, Divanne entered PS 187. She found there a disciplined but welcoming school with high standards, run by a principal who was an ex-nun. Divanne thrived in its bilingual education program, the first step in an educational trajectory that took her to St. Pius V High School in the Bronx, Boston College, and Columbia University.[96]

Divanne's success at PS 187 was a testament to her own hard work and the strength of the school. It was not, however, a sign of the health of public schools throughout northern Manhattan. The local school board continued to be the focus of faction fights, ethnically and racially charged politics, and struggles to resolve problems that outstripped the capacities of northern Manhattan and the city around it. As Katznelson observed at the end of *City Trenches*, "The gap between rich and poor in northern Manhattan, in New York City, and in urban America more generally has continued to grow in the 1970s, while social peace has been maintained. If this is a tale of success, the term requires a very special definition."[97]

In 1962, Ellen Lurie had gazed out from Fort Tryon Park and mused about the enormous potential in her neighborhood. By the early 1970s, much of that potential had been dissipated in school wars. For Jewish, Irish, and Greek residents, there was a growing sense that the "old days" of the 1940s and 1950s, when schools and municipal institutions had served them fairly well, were fading. For blacks and Latinos, who had come to Washington Heights seeking better lives, there was a fear that the segregation, inferior schools, and limited economic opportunities of the past would continue into a bleak future. Into this troubled environment came the next group whose presence would redefine Washington Heights, the Dominicans.

Unlike the Irish and the Jews, who tended to see the United States as a refuge from troubles, Dominicans knew the United States as a country that

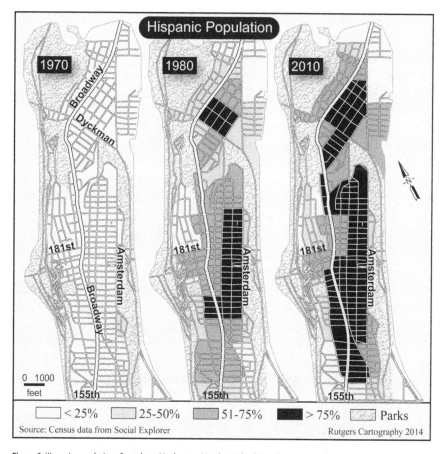

Figure 8: Hispanic population of northern Manhattan. Map by Michael Siegel, Rutgers Cartography, 2014.

was deeply implicated in many of their homeland's problems. Dominicans' national hero might be Juan Pablo Duarte, who led the rebellion in 1844 that drove out the Haitians, but much of their history was shaped by the effects of U.S. imperialism. In "There Is a Country in the World: A Poem, Sad on More Than One Occasion," the Dominican poet Pedro Mir described the Dominican Republic as a place "Situated / in an improbable archipelago / of sugar and alcohol" where "the limbs of the simplest man / belong to the company." To Dominicans, as Mir observed in his poem "Countersong to Walt Whitman," the United States was both the home of the democratic poet Whitman and an imperial power.[98]

When Dominicans cut sugarcane, it was likely processed in refineries owned by U.S. businesses. When they played baseball with incomparable skill and flair, they played a game born in the United States and transported to the Dominican Republic by U.S. interests. U.S. economic domination of the

Dominican Republic was thus well established by 1916, when the U.S. Marines invaded, fought a nasty war against Dominican rebels, and governed the country until 1924.[99]

Rafael Leónidas Trujillo, the dictator who ran the Dominican Republic with ruthless cunning, emerged from a Dominican national police force entrusted with keeping order on terms congenial to U.S. interests. Trujillo ran what the historian Frank Moya Pons has described as "a regime of plunder." In one of the less-known genocides of the twentieth century, Trujillo's forces in 1937 massacred some eighteen thousand Haitians and Dominicans of Haitian descent to preserve his nation's presumed racial purity. Eventually, his regime became an embarrassment to the United States. In 1961, Dominican officers and civilians aided by the CIA assassinated him.[100]

Two years later, the Dominican military toppled his democratically elected successor, the populist Juan Bosch, and established a junta. When dissident soldiers, urban workers, and leaders of Bosch's Partido Revolucionario Dominicano (PRD) tried to restore Bosch to power in 1965, President Lyndon Johnson sent in U.S. troops. Officially they were peacekeepers, but their real impact was to restore order by putting allies of Trujillo back in power. Johnson, amid the Cold War, was opposed to anything that might be interpreted as a repetition of the Cuban revolution in the Caribbean. Bosch was a democrat, but U.S. leaders feared his openings to the Dominican left.[101]

With order restored in the Dominican Republic, the Johnson administration worked on policies to shape immigration between the United States and the Dominican Republic. In fact, as Jesse Hoffnung-Garskof points out, with the death of Trujillo in 1961 and the lifting of the dictator's travel restrictions, Dominican immigration to the United States had been growing already. Indeed, U.S. officials in the Dominican Republic saw immigration as a way "to push troublesome actors out of the country," while Dominicans sought a way out of turmoil. The pressures of law, memory, and politics combined to shape Dominican immigration in complex ways. The Johnson administration's 1965 immigration reform law is remembered for abolishing national origins quotas, but in a nod to conservative concerns about the immigration of Mexicans and West Indian blacks, it also placed unprecedented limits on immigration from the Western Hemisphere. Among those affected would be Dominicans, who could now leave their homeland but faced limits on how many of them could enter the United States. The combination of the push from conditions in the Dominican Republic and the new limits established by law set the stage for immigration outside the law.[102]

For Dominican leftists and patriots, the legacy of Johnson's intervention meant going to a country that had twice invaded the Dominican Republic. For

Dominicans of less political minds, the new U.S. visa restrictions narrowed the Golden Door of immigration when they desperately wanted it open. Nevertheless, the push of hardships in the Caribbean and the pull of New York led Dominicans to negotiate these limits. Some left in legal ways (getting "a visa for a dream," as one merengue lyric put it) and some in less than legal ways, like going to Puerto Rico in an overloaded boat across the dangerous Mona Passage and then flying on to the United States. The ambivalence that accompanied decisions, which could be profound, was expressed in graffiti seen in Santo Domingo. "Fuera Yanqui!" someone wrote, to which another writer added, "y llévame contigo." Yankee go home and take me with you.[103]

By the early 1970s, Dominicans arriving in Washington Heights found a neighborhood in transition and schools turned upside down by demographic changes and the political aftershocks of the school strike. Nowhere was the turmoil greater than in the hallways and classrooms of George Washington High School, popularly known as G-Dubs, where students of different races and nationalities jostled each other, eyed each other, and responded to each other with everything from interest to animosity. With drugs, dealers, gangs, and muggers inside and outside the school, and the spirit of insurrection that animated so much of youth culture in the 1960s and 1970s, the atmosphere was combustible. On top of all this, there were the lingering issues of the school strike: a UFT eager to preserve its authority, community control advocates eager to remake the schools, and students torn between making revolution and staying alive.[104]

The March 26, 1970, issue of the *Cherry Tree*, the student newspaper, reflected the fractured identity of an institution with a small population of college-bound students, most of them white, and a much larger number of students, most of them African American and Latino, whose futures after graduation were uncertain. The lead story covered a dispute over how to fix the high school's inadequate academic advising and guidance. Also on the front page were a story about the new principal assigned to the school, an article about the debate team, and a piece about a George Washington team's appearance on the television quiz show, *It's Academic*. (George Washington came in second in a field of three.) Inside the paper were a rave review of a Sly and the Family Stone concert, a piece on a "favorite teacher" contest, and an editorial, "Drug Scene Is a Drag." Indeed, much of the paper suggested that George Washington was an academic high school touched but not upended by the spirit of the counterculture.[105]

In the margins of the paper, however, George Washington appeared to be something more. On page two, under the heading "Amigos," were four short news briefs in Spanish that took up barely six column inches. Also on the same page was "Latino Lingo Lives," about a Spanish literary magazine. The two stories on that page hinted, briefly and awkwardly, at a Latino presence at George Washington High School that was actually growing. The school, according to statistics obtained by Ellen Lurie, was 30 percent African American, 24 percent Puerto Rican, and more than 20 percent "other Spanish." In northern Manhattan, "other Spanish" increasingly meant Dominican.[106]

Among the Dominican students was a young woman with a vision of education as a means to personal and collective liberation, Nelsy Aldebot. Born in 1950, she enrolled at George Washington after she arrived from the Dominican Republic in 1967. She had already lived in New York City for a year in 1963, when her passion for the freedom of Manhattan life and her studies at Joan of Arc Junior High School ended with her reluctant return to the Dominican Republic to care for a widowed grandfather. Aldebot entered George Washington to get an academic education that prepared her for college. Inside the school, she discovered its tracking system, with its division of commercial and academic courses. Aldebot also noticed the tendency for white students to be in the academic tracks, with Hispanic students more in general courses that were not academically oriented. White and Hispanic students were in different worlds, Aldebot thought. She herself lived with "one foot in one world, and the other foot in the other world." Black students, she believed, were somewhere between the two. In her general courses, Aldebot sank into despair when she saw her friends "fooling around with their lives" and "killing themselves academically" by goofing around in class. In her academic courses, she worked alongside well-prepared black students and white kids, most of them Jewish. She found it hard to keep up at first, but persevered and did well. She fell in love with the study of science.[107]

Among her fellow students was Sara Lurie, Ellen Lurie's daughter, who began attending George Washington in 1969. Sara, like Aldebot, recalled a school that seemed to be divided into separate worlds. White students were in the college preparatory track, but Latino and African American students were mostly in general and vocational tracks. Sara spent a lot of time in the hallways instead of going to classes. There was a lot of hanging out, going out to eat Cuban sandwiches, and joining in demonstrations against everything from school policies to the Vietnam War. The personal became political in new ways as Jewish girls dated African American and Latino boys. Once, Sara recalled, a black youth asked her out on a date. Her mother had no problem with that but offered some tough-minded advice: if things get frisky, you have the right to say no. And if he says that makes you a racist, don't fall for it. The evening went as Lurie predicted. Sara felt strong enough to say no, and all ended well.[108]

Starting from different places, Aldebot and Sara both noticed the problems of the school's tracking system. But for Ramona De La Cruz, who was born in the Dominican Republic in 1953 and entered George Washington in 1969, the problem was not so much tracking as a general sense of disorder. De La Cruz approached high school with confidence and aspirations for a career in business, but entered a school where rivalries between African American and Dominican students made the hallways tense. "You didn't have to look for trouble," she recalled, "trouble was looking for you." Although she made friends with all kinds of students, she was still frightened. Dominicans, with their range of skin colors, didn't fit into American categories of black and white. Some of her friends were cornered in hallways and asked, "Which side are you on?" De La Cruz, raised in a family where she was taught to respect elders and teachers, found the chaos and violence jarring. Resolutely, she pursued her goal of graduating with a commercial diploma and starting a career in a business. To avoid being singled out, she stuck with a pack of students when changing classes. She also stayed away from the lavatories, which had reputations as dangerous places. In four years at George Washington High School, she never once used the girls' room.[109]

The turmoil at George Washington High School was not exclusively social and cultural. The political protests that rocked colleges and universities in these years also had their counterparts in high schools, including those of northern Manhattan. Students at New York City high schools organized to demand rights and forged new identities. As early as 1967, as Hoffnung-Garskof's research has shown, a group of Dominican students nicknamed the *filósofos*, or philosophers, studied politics, philosophy, and literature together, and reached beyond their school to protest against U.S. foreign policy and the Joaquín Balaguer regime in the Dominican Republic. Girls at George Washington demonstrated in January 1969 for the right to wear pants instead of skirts. Dominican and Puerto Rican students joined the Asociación de Estudiantes Hispanoamericanos. Aldebot helped found the Asociación and served as its vice president. African American students formed Umoja, and argued for hiring more "minority" teachers and the introduction of more courses relevant to "minority" concerns.[110]

Aldebot—driven by her own intellectual independence and inspired by Dominican revolutionaries—grasped education as a means to personal and collective liberation. She studied hard with memorably good teachers and worked with black and Hispanic students to change the school's educational practices. Outside of school, she supported the United Farm Workers' boycott of nonunion grapes to such an extent that one of her friends nicknamed her "grapes." Aldebot also participated in Juventud Obrera Christiana, and talked with Belgian priests about working-class life, the oppression of the poor, and social justice.[111]

In the spring of 1969, Aldebot's work with the Asociación and Umoja led her to join in a schoolwide strike. She remembers arriving at George Washington High School in a green raincoat and yellow rain hat, feeling very afraid and wondering if she would wind up dead or in jail. She was standing on a student picket line when a teacher stopped to tell her that she didn't belong there because she was a "good girl." She thought to herself that the teacher didn't really know her.

The strike, for Aldebot, ended in disappointment. Even though black, white, and Hispanic students and a student government representative negotiated with administrators, the students were defeated. People were dishonest, she concluded; people could be bought out. Contrary to her fears, participating in the strike did not result in her going to jail.

The disputes within George Washington High School took place against the backdrop of citywide debates about the purposes and practices of education. Some, like Mario Procaccino—a conservative Democratic mayoral candidate in 1969—blamed the crime and disorder at George Washington High School on the Lindsay administration. But Ellen Lurie and her allies thought the problems at George Washington had complex causes: shaky leadership; poor advising; a curriculum that was inadequate for the school's changing population; friction between Dominicans and African Americans; and a tracking system that further divided students.[112]

As a solution, Lurie and like-minded parents proposed to establish an information table in the lobby of the school. In March 1970, after student demonstrations that shut down the school, a principal's resignation, and wary discussions with school administrators and representatives of the Board of Education, the plan went into effect. At the table, students could ask parent volunteers about graduation requirements, drugs, rights, suspension, and any other problems they encountered.[113]

The administration at George Washington High School may have wanted nothing more than compliant assistance from parents. To the UFT, however, the demands of the parents and students who gathered around the table amounted to an effort to create an alternative source of power and information to change the school. Even though George Washington did not fall under the purview of the local school board because the central board still controlled high schools, the issues that surged through the high school were the same kind of grievances that had animated the strike. To the UFT, its supporters in the neighborhood, and the Council of Supervisory Associations (which represented principals), giving authority to the community opened up the prospect of more disorder. To African American and Latino students who were confounded and undermined by the school's courses and procedures, the table offered help. Among members of the UFT and its allies, the group around the table threatened to open the door to angry activists who were not above using threats and intimidation to get their way. To Jews with memories of the chaos and crackdowns of Germany, the turmoil in the school smelled of danger. To parents of all races whose children just wanted to get through school quietly and successfully, the debates around the table were one more volatile element in a tumultuous school.[114]

Anger and mistrust eroded scarce common ground. Richard J. Margolis, a writer who covered subjects such as rural poverty, housing, and education, published an article about the situation at George Washington in the *New Leader*. He described the school as a place with real problems where all parties claimed to speak the truth, no one could agree on what was happening, and no one was at a loss for rhetoric.[115]

Through the spring of 1970, George Washington High School was rocked by demonstrations, classroom confrontations, and violence. Sara Lurie saw a Molotov cocktail thrown inside the school. Although she felt no fear, she avoided using the lavatories. Her mother had always envisioned schools with doors open to their surrounding communities in healthy and nurturing ways, but around George Washington it was too often the poisonous, violent, drug-ridden aspects of the streets that leached back into the school. News stories, letters to the UFT, letters to the Board of Education, and reminiscences all convey the sense of teachers, students, parents, and administrators locked in a many-sided conflict over order, legitimacy, and learning. In a revealing succession of letters written in March 1970, fourteen Protestant ministers and Roman Catholic priests from across northern Manhattan acknowledged the prerogatives of "teachers and guidance leaders" at George Washington, but encouraged everyone to give the table experiment the time and opportunity to succeed. In contrast, a letter from rabbis in northern Manhattan—Reform, Conservative, and Orthodox—deplored "the violence and acts of defiance of authority" at George Washington and concluded with the "hope that the spirit of cooperation will prevail over the spirit of undemocratic fanaticism."[116]

Demonstrations, UFT walkouts, and lawsuits over the table riled the school. In April, seventeen men and women wrote Mayor Lindsay to demand a reopened school, the assignment of as many police officers as necessary to guarantee safety, and the "PERMANENT REMOVAL" of any student who committed violence against a student or a staff member. In the same month, some fifty-eight parents of George Washington students sent a telegram to Superintendent of Schools Irving Anker, copied to Albert Shanker, demanding a "meaningful, uninterrupted" and safe education for their children. Judging from the signatures on the letter and telegram, Latino, Jewish, and African American parents were all concerned. In May of 1970, dissident teachers criticized both the administration and the UFT for their intransigence on the table, pointed out the students' legitimate grievances, and insisted that parents, teachers, and administration learn to work together to prevent a bad situation from getting worse.[117]

Troubles continued in the fall. Poignant recognition of deep problems and the difficulty of getting people to work on solutions came in a pair of letters from Rosemary Strauss, a UFT member and adviser of the Student Government Organization (SGO) at the school.[118] Writing to Bob Miller, the UFT chapter chairman, she began: "I think the UFT will be making a big mistake if some positive plans are not proposed to solve problems magnified by the current crisis. Many students in the S.G.O. feel that union teachers only use their union to protect their job rights. It's all the students have known. When have G.W. teachers taken strong union action to improve the school?" Strauss identified the students' problems: "red tape," "terrible anonymity," and the absence of a "friend at court" when students landed in trouble. She raised possible solutions—identifying someone on the staff who would be a clear source of information, or a paid ombudsman. Then she concluded: "Maybe we haven't done enough as a union to earn the respect of students. (At least that's a fraction of the complex story.) I don't want in any way to lessen our justifiable response to the violence & capitulation of the past 2 wks., but I would hate for us only to respond in terms of an eye for an eye."

Strauss wrote again later in the year. This time it was to report the theft of her "handbag" while she was at George Washington. Under the terms of her contract she requested reimbursement for everything she lost: a change purse worth $7.95, her driver's license, a Parker pen worth $10, and $20 in cash.

Despite Strauss's suggestions, violence and confusion continued. Incidents were both murky and frightening. Curtis Francheschi, an African American youth, belonged to the Brotherhood—a black organization that fought with security guards and drug dealers alike. Francheschi had clashed with teachers and supported the table group; the UFT wanted him removed from the school. In October, Francheschi was spotted pounding on a youth outside the school. Whatever the explanation—he might have been beating up a pusher, it might have been a mugging—the police took him away to spend a night in jail at Rikers' Island. Francheschi's supporters, unaware that Ellen Lurie had already pulled together bail money for Francheschi, stalked through the school. They barged into classes to ask for bail money and shook down students in the halls. (In a letter to Nat Hentoff of the *Village Voice*, Lurie called this fund-raising of "a rather unorthodox fashion.") She went on to explain to Hentoff: "One student who did not understand much English pulled a knife on the fundraisers, and before the fight ended, four black kids were stabbed." When black kids retaliated by attacking the knife-wielding Dominican youth, she added that "two parents (both black) from the parent table threw their bodies on top of him and literally saved him from death." Afterwards, the school was shut down for a week. In the same month, the table vanished. The shutdown, the disappearance of the table, and an effort to transfer out students who were making trouble (which could cover everything from political agitation to robbing people) made things no better.[119]

Looking at the crisis in retrospect for the *New Leader*, Margolis described a complicated standoff. Supporters of the table were probably correct, he wrote, when they said they kept students from acting even more violently. Yet the UFT was probably also correct, he noted, when it argued that supporters of the table group used the disorder in the school as a "trump card" to get their way. Still, Margolis concluded, "It is just possible that if the UFT had understood the table proposal as a desperate plea for reform, rather than as 'a power play to gain control of the high school,' the ensuing conflict could have been averted."[120]

In December 1970, that possibility seemed long past. Students and security guards continued to fight. In one confrontation, guards beat the students so badly that one had a broken arm and another needed forty stitches; police were summoned to restore order. For everyone who read about the incident in the *New York Times* under the headline "2 Hurt, 3 Seized in School Melee," it looked like George Washington High School was careening out of control. In fact, better days were coming. They would be built by a principal with a passion for literature who valued education as much as security.[121]

Samuel Kostman was born at sea in 1928 on the French ocean liner *Isle de France* as his parents steamed from Poland to America. After they landed, the family settled in Borough Park, Brooklyn, and his father found a job delivering mattresses. Kostman grew up in an Orthodox community and studied at yeshivas through high school. "I lived in an enclosed world, in a sense it was like a cocoon," he recalled. His first sustained contact with the world beyond his Orthodox community came when he registered at Brooklyn College. His cocoon "burst," he remembered, and he experienced "a whole revelation." Working in a belt factory by day and taking courses at night, Kostman studied literature, history, sociology, and psychology. Outside of class he listened to classical music, attended plays and lectures, and developed a love for the writings of Thomas Wolfe. Taking advantage of free tuition at Brooklyn College, he earned his BA in 1950 and an MA in 1952. Substitute teaching in public schools, after-school work teaching Hebrew, and summertime work at Jewish sleepover camps confirmed his passion for working with students.

After a year at JHS 109 he settled into teaching English and Hebrew at Midwood High School; he then moved on to teach and chair the English Department at George Wingate High School from 1965 to 1970.[122]

Through study and exams, Kostman built up the credentials needed to become an assistant principal and then a principal. Critics of the prestrike order said this bureaucratic system limited the available pool of principals. But as he passed the tests required for promotion and observed the careers of principals and superintendents who preceded him, Kostman gained confidence that he was advancing on merit and gaining the skills to handle anything the system might throw at him. He was as much a learner as he was a teacher and administrator—reading endlessly and establishing book clubs. He asked prospective teachers what they were reading to assure himself that they had active minds. He was also a member of the UFT. In 1968, at Wingate High School in Brooklyn, in a neighborhood wrestling with racial transitions, he went on strike because he thought teachers had to be defended, especially Jewish teachers. During the walkout, he taught English at a freedom school so that students could learn without crossing a picket line.[123] In November 1970, Kostman was asked to become principal of George Washington. He thought hard and said yes because he thought he owed it to the city and saw it as a good opportunity to become a principal. The *New York Times* reported the news on December 3 under the headline, "Washington High Gets Fourth Principal This Year."[124]

If the information table pushed by Lurie was an attempt to fix George Washington from the bottom up, Kostman's appointment was part of an effort to fix the school from the top down. When he arrived, students deemed troublemakers had already been pushed out and officials in the central board moved to put an end to the parents' table.[125] By the end of January, the table was long gone and the transfers had stopped. Although this suggested a standoff between the old and new regimes at George Washington, familiar problems remained. On December 17, a twenty-three-year-old English teacher was beaten unconscious and robbed of her wallet in the ninth-grade annex of George Washington at 183rd Street and St. Nicholas Avenue; a fifteen-year-old student at the school was arrested in the case. On February 3, 1971, Sara Lurie and three members of George Washington's Consultative Council wrote the Board of Education to say that there was still no way for students to speak out and voice their grievances. And on February 19 fighting erupted at the school after African American girls robbed two Dominican girls. Five students were injured and five more arrested.[126]

On the following Tuesday, Kostman read an announcement and sent copies to students' parents. The new principal warned everyone that all students who were not registered in classes, who roamed the halls, or who refused to

leave the cafeteria when they had no cause to be there had an absolute obliga-
tion to comply with requests for proper conduct. If they did not they would
be suspended immediately and would bring upon themselves "the most serious consequences." The written message concluded with a plea to parents:
"Please enlist the cooperation of your children and help us establish a via-
ble educational atmosphere at George Washington High. The very life of the
school is at stake."[127]

The announcement was the first part of a carrot and stick strategy. The stick
was wielded prudently and with Kostman's personal example. In the morning,
he greeted students as they entered the school. At midday, he ate lunch with
them in the cafeteria. He walked the hallways and once chased a student with
drugs from the top floor of the school to the basement. When a crowd of Latinos attacked an African American student, Kostman shielded him with his
own body. Only afterward did he notice the welts on his back. To better keep
order, Kostman recruited priests, ministers, and rabbis to visit George Washington. He developed a working relationship with the local precinct (it came
in handy when he had to dispose of a pistol that a student gave to a teacher),
but usually he asked police to stay away because their presence inflamed the
students. When students staged a sit-in, he told them to go to class or go home.
With that, he led the students who wanted to go home to the subway.

The carrot in Kostman's strategy drew on his own education and his years
of teaching. For students who could not study effectively in a large high school,
he established a small satellite school, the George Washington Academy, and
ran it out of the Church of the Intercession. (Ellen Lurie, his fierce opponent
in the information table episode, called it "the most exciting and wonderful
and terrific thing going in the high schools.") He introduced speak-out sessions where students could state their complaints. Over opposition within
his own faculty, he introduced a program in English as a Second Language
to serve immigrant students. In an effort to strengthen school spirit, Kostman revived the school's football team and made its coach, Jim Walsh, head
of security. Walsh organized a winter retreat at the Hudson Guild Farm in
Netcong, New Jersey, where northern Manhattan parents had met to discuss
integration in the 1950s, so that students could learn to talk about their differences instead of fighting over them. Sara Lurie, who participated, recalled
the experience as "fantastic."[128]

In large and small gestures, the principal signaled his devotion to the
school. When student events were held on Fridays or Saturdays, Kostman—a
Sabbath-observant Jew—ate and slept at nearby Yeshiva University and
walked back to his high school to attend. "Whoever we're teaching," he said,
"they're ours. They're God's children. We've got to do this for them. We've got
to help them in every way that we can."[129]

By the end of Kostman's first year, stories in the *New York Times* noted the change in George Washington High School. As a headline in the *Times* put it, the school had gone "From Riot to Hope." In the *New Leader*, Richard Margolis wrote that everyone at George Washington—students, parents, and the UFT—trusted Kostman and his plans for the future. "They do not yet trust each other," he concluded, "but most are ready to put aside former hostilities for the sake of peace." Albert Shanker, in the column that he published in the *New York Times* in space paid for by the UFT, lauded Kostman's turnaround as a rejection of "capitulation" before militants like Ellen Lurie.[130]

The teachers and staff at George Washington worked to make their school a place where their minds could open up to new ideas and new possibilities. Students went to Princeton, Montreal, and Lincoln Center on field trips. Neighborhood residents took classes after working hours. A reorganized school week left Wednesdays open for speakers, performances, and discussions of current affairs. Students organized a gay rights group and Kostman permitted them to meet—more in the spirit of avoiding a conflict than out of a personal endorsement of gay rights, but they met nonetheless.[131]

Kostman served at George Washington until 1983, when he moved on to become the superintendent of high schools in Queens. When he left the high school, alumni and his colleagues in administration saluted him. He himself was frustrated that he could not do more for his students. So many of them, he recalled, were learning a new language, coming from homes that were either broken or under great pressure, and starting from the bottom rung of the ladder for no other reason than the "luck of the draw." Ultimately, he was sustained by the certainty that he cared and he tried.[132]

For a time, the intelligence and energy of committed students, and the dedication of good teachers and administrators, made George Washington High School a launching pad for good lives. Nelsy Aldebot graduated in 1969 and went on to Hunter College. Her interests shifted from science to education and psychology, but she was steadfast in her embrace of learning and activism for individual and collective liberation. She earned a bachelor's and a master's and worked as a public school teacher. She shocked her parents in 1974 by moving out of their home without being married to live on the Lower East Side. Four years later, sure that there was still work for leftists to do in the land of her birth, and determined to avoid getting caught between two countries, she moved back to the Dominican Republic and continued her work as a teacher.[133]

Ramona De La Cruz, who married in her senior year, spent her last year at George Washington in a cooperative program that had her studying on campus and working downtown. After graduation, she found a job at Equitable Insurance. She started in the typing pool but rose quickly to be a department secretary. She was on her way to the lifelong career in business that she had envisioned when she started at George Washington.[134]

Despite such student successes, Kostman's efforts were not enough to transform George Washington High School. Within five years of his departure in 1983, George Washington High School was cited for high absentee rates; within six years the state education commissioner rated it among the state's most academically troubled schools. One principal's leadership was not enough to halt the school's decline.[135]

For Ellen Lurie, the struggles at George Washington High School were her last major efforts in her neighborhood. She went on to work for the United Bronx Parents and to teach at the New School. Lurie saw more clearly than most that the New York City public schools in the 1960s were headed for a disaster. In an effort to prevent that she committed her intellect, her energy, and even her children. She was no limousine liberal. Hard experiences convinced her that New York's public schools had to work for all if they were to win parents' trust and reach their full democratic potential. Her insights were sound, but she could not bridge the gap between what needed to be done and what she could actually put into practice.

Lurie's enthusiasm for community control was grounded in her belief that devolving power to city neighborhoods would give residents the ability to change their schools and their school policies, hastening the arrival of integration. What she did not clearly anticipate was that power in a decentralized school system could flow not to supporters of integration and equity, but to their opponents. She also failed to consider how the bold, all-at-once integration that she so deeply desired could be accomplished only with a powerful, top-down application of municipal authority—the kind of centralized authority that she so distrusted. Yet central authority had it uses: at George Washington High School, for all her efforts to bring order and justice to the school with the table group, there is a sense that the violence in the school surpassed anything that could be addressed by her bottom-up efforts. Finally, she did not have a remedy at hand for one of the most pernicious consequences of decentralization: ultimately, it absolved this city's elites of their responsibility to provide adequate funding and political support for public education. Once schools that served neighborhoods of poor and academically troubled students were left to the care of their surrounding communities, they were far from constructive oversight and support and vulnerable to inequalities and corruption.[136]

In her book *How to Change the Schools*, published in 1970, Lurie grasped the disabling conflicts in the schools. "The school system is not able to function today, because the parents no longer believe in it," she wrote. "The community has lost its trust in the schools. Professionals are seen as the enemy—targets to be attacked and cut down." Educators, she believed, had to win the community's trust. She also thought that the schools were poisoned by the animosities among parents.

> Parents remain weak and divided because we are afraid of each other. Middle-class parents are afraid of poor parents; because of that fear they did not join in the fight for community control, even though it might have helped them improve the schools in their communities too. White parents are afraid of black parents. Black parents are afraid of Puerto Rican parents. Puerto Rican parents are afraid of Chinese parents. In every community, and between every community, there is a wall of fear and distrust which effectively keeps parents apart. When will we realize that we have much more to fear from the system than from each other?[137]

In her personal papers, which eventually went to the Center for Puerto Rican Studies at Hunter College, was an op-ed that Lurie kept from the January 6, 1977, issue of the *Heights-Inwood* newspaper. The author of the piece, Hope Irvine, was identified as a thirty-five-year resident of the Heights and local teacher who had "sat through more than her share of discussions as a member of Community Board 12." In that short piece, Irvine argued that cultural events that brought the peoples of the Heights together were an important part of building a healthy neighborhood. Portions of the piece were underlined. Decades later, it is impossible to tell who did the underlining and whether it was meant to emphasize small victories, cherished hopes, bitter disappointments, or the gap between ideals and realities in northern Manhattan.[138] Yet it seems reasonable to see some significance in a sentence, in the next-to-last paragraph of the article, that was underlined in Lurie's copy: "The riches of our neighborhoods are the people: who make time to build bridges of understanding, who find ways to bring people together in relaxed, non-threatening ways, who work towards a stronger more cohesive community which draws its strength from our rich mixture of cultural heritage." And the underlining continued, thickening through the last paragraph of Irvine's piece, which argued that "the hope of our community" lay in people's willingness to work together for each other. The last sentence in the piece was underscored heaviest of all: "When we share our arts, our foods, our fun—we can find each other; when we can share our cares and concerns—we can trust each other; when we work together for each other—we can love each other."

Eighteen months after the article appeared, Ellen Lurie died of cancer.[139]

CHAPTER 4

IN THE SHADOW OF
THE SOUTH BRONX

ON A SUMMER NIGHT IN 1978, people packed into a hot auditorium with a broken air conditioner at the Young Men's–Young Women's Hebrew Association of Washington Heights and Inwood. They had gathered to hear the new mayor's plans for their neighborhood, which was wracked by crime, racial and ethnic tensions, dirty streets, and troubled public schools. The number of abandoned apartment buildings was growing. Residents of northern Manhattan looked across the Harlem River to the Bronx, where arson turned city streets into ashy rubble, and feared that their neighborhood might be the next to burn.[1]

Just seven months into his first term, Mayor Ed Koch arrived at the auditorium on Nagle Avenue armed with a copy of the report of the Washington Heights–Inwood Task Force that he had convened in March. The crowded audience before him was mostly white and, by appearance, middle class. "Despite the large number of blacks in Northern Manhattan," the local newspaper *Heights-Inwood* observed, "only a handful attended the meeting." Also notable for its absence was the group that would soon redefine the population of northern Manhattan: "The growing Hispanic population," the paper reported, "was also lightly represented."

Mayor Koch began with an exhortation. "Washington Heights is not going to become another burned-out, demoralized neighborhood," he said. "That's not going to happen because you're not going to let it happen." He continued by emphasizing the high stakes at hand, asserting that Washington Heights and Inwood were the type of neighborhoods "which must be saved if this city is to survive." To help, he announced plans for improvements in housing, sanitation, parks, policing, and business district conditions.

Looking back on the episode it is possible to glimpse the gravity of the situation, the limits of what the city had to offer by way of assistance, and the lingering presence of the neighborhood's old European ethnic groups even as Latinos and African Americans became its new majority. The mayor, in effect, was telling the people at the meeting to stay in their neighborhood and defend it from decay. The other option—for those who could afford it—was to leave for either the suburbs or a more congenial section of the city. Poised between taking action and taking flight, balancing inclusion and exclusion, residents of Washington Heights and Inwood faced an uncertain future. Ultimately, they staved off the blight that claimed significant parts of the Bronx. Yet when Koch spoke that summer of 1978, the fate of the neighborhood was not promising. And while the mayor promised support, there were no expectations of transforming amounts of help arriving from outside northern Manhattan.[2]

Washington Heights was in the grip of a citywide economic crisis that undermined its housing stock. Some landlords, faced with weak returns on rents, scrimped on maintenance or declined to pay taxes; others milked their buildings and then abandoned them. Market-driven development, led by entrepreneurs, was not an option. Instead, community organizations and city government prodded businesses—above all banks—to work in a troubled neighborhood that many investors wanted to write off. "Neighborhood preservation" was the slogan of those most active in efforts to turn back blight. For some, the phrase meant restoring municipal services and a decent standard of living in a neighborhood that seemed to be teetering on the edge of ruin. For others, "neighborhood preservation" was more about preserving the old ethnic order of New York than it was about forging a more inclusive future.

Out of these complex motives in the 1970s, a decade that is rightly remembered as one of the bleakest in the history of New York City, people in northern Manhattan used grassroots efforts, government, and innovative financing to rescue their neighborhood from ruin. At the same time, they bequeathed to future generations a neighborhood that would be physically intact but still ethnically divided as traditional territorial disputes gave way to a new era of tensions between the old Washington Heights of Irish, Jews, and Greeks and a new Dominican community. If the preservation of housing stock was largely a victory of old Washington Heights, the effort succeeded only because Dominican newcomers arrived and settled into the rescued apartments and streets. Yet the battle for neighborhood preservation was more than a struggle to preserve the streets and buildings of Washington Heights; in the long run, it was a contest over exactly what kind of community would emerge in the streets that had been saved from ruin.[3]

In northern Manhattan, the anxieties of the 1970s had deep roots. When Jim Carroll moved to Inwood from lower Manhattan, he noticed the generally conservative tenor of the neighborhood. Carroll was Irish and a skilled basketball player, but his countercultural tendencies made him an awkward fit with his new neighbors. "Hallways in my new building and each park bench," he later wrote in *The Basketball Diaries*, "filled with chattering old Irish ladies either gossiping or saying the rosary, or men long time here or younger ones right off the boat huddling in floppy overcoats in front of drug stores discussing their operations, ball scores, or the Commie threat." Carroll described young men his own age as "strictly All American," but noted that most "do the beer-drinking scene on weekends."[4]

For Father Jerry Travers, a Paulist priest at Good Shepherd Church in the Irish section of Inwood from 1966 to 1968, one of the first signs of unease in his neighborhood was a comment he heard through an open rectory window that faced Isham Street. "They're coming up out of the subway" was the remark he heard, not knowing who said it but certain that the person was a parishioner. The Irish Catholics of Good Shepherd, like both Irish and Jewish residents of northern Manhattan, saw the world through the lenses of ethnicity and geography. Inwood was a neighborhood with a strong Irish presence, but its residents were well aware that some three miles to the south, in the lower Heights and upper Harlem, there were streets with African American majorities whose residents might well want to move into Inwood. For many of Travers's neighbors in Inwood, that prospect inspired thoughts of crowded tenements and streets rife with crime.[5]

Travers saw it differently. The Canadian-born son of an Irish immigrant, he was drawn to the priesthood by a sense of idealism and a concern for the underdog. He embraced the reforming spirit of Vatican II and, while studying in Washington, DC, he had supported the civil rights movement. In response to the comment he overheard, he preached a sermon at Good Shepherd on the need to accept change. His parishioners did not receive his message with enthusiasm. Moreover, when representatives of the Dyckman Houses, a public housing project in northeast Inwood, contacted Good Shepherd about getting Irish families to move in, Travers's superior there showed no interest.

The resistance to change that Travers found was part of a larger wave of anxiety and sometimes outright fear that swept the older Irish and Jewish sections of northern Manhattan as the 1960s gave way to the 1970s. Older white residents of the Heights and Inwood looked at the changes in their neighborhoods—rising crime, declining economic prosperity, problems in city government and city services, and the arrival of first African Americans, then Puerto Ricans, and eventually Dominicans—with a sense of dread. Many responded by leaving the city or moving to sections of northern Manhattan that seemed less susceptible to change. At the same time, newer black and Hispanic residents of northern Manhattan felt themselves either rejected by old-timers or excluded from the modest but real prosperity that had once been the hallmark of Washington Heights.

A *Times* article published in 1969 described the Heights as a place that reflected "the urban experience of a nation entering middle age," a neighborhood neither fully thriving nor fully decrepit. The population of the Heights and Inwood was declining—from 194,885 in 1960 to 191,118 in 1970. At the same time, its ethnic and racial mix was beginning to shift. Whites in 1970 remained a solid majority in northern Manhattan, but over the previous decade their share of the population fell from 87 percent to 78 percent, while blacks went from 12 percent to 19 percent and Hispanics (who were surely undercounted) grew 0.5 percent to 1.8 percent. Sections of northern Manhattan with older and more prosperous residents held their Irish and Jewish populations as African Americans and Latinos moved into less stable and affluent sections in the southern and eastern Heights. The western Heights, from the George Washington Bridge to Fort Tryon Park west of Broadway, had the most Jews and the fewest blacks and Hispanics of all northern Manhattan, plus a large percentage of elderly and long-time residents. Inwood, which the analysts defined as Fairview Avenue to the northern tip of Manhattan, had the area's highest proportion of Irish and a low number of Latinos.[6]

In a survey conducted in 1972, residents of northern Manhattan (as in other neighborhood studies) rated fear of crime as their uppermost "great problem."[7] Compared with other sections of New York City, residents of northern Manhattan were relatively satisfied with municipal services but less likely to feel that people in their neighborhood shared "positive" attributes, less likely to join neighborhood organizations, more likely to complain about conditions on their block or in their building, and less likely to think that citizens can have an impact on issues that matter to them.[8] More troubling for the prospects of bringing people together to solve problems, respondents said that two out of three times, when they had a problem they did not call anyone about it; half of all respondents said it wouldn't accomplish anything, 13 percent said they didn't know whom to contact, and more than a third said they didn't want to get involved. One survey respondent from northern Manhattan told researchers he had "no problem with crime because we never go out." Buried in that answer were attitudes of resignation and withdrawal.[9]

The sense of alarm in the Heights and Inwood touched my relatives in the city and my home in the suburbs. Through the late 1960s, in my own developing sense of the cultural geography of New York City, Washington Heights and Inwood were zones of safety. In 1966, at the age of eleven, my parents had let me take my first trip to the city on my own. I rode the 86 bus from Dumont, New Jersey, across the George Washington Bridge, walked up Fort Washington Avenue to visit the Cloisters, and enjoyed a day without any unpleasant incidents. That experience whetted my appetite for more visits to New York. Equally memorable were family trips to northern Manhattan, enlivened by my parents' stories about which article of furniture in our living room was bought in what neighborhood store, that helped me see how our suburban family life was touched by urban beginnings.

By the early 1970s, however, I sensed through family and friends the tremors of danger that reverberated around the Heights. My grandmother in the Bronx neighborhood of Highbridge, just across the Harlem River from the Heights, was mugged. My aunt and uncle in Inwood suffered a burglary and then a robbery at gunpoint. One of my dad's old friends, a bus driver we ran into at a Heights boathouse on the Harlem River, told us how he was beaten in a robbery. Even my dad's explanation of why Inwood seemed safe (which really meant that we saw mostly white people on the streets) contained a glimpse of a dark knowledge that I hadn't previously associated with him: the apartments were basically nice, he explained to me, and the people who lived there couldn't afford to move. There were also some tough young guys in the neighborhood, he said, who would take care of anyone who came around to cause trouble.

The rise in crime during the 1960s and 1970s was matched and, some would argue, caused by an equally powerful trend: the collapse of the city's industrial economy. Together, in different but equally damaging ways, the two developments remade life in northern Manhattan.

Washington Heights and Inwood were urban bedroom communities. While there were employers in the neighborhood—Wertheimer's department store on 181st Street, the Columbia-Presbyterian Medical Center, Yeshiva University, and the Kingsbridge Depot and 207th Street Yard of the city's transit system—most people left northern Manhattan to go to work. In the 1940s and 1950s, they found jobs in a New York that was above all a seaport manufacturing city. The movement of goods in and out of the harbor, and the making of light, nondurable goods that could be profitably shipped to distant markets, were the heart of New York's economy. The assembly lines of Detroit might have been the incarnation of modern mass production, but in New York people toiled in small enterprises that specialized in printing, food processing, publishing, and garment manufacturing. From the walkway on the south side of the George Washington Bridge, you could look down the east bank of the Hudson River, swirling along the flank of Manhattan, and see the piers, factories, and warehouses where workers produced New York's wealth. If you continued looking south and turned your gaze inland, you could see the skyscrapers, such as the Empire State Building and Chrysler Building, that housed New York's offices and corporate headquarters.

In the years immediately after World War II, the economic colossus that was New York looked impregnable and the massive buildings that formed the midtown skyline pronounced confidence. By the late 1960s, it was coming apart. The piers where longshoremen worked were rendered obsolete by containerized shipping. Most of the work around the harbor moved to New Jersey, where there was more room for the trucks and railroad cars that would bring the containers to and from the ships. The garment industry shrank as clothing manufacturers left the city for lower-wage locations. Corporate headquarters moved to the suburbs seeking lower taxes and easier commutes.[10] Skyscraper floors, once prime rental property, often went empty of corporate tenants. Indeed, between 1965 and 1973, New York City lost six hundred thousand jobs. From 1970 to 1975, the rate of loss intensified to an average of one hundred thousand jobs a year. The loss of corporate headquarters was equally astounding. By 1974, thanks to both corporate mergers and departures, New York lost more and more major corporate headquarters. Just across the George Washington Bridge in Englewood Cliffs, New Jersey, a stretch of Route 9W known for its offices and corporate headquarters was dubbed "the billion dollar mile." From 1968 to 1974, the suburbs' share of Fortune 500 companies tripled. Meanwhile, New York lost a third of its share. With the vanished headquarters went supporting firms and good service jobs.[11]

For older New Yorkers in the Heights and Inwood, this meant the degradation of their established standard of living. Those who had the money could follow their jobs to the suburbs (on highways built with government subsidies) and buy new houses (with mortgages subsidized by the government). However, those who stayed in the neighborhood or moved to it—particularly Dominicans—were far from available jobs and settling into streets where the standard of living declined. Worse, for working-class Dominicans, the city's manufacturing jobs were disappearing and its public services were declining.[12]

Since the era of the New Deal, New York City had been an urban social democracy—with its own public hospitals and a free public university—supported by the city's strong economy, a rich array of labor and civic organizations, and federal subsidies. As early as the Lindsay administration, however, politicians in Washington began to question this order. At the same time, the city was relying on a growing number of short-term bond offerings to plug gaps in its budget. Banks encouraged and then discouraged municipal borrowing. Unemployment climbed from less than 5 percent in 1970 to 8.5 percent in 1974 to 12 percent in the middle of 1975.[13] By 1974, this debt financing scheme was failing and Mayor Beame, elected in 1973, was making cuts and layoffs. The bankers wanted more. New York City, with too little money to pay its bills and unable to borrow, was on the brink of going broke. When Mayor Beame sought help from President Gerald Ford and the federal government, the response was summed up in a memorable *Daily News* headline: "Ford to City: Drop Dead."

Bankers, Republicans, and fiscal conservatives seized on the opportunity to discipline New York, restructure its political economy, and set an example for other municipalities that embraced anything that smacked of socialism in one city. Eventually bankers, unions, and elected officials crafted a solution, but it came at a price. New York's social services would be drastically reduced and so money would be saved. The savings were clear but so, too, was the cost. From 1975 to 1980, the city government shed more than sixty-three thousand jobs. Between 1974 and 1976, the Board of Education reduced the teaching workforce by 25 percent. More than three thousand City University faculty members were laid off. Tuition was imposed for the first time; enrollments dropped by sixty-two thousand. Fewer subways ran, and those that did were more often late. Potholes went unfilled. Uncollected garbage piled up in the streets.[14]

In Washington Heights, the magnitude of neglect and austerity was obvious in one of the old gems of the New Deal, Highbridge Park. A parks department engineer quoted in the *New York Times* in 1977 called the park "a chamber of horrors." Surveying the landscape, the *Times* reporter noticed that the park's surrounding fence was "ripped to shreds." Concrete bench frames no longer had wooden seats and broken glass was everywhere. The roof of the park house had been burned out and its interior reduced to dust and debris. Every Monday, the stretch of the park beside Edgecombe Avenue had to be "cleaned of the hundreds of auto parts thrown into it by people who use the street alongside it as a makeshift body shop." In short, the park was in an awful state.[15]

Heights residents continued to visit the park despite its decrepit facilities.[16] As they walked past trash and the scars of vandalism, or glanced toward the forested areas of the park that were littered with junked auto parts and abandoned cars, they tried to keep faith with the old ideal of public parks as places where people could connect with nature and each other. They found snatches of beauty in the view over the Harlem River, but they also encountered diminished facilities that the city was unable to maintain. There were also signs, in the garbage and automotive debris that littered Highbridge Park, that some of their neighbors were fouling their own nest. For newcomers, this looked like the city's promise unfulfilled. For older residents, it looked like the city's promise broken.

The decay of Highbridge Park was part of a larger decline in public life in northern Manhattan. By the late 1960s, for example, the Irish of Inwood sensed that the vigorous street life of their community was in jeopardy. For decades, parishes, shops, bars, parks, and street corners had defined their neighborhood. In 1968, *Goodbye to Glocca Morra,* a documentary produced for Irish television,[17] captured this tendency in scenes of crowds pouring out of mass at Good Shepherd and ballad singing in pubs. Yet the film also depicted a theater group at Good Shepherd rehearsing *Finian's Rainbow,* a Broadway musical laced with Irish nostalgia. As the cast sings "How Are Things in Glocca Morra?" the film leaves viewers with a strong sense that the Irish of Inwood in 1968 are poised between longing for Ireland and dispersal into the suburbs.

The narrator of the film described the Inwood Irish as divided between those who could afford to move out, children who were comfortable with blacks and Latinos, and older people who lived in a state of fear and hostility. In a drive through the neighborhood in a convertible, Mark Barrett—the son of a Con Edison worker and a Fordham graduate who was about to go into the army—explained the mind-set of many of his neighbors. They were fearful of crime, he said, worried about blacks arriving in the neighborhood, and increasingly willing to cast their votes for the Conservative Party. (There were also, he said, stories of armed groups formed to repel African Americans.) Working-class Irish developed a "terrible animosity" to blacks, he said, because they feared losing their jobs or homes to them in ways that middle-class people would not have to face. If a black man walked into an Inwood bar, Barrett predicted, he would be beaten up. Yet buried within this animosity, Barrett said, was a paradox: "Most of the Negroes who do move in here are the middle class of the Negro community, and they are on their way up, and they are really not too much interested in causing trouble. So in actuality, the Irish are afraid of a ghost."[18]

Under the pressure of fear and crime, Irish social life in Inwood suffered. For many of the Irish of the Heights and Inwood, local bars were a congenial aspect of life in northern Manhattan. All of that vanished when crime rose and it became risky to stroll from tavern to tavern late at night. "The fear of violence sends people home early," the newspaper *Heights-Inwood* noted in

1974, "and more bartenders are locking out persons they don't know after midnight." One article listed four holdups and shootings, two in the month of July 1974: an off-duty policeman shot in a holdup at Cannon's Pub on Dyckman Street and a bartender and a suspect shot in a holdup at the Vinegar Hill Bar at Tenth Avenue and West 215th Street. The article also mentioned a shootout in a holdup at the Park Gate Bar at Broadway and Arden Street in February 1973 and a shooting in an apparent holdup at the Inn Between Bar and Grill at 207th Street and Sherman Avenue in October 1972. The gunman there shot and killed James Rayill, owner of the bar, and wounded his brother and co-owner Brian Rayill.[19]

Bartenders no longer wanted to work nights. Bar owners put locks and buzzers on their doors. Peak business hours shifted from nights to 4–6 p.m. "Everybody who's at a bar at night is afraid," said a customer at O'Donnell's on 207th Street. "Whenever the door opens, everyone looks around."

Against this backdrop, decisions to leave the neighborhood could be sudden and sweeping. In the early 1970s, Joel Rothschild, a Reform Democrat living in the Grinnell, ventured east of Broadway in the southern Heights to canvas voters. The voter registration rolls he carried listed many Irish names, as did the labels next to the door buzzers in the apartment buildings that he visited. But when he buzzed the apartments, the people who responded were Hispanic. The Irish were gone. By the 1980s they were concentrated in the streets around Good Shepherd, remnants of an older Irish way of life that was gradually receding.

Irish residents of the Heights who went to the suburbs were bound for communities that lacked the dense mix of parishes, parks, bars, and street corners that once made parts of the Heights and Inwood feel so Irish. Still, noticeable concentrations of the Irish could be found in metropolitan New York, particularly in towns to the north like Pearl River in Rockland County. Irish police officers and firefighters tended to move to towns in Rockland and farther out where housing was affordable and the terrors of the city were far away. Similarly, Jews moved to communities that often had dense Jewish populations but otherwise lacked the vigorous street life of the city.[20]

All residents of northern Manhattan felt the presence and fear of crime, but due to racial, ethnic, and economic inequalities, the chance to leave it behind were not evenly distributed. The Irish and Jews who left northern Manhattan for suburbia benefited from the postwar real estate market. Tax deductions for mortgages made it easier for them to buy houses. Unionized public sector jobs, especially teaching for Jews and work in the uniformed services for the Irish, paid enough that they could afford their own homes. Highways and mass transit systems supported by tax dollars eased their trips in and out of the city. Religious discrimination in real estate, a bitter burden for Jews before World War II, was fading after 1948, when the Supreme Court declared restrictive residential covenants illegal.[21]

For the Jews and Irish alike, the departure from northern Manhattan was not necessarily a happy occasion. If they left under the shadow of crime, the move out of New York was likely accompanied by a sense of relief at best and feelings of bitterness, fear, and displacement at worst. If they left behind relatives, they lived with anxiety that their elders would not fare well in a changing city.[22]

Jewish departures from the Heights were broadly similar to Irish departures, but they had their own distinct geography. In general, in the 1940s and 1950s synagogues and other Jewish institutions were concentrated in the western Heights, with a cluster of German Jewish institutions along Broadway between 157th and 165th streets. From the early 1950s on, Jews moved up Fort Washington Avenue to the western Heights and settled in the area between 181st Street and Fort Tryon Circle west of Broadway.

Hebrew Tabernacle, a Reform congregation founded by German Jews in 1906 in Harlem, had since 1923 worshipped in a sanctuary at 605–607 W. 161st Street, between Broadway and Fort Washington Avenue. (Its earlier home, on West 130th Street, was sold to the Colored People's Church.) Rabbi Robert L. Lehman, who led the congregation from 1956 to 1997, participated in civil rights demonstrations in the South.[23]

By the early 1970s, however, with the northward movement of Jews in Washington Heights, the congregation was increasingly isolated in an area with a large Latino and African American population. When a large building housing the Christian Science Church on Fort Washington Avenue at 185th Street became available for purchase, the congregation sold its home on 161st Street to a congregation of Jehovah's Witnesses and moved north. In the Tabernacle *Bulletin*, Rabbi Lehman justified the move on the grounds of maintaining the congregation's vigor. Efforts to move to New Jersey or to Riverdale in the Bronx, he wrote, had come to nothing. "The point at issue," he argued, "is that we did not seek to relocate our Temple in other areas because we keenly felt the need to serve our people and we did not want to remove ourselves from them." The new location was easily accessible by bus, subway, and automobile. He added, "Our people could WALK to the new building, the streets are populated not by strangers but by your friends and mine! Finally: THE CHARACTER OF OUR CONGREGATION WOULD BE MAINTAINED!"[24]

It was a painful departure all the same. In Rabbi Lehman's final sermon at West 161st Street, delivered February 3, 1974, he spoke of how "both old-timers and newcomers alike may well find peace in remembering the babies we have named here, in the boys and girls who were Bar Mitzvah and confirmed from this pulpit, in the romances that began here, in the Shabbat kiss that united their family, in the parents blessing their children, in the joys shared and in the sufferings borne." As he warmed to his conclusion, he reminded congregants: "We leave here at a time we designate, to a place of our own choosing, in our own manner of leave-taking, and that makes all the difference. There is no Inquisitor outside to hurt us, there are no Cossacks to persecute is, there is no individual tyrant who can expel us or destroy us at his very whim and fancy." (The last point was, at least implicitly, a response to anyone who might equate the change in the southern Heights with any of the historic persecutions that had afflicted the Jewish people.) He urged his congregants to wipe away their tears, let go of their memories, and go forward to success in the future. Switching to Hebrew at the start of his last sentence, he exhorted them: "Chazak, Chazak, V'Niz Chazeik," the words spoken when Jews make the transition from one book of the Torah to another: "be strong, be strong, and let us strengthen one another."[25]

When Washington Heights residents stared across the Harlem River or into their television screens to contemplate the Bronx, the future looked ominous.[26] Particularly disturbing was the Highbridge section of the west Bronx, just across the Harlem from the lower Heights. Into the early 1960s, both Washington Heights and Highbridge had similarly Irish and Jewish populations. By the 1970s, however, Highbridge was transformed by massive population shifts, rising crime (including the mugging of my grandmother), and arson. If it could happen to Highbridge, people wondered, could it happen to Washington Heights?

Television documentaries and news reports from the Bronx offered little hope of avoiding the same fate. Too often, the implicit explanation for why the South Bronx burned was that new people, African Americans and Latinos, had ruined the place. In fact, as the historian Evelyn Gonzalez has pointed out, the collapse was the result of racial discrimination, crime, errors in government, and "economic transactions, political decisions, and human choices."[27]

Whereas many news reports framed the story of the South Bronx as one of elderly whites besieged by black and Latino gangs, in the TV documentary *The Fire Next Door* Bill Moyers showed a multiracial, multiethnic array of people who tried to live good lives in harsh circumstances—from an elderly woman to young tenants to neighborhood activists. In one scene, a woman's apartment is broken into while Moyers interviews her on the sidewalk. Through it all, Moyers concluded: "You can come here and be depressed by the slums, fires, drugs, crime and poverty," he said. "Or you can be impressed with the discovery that even in awful conditions, some people cherish common human values and try to build a decent life among the debris."[28]

Another documentary, Alan and Susan Raymond's *The Police Tapes*, had none of Moyers's optimism. The film followed police officers of the 44th Precinct in the Bronx, which contained Highbridge, through random patrols, painful negotiations with residents, and violent confrontations. The film explored the conditions that produced a culture within city law enforcement that was a volatile mix of impassive resignation, decency, anger, and a propensity to use physical force.[29] *The Police Tapes* depicted the police in the South Bronx as less a thin blue line holding back a tide of disorder than a badly beleaguered force that was, despite its best efforts, part of the disorder itself.

Whether it was the perspective offered by the Raymonds or Moyers, no one disputed that the South Bronx was disorderly, dangerous, and close to unlivable. Residents of Washington Heights, like other New Yorkers, were used to dividing the city into familiar places and unknown places, zones of safety and zones of danger. For the longest time, Washington Heights was, for them, distinct from the Bronx and free of its crime and poverty. That same attitude had also been employed, decades earlier, when white residents configured their mental maps of Washington Heights to exclude areas with black or Latino residents. By the 1970s, as great changes transformed the demography of northern Manhattan, this strategy was less effective and it was harder to think of the Bronx as a cautionary tale safely across the Harlem River. Indeed, just as had happened in Highbridge, Washington Heights was becoming more multiracial and multiethnic. The working-class and middle-class ideal of a modest but tidy neighborhood free from litter, noise, and graffiti and safe for children was also in question. Noise and litter became prominent concerns in the Heights in the 1970s and, in the same period, graffiti became a more common presence. (One of the earliest New Yorkers to decorate the city with his tags was a young Greek American from West 183rd Street named Demetrius, Taki for short.)[30] Crime, of course, continued to rise.

The changes in northern Manhattan took a toll on local businesses. The 207th Street Chamber of Commerce disbanded in 1974 because it couldn't raise money for Christmas decorations. By January 1977, more than ten businesses on 207th Street had closed their doors, including a furniture store, a supermarket, and a small department store. "Changing trends and population shifts are largely responsible for the decline," the *New York Times* reported. "In the last 15 years, many older Irish and Jewish residents have moved out of the area and have been replaced by recent arrivals from the Dominican Republic who have less money to spend." More affluent residents could drive across the George Washington Bridge to the malls in New Jersey.

Poorer residents took the subway or bus to cheaper stores on 14th Street in Manhattan or Fordham Road in the Bronx. In either case, the merchants of Washington Heights and Inwood suffered. Matters only got worse that summer.[31]

A power failure on the night of July 13, 1977, plunged New York City into darkness. Unlike a blackout in 1965, which was remembered as a night of good-humored endurance, the blackout of 1977 would be remembered as "the night of the animals." While civic-minded residents used police flares and flashlights to illuminate the intersection of Broadway and Dyckman Street, farther east looters wrecked stores. Ten minutes after power failed on Dyckman Street, Detective John Collich (who in all likelihood was the same Officer Collich who heard Michael Farmer's last words twenty years earlier) made the first of fifteen arrests in the 34th Precinct. By a local newspaper's count, forty-two stores were broken into north of West 155th Street. At Dyckman Street and Post Avenue, the Sight and Style optometry shop was emptied; the looters left behind only broken glass. At Crest Radio and TV, 1635 St. Nicholas Avenue, operated by the Rose family for twenty-five years, a call from the police brought them to the store at 12:30 a.m. Afterward, they endured the sight of boxes that had once contained their goods littering the street and the laughing taunts of teenagers outside their store.[32]

The same summer, a deranged gunman who called himself Son of Sam stalked and killed six women in Queens, the Bronx, and Brooklyn before the police captured him. Predictably, the *Daily News* and *New York Post* covered the murders and the blackout in blazing headlines. What was new in the journalistic equation was the editorial tone of the *Post*. Under its new owner, the Australian newspaper magnate Rupert Murdoch, the formerly liberal newspaper was becoming a voice of angry, conservative populism. It would speak loudly in the mayoral election of 1977.

While some argued that the looting was the product of worsening social conditions after the fiscal crisis, the politically dominant analysis condemned the looters, savaged liberals as their softheaded enablers, and demanded a restoration of order. That tendency suggested that a candidate who could legitimately appeal to voters looking for a return to "law and order" would enjoy significant support. In the weeks that followed, that candidate turned out to be a Democratic congressman from Greenwich Village with a reputation as a reformer, Edward I. Koch.[33]

In truth, by 1977, Koch's most prominent days as a reformer were well behind him. Koch defined himself as "a liberal with sanity"—a stance designed to retain some of his old liberal supporters while winning new votes from more conservative Catholics and Jews. Koch proclaimed his support for the death penalty, criticized "poverty pimps" in social welfare agencies, and called for professionalism and fiscal austerity to restore the city's finances. He was also increasingly alienated from liberals, whom he often described as humorless, strident, and conspiratorial "hairshirts." And he seemed to be uninterested in courting black or Latino voters. Rather than currying favor with what might be presupposed to be his Democratic base, he relished debate, cherished his grudges, and enjoyed tweaking people from old money as he proclaimed his affinity for people of self-made wealth. In short, he had adopted stances that would play well in conservative neighborhoods, including parts of northern Manhattan.[34]

Northern Manhattan warmed gradually to Koch. In the Democratic primary, he carried neither the Heights nor Inwood. In the 74th Assembly District, which covered the lower Heights and upper Harlem, he trailed well behind Percy Sutton (an African American candidate), Bella Abzug, and Herman Badillo—a sign that liberal and minority voters had other preferences. In the same Democratic primary in the 73rd Assembly District, covering the northern Heights and Inwood, Koch ran second to Beame and ahead of Abzug—a sign that the further north you went in Manhattan, the more congenial the territory was for a moderate to conservative Democrat. In the Democratic runoff, Koch defeated Mario Cuomo in both the Heights and Inwood. In the general election Koch easily won all of northern Manhattan, presenting himself as a moderate who could still reach out to liberals with appeals to honest, effective government and a broad sense of social liberalism. (Any suspicions that the bachelor candidate might be gay were checked by his frequent appearances with Bess Myerson, the first Jew to be named Miss America and a former Consumer Affairs commissioner in the Lindsay administration.) Before and after the election, he was in touch with local politicians and community organizations—among them the Jewish Community Council and Saint Elizabeth's—and elected officials, who wanted to see the Koch administration stabilize and revive a shaky northern Manhattan.[35]

Ultimately, the Irish and Jewish sections of the Heights and Inwood were congenial territory for Koch: sufficiently Democratic in that they would prefer a Democrat to almost any Republican, and home to enough moderate Democrats that many—especially in the northern Heights and Inwood—would find the centrist to conservative Koch appealing. There was also in northern Manhattan a rising generation of elected officials from the reform wing of the Democratic Party—Franz Leichter in the state senate, Edward H. Lehner in the state assembly—whose supporters could still see in the Koch of 1977 a politician with reform roots.[36]

Yet Koch's political evolution was taking him in a distinctly conservative direction. Indeed, the night after the election, Koch told a friend how he wanted his mayoralty to tackle the many problems of New York City and "make it like it was." Among the newer residents of Washington Heights, the phrase had little meaning and, to the extent that it did, seemed hardly a message of reform. For Dominicans, New York was not a place of past glories to be restored but a place to build a better future. African Americans might remember some good things about the best of New Deal New York. (The Rev. Calvin Butts, recalling the optimism of African Americans of New York in the 1950s, once paraphrased Langston Hughes and said that America never was America for him, but once New York City almost was.) Cubans and Puerto Ricans had long made homes for themselves in the Heights and Inwood, but had yet to experience anything like a golden age.[37]

Although older white ethnic residents might gild their memories of midcentury New York with a nostalgia that obscured racist housing covenants, anti-Semitism, and gang fights between white, black, and Latino kids, it was true that Washington Heights (or Inwood) in the 1940s and 1950s had provided them with a standard of living that their grandparents had rarely known. By the late 1970s, the New Deal order had crumbled and left them behind, clutching their memories of economic security in ethnically homogenous enclaves.

In his inaugural address, Mayor Koch responded to the concerns of these older residents of New York, including northern Manhattan. He spoke less as an outright conservative than as a chastened version of his older liberal incarnation—a rhetorical stance that made his conservative shift seem like simple common sense to which there was no alternative. He extolled the city's diversity, but vowed to support only those poverty programs that really helped the poor. He vowed to end waste and provide "better services for the middle class and a healthy climate for commerce and business and industry." He called the city's residents its "first line of defense" and asked them to set a standard for city employees, a point that implicitly criticized municipal workers. As he moved toward his conclusion, he challenged Americans to reverse the westward trek of the pioneers and join "the urban pioneers of this generation" in a great task: "There are homes to be rehabilitated and maintained, schools to be reclaimed and preserved, neighborhoods to be freed from the oppression of crime and the stranglehold of unemployment." Koch never used the word gentrification, but as the historian Jonathan Soffer notes, this was a plan to revive the city by making it more attractive to people with money. But would this vision improve the city for all? Or would it embed existing racial and economic inequalities and even create new ones? At the beginning of the Koch years, the city was so broke that there was no sure answer to any of these questions, much less to whether the mayor would be able to "make it like it was." Yet even before the Koch administration was one month old, it was planning an effort to preserve, stabilize, and rehabilitate Inwood and Washington Heights.[38]

By the summer of 1978, when Mayor Koch arrived at the YM-YWHA to assure the residents of Washington Heights and Inwood that their neighborhoods had a future, people were already at work to save or transform their streets. Northern Manhattan was strongly Democratic, but within that party identification there was room for all sorts of political distinctions ranging from moderate Democrats (think of all the Beame supporters in the northern Heights and Inwood) to staunch liberals. These Democrats were complemented by leftists; together they gave Washington Heights a distinct political punch in an otherwise conservative time. The neighborhood was not associated with radicalism in the spirit of Greenwich Village, the Lower East Side, or the Allerton Avenue cooperatives in the Bronx, but the Heights was home to a significant number of leftists whose ideology led them to action and practical politics. Communists, for example, played an important role in organizing the hospital workers of Columbia-Presbyterian into Local 1199 in 1973. In my parents' old residence at 550 Fort Washington Avenue and in the majestic Grinnell at 800 Riverside Drive, varieties of leftists played important roles in turning economically moribund buildings into low- and moderate-income cooperatives run by their residents. And on the border of Harlem and Washington Heights, Albert Blumberg, a Communist from the 1930s to the 1950s and a professor emeritus of philosophy at Livingston College of Rutgers University, was a leader in the Audubon Reform Democratic Club, founded in 1966 by opponents of the Vietnam War.[39]

Far more numerous than Communists and ex-Communists were liberal Democrats who rose to dominate the Heights and Inwood in the 1970s. Until then, politics in the Heights was dominated by the Washington Heights Progressive Democrats, which despite its name was a club of Democratic regulars led by Joseph Zaretsky, the leader of the Democratic minority in the state senate. In the 1940s, Zaretsky had overcome Irish political dominance among Democrats in northern Manhattan to win his seat; he became the senate's Democratic leader in 1958 and went on to establish a friendly relationship with Governor Nelson Rockefeller, a Republican whose fiscal largesse and fondness for public works projects enabled him to build common ground with many Democrats. By the 1970s, however, Zaretsky and the Washington Heights Progressive Democrats were a fading force. In 1972, the reformers scored their first major local victory when Edward H. Lehner, a veteran of

Eugene McCarthy's antiwar presidential campaign in 1968 and a member of the local Concerned Democratic Coalition club (and a graduate of PS 187), won a seat in the state assembly to represent the Heights and Inwood.[40]

An even more significant victory for reform forces came two years later when Franz Leichter, the son of Austrian Jewish socialists who came to the United States as a refugee from Hitler in 1940, defeated Zaretsky, and assumed his seat in the state senate. Leichter, who had already served in the state assembly, had campaigned in the Heights with both Eleanor Roosevelt and the Reform Democrat William F. Ryan. To Leichter, Zaretsky was an ineffectual leader who prospered by lining up Democratic votes for the Republican governor, Nelson Rockefeller, and dissuaded challengers with offers of patronage jobs. Leichter would spend the bulk of his career in the state senate as a gadfly from a minority party, but he used his office to address issues such as housing, jobs, redlining, and economic development that were major concerns in northern Manhattan.[41]

The strength of liberal Democrats in northern Manhattan grew in 1977, when Stanley Michels—whose membership in the Progressive Democrats gave him a reputation as a "regular"—pivoted and ran for the northern Manhattan city council seat with the support of two reform clubs, the Audubon Democrats and the Concerned Democratic Coalition. Their support, and Michels's evolving work with reformers, contributed to Michels's becoming a liberal Democrat with a reputation as a strong advocate for tenants, parks, and environmental causes.[42]

With John Brian Murtaugh, a Democratic district leader in the Heights and Inwood during the 1970s who went on to serve in the state assembly of New York from 1981 through 1996, the rise of liberal Democrats grounded in the old ethnic communities of northern Manhattan was complete. Murtaugh, an Irish Catholic merchant seaman living in Inwood with strong family roots in the military and the Democratic Party, was superficially aligned with the old face of his neighborhood. In fact, he was a McGovern delegate to the 1972 Democratic convention and a tenant activist who developed a following among Jewish liberals. As a district leader and assemblyman, he contributed to the political dominance of liberal Democrats in Washington Heights and Inwood.[43]

This political sea change of the 1970s in northern Manhattan meant that the challenges of navigating the bleakest years of the urban crisis would fall not on old-style Democratic regulars, but on liberal and reform Democrats. Elsewhere in the United States, and even in New York City, the 1970s have been seen—correctly—as a decade when politics turned in a more conservative direction. In Washington Heights, however, local officeholders were distinguished by their liberalism. To be sure, the liberalism of the Democrats who held office in northern Manhattan from the 1970s on was not a continuation of the New Deal. The political alliances and institutional alignments of New Deal New York had already died a painful death in the 1968 school strike. Also gone were the New Deal's expansive optimism and its emphasis on city, state, and federal government as providers of expansive social services. Compared with their predecessors in the years of La Guardia and Roosevelt, Washington Heights Democrats were constrained, besieged, and underfunded. Although they held to an activist conception of government, they had to navigate unfavorable terrain with policy improvisations and public-private partnerships that would not always match the needs of their neighborhood. Their achievements would be shaped by the Koch administration, conditions on the ground in Washington Heights, and local initiatives that emerged from the bottom up.

No issue was more important to activists, journalists, and elected officials in the Heights and Inwood in the late 1970s than housing. Since the late 1960s, in a weak market for private real estate, large parts of Manhattan, the Bronx, and Brooklyn were devastated when landlords who couldn't or wouldn't pay their taxes abandoned their buildings. The orphan buildings fell into municipal ownership. By some estimates the City of New York became the landlord of last resort for at least one hundred thousand tenants and the manager of four thousand landlord-abandoned buildings.[44] The trend did not spare Washington Heights and Inwood. Indeed, the report Mayor Koch brought to the YM-YWHA in 1978 depicted a neighborhood poised between survival and decay. "While the basic housing stock is generally sound," the report said, "much of it shows the effects of undermaintenance and neglect." The report went on to state: "Spiraling costs, insufficient rent rolls, inexperienced management, the limited availability of financing for rehabilitation and repair, and the increased difficulty of securing property insurance at reasonable rates present obstacles to conscientious owners who wish to maintain their properties. Other owners, less interested in maintaining their property, have deliberately reduced services." Ominously, Koch also provided evidence of the growth of apartment building abandonment in Washington Heights. As grim as the picture appeared, however, efforts were already under way to prevent northern Manhattan from going the way of the South Bronx.[45]

During the Lindsay administration, Washington Heights and Inwood were among the first sections of the city selected for a program that helped landlords get low-interest loans to fix up their buildings. The program eventually died in the fiscal crisis, but as early as 1974 another effort was under way to address the citywide problem of decaying and abandoned housing.

A consortium of commercial banks brought together by David Rockefeller, and later supported by savings banks, founded the Community Preservation Corporation (CPC) to create financial resources for housing rehabilitation. The CPC's earliest work focused on Crown Heights in Brooklyn and Washington Heights and Inwood. In northern Manhattan, its efforts were led by Michael Lappin, a native of Buffalo, New York, who had served as a Volunteer in Service to America (VISTA) volunteer in western Kentucky, did graduate work in philosophy at the New School, and worked for New York City's office of Housing Development Administration (later renamed the Department of Housing Preservation and Development). By 1975, Lappin and the CPC were hard at work in the Heights and Inwood.[46]

Lappin looked at Washington Heights and Inwood and saw a neighborhood whose old ethnic mix reminded him of Buffalo. He also recognized that a significant percentage of the housing was owned by small landlords with old buildings, thin resources, and limited skills at gaining help from financial institutions. (In the 1930s in northern Manhattan, my grandfather and father had worked in this world as painters and small-scale contractors. My father remembered it as a sector of hard work, small earnings, broken promises, and unfulfilled ambitions. By the time Lappin arrived, the biggest change was that the shadow of the Great Depression had been succeeded by the shadow of the South Bronx.) In northern Manhattan, where there was little empty space for new buildings and little money for new construction, Lappin believed that repairing old buildings was the best way to improve the area's housing stock. Yet getting loans in northern Manhattan was next to impossible for landlords because banks thought it unprofitable to lend out money in what seemed to be a declining area. (Of course, refusing to make loans in a changing neighborhood contributed to its decline.)[47]

A report on redlining by State Senator Leichter and his legislative counsel, Glenn F. von Nostitz, clarified the problem. In an investigation of mortgage lending in Manhattan north of 118th Street and west of Eighth Avenue, they found that banks in the Heights and Inwood did not invest many of their deposits in northern Manhattan. In effect, the deposits of people in Washington Heights were being used to further the economic development of the suburbs. The case of the Washington Federal Savings and Loan Association was extreme but hardly unique. With deposits of $166.9 million and three branches in the Heights, it made not one loan in northern Manhattan in 1978—but it did make loans to three counties.[48]

Leichter proposed legislative solutions to this problem. In the meantime, Lappin went to work with a consortium of banks and the people he found in northern Manhattan. Refusing to disdain the hard-bitten, small-time landlords that he found in the Heights and Inwood, Lappin built on their desire to repair their buildings at a reasonable cost so they would provide a steady if modest income. At the same time, he created "one-stop shopping" that helped small landlords get financial assistance from a consortium of banks (most of them from outside northern Manhattan) and help with the physical rehabilitation of old buildings. Typically, the improvements that the CPC made possible brought rent increases, which in turn brought some complaints from tenants and wariness from some elected officials. It was especially difficult for some tenants to swallow a rent hike when the CPC project brought improvements in building infrastructure that were largely invisible to the tenant. Still, until the Reagan administration there were federal programs to help with the rent and most tenants accepted the trade-off of higher rent for a sounder building. The CPC succeeded not by unleashing the forces of the free market, but by working with both government and private investors to make possible changes that neither could produce alone. In 1979, Senator Leichter called the efforts of the CPC the only bright spot in an otherwise dismal picture.[49]

While the CPC succeeded by bringing outside resources into northern Manhattan, other important efforts grew from within the area. On a spring day in 1977, Leichter convened a meeting at his office to discuss a summer jobs program for young people. In attendance was Father Kevin Sullivan, a priest at Saint Elizabeth's, a Roman Catholic parish in the eastern Heights once largely Irish but by 1977 primarily Latino (mostly Dominicans, with a significant number of Cubans and a modest number of Puerto Ricans) and a small number of elderly Irish. Also at the meeting was Elizabeth Wurzberger, the executive director of the Jewish Community Council (JCC), an organization grounded in the Orthodox Jews of the Heights—especially the families around K'hal Adath Jeshurun, informally known as the Breuer congregation after Rabbi Joseph Breuer. The Breuer community, with its strong institutional infrastructure, was concentrated on Bennett Avenue. Sullivan recalls: "On 181st Street, I turned to Mrs. Wurzberger and said, 'These streets are filthy.' She looked at me and she said, 'You think they're filthy? Your parishioners, do they think they're filthy?' I replied, 'Absolutely, they hate the filthy garbage in the streets.' She said, 'The people in the synagogues think the streets are filthy. Can't we come together to do something about it?'"[50]

Out of that encounter emerged the Washington Heights–Inwood Coalition, one of several organizations that worked to improve Washington Heights. The participation of the JCC was significant. Fears that the Breuers would abandon the Heights, leaving a glut of apartments that would either go unrented or fill up with low-income tenants, gnawed at public officials in the Heights. Also important was the Catholic and Jewish dimension of the effort, which was underscored in an op-ed in the September 28 issue of *Heights-Inwood* coauthored by John Devaney and Father James Gilhooley, a priest with Catholic Charities whose ministry took him to northern Manhattan. The op-ed noted with concern a recent report from the Metropolitan New York Coordinating Council on Jewish Poverty on the declining Jewish population of northern Manhattan. Young Jewish couples, driven by crime and housing problems, were leaving for the suburbs, the study noted. "We would add, by way of postscript," the column continued, "that it is imperative that the Jewish community remaining within North Manhattan must be offered sound reasons to continue making their homes among us. Should a good portion of them be forced to leave, the plight of the rest of us becomes more grim and sad. We who are black, Irish, Hispanic or whatever cannot afford to lose them. They are a vital ingredient to the well-being of this human village."[51]

The column, ecumenical in spirit, went on to insist that elected officials be held accountable for the health of the community. As for solutions to northern Manhattan's problems, the piece drew on a memo from the Jewish Community Council and called for better policing, neighborhood revitalization, and rehabilitation of the streets and parks. In addition, the column demanded improved public schools (citing the NAACP) and legislation that would require municipal workers to live in the city. "This area was once the bedroom of downtown municipal workers: subway men, teachers, sanitation men, cops," wrote Father Gilhooley and Devaney. "They have led the flight from the city. Their return, however forced, would go a long way to making North Manhattan healthier."

In January 1978, less than one month into Koch's first term, informal conversations within northern Manhattan evolved into meetings of neighborhood officials, elected representatives, and community organizations with the staff of the City Planning Commission, led by Robert F. Wagner Jr.—the son of the former mayor. The most prominent of the community organizations were religious institutions—Jewish, Roman Catholic, Greek Orthodox, and Protestant. Despite Father Gilhooley's insistence on inclusion, the neighborhood's growing Dominican community was represented at best indirectly through the parishioners of Saint Elizabeth's Roman Catholic Church. Black residents of Washington Heights might expect to have a presence through the Protestant churches organized by Broadway Methodist Temple, but ultimately the strongest voices to emerge were those of old Washington Heights—Irish, Jewish, and Greek residents.[52]

The work of the Koch administration task force was more than matched by neighborhood efforts, which predated Koch's interest in the Heights and lasted long after his administration. The Washington Heights–Inwood Coalition, strongly grounded in the old Heights, included Saint Elizabeth's, the JCC, the Hispanic Chamber of Commerce (represented by a Cuban American businessman), Yeshiva University, and the Broadway Temple Methodist Church, a liberal congregation. The Hellenic-American Neighborhood Action Committee, located in Queens, worked in the Coalition through Saint Spyridon Greek Orthodox Church in the Heights. (It was a measure of the speed of neighborhood change that Greeks had built a grand church for Saint Spyridon at 124 Wadsworth Avenue in a moment of vigor and optimism in 1952, only to see the congregation depleted in twenty-five years.)[53]

The first executive director of the Washington Heights–Inwood Coalition was Beth Rosenthal, a Chicago native who had earned an undergraduate degree at Barnard and a master's in social work at Columbia, where she studied community organizing. In Chicago, she was active in the antiwar movement and took up Saul Alinsky's vision of activism, with its emphasis on winning power for communities that had been kicked around. She spoke Spanish and had traveled in South America.[54]

In Washington Heights, Rosenthal found a neighborhood where people were highly concerned with their community's future, but did not often look beyond their own ethnic enclave. While the Coalition emphasized neighborhood improvement, safety, and housing, part of her job was getting people to talk to each other about common concerns. The strong representation of the old Heights on her board reduced engagement with Dominican organizations, but her programs—tenant organizing, conflict mediation, and court monitoring for crime victims—engaged individual Dominicans. Rosenthal thought of community building and crime prevention as complementary efforts. One of the Coalition's most innovative and influential efforts was a mediation program proposed by one of her staffers, Dana Vermilye—a Stanford graduate and descendant of a Dutch settler whose name graces an avenue in Inwood. The mediation program, which eventually trained two hundred people, stopped conflicts before they escalated into crimes and encouraged better relations between potential antagonists. Senior citizens were taught crime prevention techniques and paired with young people—who helped them with errands—who might otherwise have gotten into trouble. The Coalition and its mediation program launched the careers of both Adriano Espaillat, a volunteer mediator who went on to become a state senator, and Mary Ely Peña-Gratereaux, a staff mediator who went on to found Cayena Publications, which issued works on a variety of topics that included Dominican culture and history. Rosenthal also found herself working with ethnic groups in complicated ways. The JCC, she discovered, did not have the same perspective as Yeshiva University and did not represent liberal Jews in the

Heights. Certain Roman Catholic parishes had rivalries. With her knowledge of Spanish, she uncovered a strain of anti-Semitism in the neighborhood and worked to counter the stereotyping that accompanied it. It was complicated and demanding work, but she liked it.[55]

The Washington Heights–Inwood Coalition was complemented by the Northern Manhattan Improvement Corporation, founded in 1979 with seed money from Senator Leichter and Assemblyman Lehner, who pooled their money from member items in the state legislature to set up an office that would help tenants arrest housing decay. Similar to the Washington Heights–Inwood Coalition, but more connected to elected officials, the Northern Manhattan Improvement Corporation grew into a major social service agency that has worked extensively on housing rehabilitation, domestic violence, childcare, and employment. Both agencies worked on housing and tenant issues, but in the long run the Washington Heights–Inwood Coalition remained smaller in scale. Their origins lay in the older Washington Heights, and in retrospect, Leichter believes, the organizations founded by the older communities of Washington Heights did not do as much as they might have to bring in Dominican leaders and organizations. Neither, however, did he think they set out to deliberately exclude anyone. At the same time, the years of the founding of the Northern Manhattan Improvement Corporation were a period of flux and change in the Dominican community in the Heights, which would itself soon produce leaders and organizations of its own.[56]

Within the Koch administration, the task of running the Washington Heights–Inwood Task Force went to Nathan Leventhal, a former chief of staff for Mayor Lindsay with experience in housing issues. Through the spring and early summer of 1978, the task force studied the problems of the Heights and Inwood and how they might be addressed by city government. In July 1978, when Mayor Koch spoke to the crowd at the YM-YWHA on Nagle Avenue, he announced plans to strengthen housing, repair parks, increase policing, and improve local business districts.[57] Less than a year later, in March 1979, the Task Force issued a second report to assess the impact of the Koch administration's efforts. Overall, the report testified to enduring problems, serious effort, and areas of success—particularly in housing. But there was still more work to do to safeguard housing in Washington Heights, and it would challenge residents' collective efficacy and their sense of economic self-interest.[58]

Some of the most imaginative housing successes in the early years of the Koch administration were the result of efforts by tenants and neighborhood organizations that seized the opportunities created by the failures of the housing market.[59] Nowhere in this effort were the stakes higher, more dramatic, and more complex than in a majestic old building in the southwest Heights at 800 Riverside Drive that had fallen on very hard times, the Grinnell.[60]

Built from 1910–11 in a renaissance revival style graced with mission style elements, the Grinnell rose nine stories above an entire triangle-shaped block. While the blocks between Riverside and Broadway in the west 150s and 160s were filled with more modest apartment buildings, the grand Riverside buildings like the Grinnell recalled Central Park West.[61] Into the 1950s the owners of the Grinnell, as in other buildings in the southwest Heights, barred black tenants. (The ban was even enforced when Charles Manuel "Sweet Daddy" Grace, the black Cape Verdean founder of the United House of Prayer for All People, owned the Grinnell. Blacks worshiped in Grace's churches, but according to Grinnell tenants they could not live in his building.) In 1959, though, the efforts of integration activists bore fruit: the writer Alice Childress moved in with her husband and the Grinnell had its first black tenants. Over time, the building became the integrated home of a mix of jazz musicians, African American government workers, interracial couples, activists, and academics. Maya Angelou lived there while she wrote *I Know Why the Caged Bird Sings*.[62]

The Grinnell was also, like other buildings in the southern Heights, the home of a modest but committed number of radicals and staunch liberals. Among them was Joel Rothschild, a biologist with a PhD from Columbia who moved into the Grinnell in 1964 with his wife and children. A member of the Communist Party from the 1930s to the 1950s, he gravitated to local reform circles in the Democratic Party and served as founding treasurer of the local Audubon Democratic Club. As a public school parent, he and his wife were active in the myriad struggles over community control that roiled the Heights in the 1960s.[63]

Rothschild and former Grinnell residents of the 1960s recall an integrated building where children played up and down the halls and in and out of open apartments. Families gathered in the courtyard to sing carols at Christmastime. At its best the Grinnell was something of an island, a place that was friendlier and safer than the deteriorating streets around it. By the mid-1970s, however, the building was falling into disrepair and disarray. To generate more revenue the landlord moved in African American families on welfare, providing the owners with guaranteed income because they were paid directly by the city. Middle-class African American tenants, however, grew angry and resentful. In one apartment, a gypsy cab company set up a dormitory for its drivers; it eventually became a brothel. In response, tenants sat down on the lobby floor to impede the passage of johns.[64]

Tenants organized a long rent strike and strategically negotiated to trade their withheld rent monies for improvements in the building. The effort built unity among a core of active tenants, but conditions in the building remained bad. The winter of 1976–77 was the worst of all. When the heat failed, people put on gloves. When the hall lights failed, they opened their doors so the lights from their apartment would shine into the hallway. When the elevators broke down, they trudged up the stairs.[65]

The Grinnell tenants were beleaguered but not alone. In school wars, struggles over public heath, and Democratic Party politics, Rothschild had built up a reservoir of political support among elected officials. In consultation with local Democrats, he organized tenants to take control of the building by petitioning for the appointment of a "7A administrator," a court-appointed manager empowered by state law to collect rents and make necessary repairs in abandoned buildings. In a scene that testified to the tight-knit nature of political life in the lower Heights, and the spacious nature of Grinnell apartments, one set of tenants trooped into Rothschild's kitchen to sign a petition (notarized by the local Democratic activist David Dinkins) to establish a 7A administrator while in another part of Rothschild's apartment the Audubon Reform Democrats interviewed aspiring mayoral candidates.[66]

Eventually, Rothschild became the building's 7A administrator. The majority of tenants paid him their rent without prompting, but already there were signs that economic interests would lead tenants in different directions. There were squatters in the building—about twenty-three of them had settled in during years of chaos and the rent strike—who undermined the rent rolls. Some Grinnell "tenants," who were doing fine by subletting their apartments to others at a profit, saw no need to disrupt their arrangements. Other tenants feared the responsibility and expense of running the building on their own. From within the building, some tenants questioned Rothschild's decisions; by 1979 he stepped down as 7A administrator. Leadership of the Grinnell Tenants Association, in effect managers of the building, passed to a different set of tenants who confronted a new problem. From outside the Grinnell, the actions of city government both helped and hindered the Grinnell tenants' efforts. For example, while under the law tenants could buy the building from the city and run it as their own cooperative, the city typically upgraded buildings before selling them. If that happened, the price of the building would rise beyond tenants' reach.[67]

Demonstrations and complex negotiations with the city government followed. Residents resisted a mortgage holder's effort to retake control of the building. They also negotiated a city loan to support repair of the Grinnell, premised on the belief that revenues from the sales of apartments would also fund repairs. Eventually, after much debate, 60 percent of the tenants agreed to buy their apartments. Having met the required threshold, in November

1982 the Grinnell Housing Development Fund Corporation purchased the building from the city for $250,000.[68]

The Grinnell became what was typically referred to as an HDFC cooperative. There were forty-seven of them in lower Washington Heights, part of a larger total in the area of seventy-nine buildings that were saved from abandonment or ruin by tenant action. Despite rules on the allowable income levels of future residents, there was no limit set on the future sales prices of Grinnell apartments. In the long run, in a flush real estate market, this possibility could be exploited to make an HDFC cooperative like the Grinnell something other than a home for people with low or moderate incomes.[69]

After years of neglect, there was much work to be done on the Grinnell but few ways to pay for it. In a big building with spacious apartments and relatively few tenants, major expenses were spread over a thin base. Anticipated revenues from the sales of apartments failed to appear because people contemplated the poor state of the real estate market (and a 50 percent tax on the profits of apartment sales for the cooperative's first ten years) and held onto their apartments in hopes of selling in more lucrative times. Residents clashed when the cooperative's board raised maintenance fees and levied assessments. Grinnell residents who thought of the cooperative as a community for people with low incomes wanted to run the building modestly. Others, who wanted to sell their apartments for the best possible price, felt it made sense to renovate the building extensively and staff it generously to raise its market value. These two perspectives were difficult to reconcile. As Grinnell resident Wayne Benjamin observed in retrospect, having beaten the landlord the residents turned on each other like "the Hatfields and the McCoys."[70]

In difficult times, working with courage and ingenuity, residents of the Grinnell had saved their building from ruin. They displayed an impressive degree of collective efficacy, extracted homes from a collapse in residential real estate, and created a livable environment for people of limited wealth. Ironically, their success was bound up with the economic crisis of northern Manhattan. Only in a period when landlords were abandoning their properties could tenants hope to take over their dwellings and turn them into cooperatives with the blessings of city government. More troubling for the future of low-income cooperatives was the range of residents' commitments to cooperative ideals. In the long run, resale policies left open the possibility of individuals selling their apartments at high prices. If that happened, an individual cooperative member would reap a great financial reward but their apartment would be lost to Manhattan's stock of low-income housing.[71] The goals of making money and building a community for people with limited incomes existed in a certain tension with each other. In 1982, however, it was difficult to envision a lucrative market for real estate in southern Washington Heights.[72]

The Koch administration initiatives in northern Manhattan were early efforts at what would become, as the historian Jonathan Soffer argues, Koch's greatest success: the creation of affordable housing on a vast scale. Despite Reagan administration cutbacks that limited federal support for affordable housing, Koch used capital funds and other sources of financing to undertake a major housing program. By the time Koch left office in 1989, his administration had renovated three thousand apartments, had thirteen thousand more under construction, and had design work under way on twenty thousand more.[73]

Yet the legacy of Koch era housing policies was contradictory. The Koch administration's housing effort was a dramatic example of municipal government's power to address a serious problem, but Koch himself would do more than any of his predecessors to extol the power of the market, unfettered by government, to revive the city. Indeed, a significant part of Koch's housing efforts were aimed at encouraging gentrification in order to revive the city's economy. Within the Koch administration, Bobby Wagner argued strongly that real estate development—especially at the high end of the market—was one of the best ways to revive the city's economy and increase tax revenues. Industry was contributing ever less to the city's economy, and at least high-rise apartments couldn't move out of town the way factories did. On the other hand, revival through gentrification set off waves of building and speculation that would be difficult to control and sharpened the contrast between housing for the rich and poor.[74]

In northern Manhattan the Community Preservation Corporation, working with the city's Department of Housing Preservation and Development, would by 1988 be credited with financing the rehabilitation of 10 percent of the housing in Washington Heights and Inwood. Another 8 percent was improved with city and federal money. Alongside these efforts the Northern Manhattan Improvement Corporation, the Washington Heights–Inwood Coalition, the Grinnell residents, and other founders of cooperatives prevented the collapse of Washington Heights housing. In a spate of newspaper articles that appeared in the early 1980s, Washington Heights was depicted as a neighborhood that was working its way out of a crisis. There was some truth to this claim, but it was strongest with regard to the western Heights—which was always whiter and more prosperous than most other parts of northern Manhattan. In the 1980s, the transition to poverty continued across much of Washington Heights.[75]

Moreover, the Heights and Inwood continued to lose population. In 1940, Manhattan north of 155th Street was home to 214,099 residents. By 1980, it held only 188,208 people—and by some municipal calculations, the total in 1980 was even lower: a report from Community Board 12, which served Washington Heights and Inwood, stated that in 1980 the board served a total population of 179,919. The alignments of older ethnic groups changed as Greeks declined in number. The Jewish population gained immigrants from the Soviet Union, many of them professionals, artists, and intellectuals who liked the Heights for its available apartments and its ease of access to Manhattan's cultural institutions. (Jews from the Black Sea port of Odessa, whose idea of a good time was consistent with that city's easygoing reputation, tended to settle in the larger Jewish community of Brighton Beach in Brooklyn. Northern Manhattan gained cultural and intellectual capital, but lost an opportunity for a better nightlife.)[76]

As the population of northern Manhattan declined, the proportion of African Americans and Hispanics grew. In 1970 northern Manhattan was 78 percent white, 19 percent black, and 1.8 percent "other," which is best interpreted as Hispanic. By 1980, it was 39 percent white, 19 percent black, and almost 38 percent Hispanic, with Hispanics in all likelihood undercounted. The African American population, as would become clear in subsequent years, was reaching its historical height. A new Hispanic majority, dominated by Dominicans, was emerging in a neighborhood with less than promising economic prospects. The newcomers had to make a place for themselves in an area that was at best unfamiliar and at worst hostile.[77]

In the streets of Washington Heights, you could see both the symptoms and the causes of a poorer, more insecure neighborhood. Hospitals that for decades had been familiar parts of the city landscape closed, undone by changes in Medicare and Medicaid funding, the departures of both doctors and patients for the suburbs, and a new medical economy that rewarded specialization and research rather than care for the urban poor. Between 1967 and 1983 five hospitals closed in the Heights and Inwood: Mother Cabrini (1967), Frances Delafield (1975), Wadsworth (1976), Saint Elizabeth's (1981), and Jewish Memorial (1983). In Washington Heights, the closings left Columbia Presbyterian, a major medical center at West 168th Street and Broadway with developed facilities for teaching and research, in an increasingly poor neighborhood with a pressing need for primary medical care. Neighborhood residents went to Columbia-Presbyterian clinics and emergency rooms for everyday treatment, but the mismatch between the hospital's conception of itself and the needs of the community around it was glaring.[78]

To Columbia, the medical center was hemmed into a declining neighborhood with a worsening reputation for crime, drugs, and AIDS. The armory

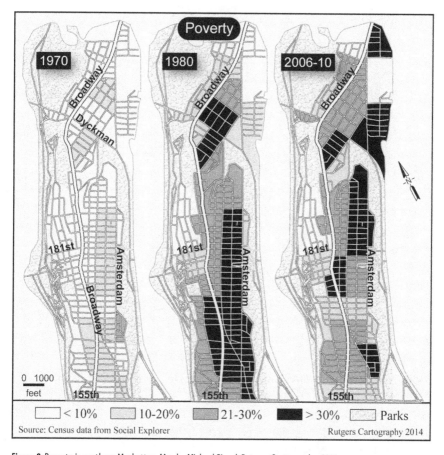

Figure 9: Poverty in northern Manhattan. Map by Michael Siegel, Rutgers Cartography, 2014.

across the street from the hospital became a vast shelter for homeless men. Hospital and medical school officials said Washington Heights' reputation made it difficult to recruit and retain staff and students. Perceptions of the situation were not helped by the November 1981 slaying of Dr. John Chase Wood Jr., a resident surgeon at the medical center. The musician, rugby player, and married expectant father was fatally shot in a mugging near 165th Street and Riverside Drive.[79]

Like so many families, businesses, and institutions, Columbia contemplated whether to keep the hospital based in the Heights or to leave. Unlike the decisions made by individuals and smaller institutions, this decision would, one way or another, have a major impact on northern Manhattan. The neighborhood's long-term prospects received a boost in 1982 when a Columbia long-range planning committee decided to keep the medical center in Washington Heights as a medical school and research hospital. Admittedly,

Columbia Presbyterian's emphasis on research and teaching meshed awkwardly with the needs of its surrounding community, where residents needed better everyday care. The medical center also had a reputation as a powerful and overbearing presence in real estate matters. Nevertheless, the decision to keep the medical center's jobs and facilities in Washington Heights gave the neighborhood a much-needed jolt of stability in an unsettled time.[80]

As the neighborhood's old structures of public health were being hollowed out, an informal economy that reflected the decreased regulatory capacities of government, greed, and the desperate needs of a population of new immigrants was growing. This new economy took the form of labor done inside homes, such as childcare, sewing, and knitting, as well as street peddling, automobile repair, and sweatshops. By 1978, sweatshops doing work for midtown garment firms could be found in the southeast section of the Heights, from Broadway east to Amsterdam between 155th and 180th streets. Ironically, an earlier generation of Heights residents included garment workers or children of garment workers who used union wages to escape the sweatshops of their own time and to find better lives in Washington Heights. (Alex Rose, the millinery worker who helped organize the American Labor Party, and then led the Liberal Party, lived at 200 Cabrini Boulevard until his death in 1976.) In the late 1970s, however, new immigrants—many of them Dominicans—found sweatshops in the Heights. For older residents of the Heights, particularly Jews who thought of the sweatshop as part of an era best left behind, the new sweatshops turned familiar ideas of progress upside down. For Dominicans, they were part of the badly skewed opportunities that they found in New York.[81]

Senator Leichter issued a report based on the inspection of twenty-five sweatshops. (There were more, hidden in basements and apartments, that could be not be examined.) Workers manufactured garments for piecework rates that amounted to wages of $50-$60 per week with no benefits, the report found. The workers were undocumented immigrants from the Caribbean, including a substantial number who were probably Dominicans. Repeating an old pattern in the history of labor and immigration in New York City, they worked in such establishments—sometimes eagerly—because the wages were better than in the land of their birth. A few shops were run well, Leichter found, but most were unhealthy firetraps. His report documented conditions at Neida Sportswear, 500 W. 170th Street: "19 sewing stations and several steam pressing machines. Room appears to be about 20' by 30'. Rear door is sealed with a padlocked sliding door. Front entrance is small and partially blocked by garment racks. Floors are littered with piles of garments, blocking aisles. There is one small, closed window, barred shut."[82]

Dominicans had been a growing presence in northern Manhattan since the mid-1960s but did not begin to achieve political power until the 1980s—in part because of the organizational challenges of building a political base, and in part because of their ambivalent relationship with the United States. The Dominicans' predecessors in northern Manhattan, especially the Irish and the Jews, had found respite from past injustices and a chance to start over. Irish immigrants and their children said good-bye to life in the shadow of Great Britain, stepped aside from the painful politics of the Irish civil war, and took their chance at earning the kind of economic prosperity missing in Ireland. Jews, especially the German Jews who arrived before World War II, found a sanctuary from Hitler.

Dominicans, living under the imperial power of the United States in the Caribbean, brought to Washington Heights a more complicated relationship to the United States. Of course, for Dominicans, immigration to the United States brought the possibilities of earning more money than they ever could at home. As a Dominican woman who had ventured north and returned once said, "In the Dominican Republic, there are three kinds of people: the rich, the poor, and those who travel to New York."[83] As long as New York had a

Figure 10: Dominican Day Parade, Amsterdam Avenue, 1982. Courtesy CUNY Dominican Studies Institute Archives.

firm industrial base, Dominicans who immigrated to the city had a chance at blue-collar prosperity.

For example, Sixto Medina, a country boy from Cibao who in his teens worked in a restaurant in Santiago in the Dominican Republic, immigrated to the United States in 1963 to find work. He settled into Corona, Queens. Three days later he was working in a Jackson Heights factory making metal cabinets, then living in Washington Heights and working at a luggage factory on the West Side of Manhattan. In his off hours, he studied English by watching television shows and old movies. During a stint in the Job Corps, he learned English, earned his GED, gained specialized mechanical skills, and won recognition for his leadership abilities. He then went on to work as a mechanic in a taxi garage. When he overheard Cuban men in a restaurant talking about jobs at the General Motors plant in North Tarrytown, New York, he seized the opportunity. He started at the plant in September 1967, joined United Auto Workers Local 664, and worked there until the plant closed in 1996.[84]

For middle-class Dominican immigrants, there were opportunities for work in the Dominican business sector that sprang up with impressive vitality in northern Manhattan. But by the 1980s, as the number of Dominicans moving to the United States increased, migrants were ever more likely to be working-class people whose skills were poorly suited for the new economic order of New York, with its emphasis on finance, media, and real estate.[85] And if the political and economic consequences of immigration were not jarring enough for Dominicans, their treatment in New York complicated their racial and ethnic identities. The older white, European ethnic groups were likely to see them as Hispanic. Many Dominicans were partly of African descent, a fact that discomfited many of them because they associated Africa with Haiti and blackness. All the more baffling for them, then, when some in the United States identified dark-skinned Dominicans as black. Despite the old Trujillo dictatorship's emphasis on Dominican whiteness, Dominicans are in fact a multiracial people who transcend conventional U.S. categories of white, black, and Hispanic. Yet this complexity was awkwardly received in the city of New York.

Many Dominicans, out of a love for their first country and as a kind of solution to the cultural, political, and economic challenges of life in northern Manhattan, embraced a transnational way of life. For Dominican leftists in the late 1960s and most of the 1970s, New York was a base for political action aimed at overturning the conservative rule of the Joaquín Balaguer regime. The Partido Revolucionario Dominicano, the leftist opposition to Balaguer, annually paraded in the Heights. For less radical Dominicans, who simply wanted to live a better life in the land of their birth, New York was a place to make money on a temporary sojourn. The dream of returning to the Dominican Republic might be endlessly deferred and scaled down to an annual Christmas trip loaded down with suitcases full of gifts for friends and family, but the dream remained and sustained people in crowded Washington Heights apartments and during long hours of work cleaning offices, running a bodega, or driving a livery cab.[86]

These transnational immigrants lived, as they said, *"con un pie aquí y el otro allá"*—one foot here, the other there. They came to call their part of northern Manhattan not Washington Heights, but "Quisqueya Heights"—an adaptation of an indigenous name for the island that the Dominican Republic shares with Haiti. The name "Quisqueya Heights" stamped the neighborhood with a Dominican presence, but begged the question of what Dominicans would find there and what the changing neighborhood would mean to residents who did not trace their ancestry to the island of Hispaniola.[87]

Among the old residents of Washington Heights, particularly Irish and Jewish residents, there was a tendency to view this phenomenon with alarm. To European-born residents of the Heights and their children, Dominicans could seem like sinister birds of passage who changed the neighborhood without really settling in for good. The older Irish, Jewish, and Greek residents of the Heights had come of age in the era of World War II and the Cold War, when national spirit in the United States was particularly strong. In judging the Dominicans, they were sometimes quick to forget that transnational attachments were part of Washington Heights from its earliest days. In 1933, for example, Armenian nationalists with radical views on how to represent and define their nation entered the Holy Cross Armenian Apostolic Church in Washington Heights and assassinated Archbishop Leon Tourian. Greeks with family members living under Turkish rule knew that tensions in Istanbul could send relatives fleeing to Washington Heights. Many Jewish and Irish Heights residents adhered to Zionism or Irish Republicanism, both strongly international movements. In Washington Heights, politicians who wanted to win Jewish votes were expected to support Israel. In the 1980s, the Irish Northern Aid Committee, which supported the republican movement in Ireland, maintained an office in Inwood. At the same time, the transnational dimension of Dominican life in the Heights, aided by media connections, affordable airfares, and the relatively short distance between the United States and the Dominican Republic, encouraged vigorous links between the two countries. Irish and Jewish Americans might make sentimental trips to Ireland and Israel, but Dominicans packed themselves up and moved bodily to the Dominican Republic for months at a time. And while participation in Dominican and U.S. politics were not mutually exclusive, Dominican commitments to both countries carried the risk of making them less vigorous participants in northern Manhattan's public life than they might have been.

They also diverted money to the Dominican Republic that might otherwise have supported people and institutions in northern Manhattan.[88]

Over time, Dominican activism shifted from athletics, hometown associations, and a concern with the politics of the Dominican Republic to an emphasis on meeting the human needs of Dominicans in Washington Heights. For example, the Club Deportivo Dominicano was founded in 1966 to encourage athletics and give Dominican families an alternative to the streets and bars in their leisure time. The shift from a Dominican orientation to a New York orientation was never exclusive, however. From 1982 to 1984 the Association of Dominican Women marched down St. Nicholas Avenue to protest rape, picketed a sweatshop on 184th Street, ran a health fair—and conducted multiple events to link political questions in the Dominican Republic and the United States. Eventually, differences between women with commitments to political parties in the Dominican Republic and politically unaffiliated women produced splits and the organization's eventual dissolution.[89]

Women made up a majority of Dominican immigrants. By the 1980s the substantial number of working-class women among them faced weak economic opportunities in New York, sexism, and racial and ethnic prejudice. One response was the creation of the Dominican Women's Development Center, formed in 1988 in a meeting at the Broadway Temple where thirty women gathered, passed a hat, and established a treasury of $30. Their initial efforts emphasized education, personal development, and economic development. Other women's organizing efforts were either more informal or located within larger organizations, like the Alianza Dominicana and its social service projects.[90]

In this complex context, one of the first Dominicans to gain political prominence was Maria Luna, who had immigrated to the United States with her widowed mother and two sisters in 1961 and settled in the Heights. She was encouraged to get into politics by Albert Blumberg of the Audubon Reform Democratic Club, who thought an important part of his job was getting Dominicans into political life. Blumberg had a knack for working with everyone from radicals to organization Democrats and approached politics with a mixture of principled pragmatism and an appreciation for social forces. In 1983, urged on by Blumberg, Luna was elected a Democratic district leader from the Audubon Democrats. She would go on to become a member of the Democratic National Committee (and Blumberg, in 1985, would lose his own position as district leader to a Dominican challenger).[91]

Other Dominicans entered politically charged realms of public life—although not necessarily elective office—through community-based organizations that provided social services. Washington Heights was a neighborhood of immigrants with low incomes, crowded schools, crowded housing, and families undergoing the strain of adapting to life in the United States. The need for social services was urgent and inadequately met. Into this environment entered Moisés Pérez and Milagros Batista, graduates of Brooklyn College working at a downtown youth program and looking for recruits. (Batista was much influenced by having studied with Richie Pérez, a founder of the Young Lords Party who mixed radicalism, Puerto Rican activism, and community organizing.) Their effort to bring kids downtown didn't succeed, but the two saw in Washington Heights a neighborhood where Dominican kids were "in trouble." They also found a group of Dominican activists interested in gaining power for Dominicans in Washington Heights. From these encounters emerged, in the early 1980s, the social services agency Alianza Dominicana. Of course, obtaining funding for social services would inevitably involve lobbying and the cultivation of politicians. In this respect, as the sociologist Nicole Marwell has observed, organizations like Alianza became deeply embedded in political processes and structures that were grounded in Washington Heights but eventually reached up to elected officials and power centers at the city and state level. At the same time, in Alianza, Pérez and Batista, along with Dr. Rafael Lantigua, a physician at Columbia-Presbyterian, created an agency that would work to serve the pressing needs of Dominicans in the neighborhood.[92]

Alianza opened its doors on Amsterdam Avenue, just across from Highbridge Park. First came city funding, then state funding. Its first projects, which Batista worked on, addressed the problems of teenage pregnancies and violence. Batista brought in boys and girls to get them talking about sex and babies and contraception. She talked with girls while crocheting and got boys thinking about what it meant to be a man. Part of the challenge was connecting Dominican parents and their children. The two might be living together in the same crowded apartment, but otherwise they could be in different worlds. Batista tried to get them to communicate.

Dominican parents were deeply concerned about their kids and strict within the home, yet the structure of many Dominican families was flexible. As in the Dominican Republic, couples with little money lived together without the expense or formality of marriage sanctioned by law or church. Within families there was a tradition of custody that made for blended families and lots of half brothers and sisters. Dominicans could take pride in this as a sign of their generous, accepting way of life. Under the pressures of immigration and urban poverty, however, such families could come apart.[93]

Spouses, along with parents and children, could be separated for long periods of time while one parent worked in New York, hoping to bring the rest over. Even when families were united in one (crowded) apartment, strict gender roles put both young men and young women in difficult situations. Parents tended to let their boys run loose while expecting their daughters to do a lot of work at home. Parents were aware that kids on the street could get in trouble, but when Batista took some girls to a family planning clinic, one parent was angry.

Men who saw themselves as breadwinners were humiliated and angry when they couldn't find work. When that happened, they might become abusive or abandon their family—leaving a disproportionate number of young Dominican women to live as single mothers with limited incomes.

Over time, in response to such conditions, Alianza Dominicana would grow into the largest social service agency in northern Manhattan. Dominican immigrants and their children brought to it questions such as "I need to get help so my kids can do their homework," "I need to apply for Medicaid," and "I am worried that my children will lose touch with their culture and roots." Alianza became, in the words of Miriam Mejia, its associate director, "the genuine expression of a community that develops in the midst of pain and desperation." It was also, she noted, a place of "hopes and dreams" for "a community in which nostalgia is intertwined with life in a new country."[94]

Although the founding of Alianza was a direct response to conditions in Washington Heights, the transnational nature of Dominican life ensured that events in the Dominican Republic would also echo in New York City. Since 1966 the Dominican Republic had been governed by the Balaguer regime, which repressed opponents on the left and failed to generate a sustainable, broad-based prosperity. Imprisonment, censorship, and death squads underpinned Balaguer's rule. At moments, this could give the lives of Dominican radicals in New York a great sense of urgency: an assassination in the Dominican Republic could be followed by a demonstration at the Dominican consulate in New York City. In 1978, however, Balaguer was defeated by a candidate from the moderate leftist Partido Revolucionario Dominicano (PRD), Antonio Guzmán. For leftist Dominicans in New York, the PRD victory changed the terms of their engagement with homeland politics. They could go home if they wished or they could stay in New York and focus their energies on Washington Heights. (When the PRD itself governed poorly, there was that much more incentive to concentrate on what might be done in New York.)[95]

Dominican leftists in New York, like Jewish socialists before them, had immigrated with radical political visions. They could speak, in Spanish or newly acquired English, a language of class, revolution, empire, exploitation, and labor that was outside the mainstream of the American electoral system. With pride, they might think of themselves as members of political bodies defined by heroic dates and struggles in the history of the Dominican Republic, such as the Movimiento 14 de Junio or the Linea Roja. The auto worker

Sixto Medina was a member of the Movimiento 14 de Junio in the Dominican Republic. In New York he was a supporter of Fidel Castro and a member
of a Communist caucus in the United Auto Workers. Yet to elected officials in
New York City, the names and dates that Dominicans like Medina held dear
were bewildering and irrelevant to tasks like lobbying for a summer youth
program. By the late 1970s, the men and women of the Dominican American left faced a profound turning point: if they were to become active in
mainstream American politics, they would have to reorient themselves more
(although not necessarily exclusively) to New York City and calibrate their
politics to the more modest range of ideological differences promoted by the
legacies of American history and the two-party system.[96]

The choice mixed principle, pragmatism, ambition, and a sense that the
concerns of an older generation were less than compelling in New York City.
As one young Dominican American quipped to a social scientist, "They kept
talking about going to the mountains to fight the revolution. What mountains? The Catskills?" Still, the decision to engage American politics, even
on the relatively Dominican terrain of Washington Heights, could mean a
trimming of radical expectations. It also would lead to conflicts over political
representation and municipal resources in a city that was moving in a more
conservative direction politically, a city ever further from the kind of fiscal
generosity that defined it in the era of La Guardia and the New Deal.[97]

One of the foremost organizations to emerge from this moment of realign-
ment was the Asociación Comunal de Dominicanos Progresistas (ACDP),
founded in 1979 by activists from the New York branch of Linea Roja, a Dominican leftist party. The founders of the ACDP left Linea Roja when they
concluded that the focal point of their political work (without ignoring conditions in the Dominican Republic) would be the Dominican community
in New York City. The name of the organization, translated as the Community Association of Progressive Dominicans, hints at a political orientation
somewhere between Latin American radicalism and American liberalism. Its
founding members came from a younger generation of Dominicans, educated in New York if not necessarily born in the city. Among them was Guillermo Linares, born in 1951, who came to New York as a teenager.[98]

In Cabrera, on the northern coast of the Dominican Republic, Linares's
father worked as a tailor and his mother as a seamstress. The family's home
had a dirt floor. The nine Linares children grew up, as was common at the
time, with a picture of Trujillo and the national motto of "Dios, Patria, Liber-
tad" on the wall. (When a radio bulletin announced El Jefe's death, the family took down his picture. When a subsequent report suggested that Trujillo

might still be alive, the family looked frantically for the picture for fear of being caught in an act of disloyalty. When it was clear that the dictator was really gone, Trujillo's picture disappeared for good.)

His parents traveled to New York City on tourist visas, stayed on, found work in the garment industry, settled in the East Tremont section of the Bronx, and eventually obtained green cards. Guillermo, the oldest, stayed behind on his grandparents' farm and then followed at the age of fourteen. He struggled through high school, learning English along the way, worked in a supermarket, and then—with his mother's encouragement (but not his high school guidance counselor's)—made his way to City College. He put himself through college driving cabs, and became a bilingual teacher at an elementary school in Washington Heights. If the kids in his classes seemed like younger versions of himself, the gulf between their educational needs and the crowded conditions in their schools made him concerned about their future.

The ACDP became the base of Linares's efforts to run for the District 6 school board, with the goal of making it better serve Dominican children. A decade earlier, the political battles around the school board were largely the issues of the 1968 strike pursued by other means. Now the board faced serious problems with overcrowding and new lines of political conflict that embroiled the "minority majority" of northern Manhattan. In 1983, Linares was elected to the school board on the strength of a campaign that mobilized Dominican parents, who could vote in school board elections whether or not they were U.S. citizens. By 1986 the District 6 board had four Latino members and two African Americans. Yet the newly constituted school board faced dire and complex problems in the schools and in its own governance.[99]

The Dominican migration to northern Manhattan had produced painfully overcrowded public schools. In 1984, District 6 had 20,395 students crowded into schools designed to hold 17,065. Even PS 187, once criticized for being underused, was overcrowded. Classes met in hallways and storage rooms. Teachers and parents complained of rooms so crowded that they posed fire hazards. Ninety percent of the students who crowded into the classrooms of District 6 were poor enough to qualify for a free lunch. Eighty percent were Latinos, the majority of them Dominicans making the difficult transition to a new language. In District 6, poor conditions inside schools made a trying situation worse. Pupils in northern Manhattan regularly produced low scores on citywide achievement tests. In 1984, only 35.2 percent of the students in District 6 were reading at or above their grade level, the lowest percentage of all the city's districts. Citywide, the figure was 52.9 percent.[100]

Sometimes, solutions brought their own problems. In District 5 in Harlem, there were empty classroom seats just a twenty-minute bus ride away. Over angry protests from uptown parents, school buses transported children from District 6 south to District 5. Stanley Michels, the city councilman from Washington Heights, criticized this as an effort "to fill up empty seats by busing our children." Luis Rivera, president of community school board of District 6, spoke against busing. "All the children in the city go to neighborhood schools," he told the *Times*. "Why should we be different?" Latino parents in Washington Heights, in their own ways, were as attached to their local schools as Jewish parents were a generation earlier. Dominicans, who had fought for years to have a say in their children's education, now faced the prospect of having them educated in a district where Washington Heights parents would have no say. Equally significant, educators and local officials feared that if students from District 6 were bused elsewhere, city funding for running existing schools and building new ones in northern Manhattan would be reduced. Despite their concerns, busing continued. By the 1990s, students from Washington Heights were sent to schools even further south, in District 3 on the Upper West Side.[101]

Just as in the earlier years of struggles over integration, planning for schools meant thinking about the geography of northern Manhattan. One solution to the crowding of District 6, a *Times* article pointed out, would be to redraw the boundary between District 6 and District 5, which served central Harlem—a largely African American neighborhood. But this would fly against the logic of decentralization and community control. At the same time, within District 6 there was limited room for new school construction and sharp disagreement, in at least one case, over the site of a new school.[102]

Debates about school sites are often contentious in New York City. They can become especially bitter when they intersect with the ethnic fabric of a changing neighborhood. In Washington Heights, ethnic politics could resemble the pattern of siege within siege that the Irish poet Seamus Heaney observed in Northern Ireland, where a Catholic community felt itself threatened by a larger Protestant community that in turn felt threatened by the larger Catholic population of Ireland. In northern Manhattan, this took the form of small, remaining Irish and Jewish communities, whose members often felt encircled and dominated by a growing Dominican community. Dominicans in turn felt themselves beset by people, institutions, and social forces beyond their control. In this climate there was little that was conducive to empathy and bridge builders were rare, producing a nasty dispute around the construction of PS 48.[103]

Discussions of a new school to be built on the east side of Broadway on a lot between 185th and 187th streets dated to 1970, but were initially delayed by the fiscal crisis. In the 1980s, with growing crowding in Heights public schools, new residents of the neighborhood—especially Dominicans—saw an urgent need for the school. Jews could be found among supporters and opponents of the idea, but the Breuer community on Bennett Avenue one block west of Broadway prominently opposed construction on the Broadway site. Explanations for their opposition varied, but from the start it was highly unlikely that Breuer children would attend the school. Sometimes opponents said they were simply concerned with the safety hazard of locating a school on a busy avenue. More often they seemed to fear that public school students would harass yeshiva students and bring mayhem to Bennett Avenue (which was already a block west of Broadway, with the proposed school on the eastern side). The Breuer fears were a mix of insularity, real concerns about street crime, an inability to distinguish young students from threatening muggers, a lack of faith in the ability of the police to keep order, and memories of anti-Semitism. Their opponents in the dispute, especially blacks and Latinos, brought their own memories to the issue. Beyond the immediate crisis of crowded schools, African Americans and Dominicans had long known Bennett and Fort Washington avenues in the western Heights as places where people with dark-colored skin would have trouble getting an apartment.[104]

The Breuer community, which traced its roots to Frankfurt, had once held itself apart from other Jewish groups in the Heights. (Its leaders, the historian Steven M. Lowenstein noted, thought the Modern Orthodoxy of Yeshiva University insufficiently rigorous and utterly mistaken in its Zionism.) Since the late 1960s, however, the Breuers had become ever more active in efforts to preserve a Jewish enclave in Washington Heights. Their network of institutions, their devotion to their own version of Orthodoxy, and their substantial numbers—among them young families with children—made them a significant presence in the Heights. Their decision to stay in the neighborhood when others were leaving in the 1970s earned them a reputation as a force for stability. (Father Sullivan thought this was an important factor in steadying the neighborhood in an uncertain time.) Their ability to work their presence and reputation to their own advantage was formidable. Michael Cohn, who did not share their version of Judaism and had a more embracing view of life in a multiethnic community, viewed their lobbying efforts with concern. Elected officials took the Breuers' views seriously—in part because they did not want to offend a potential voting bloc.[105]

The Breuers were prominent in the Jewish Community Council, a communal organization in northern Manhattan that did valuable work in the Washington Heights–Inwood Coalition but did not, despite its name, represent all the Jews in the neighborhood. It did not speak for secular or politically liberal Jews in the Heights, and it certainly didn't speak for Beth Am, a small Reform congregation also located on Bennett Avenue. Beth Am's social action committee (which I served on even though I lived well south of Washington Heights) reached out to Dominican groups and ran forums on school board elections. When the JCC presented itself as the voice of the Jewish Heights, it erased the presence of Jews who supported construction of PS 48 and set up the framing of the dispute as "the Jews against the Dominicans." That was a false description: there were Jews—in Beth Am and in all walks of public life—who supported the swift opening of a fully developed school.[106]

The delays in building PS 48 were not, by themselves, the cause of school crowding in Washington Heights. Still, a prompt opening of the school would have made a dent in the problem. In 1986, the Koch administration brokered a compromise: PS 48 would be built, but classroom space in the school was reduced and it would teach only grades K–4. PS 48 students, when they finally did arrive, would be younger and fewer in number than originally anticipated. A headline in the *Uptown Dispatch*, a local newspaper, summed up the story: "There are no winners in the battle over P.S. 48." Due to construction delays, the doors of the school would not open until 1993.[107]

If the struggles over PS 48 replayed battles between old and new residents of Washington Heights, in the mid-1980s a new round of school board debates pitted relatively new arrivals in northern Manhattan's power structure against each other. Although the board elected in 1986 had four Latinos and two African Americans, they did not form a "minority majority" board of unified perspectives. The disputes among board members have been described as pro- and anti-UFT, which certainly has some legitimacy. In troubled school districts with weak administration, the UFT had virtually come to run the schools. (Perhaps the only example of anything like unity among the board, local officials and residents came in 1983 and 1986, when Councilman Michels, Senator Leichter, Mayor Koch, and U.S. Senator Daniel P. Moynihan successfully rallied voters against candidates for the school board put forward by Lyndon LaRouche's National Democratic Policy Committee. A neighborhood weekly announced the LaRouche faction's candidacy in 1983 with the headline "Neo-Nazis Running in School Board Elections.")[108]

Some board members had faith that the school system could be made to work for Dominicans in Washington Heights, others wanted as little to do with the existing system as possible. Some parents believed that only local leaders, teachers, and administrators could help northern Manhattan, while others were comfortable with experts from outside the neighborhood. Some Spanish-speaking parents put great faith in bilingual education; others thought it a flawed strategy. Allegations of corruption deepened divisions. Opponents of the status quo attempted to create change, while their adversaries believed that the district needed some stability if it were to accomplish anything.

Allegiances and perspectives were not easily predictable. Sixto Medina, the radical auto worker who lived at 359 Fort Washington Avenue, grew active in school politics when he observed the lunchroom mess and overcrowded classrooms conditions in his own children's school, PS 173. In 1980, he was elected to the local school board on a slate with Dave Dubnau of the Riverside-Edgecombe Neighborhood Association (RENA) and Gwen Crenshaw. Medina pushed for more school construction and better classroom instruction, but he opposed bilingual teaching. He wanted his children to learn English, and thought that bilingual education amounted to a jobs program for Puerto Rican teachers. In the complex ethnic politics of Washington Heights, he found negotiation with the Breuers difficult but admired the district's deeply committed Jewish teachers. Laura Altschuler, a close observer of the board, thought Medina had become a constructive bridge builder. He ran for a second term and lost, however, and blamed his defeat on factionalism among Dominican politicians.[109]

Battles on and around the board crested in March 1987, when Chancellor Nathan Quinones suspended the school board of Community District 6, arguing that bad leadership, poor pupil performance, mismanagement, and improper personnel procedures were undermining the district. Members of the local board appealed the suspension to the Board of Education and to the New York State Commissioner of Education. Both endorsed the suspension. For two years, appointed trustees and a new superintendent, Anthony Amato, ran the district. In 1989, school board elections resumed in District 6: Gwen Crenshaw, Robert Jackson, and Guillermo Linares were all elected.[110]

The struggles of the District 6 school board illuminate the complex currents of community, identity, and power that swirled around Washington Heights. Old Washington Heights had saved the physical structure of the neighborhood, above all its housing. The Dominicans who filled the stabilized apartment buildings and the neighborhood's schools protected northern Manhattan from the catastrophic population losses that undermined parts of the Bronx. By the 1980s, in organizations like the Alianza Dominicana and the ACDP, Dominicans were increasingly making northern Manhattan the focus of their political and community-building efforts. Dominicans might live transnational lives, but it was increasingly clear to many of them that they would stay in New York City for more than a brief phase in their lives. Yet exactly what Dominicans could achieve in the Heights was uncertain.

Washington Heights was one neighborhood in a city going through a wrenching economic transformation that would make New York a less rewarding home for unskilled and semiskilled workers. Dominican entrepreneurial abilities were abundantly evident in the bodegas of Washington Heights, but they catered to an economically poor community that offered small business operators few opportunities to get rich. The garment industry that had employed earlier generations, including Dominicans, was contracting. Waterfront labor, which would have been a natural source of income for Dominicans in another era, was a memory in New York. As remunerative blue-collar jobs vanished to low-wage climes, the low-wage service jobs in the city that could not be sent overseas—such as food preparation or domestic work—remained stubbornly underunionized and low paying. Dominicans wanted to work, but the jobs available to immigrants lacking the skills to thrive in a new economy paid poorly.[111]

Beyond all these challenges, Dominicans were trying to use incomes earned in New York to support relatives in the Dominican Republic. The budget of Martin Gomez, a Dominican man who lived in Washington Heights and crossed the George Washington Bridge to work in New Jersey cleaning offices and factories, is illustrative. As the *Times* reporter Sara Rimer learned, his regular expenses in 1991 were $212 a month in rent for a share in a two-room apartment with no kitchen; $175 a month for meals cooked by a woman in the Heights, including the rice and beans he ate for lunch; $300 a month to be put into his savings account; and $300 a month for his wife and three children in Santiago, Dominican Republic (plus the annual expense of a flight home at $489). His wages varied with the amount of overtime he earned, from $1,000 a month to $3,200. A bad month left him with only $13 to spare.[112]

The lives of immigrants like Gomez, grounded in Washington Heights but connected to New Jersey and the Dominican Republic, were at once metropolitan and transnational. They could vote in school board elections. But they could not overcome the inequalities that surrounded their lives. Local boards (and this was how decentralization could perpetuate inequalities) were no match for the overwhelming social and demographic forces that reshaped school populations and redefined the educational needs of children. As the struggles over PS 48 showed, the provision of resources from outside Washington Heights could be stymied by local efforts. To change the larger contexts of their lives, Dominicans had to engage in politics beyond the confines of School District 6. Efforts at this were under way by the end of the 1980s. Both the Alianza and the ACDP started with roots deep in Dominican experiences, and both produced leaders who would engage in politics well beyond the confines of the Dominican community.[113]

Yet for all of Dominicans' institution building in northern Manhattan, as the 1980s ended there were no Dominicans in the main branches of city government. Councilman Michels, Assemblyman Murtaugh, and Senator Leichter represented Dominicans in Washington Heights and Inwood alongside the rest of their constituents, but Dominicans could not see one of their own in the central bodies of city government. The possibility of change emerged in 1989, when New Yorkers approved changes in the charter that set the basic structure of city government. Among the changes was an expansion of the city council from thirty-five seats to fifty-one to make it more representative of the city's racial and ethnic diversity. Depending on the boundaries, it would be possible to create a district in northern Manhattan that could elect a Dominican to the city council.[114]

On the night of November 27, 1990, activists, residents, and elected officials gathered at Columbia Presbyterian for a forum on redistricting. Once again, geography was at the heart of their concerns. For all the growth of the Dominican community in northern Manhattan, it was still concentrated on the streets east of Broadway. If the goal of politics was building bridges between the east and west sides of Broadway, what was the value of setting up a district that was confined to the east side of Broadway? Yet given the realities of demography and voter registration, only a district on the east side of Broadway would have a good chance of electing a Dominican representative. Speaker after speaker, among them the most venerable of Dominican activists in northern Manhattan, rose to explain why it was necessary to create a city council district in northern Manhattan that would send a Dominican representative to the city council.

Their arguments blended the particular and the universal, the pragmatic and the idealistic. All recognized the large number of Dominicans in northern Manhattan and their need for representation, but brought out different points on the proposal's value and justice. Maria Luna, whose ascent to the position of district leader with the encouragement of Albert Blumberg was an early sign of Dominican political presence, spoke the language of pluralism and the equitable division of resources: "We are ready to sit at the same table with other groups and discuss our demands, our fair share." Rafael Lantigua, one of the founders of the Alianza Dominicana, a member of the Dominican PRD, and a member of the North Manhattan Committee for Fair Representation, stressed that Dominicans were the largest group in a neighborhood with great problems. He recognized that a council seat was not a "magic wand" that would solve everything, but affirmed that Dominicans had to become politically visible if the problems of northern Manhattan were to be addressed. "We know that Hispanics, African-Americans and whites, must unite to reclaim our community," he said, "but this can only happen when we all recognize the reality of our community, or else the problem will persist."[115]

Repeatedly, speakers framed the issue in the contexts of immigration, the history of immigration in New York, and the succession of ethnic groups in northern Manhattan. If this suggested a moment of Dominican ascendancy over earlier arrivals, it also suggested that Dominicans were immigrants with a lot in common with their predecessors. In New York City, where narratives of immigration are an important part of civic culture, this was a significant stance that did much to "normalize" the Dominican experience. Adriano Espaillat, president of the 34th Precinct community council, introduced himself as "an immigrant" and "the son of an immigrant and the grandson of an immigrant that lived here before I was born." He welcomed the districting commission to northern Manhattan and emphasized, "The contributions and the legacy of our Irish, Jewish and Afro-American neighbors can be looked at with pride, and as a constant reminder of the difficulties faced by these groups, while striving to better themselves to reach fair representation and participation in government. It is exactly this concept of inclusion that we are here to defend."[116]

Guillermo Linares, by now president of Community School Board 6, did not speak in the language of the old Dominican left. But he did stress his own heritage as an immigrant, the value of hard work in a good cause, and the struggles to make northern Manhattan a good home for Dominican newcomers. "We should not kid ourselves and pretend these changes have not taken place without conflict," he said. "Old neighbors and new neighbors have been involved in struggles over the distribution of power and availability of resources. But, out of this conflict, resolutions have emerged that make our community stronger. And, this is possible because, historically, northern Manhattan has been a community of immigrants. A new wave of immigrants have fought and worked together with other immigrants to build a better and stronger neighborhood. Today, it's no different from yesterday." Linares concluded by urging the commission "to do the best possible job, juggling many interests and sometimes conflicting objectives," to create a district with "a clear Dominican and Hispanic majority." He also affirmed that a Dominican legislator would meet the challenges of democratic representation and "represent all of the people in this area: Jewish, Greek, Irish, white, black and Hispanic."[117]

As would be expected, most of the speakers were Dominican. But Franz Leichter also endorsed the creation of a new district, as did Stanley Michels. In a formal statement attached to the record of the meeting, the North Manhattan Committee for Fair Representation backed the creation of a new district so that "the second largest immigrant group in the city has the recognitions and tools with which to exercise their democratic rights." The group counted Albert Blumberg and Richard Crenshaw on its steering committee and Joel Rothschild as a member of its research committee.[118]

Eventually, a new council district, the tenth, was established. It ran from the northern tip of Inwood south to West 159th Street east of Broadway. (The district of the incumbent city councilman for northern Manhattan,

Stan Michels, was redrawn; it retained the western sections of the Heights and Inwood, but reached down into Harlem and Morningside Heights.) The new district embraced the predominately Latino and Dominican sections of northern Manhattan, which were much poorer than the streets to the west.

The competition for the new seat was fierce. Within the tenth council district, with its large Dominican population, candidates vied to present themselves as the fittest representative of a very Dominican district. Guillermo Linares won a five-way primary race that included three strong Dominican rivals. Nationalism, and not for the last time, played a strong role in uptown Dominican politics. In his campaign he stressed Dominican power and handed out Dominican flags. Linares received 30 percent of the vote, Luna 26 percent, and Espaillat 25 percent. In northern Manhattan, where Democrats were a strong majority in all ethnic groups, the victory in the primary assured Linares's entry into the city council. Politically, Dominicans had the basis for power and visibility. What they could do with them remained an open question. Would they transform politics in northern Manhattan or become, as the testimony on redistricting suggested, one more ethnic group to call Washington Heights home? The full answer to this question would emerge only over decades, but a new chapter in the history of Washington Heights was about to begin.[119]

The fear that Washington Heights would burn like the South Bronx never materialized, thanks in large measure to the determined efforts of activists, residents, and elected officials. The Koch administration also helped strengthen Washington Heights in a difficult decade, even though its plans for recovery through gentrification would one day trouble Heights residents with modest incomes.[120]

The revival of Washington Heights was, as Father Sullivan says looking back, both a bottom-up and top-down effort. It impressed him with the importance of getting beyond stereotypes, getting people to talk to one another, and recognizing that deep down most people want similar things: good schools for their kids, the ability to walk the streets without fear, good housing, and a job. When he arrived at Saint Elizabeth's in December 1976, it seemed to him that Washington Heights would go the way of the South Bronx. When he left in August 1983, he thought it probably wouldn't.[121]

Yet even as the familiar landscapes of Washington Heights endured, they were fought over in new political alignments. By the 1980s, Dominican activism gave the newest immigrants in Washington Heights a greater place in the city's politics and more power over their own destiny. The growth of Dominican political power in northern Manhattan was fundamentally a Dominican achievement, but it is important to recognize the contributions of older residents and ethnic communities in the Heights for aiding (or at least not fatally resisting) that achievement. At their best, the liberal Democrats of northern Manhattan maintained a politics of inclusion and justice that preserved the physical structure of Washington Heights and opened up democratic possibilities to the newest immigrant group in Washington Heights. In turn, Dominican arrivals and community building in northern Manhattan saved the area from decay and catastrophic population losses.

Yet this would not be a neat and easy story of ethnic succession and prosperity. In the economic geography of northern Manhattan, the new "Dominican" district was concentrated in the area that had been, since the 1970s, the poorest part of the Heights and Inwood. Increasingly, economic security in the city required levels of high school and even college education that were not guaranteed in the troubled public schools of northern Manhattan.

As the peoples of Washington Heights grappled with the challenge of educating a new generation of New Yorkers, a new threat emerged: a violent trade in crack, a form of processed cocaine that could be sold cheaply. With crack, the champagne drug of the 1980s could be mass marketed to both the poor and the middle class. The crack trade, which was initially decentralized and competitive, scarred parts of Washington Heights with gunfire and violence. In 1986, in case anyone failed to notice how bad it was, U.S. Attorney Rudolph Giuliani and U.S. Senator Alphonse D'Amato put on disguises (a Hell's Angels vest and a nondescript windbreaker) and ventured to 555 W. 160th Street (with plenty of police protection) to buy two vials of crack for the benefit of reporters. As a war of bullets broke out on the street, a war of words and images began about what the Heights meant for the city and its future.[122]

CHAPTER 5

CRACK YEARS

ON A CRISP WINTER NIGHT IN 1990, the east side of Broadway in lower Washington Heights was crowded with young men who shuffled to keep warm. Lights were on, stores were open, and cars jockeyed for parking spots. As we navigated the busy sidewalks, swarms of young men parted to let us pass and closed up as we walked on. From a distance, it looked like a lively shopping district. In fact, the bustle was the product of a devastating drug trade.[1]

For a week, as part of my research on crime and the media, I accompanied police officers from the 34th Precinct on patrol in Washington Heights. One night, I walked with an officer along the east side of Broadway in the southern Heights. The guys on the corner, the policeman explained, were there to attract customers who had come to the Heights to buy drugs. They escorted customers to the men in front of side street buildings, where a small purchase might be made on the spot. Bigger buys, which had the potential for a bigger criminal charge in the event of a bust or a bigger loss in the event of a robbery, took place upstairs. The men looking down from upper-story apartments were lookouts. In buildings where dealers worked, drugs and money were often stashed in separate apartments: if one of the apartments was robbed or raided, whatever was hidden in the other remained secure.

The drivers of the flashy cars that zipped past us were probably running errands for dealers; the oddly parked cars most likely belonged to their customers from the suburbs. Among the businesses that were open, the storefront *envios* wired both drug trade earnings and the hard-earned pay of factory workers. The men behind the cash registers in the bodegas, the officer explained, had a variety of motives: some were the dealers' partners; others were broke but trying to make some money despite the risk; and others were intimidated into cooperation.

The policeman I walked with was skeptical about whether anything could be done to reduce crime in the neighborhood, but he came down hard on cars parked illegally next to hydrants. He couldn't bear the thought of kids dying in a fire because firefighters couldn't get to a water supply. He grilled white suburban kids in the neighborhood because he thought they were probably there to buy drugs; they responded to him with panicky promises to leave. Aside from a few Dominican women who were girlfriends of police officers he knew, he had little contact with the locals. He said the western Heights, where my parents had lived, was still basically safe. But he said if I wanted to patrol in the eastern Heights in the 160s, around Amsterdam Avenue, it would be best if I wore a bulletproof vest.

The violence that surrounded the crack trade generated feelings of fear, despair, and withdrawal. A team of Columbia University researchers interviewed 100 people who lived or worked in northern Manhattan and reported:

> People are afraid to exert leadership because leaders get their heads blown off in the lobbies of apartments; drugs and gangs provide youth with what a family cannot; the streets are filled with garbage and urine because people don't consider the neighborhood their home so there is no point in taking care of it; drug dealers intimidate store owners and landlords into giving up their careers and buildings—if they don't comply, they might get shot; it is better not to do anything when a neighbor is in distress because helping out might get you shot; if you walk on the wrong side of the street you might get shot, if you call the police you might get shot, if you carry your Bible past the Latin Kings, or enter your apartment when someone happens to be taking twenty dollars off your dresser, or put your bed too close to the window, you might get shot.[2]

At stake in Washington Heights was not just the physical safety of residents and police officers—as important as these were—but fundamental questions about order and fear in the city. Whose definitions of order would prevail?[3] What would become of a neighborhood where fear leached into sidewalks, parks, and apartment building hallways? Would residents and police officers ever find a way to work together in northern Manhattan? And could Washington Heights find a way to reform itself?

The murders of the crack years took place in an area that already had been rattled by two decades of rising crime, particularly in the southern parts of the Heights.[4] Residents were well aware that the combination of violence and racial and ethnic change in the neighborhood frightened people and drove them apart. In 1966, after candy store owner Morris Goldstein was murdered in his shop at 1 Fort Washington Avenue, more than one hundred people (including state assemblyman David Dinkins) marched to the police station at 152nd and Amsterdam under the leadership of the Riverside-Edgecombe Neighborhood Association to protest the lack of police protection in the neighborhood. The *New York Times* reported that the protest was "an effort to keep what was once a pleasant middle-class neighborhood from degenerating" amid crime and efforts by blockbusting landlords to drive out white tenants, pack in black tenants, and charge them higher rents. "Negroes and whites in the gathering yesterday said they were trying to maintain the present flavor of integration in the area," the *Times* reported. "In some apartment buildings there are Negro and white floor captains working together, they said."[5]

As much as the Riverside-Edgecombe Neighborhood Association encouraged people to take collective action against crime, it was hard to generate sustained solidarity in a fearful and changing neighborhood. More common were improvised individual responses to crime, which ranged from wariness in public to staying off the streets. Ralph Ellison, author of *The Invisible Man*, carried a knife to protect himself from muggers when he walked his dog near his cozy apartment in a grand old building at 730 Riverside Drive on the corner of 150th Street.[6] In the pages of the neighborhood weekly *Heights-Inwood*, an intelligent and responsible newspaper edited by Barry Dunleavy in the 1970s, Jim Krislas described being mugged—twice—in a series of op-ed columns. He recalled the loss of dignity as his pockets were emptied; the way the episode replayed in his mind like an endless loop of film footage; the lingering memories that made him fearful of dark places and suspicious of people in apartment foyers; and the way that it took thirty-six hours after the crime for him to notice "the burning sensation from a knife crease across the front of my neck." (The first mugging was at gunpoint.) The series ended with the identification of one of the assailants in a mug shot but no report of prosecution—making street crime in northern Manhattan seem like something that would be endured but not solved.[7]

The thought of what might happen made people as nervous as actual crimes. Even with the best efforts of local newspapers, most street crimes fell beneath the radar of news reporting, forcing people to rely on rumors, hunches, and word of mouth to understand what was happening around them.[8] Residents' confidence, along with the morale and the reputation of the police, suffered. When smoldering concerns about crime and policing met "the oxygen of publicity," the consequences could be fiery. In 1966, Mayor Lindsay attempted to make the police department more responsive to complaints about police misconduct by appointing a majority of civilians to the Civilian Complaint Review Board—a panel that had been previously made up entirely of police officers. He was met with a furious backlash from the Patrolmen's Benevolent Association (the equivalent of the policemen's union) and the Conservative Party, which successfully petitioned for a public referendum on the board.[9] New Yorkers voted in November 1966 by a margin of 63 percent to 36 percent to shut down the civilian majority board. Analysts interpreted the citywide vote as a stunning defeat for civil rights activists, a repudiation of liberalism, and evidence of a split between liberal Jewish professionals and more conservative working-class and lower-middle-class Jews.[10]

In northern Manhattan, the referendum results suggested that depending on who you were and where you lived, it was possible to see both crime and the police as problems. In the lower Heights and the adjoining section of Harlem, crime was relatively high and the population more racially and ethnically mixed. Voters in these areas favored retaining the civilian review board. In the upper Heights and Inwood, voters by a wide margin favored abolishing the civilian review board. These whiter areas, even though relatively safe, worried more about crime and were comparatively more willing to let the cops work without strong civilian oversight.[11]

By the 1970s, police officers had even greater reasons to fear for both their reputations and their physical safety. In May 1971, one week after jurors unanimously acquitted all the Black Panthers accused of engaging in a bombing plot, members of the Black Liberation Army ambushed and killed two NYPD officers. The assault on officers Waverly Jones, who was black, and Joseph Piagentini, who was white, took place at the Colonial Park Houses, a public housing project beneath Coogan's Bluff at 155th Street. Jones died quickly. Piagentini was shot thirteen times at close range while he begged for his life.[12] A year later, the Knapp Commission hearings of 1972 probed corruption in the NYPD and left a damaging image of a force in which corruption was "widespread."[13] Cops were enmeshed in a war fought with headlines and gunfire. From the perspective of police officers in northern Manhattan, the circle of violence tightened in July 1977 when police officer Edward E. Mitchell of the 34th Precinct was shot to death. Mitchell, one of the relatively few African American officers on the force at the time, was trying to handcuff a robbery suspect when the situation exploded into a shootout and hostage taking. Five thousand officers attended his funeral at Holy Trinity Episcopal Church on Cumming Street in Inwood.[14]

It did little good to tell residents and police officers that crime in the Heights and Inwood, even in the 1970s, was lower than in neighborhoods like Harlem. In northern Manhattan, everyone knew that their neighborhoods were more dangerous than they used to be and they didn't like it. Then came the crack epidemic and with it more killings. By 1989, turf wars between drug dealers had driven the number of murders in the Heights—and the city—to unprecedented levels. The citywide murder rate of 7.6 per 100,000 people in the early 1960s topped anything seen before (even during Prohibition, with a rate of 7.4), but it was just a prelude to much higher rates: 24.9 per 100,000 from 1981 to 1985 and then 25.4 per 100,000 from 1986 to 1990. On a per capita basis New York was not the most dangerous city in the country. Its prominence as a media center and a symbol for urban life, however, made crime and violence in Gotham echo widely. The rise of crack only made this problem worse, especially in Washington Heights.[15]

The crack trade was concentrated in the southeast section of the Heights, but its damage rippled throughout the neighborhood. And lurid reports in the news media, with a poor grasp of the subtleties of local geography, gave the impression of an entire community aflame with violence. While many of the customers were white suburbanites who used the George Washington Bridge and northern Manhattan's good highway connections to get in and out of the Heights, Dominicans in the neighborhood were blamed for the drug trade and its violence. In fact, a relatively small number of armed men perpetrated a climate of killing that had a devastating impact, scarring the neighborhood's reputation and its residents' lives.

Leo Fuentes watched the growing impact of the drug trade in Washington Heights and concluded that it had turned his neighborhood from "a poor but mostly peaceful place to an outright war zone." Fuentes, born in New York City in 1974, lived briefly in the Dominican Republic but grew up at 382 Wadsworth Avenue near 192nd Street. At home with his mother, a factory worker, he lived a life governed by Dominican culture and customs. Outside, he was in a more American world of hip-hop, graffiti, and rap music. As with so many other Heights residents, Fuentes's world was a small and territorial one, defined by his block and its immediate surroundings. Living on 192nd Street, he and his friends (who were mostly Dominican) called the nearby 194th Street "fourth"; there was no need for a more elaborate reference because no one would normally walk the ten blocks to 184th. Sports and graffiti reinforced loyalties and identities. Young men from Fuentes's block competed against other blocks in sports, with "your block against everybody else."[16]

Crack dealers organized crews that took the fierce loyalties of some young men—previously expressed in things like allegiance to their block or pride in graffiti—and directed them toward fidelity to a crack crew. The strictness of

Dominican parents at home, which kept order in individual apartments, was no match for drug dealers' power on the streets. Young people took the kind of energy that his parents' generation applied to legitimate labor and directed it to drug dealing. "The money that flowed into the neighborhood corrupted everything it touched," Fuentes reflected years later. Crack heads took over the big rock in Highbridge Park where he and his friends went to make out with their girlfriends in junior high school. Police officers routinely stopped Fuentes and his buddies to search them; they learned to comply in order to avoid an arrest, a black eye, or worse. Fuentes stayed away from involvement in the drug trade; he veered into illicit income only once, when he stopped a man and dug into his pockets for his money.[17]

Other kids took a different path. The dealers recruited young people; kids who had grown up in the Heights were particularly useful because could tell locals from strangers, remember which alley was best for a getaway, and who in the neighborhood could be intimidated if business required it. For people who lived in the western Heights or Inwood, far from the drug bazaars, criminals were likely to be total strangers. But if you lived in the middle of the drug wars, the young man who confronted you or who died too soon might be someone you had known as a small boy.[18]

For Dominican young people, living in a low-wage neighborhood surrounded by the temptations of consumer culture, a rock of crack offered the prospect of a cheap high and quick money. Young people made more in the drug trade than hard-working adults in legitimate jobs, turning generational authority upside down. Adults were aghast as familiar faces wore the glassy expression of an illicit high.[19]

The drug trade frightened and confounded grown-ups. The challenges that face immigrant parents who raise American children are well known in New York City, but the Dominicans who brought up children during the crack years faced much more than a generation gap and cultural differences. Parents kept their kids inside when they should have been sent out to play. Teachers worried that the money and arrogance of the dealers made students think that learning was for losers. People stayed home instead of going out but even then found little sense of security. As the social scientists Jeffrey Fagan and Garth Davies observed, in city neighborhoods certain conditions set the stage for murder and violence: "weak social control, poorly supervised adolescent networks, active illegal markers where violence is the primary regulatory device, widespread perceptions of danger and the demand for lethal weapons, and the attenuation of outlets to resolve disputes without violence." They might well have been talking about southern Washington Heights.[20]

In buildings inhabited by Dominicans, researchers learned, only newcomers met in the hallways or left their doors open. Tenants who knew the realities of life in the neighborhood kept their doors tightly locked. Once they stepped out of their apartments, the layouts of apartment buildings discouraged social interaction. The blocks outside were not congenial either. The only places left to gather were in parks or bodegas, and in both the worst elements of the street could be too close for comfort. People worried about burglars who posed as police officers or electrical repair workers. One young Dominican man, with experience of life in New York, observed that newcomers from the Dominican Republic were easy to recognize: they were either too scared or too friendly.[21]

There seemed to be nowhere to turn for help. Dominicans who had experienced violent and corrupt authority at home were not likely to trust authority figures in America. Police officers' failure to have a decisive impact on the drug trade made them look weak and ineffectual. Some residents feared that helping the police would brand them as informers and leave them vulnerable to the dealers' retribution when the police were not around.[22]

Worst of all were the rumors of police corruption. While the 34th Precinct was never hit with a major scandal during the crack era, suspicions swirled around it. Residents wondered aloud how the drug trade could flourish so openly without the cooperation of corrupt officers. And if that was the case, why give a tip to a policeman if there was just the slightest chance he was friendly with a drug dealer?[23]

In such circumstances, it made a certain kind of sense to keep your head down, pretend to not notice things, and never contest the authority of the young men on the corner. The dealers could indeed be friendly if you let them go about their business. If you got in their way, or challenged their control of the sidewalks, they might intimidate you, beat you, or kill you.[24]

In sections of the Heights infected by the drug trade, relations between the police and the community were riddled with mutual distrust. Each side felt the other could break the law with impunity. Neither felt the law would protect them.

For the police, the killing of Officer Michael Buczek in 1988 was a case in point. The officer, responding to a routine call from a woman with a stomachache, wound up in a confrontation with a Dominican man who made money robbing drug dealers, who fatally shot Buczek. Buczek was mourned in a service at Saint Elizabeth's Church, but officers complained that otherwise they received too little help from residents in solving the case.[25] By the time an indictment was handed down in Buczek's murder, the suspect had fled to the Dominican Republic. After strenuous lobbying by the United States, Dominican authorities agreed to turn over the suspect. Yet he never made it into U.S. custody. Shortly before he was to be transferred to U.S. authorities, while he was in the custody of the Dominican National Police, the suspect fell to his death from the third floor of a stairwell at police head-quarters. Dominican authorities called it a suicide. In time, residents named a public school and a little league in Buczek's honor.[26]

For Dominicans, the Occhipinti case was proof that the law would not protect them. Joseph Occhipinti, a much-decorated agent in the Immigration and Naturalization Service who had assisted in the investigation of the Buczek case, was convicted of civil rights violations and sentenced to thirty-seven months in prison for his role in raids on bodegas conducted in 1989 that turned up money, drugs, and weapons. Occhipinti's supporters—among them Guy Molinari, the Republican borough president of Staten Island, the newspaper columnist Mike McAlary, who bounced between the *Daily News* and *New York Post* in the early 1990s, and Manuel de Dios Unanue, an edi-tor and muckraker in the Spanish language press—claimed he was framed. Nicholas Estavillo, commander of the 34th Precinct during the crack years, thought Occhipinti's conviction emboldened drug dealers.[27]

In the last days of the Bush administration, the president commuted Oc-chipinti's sentence (which was not the same thing as pardoning him for a crime he never committed). To Heights residents who felt that the investiga-tion Occhipinti conducted in their neighborhood was aggressive and unfair, news of the commuted sentence confirmed suspicions that misdeeds by law enforcement would go unpunished.[28]

The violence of the crack years also undermined the public parks that had made life in Washington Heights attractive. At Highbridge Pool, where families still brought their children to swim, gang members—not necessar-ily drug dealers, but angry kids who became quick to resort to violence—claimed turf and battled at the slightest provocation. In July 1989, some girls went after each other with broken bottles and knives. The police had a hard time breaking up the melee.[29] A week later, a lifeguard asked a swimmer to leave a closed section of the pool. The man stalked off, returned with a gun, and opened fire. Christine Nobile, a thirteen-year-old from the Bronx, was shot dead as she was drying off after a swim. The lifeguard and two other men were injured. The gunman, who fired as many as ten rounds, got away.

Newsday columnist Jimmy Breslin visited the pool after the incident. He heard that the gunman had procured his weapon at 160th Street and Broad-way, in the heart of the crack dealing area and near where Officer Buczek was shot to death the previous October. In Breslin's mind, the convergence of the two stories was more than a coincidence; both were part of "the maim-ing of our city." In the aftermath of the shooting, Breslin saw beautiful trees around the pool and a blue sky overhead. The sight of workmen stringing razor wire atop a fence insulted his eyes. He also noticed that the pool, on a hot and sunny Sunday in a neighborhood of crowded streets, was all but empty. If mothers from Washington Heights wouldn't take their children to Highbridge Pool on such a day, he concluded, "what chance do we have of keeping people with children everywhere in the city from considering living in places that offer less threat and pain?"[30]

A few months later, David Dinkins was narrowly elected the city's first African American mayor. He defeated Rudolph W. Giuliani, a Republican and a former federal prosecutor who ran on both the Republican and Liberal party lines. In his inaugural address, Dinkins vowed to be the "toughest mayor on crime the city has ever seen" while protecting civil rights and promoting racial harmony in the city he described as a "gorgeous mosaic." Dinkins, who lived a short walk from the Grinnell at 157–10 Riverside Drive, remained committed to interracial politics even as other African Americans embraced black nationalism. Although he entered politics with Harlem Democrats who valued order, hierarchy, and party discipline, he counted among his friends and advisors Albert Blumberg, the former Communist in the Audubon Reform Democratic Club, and Paul O'Dwyer, an Irish American Democrat and a happy warrior in a host of left-liberal causes. The new mayor combined within himself a party regular's appreciation for orderly dealings and the quiet resolution of disputes with a progressive Democrat's pursuit of social justice.[31]

Framing the issue of crime in ways that would have special resonance for African Americas, Dinkins said that "freedom from crime is a basic civil right of all our people, as fundamental as the franchise and fair housing" and that police-community relations had to be improved. Drawing on his own experiences with crime (he never tired of telling his staff that he had once been through a holdup in a bodega), the mayor encouraged all New Yorkers to demand "discipline and respect for the law and for each other from all who share this city."[32]

The new mayor's vision of lower crime and better race relations would be tested in Washington Heights, the writer Lewis Cole argued in the weekly *7 Days*. The neighborhood had changed since Cole grew up there thirty years earlier, but Washington Heights and the city both showed promise.[33] Citing the historian Fernand Braudel, Cole described cities as "electrical transformers," places where people "enter the realm of possibility, the living forges of culture, knowledge, and democracy from which come our artists, thinkers and leaders"—people ranging from Spike Lee to Grace Paley to Ed Koch. "This ideal of civic and civil life has gone unspoken and unfought for in New York during the last 12 years. But it is the vision that inspires Dinkins. And it is in his backyard that he can start to bring it to life."

Dinkins sought to fight crime, reform the police, and build bridges between his city's different communities. The odds for success were small from
the start, and the effort to govern at the volatile intersection of race, crime,
and policing frequently left him reacting to events even as he attempted to
lead with a new logic of law enforcement.[34] Dinkins's police commissioner,
Lee Brown, was committed to community policing, a phrase that meant
many things to different people. Rather than have officers patrol in cars—a
strategy designed to limit direct contact with residents and thereby mini-
mize corruption—Brown called on officers to embrace communities. At
a minimum, local residents would be officers' eyes and ears on the street.
Brown's more expansive vision would make police officers problem solvers
who worked with communities to develop shared strategies for maintaining order. The poor relations between police and residents in the sections of
the Heights that were poisoned by the crack trade suggested the value of this
goal.[35] Under a plan called "Safe Streets, Safe City," Dinkins hired almost five
thousand more cops and put them to work under a strategy of community
policing. The plan was met with some doubts: there was a widespread belief
that the police could have little impact on crime, concern that the hires would
cost too much money, and skepticism among critics of Brown and the mayor
about their ability to effectively administer such an ambitious program.[36]

Yet Dinkins and Brown's plan for community policing took on serious
problems that their critics preferred to ignore. The crack epidemic and its
accompanying murders made crime a political issue of the highest order.
A mayor who made a significant dent in crime would reap both genuine
thanks and political capital. Crime was also an issue of considerable urgency.
Dinkins had an expansive liberal vision when it came to social services, but
there was little likelihood of realizing its full breadth until the city became
safer and more peaceful. And as Dinkins himself knew from direct experience, the neighborhoods that suffered most from crime were typically the
ones inhabited by poor people of color who had enough problems in life
without having to worry about muggings and shootings. Finally, relations
between the police and the communities they patrolled were in many cases
poor, especially when white cops confronted black and Latino residents in
volatile circumstances.

For decades, the issue of "law and order" had been the political monopoly of conservatives. They had used it to attack the civil rights movement,
demonize blacks, and cultivate angry and fearful white voters. Ed Koch's
embrace of the death penalty (an issue over which a New York City mayor
has no control) was part of this pattern and part of his own conservative
turn when he first ran for mayor. As murders mounted in the crack years, it
was painfully clear that conservatives and conventional thinkers had little to

show for their domination of the issues of crime and criminal justice. Mayor Dinkins was a cautious executive, but in taking on crime he was committing his administration to the solution of a major problem that was not associated with liberal mayors. In his embrace of community policing he also took on the reform of the NYPD. The last liberal mayor to tackle police reform, John Lindsay, found himself embroiled in bitter controversies and was defeated on the question of civilian review of police conduct.

Dinkins's vision of a new kind of policing, with a new relationship between police and their communities, was tested in Washington Heights. My week patrolling with policemen in the 34th Precinct increased my respect for the officers there, complicated my understanding of their work, and left me wondering if it was possible to do anything that would reduce violence in the neighborhood and bring down the drug trade.

I learned that much police work—contrary to television shows and news reports—amounts to muscular social work. In a neighborhood with lots of problems, a lot of the work I observed didn't seem to resolve anything. I stood with two officers for endless minutes peering at the body of an elderly Chinese immigrant who died alone, covered in his own excrement, as we tried to determine whether we had reached him at the moment of death or just afterward. (The procedural implications for this with regard to the handling of the man's body were significant.) We also stood clueless and ineffectual while listening to a mother—a nurse who was the epitome of respectability—as she lamented that her sullen teenage daughter was carrying on with an older man. As we left without solving the problem, the mother's voice rose up behind us in a scream that gave way to a wail. As part of their daily routine, the two officers I patrolled with entered walkup buildings with unlocked front doors, trudged to the top of the stairs, woke the sleeping addicts on the top landing, and told them to get out of the building. It was obvious that the junkies would return. Whenever we performed this task one of the officers looked at me, shrugged, and said, "It's the American way."

Among the officers I met, attitudes toward neighborhood residents ranged from sympathy to bewilderment to contempt. One policeman, a Cuban American, found the Dominicans in the 34th Precinct baffling. Nevertheless, when we walked into an apartment where a family was crying with despair over a relative's high fever, his fluent Spanish lowered the emotional temperature. I heard complaints that the cops in the 34th Precinct could be heavy-handed with residents, even brutal. But as I rode in patrol cars I was astounded at how people flagrantly broke traffic laws and double-parked even when policemen were nearby.

Over the course of a week in a precinct with a reputation for high crime, I saw little that reflected Washington Heights' murderous reputation. One day in the precinct house there was a palpable rise in tension when an officer reported a gun incident. In a night walking up and down lower Broadway with a foot patrolman—when I gazed at the lookouts for crack dealers silhouetted in upper story windows and wondered what, if anything, could put them out of business—we narrowly missed apprehending a mugger in flight because he ran directly into the path of another officer. Still, in watching two officers do their jobs well, one of them gave me an unforgettable explanation of how relations between the police and the people they serve can turn bad.

I was with two officers who were summoned to the neat apartment of a dignified, elderly, Spanish-speaking woman whose mentally ill son preferred illegal drugs to his prescribed psychiatric medicine. He stole from his mother to buy drugs on the street until his mother took out a restraining order against him. Her bilingual daughter interpreted while the policemen tried to figure out if the son had violated the order. After a long conversation, the officers concluded that he had. We went downstairs and soon found the son on the street. When the officers moved to arrest him, he squirmed and shoved to get away. With relentless but controlled strength, they wrestled him into handcuffs and put him in the back seat of their squad car. The son said he was the victim of police brutality, but I saw nothing that fit the term. When it was all over, one of the officers turned to me and said something like this: "That lady upstairs is a good person, but her son is a lot of trouble; the problem with some cops is that they don't make the shift from dealing with guys like him to dealing with people like her."

Despite this environment of danger and distrust, residents marched to take back their streets in the bleakest years of the crack epidemic. In the snows of January 1986, carrying signs that read "Drugs kill" and "No renting to pushers," chanting "Children yes, drugs no," they marched from 157th and Broadway to the police station at 182nd and Wadsworth. They were residents of the southern Heights, elected officials, and activists. At 181st and Broadway, they stopped to hear State Senator Leichter and Assemblyman Murtaugh demand police action to root out the drug trade. The marchers were battling a business made possible by violent dealers, high demand from drug users inside and outside the city, an overwhelmed criminal justice system, and a skewed urban economy that made the gains of drug dealing attractive to young men who wanted money in a hurry.[37]

The marchers of January 1986 were not alone. From the mid-1980s into the early 1990s, as murders soared in Washington Heights, Moisés Pérez of the Alianza Dominicana watched meetings on the crack crisis draw ten people, then twenty-five, then finally enough to stage a march up Broadway.

Protestors carried pictures of the people lost to drugs and the names of mothers who had lost a daughter or a son to the violence that surrounded the drug trade. Others marched on other days, among them the Community League of West 159th Street, the Dominican Women's Development Center, and the Asociación Comunal de Dominicanos Progresistas. At Saint Elizabeth's Church, on Wadsworth Avenue just below 187th Street, Msgr. Joachim Beaumont, from Spain, led his Dominican parishioners, clergy of all faiths, and elected officials on a march against the crack trade. They walked north along Wadsworth, pausing at buildings where dealers worked to identify the source of the plague in their community and show people that it was possible to fight the drug trade. Beaumont went further: he opened up his church, redefined it as a public hall, and invited everyone in to discuss the problem that afflicted them all.

Residents offered their own suggestions to fight crime. One idea, which drew on knowledge of local geography and gained favor as the situation worsened, was to divide the 34th Precinct into two. The 34th, from 155th Street north to the tip of Inwood, was difficult to police. Yet if the same area were divided into two precincts, greater police efforts could be brought to bear on trouble spots. Officers might be able to become better acquainted with residents. Equally significant for crime statistics and perceptions, the move would separate the southern Heights—long a trouble spot for crime—from the comparatively safer areas of the northern Heights and Inwood. In one stroke, the residents of the upper part of the Heights and Inwood would see themselves as inhabitants of a statistically safer neighborhood.

Turning such proposals into policies and realities took time. Individual residents could act more quickly as they wrestled with whether to stay in the neighborhood or leave.[38] Compared to the Jews and Irish who left northern Manhattan in the 1960s and 1970s, the Dominicans who faced the crime and violence of the crack years had few suburban options. In general blacks and Latinos did not enjoy the same access to suburbia as whites. Lower wages, difficulties getting mortgages, and outright racial discrimination often locked them into New York City. The white ring around Gotham trapped many Dominicans in New York. Some, however, moved to smaller American cities, like Lawrence, Massachusetts, that offered the prospect of jobs and safer neighborhoods.[39]

For some Dominicans, the uncertain prospects of New York City in the crack years were a reason to keep up ties to the Dominican Republic. Among the small but conspicuous criminal element in the Dominican community, a flight to the Dominican Republic was a way to invest ill-gotten gains, evade prosecution in the United States, or simply live in luxury far from a dangerous workplace. Far more common was the tendency of ordinary Dominicans to maintain lives in two countries, driven by love for the Dominican Republic and frustrations in the United States, in the hopes that the merits of one country would compensate for the demerits of the other. Entrepreneurs could invest in businesses. Aspiring homeowners could buy or build a dwelling of their own. Political people could maintain ties with the parties at home. Overworked residents of the Heights who missed their families could fly home, laden with gifts, for extended vacations. Parents who thought the New York streets corrupted their children sent them back to spend times with relatives in the hopes that they would acquire proper behavior and good character.[40]

In the Dominican Republic, overworked office cleaners from New York could see the walls rise in a house where they hoped to someday enjoy family vacations. In the meantime, though, the money that went into a house in the Dominican Republic was not available to make life easier in New York. Moreover, balancing lives between the Dominican Republic and the United States could leave Dominicans vulnerable to problems in both countries. As the sociologist Peggy Levitt has observed, "Transnational migration opens up opportunities for some and constitutes a deal with the devil for others. One factor shaping this relationship is class. Those who start with more generally finish with more."[41]

The Dominican film *Nueba Yol*, released in 1995, presented a bleak view of a Dominican immigrant's life in New York City. The film featured Luisito Martí, a major actor and comedian in the Dominican Republic, in the role of Balbuena, a widower with poor economic prospects in the Dominican Republic who travels to New York on a forged visa in hopes of getting rich. In New York Balbuena meets a woman he eventually marries, but overall he experiences the city as a dangerous and exploitative place that destroys the bonds of Dominican families, instills bad manners in Dominican children, and turns immigrants into criminals. The "important thing" about New York, he concludes bitterly, is going home to the Dominican Republic "with a clear conscience." That Balbuena does, after narrowly surviving a robbery and a shootout.[42]

Staying in Washington Heights was much more complex than leaving, especially if you wanted to try to do something about the problems of crime and fear. Barbara K. Lundblad, pastor of Our Savior's Atonement Lutheran Church, recalled that older women could not attend evening meetings of any kind unless someone drove them. Residents of Manhattan north of Dyckman Street would emphasize that they were from Inwood, and not Washington Heights, because they did not want to be associated with what one policeman called "the crack capital of the world." The historian Deborah

Dash Moore, who moved to 620 Fort Washington Avenue in 1981, recalls that friends downtown would not travel north to visit her. After a gunman shot up the streets around Yeshiva University three times, the school narrowed the stretch of Amsterdam Avenue that ran through its campus to two lanes and created a pedestrian mall alongside it. The goal was a more secure campus, but the change prompted charges that the university was a bad neighbor that took away parking spaces.[43]

In a time of fear, taking action could give people a sense that they were not helpless. Some residents organized in their apartment buildings. Moore's building on upper Fort Washington Avenue, which housed so many Jewish clergymen that it was informally called "the Rabbi's Building," was also the home of a Jewish crack addict who lived on her floor; she saw the vials he dropped in the snow. She talked to the addict's mother, explained her concerns, and ensured that no harm came to her children from the addict or his dubious visitors. When another tenant was mugged in the entrance, residents pooled their money and matched the landlord's contribution to hire a guard at night. He was so old that he posed no threat to a robber, but he gave residents a feeling that they could regain control over their homes and their lives.[44]

By itself, protecting yourself or your building from crime did not reduce the isolation that made the years of high crime so bleak. Strengthening the fabric of northern Manhattan's beleaguered communities meant looking outward—which did not always come naturally in Washington Heights. Yet this is exactly what was done during the mid-1980s and 1990s at Beth Am, The People's Temple. The Reform synagogue, seeking to rebuild itself and rebuild the community around it, worked to connect Jews, Christians, and Dominicans in everything from religion to politics.[45]

Beth Am, founded in Inwood in 1950, had once been a large and vigorous congregation. By the time I discovered it in 1989, however, it had left behind its old home and rented space in the Cornerstone Center on Bennett Avenue, owned by Our Savior's Atonement Lutheran Church. Beth Am was smaller than it was during its Inwood days, but its members and rabbi, Margaret Moers Wenig, made up in energy and ideas for what the congregation lacked in size.[46]

Rabbi Wenig began her time at Beth Am in 1984, where she found a small but smart congregation—including some elderly German Jews—living through the transformation of Washington Heights. Creatively invoking the Hebrew maxim of *al tifrosh min ha tzidur*, or "don't separate yourself from the community," she resolved to keep Beth Am in touch with its community—as broadly defined as possible—as it changed.[47]

In eclectic and intellectually challenging services that drew on everything from Orthodoxy to old Reform practices, she pushed worshippers to expand their ideas about Judaism. She encouraged Beth Am to discuss Judaism's understandings of life after death. In an acclaimed sermon, she asked us to think of God not as an all-powerful patriarch, but as an aging woman who longs for company. In sermons and discussions, refugees and the children of refugees exchanged stories that they had never told anyone. Guest lecturers expanded worshippers' sense of their community. A homeless man who lived at the Armory shelter in Washington Heights, Patrick Flanagan, described his life in detail. (He enjoyed the experience so much that he eventually converted to Judaism.) With Rev. Lundblad, Beth Am organized services on Thanksgiving and Martin Luther King Day with the Lutherans and Urdu-speaking Seventh Day Adventists who also worshipped at the Cornerstone Center. With the ACDP, one of the major Dominican organizations in northern Manhattan, Beth Am members worked to improve public education in the neighborhood.[48]

Efforts to make the synagogue a place "where gay and straight folks feel equally at home" prompted some criticisms. Over time, however, and sometimes to their mutual surprise, older and younger members discovered how much they had in common. After a gay man who belonged to Beth Am was attacked and beaten as he walked out of Fort Tryon Park, members of the temple's sisterhood brought him cooked meals while he recovered. One sisterhood member, a former refugee from Germany, said, "I know what it means to be beaten in the streets simply because of who you are."[49]

Beth Am did have its share of disappointments. Efforts to bring Soviet Jews into the congregation foundered on their transience in the neighborhood and their lack of a Jewish identity grounded in religion. And even though Beth Am recruited many new members and revived its Hebrew school, its finances remained precarious.

Interfaith work in northern Manhattan wasn't always easy, but it was rewarding. As my Episcopalian wife observed at a Beth Am service with a Dominican Pentecostal congregation—an event marked by awkwardness, warmth, and welcomes—sometimes singing off-key is the first step to harmony. In a neighborhood where Jews were sometimes depicted as being locked in enduring conflicts with Dominicans, the work of Beth Am—like that of the YM-YWHA—showed that it was possible to be both proudly Jewish and concerned with the welfare of the entire community. In recognition of Beth Am's good works, the Religious Action Center of Reform Judaism gave the congregation its Irving J. Fain Award for achievements in social action.

Around the same time, some Dominican residents of northern Manhattan took on the crack trade. At the Alianza Dominicana, a woman who lost her grandson to drug violence helped organize a neighborhood chapter of Mothers Against Violence. In Highbridge Park, where a playground at 180th

Street was adjacent to an encampment of drug addicts, Mothers Against Violence sought help for the addicts while taking control of the playground gate. Under their watchful eyes, only people accompanied by children were allowed to enter. A press conference with elected officials and calls to the parks commissioner followed, and the playground was returned to the use of children and families. Here, in a new context, were mothers acting as the defenders of the neighborhood.[50]

Other actions against drug dealing grew out of networks formed in schools, the local school board, and social services. Al Kurland, an educator and neighborhood activist whose own politics inclined to the left of the American mainstream, worked with an array of Heights residents to strengthen the bonds of a shaken community. (Albert Blumberg convinced him of the value of making principled compromises to work within the system and persuaded him to join the Audubon Democrats.) Kurland and the Dominican activist Maria Luna worked together to found the Riverside Neighborhood Security Association (RNSA), which brought residents and police together to address local problems. In a time when opponents of the drug dealers faced the threat of retaliation, Kurland was awed by the determination and courage of people who responded to RNSA fliers and attended its monthly meetings. The RNSA collected three thousand petition signatures and some thirty letters of institutional support that State Assemblyman Denny Farrell used to press for an increased police presence to fight the drug trade in the neighborhood. The violence, subterfuge, and fear of the crack years destroyed trust between people in the Heights, Kurland explained, which made it all the more important to build and maintain bonds between those who could be trusted. Police officer Tommy Gallagher met with the RNSA to discuss combining anticrime activity with tenant organizing to bring people together for mutual support.[51]

Dave Crenshaw and Kurland's work brought them into contact with Blanca Battino, principal of PS 128 at 560 W. 169 Street. Battino, a Puerto Rican from the Chelsea section of Manhattan, was a proud product of Cathedral High School, Hunter College, and New York University. She had taught at PS 25 in the South Bronx, where Principal Hernan LaFontaine affirmed the value of bilingual education and "teaching the whole child." At PS 128, Battino forged a school that blended progressive ideas about active learning, traditional ideas about standards and accountability, and extensive outreach into Washington Heights. Her allies included Kurland and Crenshaw, who in 1984 created a youth program that brought together (in the intricately divided world of the Heights) two groups of kids who might never have met or, worse, met under unfriendly circumstances: Dominican teenagers from the West 170s and African American teens from the West 160s.

Crenshaw, the son of the school board member Gwen Crenshaw and the political activist Richard Crenshaw, worked with Kurland to organize athletic programs in the southern Heights that gave kids an alternative to the crack world. Crenshaw, known in this neighborhood as "Coach," understood that while drug dealers might organize barbecues or basketball tournaments for their blocks, it was never at any great economic cost to themselves and was, in effect, a way of bribing people to look the other way. Moreover, in their control of the streets and apartment buildings, dealers took away kids' opportunity to play in the streets, on rooftops, and in basements. After Crenshaw and Kurland worked with teens to clean up a grimy, underused playground at 165th and Edgecombe, they ran basketball tournaments and at night showed movies by projecting them on the wall of a handball court. Kurland and Crenshaw's programs stressed education, athletics, community service, and equality for girls. Calvin Thomas credits Crenshaw with nurturing a work ethic that carried him from athletics to after-school jobs to a career as a police officer and a retirement career running a small business. Gustavo Cruz, another alumnus, went on to run Police Athletic League youth programs at the Washington Heights Armory.[52]

Programs grounded in PS 128 eventually attracted wide-ranging support, including Yankees star Derek Jeter's Turn 2 Foundation. Battino broke the barrier between Columbia Presbyterian and its surrounding neighborhood, enlisting the help of Dr. Mary McCord at the hospital to get medical care for her students. Eventually, Columbia Presbyterian and the Turn 2 Foundation mounted a major effort out of PS 128 to promote "health and education in northern Manhattan."[53]

In a changing neighborhood under stress, it was difficult to translate your own particular experience into something that invited other people to make common cause. Concern about crime was widespread, and by the 1990s liberal Democrats and conservatives alike saw effective policing as part of the solution. Yet liberals and conservatives differed over how the ethnic changes in Washington Heights and Inwood intersected with the rise in crime.

In the *Heights Citizen and Inwood News* in 1990, Bob Grant of Inwood looked at the neighborhood around him in disgust and saw the solutions in capital punishment, prisons, and less concern for "oppressed youth."

In the New York of the 90's our senses are assaulted 1000 times a day. Loud music, which we don't want to hear, is blared at us. Our eyes are offended by the ugly graffiti that is everywhere. You have to hold your nose every time you enter a subway, but keep your eyes open, as your chances of being mugged are increasing every day.

What went wrong? Liberalism—that's what.

Grant received a response in the next issue from Michael Cohn, a German Jew who had immigrated to Washington Heights in the 1930s. Cohn, the son of a German leftist, served in the U.S. Army in World War II, married, and eventually settled in Washington Heights—where he and his wife found a political home in a club of Reform Democrats around William F. Ryan. He had been mugged and didn't like it, but he was still proud to call himself a liberal Democrat and a union member. "I am an immigrant," he wrote in response to Grant.

> As an immigrant I wasn't always popular in Washington Heights. Like all immigrants, we jammed too many people in one apartment. We talked German on the streets. I am confident that the new immigrants, like ourselves, will learn English without having to give up all of their former cultures. It will take awhile, it always has.
>
> As a liberal I have made mistakes, no question. But I prefer to go forward as a liberal Mrs. Roosevelt said while campaigning in Washington Heights, "Let us light a candle rather than curse the darkness."[54]

Cohn's letter attempted to match the highest ideals of his liberalism with the problems of the 1990s. It was a good credo for his life as an activist, author, archaeologist, and historian, but it couldn't keep him and his wife in Washington Heights. Eventually, muggings and hassles were too much. Cohn and his wife left for the safety of a doorman building on the Upper East Side.[55]

Against all odds, the inclusive and optimistic spirit that informed Cohn's letter took physical form in Coogan's, a bar and restaurant at 4015 Broadway and West 169th Street that opened in 1985. Named after the nearby Coogan's Bluff, where sports fans once gathered to look down into the old Polo Grounds, Coogan's flowered under the leadership of Tess O'Connor McDade, who immigrated from Ireland in 1988, and her two more visible partners, David Hunt and Peter Walsh. Hunt, from Inwood, had taught migrant farmworkers' children in Wisconsin as a VISTA volunteer in the 1960s and then worked as a bartender in Greenwich Village. Walsh, a singer and Marist College graduate, ran race relations workshops for the Army during the Vietnam War, when tensions between black and white GIs reached explosive proportions. (He was a conservative when he enlisted, but he joked years later that wartime service made him a liberal.) He earned an MA in theater and literature at Trinity College in Dublin, studied further at NYU, and for a time owned a pub in lower Manhattan. Both men brought something of their earlier lives to the job. Hunt, who had studied sociology and urban studies at Fordham, found that running a saloon was "a living sociology experiment." Walsh turned the back room of Coogan's into a theater and staged plays and poetry readings.[56]

Coogan's initial prospects were daunting. Drug dealers worked nearby streets, and the armory across 169th Street was the site of a large homeless shelter. Walsh and Hunt, however, recognized that Washington Heights was more than the sum of its problems. By recruiting as customers Columbia-Presbyterian employees next door and police officers on their way home to the suburbs, Hunt and Walsh turned Coogan's into one of the most amiably integrated institutions in the city of New York. The walls at Coogan's, which displayed everything from street signs to photos of politicians to runners' jerseys, became a gallery that revealed layers of the neighborhood's history. Heights residents, off-duty police officers, Irish Americans, Dominican politicians, neighborhood activists, elected officials, and Van Morrison all found their way to Coogan's.

Irish life in northern Manhattan, with its awareness of parish boundaries and neighborhood loyalties, always had a strong territorial dimension. The founders of Coogan's took that tendency in a new direction: they claimed the corner of 169th and Broadway and then, instead of defending it against all comers, invited in the whole world. There were many sources for Coogan's success, but most important was that it was centrally located (next to the 168th Street subway station where the A and 1 trains intersect), very Irish, and very inclusive. Whoever you were, you could find a place at the bar, a table for dinner, and a picture on the wall that reminded you of someone you knew.

Coogan's was an oasis of safety, but danger loomed a short walk away, as Jose Reyes learned in 1991. Reyes and other residents took comfort from the fact that the murders and robberies that surrounded the drug business were largely confined to the east side of Broadway. Living west of Broadway with his sister Nellie, at 614 W. 157th Street, Reyes had reason to think of himself as being in a safe zone.

A slender man with gray hair, Reyes was born in Coamo, Puerto Rico. He attended college in Chicago and settled in New York. He worked ten years for the city's welfare department and then twenty years with an import-export firm. Even in retirement, he still had a social worker's way about him. He was cheerful, outgoing to the point of sticking his nose in other people's business, and concerned about the welfare of his neighborhood. He used his knowledge of English and Spanish to help neighbors in transactions with businesses or city government; he busied himself so much around his apartment building that one man mistook him for the super. In a neighborhood of changes and dangers, he was a one-man force for friendliness and stability.[57] And that put him on a collision course with a crew of drug dealers called the Jheri Curls.

The Jheri Curls worked out of apartments in 550 W. 157th Street, on the east side of Broadway. In an industry where presence and reputation were important, they sported haircuts with close-cropped sides and longer, curly hair on the top of their heads, all of it made shiny with hair styling gel that gave them their name. The leader of the Jheri Curls was Rafael Martinez, who arrived in New York from the Dominican Republic illegally in the mid-1980s when he was still a teenager. He first gained a reputation as a car thief but later moved into the drug business.

In the fragmented geography of Washington Heights, the Jheri Curls were well outside of Reyes's world as long as they stayed east of Broadway. But in the early months of 1991, in the wake of police searches at 550 W. 157th Street, the Jheri Curls sought new surroundings just west of Broadway. They congregated outside 600 W. 157th Street and worked out of an apartment at 614 W. 157th, where Reyes and his sister lived.[58]

On West 157th Street, as in other parts of Washington Heights, some people coped with dealers by learning to see and not see, as a sociologist who studied the neighborhood observed. The dealers' capacity for violence against informers was well known, and the police couldn't guarantee people's safety. Officer James Gilmore, an African American community policing officer with a firm bearing, whose beat included West 157th, would stand in front of the Jheri Curls' old building for hours at a time to drive them and their customers away. But there were still plenty of hours in a day when he wasn't around and residents were at the Jheri Curls' mercy. Most avoided the gang members or treated them with deference.[59]

As the whispered tips and surreptitious photographs delivered to Officer Gilmore suggested, there were, in fact, people in the neighborhood who wanted the Jheri Curls put out of business. The boldest of them was Jose Reyes.[60]

When the Jheri Curls appeared in his building, Reyes spoke to them. They found his intervention laughable and irritating. Then Reyes posted flyers in the elevator and on the first floor: he announced the presence of drug dealers and invited fellow tenants to meet to clean up the building. (The Jheri Curls tore down the signs.)[61] Policemen augmented Reyes's efforts. Officer Gilmore went outside the boundaries of his beat and followed the Jheri Curls to 614 W. 157th. There, he spoke with tenants and found evidence of drug dealing in apartment 4B. Officer Thomas Hilbert, another community policing officer whose beat encompassed 614 W. 157th, undertook repeat visits to 4B, made arrests, and changed the locks on the door. The Jheri Curls wouldn't back down. On Hilbert's fourth visit to the apartment, on May 7, he cut a hole in the wall outside of the door jam, then ran a chain through it and out through a hole in the door. Then he padlocked the door shut.

The Jheri Curls sensed that the police weren't acting alone. There was talk about a *chota*, an informer in the building, who was talking to the police.[62] On the afternoon of May 23, 1991, Jose Reyes went out for his usual walk and stopped for coffee at a doughnut shop on Broadway at West 158th Street. Around 4 p.m., when he left the shop and resumed his walk up the west side of Broadway, a gunman fired a bullet into the back of his head.[63] Reyes fell face down on the sidewalk. A woman screamed. The gunman fled without stopping to take the money in Reyes's pockets.[64]

Police officer Paul Bailey, dispatched to the scene, dispersed the crowd that had gathered. The emergency medical service took Reyes to the hospital, where he was pronounced dead on arrival.[65] Police investigations were hampered by one problem: in a murder that took place in broad daylight on a busy street, witnesses were reluctant to describe the shooting.[66]

Reyes's death took place on the west side of Broadway, which was widely understood to be the safe side of Broadway. The crack trade had come to him, however, in the person of the Jheri Curls. Reyes's death was a reminder not only of his own individual courage, but of the crack trade's ability to cast a shadow over parts of Washington Heights that were far from the drug trade's epicenter. Leo Fuentes, for example, lived on Wadsworth Avenue near 192nd Street, more than a mile from the acknowledged center of the crack trade. Yet even at that distance, the presence of the crack heads, dealers, and police made life on his block feel like "living under siege."

As the crack trade choked his neighborhood, Fuentes found a way out through school. While he had some good teachers in elementary school, his life was transformed when he arrived at the Bronx High School of Science. An African American youth there from Harlem introduced him to *The Autobiography of Malcolm X*. The book got Fuentes thinking about politics, culture, and his own place in the world. He gravitated to the world of hip-hop in the spirit of knowing himself and his history.

As the July 4 weekend began in 1992, Fuentes, equipped with a camera and accompanied by a friend, walked downtown at night. The atmosphere in Washington Heights in those years was normally vibrant, but he sensed anger in the air. When they reached 163rd Street, he was astonished to see the "street cats" battling the police—throwing bottles at them and setting fire to anything that would burn. Fuentes wasn't sure exactly what was happening, but he sensed that it was important. He took out his camera and started to take pictures.

He later learned that a police officer had shot and killed a Dominican man, Jose Garcia, nicknamed "Kiko." The police officer was Michael O'Keefe, a member of the 34th Precinct's anticrime unit, which was nicknamed "Local Motion." Police officers admired O'Keefe's reputation for toughness in the pursuit of criminals, but some residents complained he was rough in making arrests and a judge once reprimanded him for being evasive on the witness stand. That night, rumors spread quickly. Within twenty-four hours, streets near the shooting were littered with garbage and broken glass. Outside 505 W. 162nd Street, where Garcia was slain, people built the kind of sidewalk memorial that had become all too common in the crack years: two photographs surrounded by white candles and wreaths of flowers.[67] The dead man's relatives and neighbors told reporters that Garcia was beaten and executed while he pleaded for mercy. The police department said little, largely because O'Keefe was on sick leave and had not yet been interviewed. On Monday morning, suspicions and fears took the form of blazing tabloid headlines. In the *Daily News*, "HE BEGGED FOR LIFE" stretched above a photograph of a young woman carrying a baby past a wall bearing a message written in Garcia's blood: "KIKO WE LOVE YOU." In the *New York Post*, the headline "NAPALM THE HOOD" summed up an officer's wisecrack heard over a police radio.[68]

For the next two days, demonstrators, rioters, police, residents, elected officials, and mediators were embroiled in tense, volatile confrontations. Dominicans carried Dominican flags in their protests, expressing both unity

Figure 11: Demonstration after the shooting of Kiko Garcia, 1992. Photograph by Ricky Flores.

and a wounded sense of national pride that was not open to redress in the legal confines of the episode. Police officers criticized Mayor Dinkins for giving them insufficient support in the case, releasing stored-up anger that spoke volumes about how they felt about their work and the mayor. Neither group got exactly what it hoped for. Police officers wanted backup that reached all the way to city hall. The most vocal Dominican residents of the Heights wanted justice, which many seemed to define as the conviction of O'Keefe. Anyone who attempted to mediate between these two perspectives was likely to disappoint someone.

On Monday Mayor Dinkins met with Garcia's family and told them there would be a complete investigation of the shooting. In an effort to calm things, the Dinkins administration covered the cost of the funeral and shipment of Garcia's body home to the Dominican Republic. Most news coverage viewed O'Keefe through suspicions of police brutality and corruption, even though Ray Kelly, the department's first deputy commissioner, defended O'Keefe as an "aggressive, active and good officer." Garcia was depicted as the son of a grieving family and community.

Local elected officials—including Guillermo Linares, the Dominican-born city councilman; City Councilman Stanley Michels, who represented the western part of northern Manhattan; and Manhattan borough president Ruth Messinger—tried to calm the crowds. One reporter noted Linares, an uncomfortable look on his face, carrying two Dominican flags, as he unsuccessfully tried to lead demonstrators in a peaceful direction. Linares, Michels, and Messinger, with some Latino officials from the Dinkins administration, locked arms to separate the crowd and the cops in a confrontation on 181st Street, Juan Gonzalez of the *Daily News* reported. Then protestors threw bottles at the police, taunts ripped the air, and the thin line of officeholders lost any semblance of control.[69]

Crowds smashed windows, looted stores, overturned trashcans, and broke windshields. By 9 p.m., Audubon Avenue north of 162nd Street was thick with black smoke from fires in automobiles and trashcans. As a police copter hovered overhead, firefighters fought blazes. Rioters threw bottles and rocks and squads of police officers chased after them. At 145 Audubon Avenue, a bottle thrower in flight from the police, Dagoberto Pichardo, fell to his death; early reports repeated residents' claims that he had been pushed.[70] Mayor Dinkins broadcast a fifteen-minute appeal for calm on the Spanish-language television station, WXTV, but rioting reached as far south as 135th Street.

On Tuesday morning Dinkins released a statement. Describing himself as a "longtime resident" of Washington Heights who had raised a family there, he said it hurt him "deeply" to see the neighborhood damaged. "Last night, the violence that erupted was absolutely unacceptable. Let me be clear: it must stop—and it will stop," he said. He acknowledged anger at "the death of Jose Garcia and other incidents" but added, "You do not obtain justice by being unjust to others." He described "the vast majority" of New York's police as "brave, hard-working, dedicated public servants" who were "heroes and role models for the rest of us." He promised to deal with "the handful" that were not, but added it was "wrong to hold the actions of the few as representatives of the many."[71]

At a packed forum, Cardinal John O'Connor proclaimed his absolute trust in the mayor and pledged to see the crisis through. In the streets Pete Hamill of the *New York Post* watched protestors fill St. Nicholas Avenue, pumping their fists in the air as they chanted "*Justicia, justicia, justicia, justicia.*" He noticed one teenager—"part act, part heat, part a kid trying to be a man"—taunt impassive police officers with, "Watch yo ass tonight, *maricón.*"[72]

Craig Wolff of the *Times* saw police officers report to a "station house under siege" at the 34th Precinct. One officer, insisting on anonymity, said to him: "Before all the lights and cameras come up here, you should know this: We've been up here for a long time fighting this fight. You want to join the bandwagon that all cops here are bad and dirty, go ahead, but the truth is, most of us are just plain scared."[73]

Members of community organizations and elected officials worked to keep the peace. The Alianza Dominicana sent out people; Milagros Batista recalls with pride that members of Mothers Against Violence joined hands around an excavation site so that young people could not pick up rocks and throw them at the police. Informal efforts helped as well: Assemblyman Brian Murtagh noticed Dominican families keeping watch over their blocks. Calvin Thomas, a police officer raised in the southeast Heights and a graduate of Dave Crenshaw's "Dreamers" program, saw African American men on the edge of Sugar Hill standing outside to keep things calm. Despite all such efforts, however, hurled bottles, cars set aflame, and gunshots made cops edgy and fearful.[74]

On Tuesday night, a crowd marched from the Rivera Funeral Home on St. Nicholas Avenue, the setting of Garcia's wake, to 162nd Street. There, the bad-mouthing and garbage can fires of earlier nights resumed. Unlike other nights, it got no worse. On Wednesday morning, reporters noted that the riotous sections of the Heights were beginning to calm down. Some residents even chatted amiably with the police. When Mayor Dinkins walked along 181st Street with Police Commissioner Brown and the salsa star Willie Colón, he was met with smiles. At the 34th Precinct, however, officers were angry that the mayor had met with Garcia's family and angry that he had paid for his funeral. The mayor's argument that paying for the funeral defused the situation in northern Manhattan did not change their feelings. Neither did subsequent announcements that the city would send more officers to the precinct, institute courses in Dominican culture and history to improve relations between officers and residents, and perhaps even divide it into two precincts that could be more effectively policed.[75]

A battle fought with bottles and nightsticks morphed into a war of words.[76] In the *Daily News*, Manhattan borough president Messinger, an ally of both the mayor and Councilman Linares, argued that the events of July needed to be understood not just in the context of crime and drugs, but in the city's neglect of schools, youth services, housing, and health services in northern Manhattan. In the *New York Times*, Dinkins' former electoral opponent Giuliani argued that the mayor had undermined the police, turned Jose Garcia into a martyr despite evidence that he was a drug dealer, and once again "ceded neighborhoods to the forces of lawlessness."[77]

In September, a grand jury provided answers to festering questions. District Attorney Robert Morgenthau announced that criminal charges would *not* be brought against Officer O'Keefe in the death of Jose Garcia or against Lieutenant Roger Parrino in the death of Dagoberto Pichardo. The man who accused Parrino of pushing Pichardo to his death admitted that he was lying. Evidence supported O'Keefe's claim that he shot Garcia (a drug dealer who chronically inhaled his own product) in a legitimate struggle and contradicted the women who accused the officer of beating and executing Garcia. "Moreover," Morgenthau concluded, "transmissions broadcast by Officer O'Keefe over his police radio reveal an officer in the midst of a struggle, desperate and frightened—not one engaged in an unprovoked assault and about to shoot an unconscious man."[78]

Immediately after the verdict was released, Dinkins went to Washington Heights, walked along 181st Street and visited the 34th Precinct. One of the officers there, Thomas Barnett, had already published a statement in a neighborhood newspaper criticizing Dinkins for consoling the Garcia family and accusing him of condemning Officer O'Keefe without the facts. Addressing officers at roll call, Dinkins acknowledged that they had difficult jobs and praised them for putting themselves "between good citizens and lawlessness." Barnett cut him off and said, "I believe you're an honest, sincere, caring man, but what you did that day still leaves a sour taste in our mouths." Barnett was referring to Dinkins's meetings with the Garcia family.

"I'm older than I guess anyone in this room," Dinkins said, "and I've been around a long time. People die in riots, you know. Sometimes there are police officers who die in riots," he said. "It's utter bullshit to suggest that if you comfort a family that you have taken sides against a police officer."

"That's the way it looked to us," replied Barnett.

Dinkins, with rising anger, reminded the officers that he had expanded the police department, even when other city agencies were suffering budget cuts, in the face of criticism that his cuts were "taking milk away from little babies."

"Where is it that I am the enemy of the police officers?" Dinkins said. "The one who has stood up and produced more for the Police Department than anybody in recent years. Now you may continue to feel the way you do until the day you die and the day I die, but sir, you are wrong. You are dead wrong. And so, I am going to continue to do what I think is right."[79]

Fuentes came away from the nights of rioting with photographs of a burning car, smashed windows, and a shattered bus stop. He could not fully grasp what he had witnessed, but he knew it would have an impact on his neighborhood. The city's press, at least in its initial coverage of the crisis, had not been much help in figuring out what was happening. In retrospect, as newspaper columnists and media critics argued, the early coverage of the shooting in the Heights assumed the best of Garcia and the worst of O'Keefe. There was every reason to investigate an allegation of a policeman shooting an unarmed man, but too often the coverage of the shooting suggested that O'Keefe was guilty. Mayor Dinkins's attention to Garcia's family probably helped keep the rioting from getting worse, but the absence of mayoral attention to O'Keefe could be interpreted as a sign that there was really only one suffering party in this death—the Garcia family. O'Keefe was written out of the circle of official sympathy. Equally important, the police department was slow to release the recordings of police radio transmissions that would have clarified the situation and changed perceptions of O'Keefe.[80]

Writing in *New York Newsday*, Murray Kempton found the grand jury's verdict sound, but feared that the events in Washington Heights cast a deep shadow over the future.[81] "What remains intractably unresolved in this report," he wrote, "is the impossibility of the rule of law in a city where all sense of common community has given way to tribal passions. Every tribe is alien to the other on streets like these; when the neighborhood looks at the policeman and the policeman looks at the neighborhood, each sees no more than a dangerous animal."

The 1992 rioting in Washington Heights was hardly the worst seen in the nation that year. In Los Angeles, only two months before the events that scarred northern Manhattan, more than sixty people died in rioting after the acquittal of police officers on charges of using excessive force to subdue an African American, Rodney King. The outbreak in Washington Heights was limited and far less deadly. Dominican traditions of protest that stopped short of deadly violence, honed in confrontations with repressive governments in the Dominican Republic, were acted out on the streets of northern

Manhattan in ways that stopped short of the worst possibilities. The NYPD acted with strength and relative restraint, making it clear—without forcing an all-out confrontation—that violence would be contained and put down. There was no shortage of firearms in Washington Heights that summer, but armed residents and police officers held back from an outright gun battle. Some of the credit for this should go to the peacemaking efforts of the Dinkins administration and the presence of cool heads in the neighborhood.

Yet Dinkins, who was praised for keeping the peace in New York during the Los Angeles riots, cooled the rioting in northern Manhattan only to face condemnation from police officers. Police and angry residents of northern Manhattan may have stepped back from an abyss, but they were hardly on good terms. Indeed, even though O'Keefe was vindicated, the relative ease with which people accepted the earliest version of events—the false claim that a policeman had executed an unarmed man—suggested a deep strain of skepticism about the NYPD. The crack years had tarnished more than Washington Heights. After years of murder and drug dealing in northern Manhattan, people were willing to believe the worst of both Dominicans and police officers.[82]

Within a week of the grand jury report, some ten thousand off-duty police officers demonstrated at city hall to oppose Mayor Dinkins's plan to create a civilian review board to monitor police conduct. Some carried signs that said: "Dinkins, We Know Your True Color—Yellow-Bellied," "Dear Mayor, have you hugged a drug dealer today," and "Dump the Washroom Attendant."[83]

The march soon lost discipline. One faction broke away and surged up the steps of city hall, stopped only by barred doors. Other demonstrators moved west of the city hall complex, drank beer, and listened to speakers—among them a vocal Giuliani, who said the mayor was "trying to protect his political ass" and who dismissed Dinkins's efforts as "bullshit." A third group stormed onto the Brooklyn Bridge and blocked traffic. In a preliminary report, Acting Police Commissioner Kelly called the demonstration "unruly, mean-spirited and perhaps criminal."[84]

Faced with such opposition, the Dinkins administration scored two victories in its attempts to rein in police misconduct. Three months after the unruly police demonstration at city hall, the city council approved a new civilian review board by a vote of 41–9. In September 1993, the Mollen Commission, named for Dinkins's deputy mayor for public safety, Milton Mollen, held public hearings that exposed police brutality, corrupt officers' involvement in the drug trade, the loneliness of honest officers in bad situations, and the department's inability to police its own officers. Testimony also illuminated the often tense relationship between police officers and the public, especially in dangerous precincts where officers often viewed residents with suspicion and embraced an "us versus them" mentality behind a "blue wall of silence." It was the most searching and searing examination of police corruption since the Knapp Commission during the Lindsay administration. Yet neither the civilian review board nor the Mollen Commission succeeded in improving the tormented relationship between the police and the communities they patrolled—especially in Washington Heights.[85]

One night in October 1993, the evening after the Mollen Commission adjourned, police officer John Williamson was called away from his normal duties patrolling for the Housing Authority and sent to West 175th Street to calm residents who were angry that the Department of Transportation was towing double- and triple-parked cars. The department had made a point of enforcing parking regulations in the neighborhood since 1987, after a two-year-old Heights boy died in a fire when illegally parked cars delayed the arrival of firefighters. Since then, the towing had spawned confrontations between residents, police, and tow truck operators. Williamson was walking into a difficult situation. In addition to the towing disputes, the local mood was soured by a recent clash between residents and authorities after a police car in pursuit of a suspect struck and killed a motorcyclist. In the tensions that followed in the neighborhood, a Bronx man threw a Molotov cocktail at a fire truck. Three firefighters were burned, two of them seriously.[86]

Despite the bad mood on the streets, all seemed to go reasonably well. Then, as Officer Williamson headed toward his patrol car, someone dropped a thirty-pound bucket of Spackle from a roof six floors above, killing the officer. At the Church of the Incarnation, where the death of Michael Farmer was mourned in 1957, Msgr. Gerald T. Walsh offered a mass with two intentions. "One is for peace in the neighborhood," he said. "The other is for the soul of Officer John Williamson."

Pedro Jose Gil, who lived on West 175th Street with his girlfriend and infant daughter, was eventually convicted of manslaughter in Williamson's death and sentenced to five to fifteen years in prison. Amid confusion over whether or not the Dinkins administration was suspending the towing policy, candidate Giuliani said such a suspension would mean the city had "given in to urban terrorists." The Dinkins administration continued the towing with police officers patrolling the rooftops and helicopters hovering overhead. The mayor said the officer's death was "senseless and terrible," but warned against condemning everyone in the neighborhood. In addition to making a show of force around the towing operation, the 34th Precinct worked with Councilman Linares and the city's Human Rights Commission to reduce anger in the streets and improve relations between police and the community.[87] In Washington Heights in October of 1993, where it was possible to find people who both resented hearing their neighbors called "urban terrorists" and mourned the death of Officer Williamson, the peace held.[88]

The mayoral election came one month later. Dinkins argued that New York was a city making a comeback after difficult times. The police force was growing and crime was down. In a city where Democrats outnumbered Republicans, Dinkins stressed that his opponent was the candidate of the GOP. Giuliani, on the other hand, argued that New York had fallen into a state of crisis that could be overcome only with vigorous efforts.

Although Dinkins soundly defeated Giuliani in northern Manhattan, the citywide election was decided by the narrowest of margins. Giuliani beat Dinkins by 2 percent of the vote, roughly the same margin that Dinkins had registered in his own victory in 1989.[89] Small but significant shifts helped Giuliani. In Staten Island, a Republican stronghold where the issue of that borough's secession from New York City was on the ballot, a high turnout on the secession referendum aided Giuliani.[90]

Ironically, Mayor Dinkins—who had promised to be the toughest mayor on crime that New York had seen—had lost while delivering on many of his promises. He expanded the police force and crime was going down. At the same time, he had tried to improve relations between the police and the public. However, in cases like the riot in Crown Heights and in the police uproar over the mayor's handling of Washington Heights, the Dinkins administration appeared to be embroiled in a series of crises that it could not resolve. Crime might be down, but grim headlines and broadcasts fostered a feeling of insecurity that cost the mayor votes.

To double the irony, Dinkins—whom Giuliani criticized as overly solicitous of African American interests—lost partly because some blacks believed that the mayor had not fulfilled their expectations. The political scientist J. Phillip Thompson III, who served in the Dinkins administration, has argued that the mayor was torn between demands to "go white" or "go black." In the end, he always tried to serve more than a narrowly African American base. In the close race of 1993, it cost him.[91]

Giuliani said in his inaugural address that the years of doubt and fear were over; an era of change was about to begin. He summoned New Yorkers to dream of a better city and make it real with hard work and "one standard of fairness." (It didn't take much to imagine who the new mayor thought was not living up to proper standards.) He hailed the city's diversity as its strength, but saw even more value in the common bonds that held people together. Envisioning a city reborn, Giuliani closed by dedicating his administration to the people of New York.[92]

Like Dinkins, Giuliani committed his mayoralty to reducing crime and violence. Unlike Dinkins, he would not pursue his objective through anything that smacked of community policing. Although the Dinkins administration's Mollen Commission issued its final report in July of Giuliani's first year in office, it would have limited impact on the new mayor's administration. The Mollen Commission blamed police corruption on "greed" and opportunism, criticized the department for its inability to police itself, and recognized "a hostility and alienation between the police and community in certain precincts which breeds an 'Us and Them' mentality." The report proposed the creation of "a permanent independent oversight body," working alongside the police department yet "beyond its control," to fight corruption in the NYPD. Both Mayor Giuliani and the NYPD had no interest in suggestions of "independent oversight" of the police.[93]

Giuliani embraced a strategy of police officers as active crime fighters, guided by the strategic use of statistical intelligence and a belief that taking care of small infractions would reduce the disorder that fostered major offenses. The new mayor hired William Bratton, a career police officer who was impressed by corporate management techniques, to serve as police commissioner.[94] In his brief tenure as head of New York City's transit police, Bratton had improved morale and performance by encouraging police officers to think of themselves as law enforcement officers who attacked crime and reduced it. Especially important for Bratton's model of policing was the close statistical monitoring of patterns of crime and policing. Operating from central headquarters, department leadership could target policing strategies and demand improvements where necessary. He gave precinct commanders the freedom to devise tactics but held them accountable at headquarters.[95]

Bratton brought greater discipline, accountability, and innovation to the NYPD. He also displayed scorn for crooked cops, sympathy for honest ones, and a talent for cultivating his image in the news media.[96] Once the Bratton strategies were introduced, crime declined further. At first, the trend seemed too good to be true. It lasted, though, and Mayor Giuliani reaped enormous credit—in large measure because he made the issues of crime and policing his own. The new mayor was fierce in his defense of the police department and individual officers, but he coupled that with an insistence that he get the credit for being New York's top crime fighter. When Bratton received extensive praise, Giuliani grew jealous. Eventually, the mayor forced out Bratton and replaced him with a series of police commissioners who would be firmly under his control.[97]

Crime began to fall in Washington Heights as well, but by itself that wasn't enough to make the most troubled parts of the neighborhood feel safe for either residents or police officers. Disentangling the community from the crack epidemic and its aftereffects was a complicated business, and it didn't happen easily or all at once. Some of the episodes in the process were highly publicized, like the trials that saw the conviction of both major drug dealers and police officers charged with corruption.

The first to fall, in 1993, were the Jheri Curls—the crack crew that the retired social worker Jose Reyes had resisted with the help of police officer James Gilmore. Their conviction on drug, conspiracy, murder, and firearms charges took the crew off the streets, but with regard to Reyes the victory was incomplete. The prosecution could not find credible witnesses to testify in Reyes's death. While the authorities maintain that Reyes's killers were convicted on other charges, officially no one was punished in his death. Two years later, eight members of the Wild Cowboys, a gang with roots in the Heights that did a $16 million crack business in northern Manhattan and the South Bronx, were convicted of nine murders. Both the Jheri Curls and the Wild Cowboys met their verdicts in the courtroom of Judge Leslie Crocker Snyder, a jurist with a reputation for a no-nonsense courtroom manner and tough sentencing in drug cases. On the streets, responses to her ranged from death threats to a backhanded compliment: a heroin crew once sold bags of heroin stamped with her image and the phrase "25 to life," her typical sentence. The judge made the phrase the title of her memoir.[98]

The 34th Precinct, unlike the 30th Precinct to its south, did not see the kind of major corruption scandal that earned its neighbor the nickname of the "Dirty Thirty." In the 34th Precinct, federal investigators looked into allegations that Local Motion, the plainclothes anticrime unit embroiled in the Kiko Garcia case, had conducted illegal searches, faked arrest reports, and used unnecessary force. Of course, a New York County grand jury had exonerated Michael O'Keefe, a member of the unit, in 1992 when he was accused of executing Kiko Garcia. In 1995, however, a federal grand jury indicted a highly decorated member of the unit, Patrick Regan, on two counts of perjury. Regan's defenders, among them police officers who packed the courtroom where he was tried, called the trial unfair and wept when a jury found him guilty. Federal judges upheld the verdict on appeal.

In the same period, after years of urging by residents and public officials, the city opened the 33rd Precinct in the southern half of the Heights. The move split the territory to be policed in northern Manhattan. Starting in October 1994, one precinct, the 33rd, could concentrate on policing the troubled streets in the southern Heights.[99]

Other changes in the neighborhood were more subtle but equally important in the transformation of Washington Heights. The ravages of crack were so ugly that young people, who had seen what it did to older friends, relatives, and neighbors, turned away from the drug. Drug dealing remained in the neighborhood, but dealers started to move indoors and began to reorganize their industry so that there was less competition for territory. What went down was not so much drug use as the deadly competition between drug dealers that made Washington Heights famous for its murders. Figuring out how to apportion credit for the crime drop was complicated, but the change itself was real.

In 1990 the 34th Precinct, which covered Washington Heights and Inwood, saw 103 murders. In 1998, the same area, now covered by the 34th and 33rd precincts, saw fifteen.[100]

When the journalist James Traub walked the streets of the southeast Heights with a Spanish-speaking officer, Odanel Irias, he saw evidence of changes since the rioting that attended the death of Kiko Garcia. Drug dealing remained, Traub noted in an article published in the *New Republic* in January 1997, but much of it had been forced indoors. Far more than before, the streets belonged to the police and not to the dealers. Officer Irias was skeptical about whether the drug trade could be eliminated in the Heights, but he was convinced that his "omnipresence" in the neighborhood made a difference. When he gave men summonses for drinking on the street, their noise level went down and they stopped urinating on the sidewalk. Patting down suspects when he issued a summons made men reluctant to carry weapons on the street—which left fewer opportunities for shootings and killings. Walking the sidewalks regularly, Irias collected tips about hiding places for drugs: telephone booths, garbage cans, and the rim of an automobile roof. In earlier years, residents were afraid to be seen talking to an officer because they believed that the dealers owned the streets. In conversations with merchants, Traub sensed support for Officer Irias's work. "The police can't change the dynamic that makes places like Washington Heights ripe for violent crime"; Traub concluded, "that is, after all, the central unfulfilled task of modern liberalism. But they can change criminal behavior far more than most of us ever thought likely; and for besieged communities that is very good news indeed."[101]

Fewer murders did not, automatically, mean better relations between the police and the community around them, as officers and residents of the southern Heights learned in the death of Kevin Cedeno. Born in Trinidad, Cedeno immigrated to the United States with his mother and brother and settled into the southern Heights. Al Kurland remembers him as a kid who might have turned out okay if a few turning points had turned the other way. Detective Gilmore of the 33rd Precinct, the policeman who worked to turn around troubled kids and who had gone out of his way to help Jose Reyes resist the Jheri

Curls crew, tried to straighten him out. Nevertheless, by April 1997, Cedeno, sixteen, had served time in Spofford Juvenile Center, participated in two robberies, and was on probation.[102]

In the early morning hours of April 6, a night of drinking and partying ended with Cedeno and some friends running from a crowd of men armed with bottles and bricks. The dispute seems to have been grounded in a confrontation between African Americans and Dominicans. Cedeno went to a friend's apartment and picked up a machete that he kept there. Against his friends' advice, he went back out to confront their pursuers. By 3:30 a.m., at 162nd Street and Amsterdam Avenue, a melee was under way. A resident called the police to report what sounded like gunfire.[103]

A police officer in a squad car summoned to the scene, Anthony Pellegrini, jumped from his automobile and pursued Cedeno on foot. Pellegrini mistook Cedeno's machete, with its dark handle, for a firearm. Twice the officer called for Cedeno to stop. When Cedeno turned to his left, the officer concluded that Cedeno was turning to shoot. Pellegrini fired once. Cedeno, struck in the back, was later pronounced dead at Harlem Hospital. Initial police reports, relayed by Mayor Giuliani, incorrectly asserted that Cedeno was shot in the stomach as he lunged at a police officer.

Cedeno's neighbors set up a street altar and lit candles in his memory. His mother called for peaceful protests. The Community League of West 159th Street—which had battled drug dealers and supported the creation of a precinct for the southern Heights—invited Al Sharpton to meet with angry and distraught young people from the neighborhood. In long talks, he convinced them that demonstrating was a better response than rioting, and then led protests at the precinct house. At PS 128, Dave Crenshaw organized a session for grieving and traumatized residents. The Manhattan district attorney announced that there would be a grand jury investigation.[104]

The *Bridge-Leader*, a Heights community newspaper that had welcomed police action against the drug trade, noted how Cedeno's death opened wounds that "never seem to have time to heal" in a neighborhood where many children were "more afraid of the police than any trouble they find on the street." Cedeno's death was especially hard on local activists—who had worked with the slain youth and his friends—activists who were no friends of drug dealers but knew the pressures on both local kids and neighborhood cops. Something of this perspective appeared in a later issue of the paper. Al Kurland, taking the pen name "Meditative Militant" and describing himself as "a grass roots organizer deeply involved with the youth of Washington Heights," wrote: "In their own ways—Kevin, as an injured and isolated youth, and Officer Pellegrini, as an officer isolated from his own community—both were victims of injustice. Let us start the healing process."[105]

The difficulty of healing became apparent on the afternoon of May 27. As the *New York Times* reported the following day, Regina McKay, who worked with the Lower Heights Neighborhood Association, visited the 33rd Precinct. There, she saw a plaque honoring the "Officer of the Month." The recipient of the award for April was Anthony Pellegrini. She left the building in tears. Some one hundred people gathered again at the police station to protest.[106]

In July, the New York County grand jury delivered its verdict: there would be no indictment of Officer Pellegrini. Later, the U.S. attorney for New York looked at the case and also decided not to bring charges against the officer. In the Heights, the absence of an indictment was met with anger, confusion, and acceptance. Some residents felt that prosecutors did not take seriously the perspectives of witnesses whose observations cast Pellegrini in an unfavorable light. Bad feelings about the case would linger for more than a decade, but there was no repetition of the rioting of 1992.[107]

Five years after the rioting over the death of Kiko Garcia, Washington Heights was a different place. Not only was its crime rate lower, but its Dominican residents had elected representatives. Linares remained on the city council, while Adriano Espaillat reached the state assembly after defeating the incumbent, Brian Murtaugh, in 1996. Linares and Espaillat were fierce rivals, but once in office they reduced the sense of powerlessness that made so many people angry and edgy in the crack years. Equally important, for people outside northern Manhattan, their presence in government and in the media reduced the tendency to view Washington Heights as an anonymous, threatening neighborhood.

There was still work to be done, however, to bring greater order, peace, and justice to the lower Heights. In the 33rd Precinct that task fell to Garry F. Mc-Carthy, a Bronx native who joined the NYPD after graduating from SUNY-Albany and assumed command of the 33rd Precinct in June of 1997.[108] The new commander reached out to community groups (a breakfast meeting at Coogan's attracted more than seventy local leaders, twice the expected number), but his most notable initiative was a "model block" program for West 163rd Street between Broadway and Amsterdam Avenue. Numbers 548 and 542 summed up the block's problems: five-story walkups, owned by tenants who hoped to improve them with the help of the Northern Manhattan Improvement Corporation, where the legitimate inhabitants were overwhelmed by drug dealers. When police raided the building in August 1997 to arrest ten men and four women they found a fortified complex, with electrified wires strung across windows, holes bashed in floors and walls to create escape routes, and petroleum jelly smeared on hallway floors to trip up intruders.

The response from the 33rd Precinct was dubbed "the siege of 163rd Street." In an effort that mixed law enforcement with community mobilization, police officers arrested drug dealers and established a round-the-clock presence with barricades at either end of 163rd Street between Broadway and Amsterdam. Anyone who wanted to walk on the block had to prove that they lived there. Officers also encouraged landlords to paint their buildings and remove graffiti. They pressed city agencies to replace street signs, haul away trash, and seal empty structures. They met with residents, encouraged them to form tenant associations, and coached them to identify the lawbreakers in their midst. The effort was consistent with other strategies used in Washington Heights to deny drug dealers places to work: civil enforcement initiatives prosecuted landlords who leased apartments and even buildings to dealers; the Trespass Affidavit Program of the Manhattan district attorney's office made it easier for police officers to patrol buildings and arrest trespassing participants in the drug trade. Despite the authorities' good intentions, some residents complained and the New York Civil Liberties Union criticized the practice of blocking off streets and asking people for identification. Overall, however, by November 1997 the siege of West 163rd Street was declared a success. Police barricades were removed and replaced by a sustained but less intrusive law enforcement presence. Reporters who visited the block afterward, well aware of the history of difficult police-community relations in the neighborhood, heard residents express satisfaction with the effort.

Some bad feelings persisted, however. In 1999, when residents of West 159th Street between Broadway and Amsterdam learned that their block was slated for the tactics used on 163rd Street, some were wary. Instead of embracing the prospect of becoming a "model block," the members of the Community League of West 159th Street protested and set out to run their own safety patrols, register voters, and pressure landlords to improve their buildings. Their decision reflected lingering discomfort with the police, but it also suggested a recognition—which at least some in the police department shared—that building strong communities was a big part of fighting crime.[109]

The crime drop was a welcome relief in northern Manhattan but oddly unsatisfying to many who had invested political and cultural energy in the issue. For liberals, who believed that crime was caused by inequality, it was difficult to accept that it went down even as the city became more unequal. Moreover, when crime fell liberals lost a rhetorical weapon: no longer could they argue that conditions in poor neighborhoods had to be improved lest they produce a generation of criminals. Contrary to the old argument that unleashing the police was the solution to high crime, the strategies used in New York, such as CompStat, were largely about disciplining the police and pushing them to be productive. The police themselves fell under increasing pressure to produce bigger and deeper crime reductions. Over time, this led them to make ever more arrests to establish their own diligence. Contrary to bigots who saw crime as something that blacks and Latinos brought to New York, safer conditions in Washington Heights disproved the suggestion that a community with many Dominicans was bound to be a dangerous place.

Mayors, public officials, and police officers alike could all draw misleading conclusions from the crime drop. If the scholarship of Franklin E. Zimring established that police can take some of the credit for the change, mayors Giuliani and Bloomberg seemed to conclude that aggressive policing was the only factor that made a difference. In this view, the police and mayor did not need to concern themselves with police-community relations. Ideas about community policing devolved into strategies such as "zero tolerance" and stopping and frisking vast numbers of black and Latino men in pursuit of a handful of criminals. It also created a suspicion that police officers fudged crime statistics and made many African American and Latino men conclude that they did not have a full right to the city.[110]

The decline in crime saved many young men from early deaths and gave back to people their streets, sidewalks, and parks. For these alone, it was a welcome gift. It was natural for politicians and police to want to claim credit for the change, but their monopoly of the issue could obscure that the victory was won not just by the NYPD—as important as it was—but by a generation of young New Yorkers who turned away from guns and crack and their elders who marched and lobbied endlessly for safer streets.

Crime, as the muckraker Jack Newfield used to say, is a class issue: poor people suffer from it most. Greater safety eased the lives of the poorest New Yorkers. It was possible, as Peter Walsh of Coogan's once said to me, to be for the people and for the cops. But it wasn't always easy. It is highly desirable that police officers and the communities they serve live together in a constructive relationship, but for so many reasons that is a difficult alignment to establish. All the same, the effort is worth it if law enforcement in urban neighborhoods is to be just and effective.

Skepticism about the police lingered in the southern Heights, but the open-air drug markets and murders that once scarred the neighborhood faded away. As recently as the early 1990s, journalists, politicians, and academics had predicted that a generation of "crack babies" would grow up and stalk the streets. A coming increase in the population of young people would afflict the country with "superpredators." The Heights, as a Dominican neighborhood, was assumed to be a naturally violent place. All of these predictions turned out to be wrong—colored as they were by the limitations of predictive criminology, bigotry, and the anger and fear bequeathed by the crack epidemic.[111]

Washington Heights might be a neighborhood with many poor people and many Dominicans, but their presence did not mean that the Heights was eternally destined to be a neighborhood of high crime. What did remain in the Heights from the crack years, however, was a deep strain of fear.[112]

In 1998, *New York Times* reporter David M. Halbfinger went to the Heights to gauge the impact of decreased crime on a neighborhood that was a symbol for urban mayhem. In 1991, he noted, there were 119 killings in Manhattan north of 155th Street. Five months into 1998, there were five. Yet less killing did not mean less fear. The stoops on West 162nd Street were empty in the late afternoon, he observed, as were the parks overlooking the Harlem River. No one greeted him on Audubon Avenue. "The gunfire may have receded into memory," he wrote, "but the fear hangs on."[113]

The reduction of crime in Washington Heights was built on new police strategies and residents' determination to leave the nightmare of the crack years. What could they do about something as deep-seated and intangible as fear? As it turned out, a lot.

CHAPTER 6

A NEW NEIGHBORHOOD
IN A NEW CITY

IN THE MID-1990S, when the violence of the crack years was a fresh memory, re-searchers asked people in Washington Heights two deceptively simple questions: What is violence? And what can be done about it?[1]

Interview subjects responded that there were many kinds of violence in the world, from human rights violations to street shootings. Yet they saw two ways to deal with it: "hide or flee." In the terror of the crack years, activism was not an obvious option. It was much safer to lay low. "Neighbors," the researchers concluded in a report, "are afraid of one another."[2]

People in the Heights saw the police as part of the problem and part of the solution. Some mistrusted police officers and were reluctant to give them information for fear they might come under suspicion. At the same time, people credited police officers with bringing down crime and wanted to see more of them in the neighborhood. Police, in turn, were aware of danger in the neighborhood and the locals' distrust, but were most likely to blame this on residents' apathy and their failure to communicate with officers. People blamed Dominicans for the drug trade. Dominicans responded, correctly, that their entire community was unfairly stigmatized for the wrongs of a few.[3]

The researchers were a team from Columbia University's Mailman School of Public Health led by Mindy Thompson Fullilove, a doctor with a deep interest in the health of cities and political roots in the left. Fullilove was closely attuned to the relationships among individual health, community action, and the urban environment. She was also part of a new generation at Columbia-Presbyterian that sought productive ties between the hospital and its surrounding neighborhood. "Injury and Anomie," an article in the *American Journal of Public Health* reporting the Fullilove team's findings, showed how the fear and mistrust led to isolation and a sense of helplessness. In a report that was the foundation of the article, the team described Washington Heights as a place of deep fear and great potential.

> Adults fear youth. Immigrants fear authorities and community service institutions. People of different cultural origins misunderstand and fear one another. All of this fear is encapsulated in silence and isolation, and every single one of these conflicts points to the critical need to bring people out from behind closed doors, bring them together in environments where they can speak and listen to one another, share in a public forum what they shared individually with us: we are afraid, and we feel alone; we understand precisely why we are being choked by violence and we want it to stop.
>
> All of these perceptions, when locked tightly within the midst of thousands of individuals, do nothing but alienate, dehumanize, and generate helplessness. Unleashed—shared—they have the power to generate massive community reformation.[4]

The Fullilove team's report concluded with five steps to restore the health of northern Manhattan: foster a sense of community; provide for people who have been hurt by violence; link police and the community in a collaborative relationship that overcomes distrust; create jobs and economic opportunity; and put the public health system in charge of preventing and containing drug epidemics. In substance, each suggestion fit comfortably within the range of policies advocated by liberal Democratic politicians and community activists in northern Manhattan. Yet putting such proposals into practice was well beyond the reach of the people of Washington Heights.[5]

Nonetheless, residents managed, over time, to forge ties within their neighborhood and between Washington Heights and the larger world. They founded a community newspaper, created a dynamic arts scene, made films, wrote books, opened restaurants, and restored public parks. As they strengthened their neighborhood, a greater sense of ease and optimism came to once-edgy streets. As the twenty-first century dawned, the image of northern Manhattan began to change in the metropolitan media. Inside and outside Washington Heights, people began to see the neighborhood as something more than one big crime scene. Residents began to see one another as more than just fearful strangers.

Ironically, two tragedies in the fall of 2001 brought people together and changed perceptions of northern Manhattan for the better: the terrorist attacks on the World Trade Center on September 11, 2001, and the crash of American Flight 587 from New York to Santo Domingo two months later.

Across New York and the metropolitan area, memorial making was one of the common responses to the deaths of 9/11. Northern Manhattan was no different. The first acts of commemoration were undertaken in haste. In the ghostly messages scrawled on the dusty walls and windows of lower Manhattan, one observer noticed these words on Albany Street for a firefighter: "God Bless John Burnside, Ladder 20-Inwood Boy." Gradually, more organized efforts emerged. Vigils took place at Inwood Hill, in Mitchell Square at 166th Street, in J. Hood Wright Park on Fort Washington Avenue just south of the George Washington Bridge, and in Fort Tryon Park.[6]

In the memorials and mourning in northern Manhattan, and their coverage in the media, signs emerged of a meeting and mixing between old and new groups that belied the old days of apartness. Many of those who died on September 11 were Irish Americans with roots in Washington Heights and Inwood, but Dominicans died as well. On September 14, a vigil at Good Shepherd for the missing concluded with a march to a firehouse on Vermilyea Avenue. Marchers from other vigils joined in; together, they formed a river of candlelight that stretched for four blocks. At the firehouse of Engine 95 and Ladder 36 at 31 Vermilyea, the marchers sang "God Bless America" and chanted in English and Spanish to honor the firefighters and police, "Los Bomberos" and "La Policia."[7]

More enduring signs of mixing appeared in memorials. In Inwood, the friends and family of Brian Patrick Monaghan Jr., who had gone to the World Trade Center on a new job in construction, waited four days and nights for his return. A poster seeking Monaghan among the missing described how he had a large shamrock tattooed on his arm. Outside a bodega, Monaghan's sister Danielle and his friends Mick Fitzgerald and Rey Martinez lit three candles on a cardboard box for him.[8]

Monaghan never came home. As the days went by, the makeshift memorial was moved to 207th Street and Seaman Avenue. Police officers, firefighters, and neighborhood people visited to pay their respects and to pray. So many left behind memorabilia—poetry, flowers, and photographs—that a bookcase was brought to the site to hold the accumulating items. Monaghan's friends Martinez and Fitzgerald took on the tasks of maintenance. At a shrine with cultural roots in Latin America, crucifixes came to rest alongside Jewish yarzheit candles, a bottle of Heineken, letters, wind-up toys, Yankee caps, and a Christmas tree. The kind of sidewalk memorial that once marked the

Figure 12: Inwood memorial to Brian Patrick Monaghan Jr., who died on 9/11. Photograph by Martha Cooper/City Lore.

casualties of the drug wars became a shrine to the dead of 9/11. A practice with roots in Latin America took on meaning for many who traced their ancestry to other regions. The shrine was featured on broadcasts in the Dominican Republic and the United States. Brian's body was discovered and buried before the attacks were a month gone, but the shrine remained up through New Year's Day 2002. The day after, with permission, the New-York Historical Society and City Lore, an organization dedicated to urban folk culture, took down the shrine to present it a new venue—in their exhibit "Missing: A Streetscape of a City in Mourning."[9]

Another memorial paid tribute to a former Inwood resident, Bruce Reynolds, a Port Authority police officer and an African American. After the attacks, Reynolds raced from his patrol on the George Washington Bridge to the World Trade Center, where he was last seen helping a woman who had been burned by jet fuel. Reynolds and his parents were probably the only African American family on their street when they moved to Inwood in 1965. Bruce's father, to get him out and playing with other children, organized neighborhood kids to clean up Isham Park, which was scarred by burned benches and foul-mouthed teenagers who hung out there to smoke and drink. When Reynolds grew up, he joined the Port Authority police and married Marian McBride, an immigrant from County Donegal in Ireland. They moved to western New Jersey, and had two children. Reynolds joined the Ancient

Order of Hibernians and traveled often to Ireland. In May of 2002, the Parks Department dedicated a corner of Isham Park as Bruce's Garden.[10]

In mourning Brian Patrick Monaghan Jr. and Bruce Reynolds, it was possible to see that some of the boundaries between people and communities in northern Manhattan were more permeable than some people had assumed. Interracial and interfaith friendships, romances, and marriages had always been present in Washington Heights and Inwood, of course, but now they were public stories in the lives of honored dead, stories that people could learn from.

Barely two months after the September 11 attacks, northern Manhattan was scarred by another tragedy—the crash of American Airlines Flight 587. One of some fifty flights that coursed weekly between the United States and the Dominican Republic, Flight 587 was one of the mainstays of Dominicans' transnational way of life. The general pattern of flying home to the Dominican Republic was familiar to many residents of Washington Heights, as the journalist Seth Kugel noted: First, buy tickets from a travel agent in northern Manhattan. Then, buy an enormous suitcase to be filled with gifts for relatives. Shop the stores on 181st Street or Broadway for everything from cheap jeans and T-shirts to gifts with brand-name labels for special relatives, then jam as much as possible into the suitcase without going over weight limits.[11]

The aura around Flight 587 was so strong that it became the subject of a merengue lyric sung by Kinito Mendez and Johnny Ventura, which begins "*Llegó el avión / Es el vuelo 587 con destino a Santo Domingo*" and continues (in translation)

> The plane comes packed with luggage
> The plane comes packed with luggage
> It comes full of hope
> And also with joy
> It comes full of hope
> And also with joy
> To spend Christmas with my family.[12]

When Flight 587 crashed in the seaside neighborhood of Belle Harbor in southwest Queens barely two minutes after takeoff on November 12, 2001, 260 people on the plane died. The crash killed five people in Belle Harbor and left a burning black crater in a neighborhood of Irish, Italians, and Jews that was already devastated by losses in the World Trade Center attacks. Belle Harbor was the final stop at the eastern end of the A train. At the other end of the A train, in northern Manhattan, in an eerie replay of September 11, Dominicans rushed to call friends and relatives. Rumors spread that the plane had been taken down by a terrorist attack.[13]

Grief-stricken friends and relatives descended on Alianza Dominicana. An agency founded to help Dominicans struggling with new lives in Washington Heights now turned to serving grief-stricken friends and relatives of those who died on Flight 587. Moisés Pérez, executive director, estimated that his agency was serving 120 families stricken in the crash. Within Alianza itself, ten staffers lost family members.[14]

In media coverage of the crash, New Yorkers glimpsed fuller pictures of the Dominican diaspora and Washington Heights. Before Flight 587 plunged to earth, the human connection between the Dominican Republic and the United States was often represented in the persons of baseball players or criminals. Afterward, in newspaper stories about relatives who came to New York to claim their dead but instead found red tape, and in accounts of funerals that channeled mourning between the Dominican Republic and northern Manhattan, Dominicans became real people with real grief. In New York, a city where the story of immigration is endlessly repeated as a kind of civic religion that spans groups and generations, Dominicans were finally acknowledged in defining ways as immigrants—just like so many other New Yorkers.

Ray Sanchez of *Newsday* chronicled a sad yet illuminating funeral in the small city of Baní, in the Dominican Republic. Forty or more passengers with ties to Baní were on Flight 587. Many of them worked as grocers or gardeners, and supported relatives in the Dominican Republic. They took the flight south to join in the feasts and processions in honor of La Virgen de Regla that brighten Baní every November. When the plane crashed, the annual celebration was replaced by days of prayers for the dead. Sanchez covered the funeral for Jose Hilton Sanchez and his brother Elvis. Born in Baní, they had left eleven years earlier to run their uncle's store, Rafael Grocery, on West 134th Street. They returned in coffins. At their wake in Baní, the funeral home was packed. Chairs were set out on the sidewalk for the mourners, who dressed somberly in gray and black under a sweltering sun.[15]

Back in the Heights, grieving was both intimate and public: a gasp of recognition at a neighbor's face in a photograph enshrined in a sidewalk memorial; the sudden absence of a regular customer at a food market; wreaths of black ribbon in a hair salon. These stories of grief were shared with the rest of the city through news media that rediscovered northern Manhattan. As the *Daily News* put it immediately after the crash, appropriately mixing English and Spanish, "If a street could cry, upper Broadway wept yesterday for the victims of Vuelo 587."

After the attacks on the World Trade Center, the *New York Times* columns "Portraits of Grief" remembered the secretaries, police officers, firefighters, and restaurant workers who died—the kind of working people whose lives were typically ignored in *Times* obituaries. After the crash, *Newsday* did something similar for the dead of Flight 587. In *Newsday*, readers encountered stories of labor, sacrifice, and devotion in a frame that embraced both New York and the Dominican Republic: Tito Bautista of the South Bronx, who worked at both a meat market and bodega and changed flights three times to cover his double shift before flying south to bring his four-year-old son back to New York; Ramona Pimentel, who retired comfortably with her husband to Santo Domingo after years of running a bodega in Brooklyn; and Domingo Matias of Corona, Queens, married and the mother of five, who worked twelve hours a day in a factory and then went home to cook and clean house. Individually and collectively, such portraits gave new meanings to the Dominicans of New York City.[16]

There were some concerns that disproportionate attention was devoted to the residents of Belle Harbor. In *Newsday*, Sanchez and the novelist Angie Cruz, who was born and raised in Washington Heights, argued that the dead of Flight 587 were slighted in comparison. Sanchez blamed the problem on bigotry and a habitual lack of interest in the lives of the kind of Dominican working people who were on the flight. ("If it would have been [Dominican-born baseball star] Sammy Sosa on that plane we would have gotten more coverage," an Alianza Dominicana staffer told Sanchez.) Cruz asked: "Does the amount of compassion we feel for the families affected with any tragedy have to do with how much the media machine cares to cover?"[17]

Nonetheless, the stories of Dominican lives lost were a great departure from the ignorance and demonization of the past. Equally important were mourning rites that helped bridge the gaps between Belle Harbor and Washington Heights. At Saint Elizabeth's in Washington Heights, which held eleven funeral masses for people who died on the flight, Cardinal Edward Egan entered an overflowing mass to the hymn "Sí, Me Levantaré" (Yes, I Will Rise). Among those in attendance was Melvin Lafontaine, son of the impresario who had helped make famous the song about Flight 587. Cardinal Egan welcomed the worshippers in Spanish. "The entire community of the Archdiocese of New York is with you," he said. "We love you very much." In grief, the Dominicans of New York could be seen for what they had been all along: hard-working people who deeply loved their families. As Councilman Guillermo Linares observed, "We have been exposed as a people, that we are part of the fabric of what America is, in the tradition of fulfilling the American dream."[18]

Unfortunately, despite all the grit, energy, ambition, and determination that Dominicans shared with other immigrants, past and present, their grasp of the American dream was less than complete. By 2001 New York City was not the engine of immigrant economic mobility that it once had been because it no longer had the manufacturing and shipping jobs that once provided solid incomes for immigrant families.

The income gap between recent and older immigrant groups in northern Manhattan was visible in the casualties in the fall of 2001. The Irish dead of Inwood were members of the securely employed working class (firefighters and police officers) and children of immigrant, working-class parents who had moved up into the comforts of the middle class. Their mobility was a testament to hard work, good connections (often forged growing up in Inwood), and a lack of ethnically based discrimination against Irish Americans in the second half of the twentieth century. Their lives ended early and tragically, but in most cases their survivors could credit them with achievements that their grandparents only imagined.

For the most part the Dominican dead of Washington Heights were in the modest and insecure end of the working class—people who drove livery cabs, worked in the region's remaining factories, washed dishes, styled hair, emptied bedpans, and kept bodegas open until the late hours of the night. Their deaths were a tragic endpoint to lives that were often lived in a persistent state of longing for prosperity and reunion with loved ones. While they knew days of joy, their highest hopes were frequently pegged to the future. The crash of Flight 587 ended the dreams of both the passengers and their survivors on the ground.

Owing in part to the two tragic events in 2001, Dominicans visibly took their full place alongside the immigrant groups that had preceded them in northern Manhattan. This was itself a great achievement. But in the background a nagging question remained: Would Dominicans find the prosperity that had enriched the lives of their predecessors?

A report issued in 2003 by the Dominican Studies Institute at the City University of New York found that Dominican New Yorkers had the highest poverty rate of all the city's major racial and ethnic groups—32 percent—when the overall poverty rate in the city was 19 percent. Women headed some 38 percent of Dominican families; citywide the figure was 22 percent. Almost half of the families headed by Dominican women were poor, more than twice the rate for other families. Unemployment among Dominicans was high. There was a bright spot, however. From 1990 to 2000, per capita income for all New Yorkers increased by 9.2 percent. Among Dominicans, the increase was close to 16 percent.[19]

Reports from the New York City Department of Health and Mental Hygiene issued in 2003 and 2006 found the Heights and Inwood were far more Hispanic than the city as a whole (71 percent compared to 27 percent) and had far more immigrants (51 percent compared to 36 percent). In Washington Heights and Inwood, 31 percent of residents lived in poverty, compared to 21 percent in the city as a whole.[20] The 2003 Department of Health and Mental Hygiene report also included the results of a survey on people's feelings of vulnerability in their own community. Overall, 32 percent of New Yorkers felt their neighborhood was unsafe. In Washington Heights and Inwood, the figure was 51 percent.[21]

Despite these statistics, there were grounds for cautious optimism.[22] In both Inwood and Washington Heights west of Broadway, Dominicans could now be found in greater numbers in census tracts marked by economic security, even prosperity. In the 1970s, the Inwood streets north of Dyckman and west of Broadway, census tract 295, were the more Irish section of the neighborhood. Yet between 1990 and 2000, the Hispanic population there, strongly Dominican, grew from 38 percent of the population to 60 percent. Economic mobility, and a Latino presence in Good Shepherd Parish, helped open the area to Dominicans. In the west Heights along Fort Washington Avenue, in census tract 273, a middle class and strongly Jewish area that gentrified under the new name of Hudson Heights, the Latino percentage of the population, again strongly Dominican, grew from 26 percent to 33 percent. In the two parts of northern Manhattan most associated with economically secure Irish and Jews, Dominicans had arrived as residents in their own right.[23] The growing Dominican population west of Broadway was a sign that the Dominicans of northern Manhattan included not only the poor, but also striving first-generation immigrants and members of a second or even third generation who were making impressive strides into the middle class through politics, business, the arts, science, and medicine.[24]

Ironically, some of the unease in the neighborhood was the consequence of visible improvements. In 1979, Betty Clarke, an aide to State Senator Leichter, said she dreamed that one day the Heights and Inwood would have to worry about gentrification. It was a funny line at the time, but in less than two decades it was a reality.[25]

The historian Deborah Dash Moore, who moved into an apartment on upper Fort Washington Avenue in 1986, at first found her neighborhood "rough." Around 1990, though, she noticed harbingers of change. Musicians, priced out of the neighborhood around Lincoln Center, began to appear in her section of the Heights. Gay and lesbian residents also moved in. With musicians riding the uptown train home from downtown gigs late at night, the A train began to feel safer. Over time, the efforts at neighborhood stabilization and public officials' efforts to strengthen municipal services bore fruit. When Moore first settled in the Heights, her friends would not visit a neighborhood with a dodgy reputation so far uptown. By the early 1990s, her friends started asking for tips about finding apartments in the western Heights. By the late 1990s, the arrival of middle class families with baby carriages signaled that gentrification was a fact.[26]

An article in the October 2001 issue of *Cooperator: The Co-op & Condo Monthly*, caught the prevailing mood: "'The cat's out of the bag,' says Gus Perry, owner of Stein-Perry Real Estate, who deals mainly with Washington Heights properties. 'We've been discovered. People come to the neighborhood and realize it's a diamond in the rough.'"[27] In fact, such enthusiasm applied mostly to the western Heights, an area once known as Fort Washington, which was reborn in the 1990s as Hudson Heights. The term Hudson Heights was disparaged as a realtors' invention on the order of renaming Hell's Kitchen as Clinton. Residents, however, made a convincing claim that the term was coined in 1993 by the founders of the Hudson Heights Owners Coalition, who banded together "to maintain and enhance the quality of life and the property values in the neighborhood." While membership in the coalition was no impediment to a life of inclusive public activism, once the realtors grasped the new name its predictable impact was to conceptually separate the area from the rest of Washington Heights.[28]

This was an old phenomenon in the Heights. Earlier generations of residents had mentally drawn and redrawn the southern boundaries of their neighborhood to exclude Harlem to the south. In a time of gentrification, the use of the new name could diminish a sense of shared interests on both sides of Broadway.

Into this promising but precarious situation appeared the bilingual *Manhattan Times*, launched in 2000 by Luis A. Miranda Jr., Robert Ramirez, and David Keisman—all veterans of politics and government. Keisman was the former publisher of a newspaper in Queens. The *Manhattan Times* succeeded where other community newspapers failed because it generated readers and advertisers in both English and Spanish. In its news stories, the paper gave readers an unprecedented possibility of shared knowledge. In fighting for the neighborhood, it was a voice grounded in both sides of Broadway. Its coverage of the arts in northern Manhattan enabled residents to see themselves as inhabiting something other than a crime scene, while its attention to the growing number of local restaurants chronicled a growth industry with a significant number of Dominican entrepreneurs. The paper's real estate stories encouraged people to see the neighborhood as a place to buy or rent a home (and probably advanced gentrification as well). Its coverage of landlord-tenant issues—always a sore point in northern Manhattan—gave residents a voice in housing disputes.[29]

For the *Manhattan Times*, community building was as much a part of the paper's role as reporting the news. Indeed, one of the paper's founders, Luis Miranda, grew up in a politically active family in Puerto Rico reading the socialist newspaper *Claridad*. After a stint in the Koch administration led him to see the value of working inside mainstream institutions, Miranda and Ramirez became partners in the MirRam Group LLC, a political consulting firm. They eventually counted among their clients Hillary Rodham Clinton, the New York Yankees, and Transport Workers Union Local 100. Equally significant, Miranda's years reading *Claridad* gave him a belief in the value of a newspaper that organizes a community and solves its problems.

The newspaper's owners clashed with Republican mayor Michael Bloomberg on the editorial page and on Election Day. When Bloomberg ran for a second term in 2005, Ramirez and Miranda advised his Democratic opponent, Fernando Ferrer. The Democrat lost, but one of their editorials illuminated recent changes in northern Manhattan.[30] "Beneath the phoenix-rising-from-the-ashes story that the Bloomberg campaign has tried to sell," the *Manhattan Times* argued,

> there is a dark and ultimately unattractive truth: New York City is fast becoming defined by nothing else but the stark divisions between the very rich and the rest of us. And our neighborhood, for better and for worse, is about as clear an example of this new reality as any in New York.
>
> While we are as happy as any local resident to see that new blood is moving into places like northwestern Washington Heights (er, Hudson Heights) and western Inwood, we have watched as many local residents and businesses—including many who braved the dark days of the late eighties and nineties—have fled looking for relief from ever-increasing costs of living. How sad and ironic that many of the same people who fought to save our neighborhoods in the face of thugs and drugs have ultimately been forced to surrender their communities to the almighty dollar.[31]

The newspaper's editorial stances and its owners' political tendencies usually align, but the *Manhattan Times* maintained a broad commitment to community building that transcended the concerns of any one political party. In May 2006, the paper conducted the Bridge/Puente project to connect both sides of its community. Under rainy skies, a long line of residents and elected officials stood shoulder to shoulder across upper Manhattan along Dyckman Street—the boundary between Washington Heights and Inwood—from the Harlem River across Broadway to the Hudson. At either end of the line, participants filled large jugs with water from the respective rivers. Cheer-fully, they passed the jugs hand to hand along the line. When water from the Harlem was poured into the Hudson and water from the Hudson was poured into the Harlem, the event symbolically linked the two sides of Broadway. The future of northern Manhattan, the project suggested, was about making connections and not about enforcing boundaries.[32]

Publications on the Web complemented the *Manhattan Times* and dra-matically increased the opportunities for residents to learn about each other. From 2003 to 2012, Washington Heights and Inwood Online offered listings of events, discussion forums, local history, a photo gallery, and classified ads. Equally important was DNAinfo.com, a Web-based news organiza-tion founded in 2009, which covered Washington Heights and Inwood as well as other neighborhoods across the city. In 2010, Led Black and friends launched the *Uptown Collective* at uptowncollective.com to "document" the "verve, energy and dynamism" of "the Uptown Renaissance" and "shape its trajectory."[33]

The new media system of northern Manhattan reduced the ignorance and uncertainty that had scarred the area in its bleakest years. Also valuable, in complicated ways, was a new sense of New York emanating from city hall. Mayor Michael Bloomberg had little patience for ethnic politics, unlike his predecessors Koch and Giuliani who exploited white fears and resentments. Bloomberg, a cosmopolitan businessman with technocratic tendencies, was more interested in expanding the city's economy. In government, he val-ued competence and recruited a generally well-regarded administration. He thought of himself as a straight-talking businessman and took pride in not being a politician. That became a vulnerability because he lacked a common touch. He made himself an easy mark for tabloid wisecracks when he flew to Bermuda in his private jet, but the nagging question during his mayoralty was whether his economic vision enriched the city as a whole. He nurtured a prosperity that helped the city endure the Great Recession and promoted amenities like riverside parks, all of which made New York a more pleasant place to live and attracted tourists and residents from around the world. Such measures did not, however, raise stagnant wages or close the growing gap between rich and poor. Bloomberg's New York was safer and more dynamic economically, but it was also a place where people of low and moderate in-come felt less and less at home. While crime dropped, his stubborn adher-ence to aggressive stop-and-frisk policing angered and alienated thousands of young men of color and diminished the good feelings that might have other-wise arisen from living in a safer city.[34]

With safer streets, New York became more comfortable with its own urbanity. In Washington Heights, as elsewhere, residents stepped out of their homes, reclaimed parks and sidewalks, and overcame the fear that had driven so many people indoors during the years of high crime. In this context, one of the strongest sources of optimism about northern Manhattan's future has been a growing, multiethnic arts scene. Of particular note is the annual monthlong Uptown Arts Stroll with gallery shows, open studios, performances, and a street fair that showcases both the work of local artists and the neighborhoods of northern Manhattan. A central figure in founding the Uptown Arts Stroll was Mike Fitelson, a journalist and photographer who moved to northern Manhattan in 1999, and began looking for a place close to home to show his photographs. One meeting led to another and eventually a one-day event emerged in the fall of 2003. With the support of the *Manhattan Times*, where Fitelson worked, the Uptown Arts Stroll, or El Paseo de las Artes del Alto Manhattan, was born in 2003.[35] The event would have been unthinkable in the early 1990s, when many people associated the sidewalks of Washington Heights with drug shootings.

There had been arts organizations before in the Heights and Inwood, but in 2007 the energy that produced the Uptown Arts Stroll was also manifested in the founding of the Northern Manhattan Arts Alliance (NoMAA), a nonprofit dedicated to supporting artists and the arts funded by money from the Upper Manhattan Empowerment Zone, a Clinton administration antipoverty initiative, and the Hispanic Federation.[36] With NoMAA, artists in northern Manhattan have a strong, cosmopolitan advocate and northern Manhattan had the possible germ of a new relationship between artists and the city. By 2007, arts-oriented strategies for urban revival were nothing new. What was new about NoMAA and Washington Heights, however, was what they offered in a divided neighborhood with an uneven economy.

By the late 1980s, northern Manhattan had already attracted musicians lured north by affordable rents and sturdy, prewar apartment buildings that could contain the sounds of a practicing cellist. There were also local artists, often immigrants or the children of immigrants, whose works ranged from traditional to strongly topical. Natasha Beshenkovsky, educated in the Soviet Union, painted classical miniatures. In the same neighborhood, M. Tony Peralta, an artist and graphic designer born in New York to immigrant Dominican parents and raised in Washington Heights, grew up with the influences of hip-hop, graffiti, Marvel comics, and Keith Haring. He designed a T-shirt emblazoned "DOMINICANYORK"; its black-and-white type underlined in red recalled the *New York Post*, a paper whose coverage of Dominicans in the Heights' bleak years was not always enlightened or subtle. He also took on Dominican attitudes about race in two posters of identical Afro picks (combs) labeled *Pelo Bueno* (Good Hair) and *Pelo Malo* (Bad Hair).[37]

The People's Theatre Project, founded in 2008 by the Dominican theater artist Mino Lora and Bob Braswell, an actor with a BFA from Boston University, embraced northern Manhattan as both a theatrical subject and a source of actors and playwrights. The Project blends performance and activism to address community concerns such as deportations, housing, and obesity in programs that reach everyone from school children to senior citizens. Its plays, writing projects, and theatrical games foster an awareness of current concerns on both sides of Broadway, even as its collaborators include older institutions in the neighborhood such as New York-Presbyterian Hospital (born in the merger of Columbia-Presbyterian and New York Hospital in 1998), the YM-YWHA, and the Morris-Jumel Mansion.

Like NoMAA, the People's Theatre Project helped create an artistic crossroads. Such efforts have raised the prospect of urban revitalization through the arts that does not involve the displacement of working class and immigrant residents, but grows from their presence. Northern Manhattan could incubate, in Richard Florida's phrase, its own "creative class."

To be sure, artists in northern Manhattan faced problems, foremost among them rising rents, the lack of arts supply stores, a relative shortage of gallery space, and a relative shortage of patrons who would buy artwork in sufficient quantities at sufficient prices that an artist could make a living. Their unique individual and collective strengths, however, more than compensated for these limitations.

The arts scene was not the only crossroads in northern Manhattan. Residents also took back the streets and parks in Washington Heights and restored them to public use. As far back as the 1970s, a medieval festival in Fort Tryon Park—an outgrowth of a workshop program run by the Cloisters for young people in Washington Heights and Inwood—brought crowds to the park and demonstrated better possibilities of sharing public space. In the summer of 1977, with the looting during the blackout in recent memory, my mother wrote me in Alaska about her visit to the festival; she praised the "non-littering crowd" and said the people of New York did themselves proud that day. In 1985, Tim Page of the *New York Times* took in the exuberant crowds, the sunshine, the exhibits on black, Hispanic, Islamic, and Jewish life in the Middle Ages, and pronounced the afternoon "one to be cherished rather than merely enjoyed." When the festival faltered, Councilman Stan Michels helped revive it under the auspices of the Washington Heights–Inwood Development Corporation, a not-for-profit organization founded in 1978 to encourage local economic development. Eventually, a grand painting of the festival—with northern Manhattan notables, including Michels, dressed in medieval garb—graced a wall in Coogan's. The artist who did the painting was Sam Garcia, formerly the baritone to Jim Clarke's first tenor on the street-corner singing scene of Washington Heights in the fifties.[38]

The owners of Coogan's got into the business of reclaiming the streets for the people in 1999 by sponsoring a five-kilometer footrace—Salsa, Blues and Shamrocks. From a starting line in the lower Heights the runners plowed uphill on Fort Washington Avenue, wound through Fort Tryon Park past the Cloisters, doubled back to the finish line, and retired to a generous brunch at Coogan's. In the array of runners and the cheering onlookers, people gained an opportunity to recognize what Washington Heights looked like and to celebrate it.[39]

Yet the task of restoring the streets and public parks of Washington Heights required more than energy, imagination, and goodwill. It would also cost an enormous amount of money, as a 1990 report by the Dinkins administration noted. Fort Tryon Park, with perhaps the most glorious view in all of New York, was marred by neglect, vandalism, and graffiti. Despite the efforts of the Friends of Fort Tryon Park, it needed extensive work, including "erosion control and planting." Highbridge Park was in worse shape. There, despite "spectacular natural resources" and an extensive recreation complex that dated to the La Guardia years, the most pressing task was to remove dumped automobiles. In 1985 alone, more than three hundred abandoned cars and one hundred junked refrigerators were pulled from the park. In the same year, the pool was restored at a cost of $7.4 million in capital funds. One year later, the park's recreation center had been restored but the playgrounds, paths, basketball courts, and ball fields still were in disrepair and the Dinkins report estimated it would cost $7 million to restore them. But where would the money come from? During the crack years in Highbridge Park, Mothers Against Violence had won back a playground from drug addicts. Their action took great courage, but the heroism they brought to the park could not by itself bring in the dollars needed to rebuild what was once one of the grand facilities of New Deal New York.[40]

The dilemma of Highbridge Park was complicated by the fact that it had never enjoyed the prominence of a Central Park or even nearby Fort Tryon Park—both of which fell on hard times of their own in the bleak period from the 1970s to the 1990s. When activists and elected officials lobby government offices or foundations for help with a park, they enjoy an advantage when a park is well known and located near affluent neighbors with political power (and a desire to maintain real estate values). Fort Tryon Park benefited from

Figure 13: Reclaiming Highbridge Park: Quisqueya en el Hudson festival, 1996. Photograph by Tom van Buren. Courtesy of the Center for Traditional Music and Dance archive (www.ctmd.org).

the work of the Friends of Fort Tryon Park and later the Fort Tryon Park Trust. Separately and after they merged, they coordinated volunteers who cleaned up garbage, cultivated gardens, and worked with city government and foundations to restore the park to its full beauty. David Rockefeller, son of John D. Rockefeller Jr., whose philanthropy first made the park possible, donated $1 million to the Fort Tryon Park Trust. In 1995, the entertainer

Bette Midler founded the New York Restoration Project to help New York's less known parks—including Fort Tryon Park, Fort Washington Park, and Highbridge Park. In 2001, the project turned a very ordinary snack bar in a stone building in Fort Tryon Park into the New Leaf Restaurant and Bar—an elegant establishment whose earnings support the Restoration Project.[41]

Grants and volunteers alone could never replace the need for substantial government expenditures to keep the parks open as healthy public spaces. Still, in fits and starts, and not without setbacks, the people of Washington Heights recovered their open spaces. As early as 1996, the ACDP and the Center for Traditional Music and Dance went to Highbridge Park to mount Quisqueya en el Hudson, a festival that featured dynamic but less familiar forms of Dominican music and brought people into the park. Jon Pareles of the *New York Times* called the event in its second year "a mixture of neighborhood party and aficionados' folk festival." In his 2004 book, *Waterfront: A Journey around Manhattan*, Phillip Lopate examined the thickets, highway ramps, cliffs, architecture, and ruins found in Highbridge Park and pronounced it a complex mixture of "problem and potential." Sara M., who grew up in Washington Heights in the late 1980s and early 1990s, wrote in 2009 about the "chaos" of her young days at Highbridge Pool: "hooligans" breaking into lockers, "floating diapers in the children's pool," fights on the line for the diving board, and blasting music. In 2009, however, she found the park "all cleaned up."

> It is still very popular with the local teenagers but the bathrooms are clean, the lockers are secure, everyone has to wear bathing suits (they check to make sure there is a lining in all suits). People picnic, play and smoke blunts in the park. A good time is had by all.
>
> It's come a long way but that's a testament to the neighborhood, it's come a loooooooong way from what it once was and while some people like to talk smack about it being ghetto . . . in comparison to what it used to be . . . it's almost suburb like!

Smoking blunts was not what Mayor La Guardia had in mind when he opened Highbridge Pool, but in 2009 the park that Sara M. enjoyed was a grand public recreation area in recovery. After gang wars, decades of decay, and crack wars, the people of Washington Heights could reenter their parks, enjoy them, and get used to each other's company.[42]

As Sara M. recognized, the changes in Highbridge Park were one more sign that Washington Heights had passed through a great transformation—one of many that marked the neighborhood's passage from the era of La Guardia to the era of Bloomberg. In such moments, some older ethnic groups strove to preserve their history by writing about the neighborhood as it had been. For example, Jim Carroll in his 1978 memoir, *Basketball Diaries*, and John McMullen in his 2010 book, *The Inwood Book: Poems, Short Stories and a Novel*, wrote about the Irish experience in northern Manhattan.[43] Manfred Kirchheimer, whose Jewish family fled Germany in 1936 and arrived in the Heights in 1942, examined his community in the documentary film *We Were So Beloved*, released in 1986. Kirchheimer looked closely at German Jews' capacity for questioning the country they lived in—whether it was Germany or the United States. Kirchheimer's former neighbors criticized him for airing the prejudices that some of them held against Eastern European Jews and for relating one woman's enduring good feelings for Germans. Overall, Kirchheimer thought his film was not popular with the German Jews of Washington Heights.[44]

For African Americans, the desire to preserve an important part of their history in a changing neighborhood fueled a bitter dispute with Columbia University over the fate of the Audubon Ballroom in the southern Heights, where Malcolm X was assassinated in 1965. After the slaying, the Audubon declined and the city seized it for back taxes. In the 1980s, Columbia proposed to demolish the building to build a research center. After long and complex negotiations, a compromise preserved the Audubon's facade, let Columbia have its research center, and established a home in 2005 for the Malcolm X and Dr. Betty Shabazz Memorial and Educational Center.[45]

Sharing histories did not mean a consensus, but it did help people learn to live with the complexities of their own history. Equally important, an interest in local history could also draw people to public events, enriching the sense of ease in northern Manhattan that was so important for overcoming the sense of fear that once plagued the area. In Inwood, the writer and realtor Cole Thompson joined with Don Rice, a musician and Inwood resident, to produce monthly evenings devoted to Inwood history at the Indian Road Café. The filmmaker and realtor Vivian Ducat, living at 790 Riverside Drive, organized a series of oral history meetings where residents of her neighborhood shared memories of the past. Her efforts contributed to the designation of the area between 155th and 158th streets west of Broadway as the Audubon Park Historic District. Historian James Renner ran walking tours of northern Manhattan devoted to everything from its role in the American Revolution to its great estates to the African American enclave of Sugar Hill.

Nowhere did the past and present of northern Manhattan meet with greater humanity and artistry than in the parlor concerts of Marjorie Eliot, a pianist who moved from the Upper West Side to 555 Edgecombe Avenue at West 160th Street in 1982. Raised in Philadelphia in the African Methodist Episcopal Church in a community saturated with music, she grew up to play jazz in clubs and work in the theater. Officially, her address north of 155th Street put her in Washington Heights. As an African American who was proud of her predecessors at 555 Edgecombe—a building that was by the 1940s the home of the singer, actor, and activist Paul Robeson, the jazz musician Count Basie, the psychologist Kenneth Clark, and the actor Canada Lee—she thought of herself as a resident of Harlem. (Edgecombe Avenue is the spine of the section of Harlem known as Sugar Hill.)[46]

After Eliot's son Philip died on a Sunday in 1992, she began to put on Sunday afternoon concerts in her apartment as a way of getting her through a painful weekly anniversary. Her playing met similar needs after her son Michael died in 2006. ("It's a great joy to me, and it chases the shadows," she said.)

Eliot's parlor concerts attract jazz fans from around New York and around the world; they have been chronicled in a French documentary. They bring in comparatively few African Americans, however. African Americans are a declining presence in northern Manhattan, and even when they were more numerous they were not a large part of her audience. Still, Eliot became a beloved presence in northern Manhattan. She developed a warm relationship with Councilman Stan Michels, and in 2000, City Lore, an organization dedicated to urban folk culture, inducted her into its People's Hall of Fame.

"History will not leave you alone," Eliot says. In 2009, Ducat and the Riverside Oval Lecture Series featured Eliot and friends in a concert at the apartment of Mo Strom and Craig Ulmer in the Grinnell. The concert was conceived as an opportunity to savor the music of "jazz legends," many of them from nearby Sugar Hill, and "meet your neighbors." As at Eliot's concerts at 555 Edgecombe, most in attendance were white. Talking with the audience, Eliot said she could not shake the feeling that in crossing over to the west side of Broadway, she was going to "the other side of the tracks." With that thought in mind, her gracious, elegant, and sensitive performance created a sonic bridge across Broadway for an evening.[47]

By the twenty-first century, Dominicans had taken their place in the history of Washington Heights. In 2001, the CUNY Dominican Studies Institute at City College (founded in 1992) and the City College library mounted an exhibit chronicling "one of the largest Latino immigrant groups and the fastest growing ethnic minority in New York City." The show, *The Evolution of an Ethnic Community: Dominican-Americans in Upper Manhattan*, recognized that the formative years of the Dominican community in northern Manhattan were over. A great and tumultuous historical passage had ended. "As the 21st century begins," a label in the final panel of the exhibit said,

"Dominicans are hopeful. In the past 40 years, Dominicans have grown and matured as a community. . . . Dominicans now count on the strength of its youth and the wisdom of its elders in the land they have chosen to settle and now call home." For a neighborhood that had been painted in the media with lurid colors, the exhibit was refreshingly restrained.[48]

Sharing the Dominican experience with non-Dominicans—something the Dominican Studies Institute did generously—still meant overcoming obstacles. Ironically, the Dominican presence in upper Manhattan was so large that Dominicans in Washington Heights lived with less "diversity" than they would have found in other neighborhoods, where Dominicans were not as large a percentage of the population. If the goal was to overcome the "apartness" that defined relations within and between ethnic communities in northern Manhattan, the number of potential partners in dialogue shrank as the number of Height residents of European ancestry declined. A change from this pattern appeared, however, in a musical play.

The YM-YWHA of Washington Heights and Inwood had a long record of serving Jews and non-Jews. Still, by the 2000s it was a challenge to create programs that embraced both the large Dominican community in the area and its much smaller Jewish population. A possibility emerged in 2008 when the Museum of Jewish Heritage—A Living Memorial to the Holocaust in lower Manhattan mounted an exhibit on the little-known story of Jewish refugees who found a refuge from Hitler in the Dominican Republic, in the town of Sosúa, when most countries were closed to them. The motives of Trujillo, the Dominican dictator who accepted them, were far from pure—he hoped to whiten his population and improve his international standing. Moreover, the eight hundred Jews who made it to his country were far fewer than the anticipated number. Still, the Jews who settled in Sosúa survived the war and wrote a unique chapter in the history of Jews and Dominicans.[49]

Victoria Neznansky, a social worker and chief program officer at the Y, visited the exhibit on Sosúa and saw how its story might appeal to Jews and Dominicans in northern Manhattan. A colleague directed her to a meeting with Liz Swados, a composer and director. Eventually an idea was in motion: a play about Sosúa, performed by Jewish and Dominican young people under the auspices of the Y, *Sosúa: Dare to Dance Together*.[50]

Aside from the obvious Jewish-Dominican dimension, and the two groups' histories as immigrants, the concept had other strengths. It began with one thing that the two populations shared: an experience with dictators, Hitler and Trujillo. Unlike the situation in northern Manhattan, where an older Jewish community encountered Dominican newcomers, in Sosúa the Dominicans were the local majority meeting newly arrived Jews. Trujillo's racism against Haitians, and his slaughter of some fifteen thousand ethnic Haitians in the Dominican Republic in 1937, was set against Hitler's anti-Semitism and the Holocaust.[51]

Students researched the history behind the play, wrote and performed scenes, and wove their own experiences into the continuously evolving script. Moreover, they swapped identities: Jews played Dominicans and Dominicans played Jews. In a performance of *Dare to Dance Together* that I saw, Dominican students played elite members of the U.S. government explaining why they would not admit Jewish refugees to the United States. The actors' cutting portrayals of U.S. officials, which must have drawn on the rejection Dominicans faced in their own time, were unforgettable.[52]

Dare to Dance Together, along with the talkback sessions that followed it whenever I saw it, was a great exercise in bridge building. (Not all of the chasms bridged were the obvious ones. At one performance, I heard one cast member explain that being in the play taught him an important lesson: the students he encountered in the cast from La Guardia High School of Music and Art and Performing Arts, one of the city's elite public schools, were not all snobs.) In *Dare to Dance Together,* performed in northern Manhattan, at the Museum of Jewish Heritage, at the United Nations, and many more venues, Jewish and Dominican kids learned to explore not just their own identities but how there was also a bit of the other in each of them. One play wove together not just Nazi Germany and the Dominican Republic but both sides of Broadway.

As the historian Thomas Bender has observed, a democratic city rests on political representation and visual representation. As for political representation, Washington Heights entered the twenty-first century with elected representatives and civic institutions that could credibly deliberate the issues facing the neighborhood and present its views to the larger public. Decades of community board meetings, efforts to elect Dominicans to political office, and painstaking efforts to build alliances around common interests had all born fruit.[53]

Visual representation, the project of seeing and being seen in ways that promote respect, inclusion, and a recognition of differences within a larger collective identity, was another matter. Local media, like the *Manhattan Times,* had done important work to introduce the different peoples of northern Manhattan to each other. Introducing northern Manhattan to the rest of the city, the state, the nation, and the world was a much more difficult matter. Yet just as the Jewish Lower East Side inspired a wide range of cultural productions that defined and redefined the neighborhood over many decades, so did Dominican Washington Heights in the early years of the twenty-first century generate films, novels, and a Broadway musical that would give upper Manhattan a new face.

To be sure, the association between Washington Heights and the drug trade died hard. *El Circulo Vicioso*, a low-budget feature film released in 1999, made by a Dominican director and Dominican actors and shot in Washington Heights, sparked anger among Heights residents with its recycling of old and ugly themes. But as time passed, more nuanced depictions of the neighborhood's difficult and notorious years appeared. Crime and the drug trade are elements in *Washington Heights* and *Manito*, both released in 2002, but in complicated ways. *Washington Heights* is less a drug movie pure and simple than a story about ambition, generations in an immigrant family, and making peace with life's limitations. *Manito*, a feature film produced with a documentary feel, treats the drug trade years as the source of a toxic residue of violence, exploitation, and distrust. Contrary to the image of drug dealers as uptown Robin Hoods or eager entrepreneurs who would have become legitimate businessmen in better circumstances, the dealer in *Manito* is a selfish man who wrecks his family.[54]

Infinitely less bleak in its perspective on Washington Heights was *Mad Hot Ballroom*, a 2005 documentary about New York City public school children in Tribeca, the Bensonhurst section of Brooklyn, and Washington Heights who compete in a ballroom dancing competition. The filmmakers knew that the Heights had a reputation for poverty and crime, so they concentrated on what people didn't know about the neighborhood: the dreams and ambitions of its children. There is a sense in the film, as the *Times* critic A. O. Scott noticed, that the students from Tribeca "expect to win" the competition but the students from the Heights (or at least their extraordinary teacher) "need to win." The film's camera crew captured the eventual victory of the Washington Heights team, but left them as they took the subway uptown with their trophy. There, the camera crew missed the real ending of the competition: the crowds of Washington Heights residents who cheered the children as they emerged from the subway.[55]

Underdogs who become winners is an old theme in immigrant New York. So is getting out of your old neighborhood to seek a better life. All of these themes appeared in two feature films made about Washington Heights, *Take the Bridge* (2006) by the Chilean filmmaker Sergio Castilla, and *GWB* (2010) by Jonathan Ullman. Both are set in the years after the crime drop. In both films, drug dealers are a presence in the neighborhood that the protagonists overcome. Both films were shot with loving attention to the buzz of the street and the natural beauty of the Hudson River, and the title of each film played off the defining landmark of Washington Heights—the George Washington Bridge.[56]

For Castilla, a Chilean who made his film after many years in New York, *Take the Bridge* was an ode to New York's "last neighborhood," a place where an older city of corner stores, grandmothers watching over sidewalks, and kids playing on the street still survives. His protagonists—four young people who have all tried to commit suicide, an issue in Castilla's own family history—wrestle with whether to stay in Washington Heights or break free from it and "everything that holds us back." In they end they leave, triumphant and exultant, speeding west across the George Washington Bridge.

Take the Bridge was Castilla's farewell to New York City before he moved to Europe. For Ullman, *GWB* was film about a neighborhood he grew to love. Living at 158th and Riverside, he noticed that the neighborhood was often used as a setting for films and television series about general urban themes. Rarely, however, was it the subject of work that told Washington Heights' own stories. In a neighborhood where, as one character says, you've got to "make it to take it," two young boys run off with drug dealers' money. The drug dealers come in pursuit. Official sources of authority are not much help, so the boys rely on their friends and family to help them through the ordeal that follows.

As in *Take the Bridge*, the protagonists of *GWB* (which went into commercial distribution in 2012 under the name of *Trouble in the Heights*) eventually leave Washington Heights. In both films, the protagonists have surmounted the challenges of their neighborhood. Neither film sees the lingering shadow of the crack years as anything but a bleak remnant. Both look forward to a better future. In such stories, after many difficult years, Dominican residents of Washington Heights could claim something like a victory. For all the romance around immigrant neighborhoods in New York City, for their residents a large part of life is dedicated to making it—and for young people, as Marshall Berman observed of his beloved postwar Bronx, that usually means getting out. In the twenty-first century Dominican Washington Heights took its place in the history of New York's immigrant enclaves, alongside the Irish Five Points and the Jewish Lower East Side, in its scale, its struggles, and ultimately in its residents' willingness to leave it for better places when they had the chance.[57]

More recognition of the struggles and victories of Dominican Washington Heights emerged from Cayena Publications. Founded by Mary Ely Peña-Gratereaux—who immigrated to New York in 1965 and has worked as a mediator in northern Manhattan—Cayena in 2000 published the first of a series of books on Dominicans, the Dominican immigrant experience in the United States, mediation, and social justice. Among its productions are a book and documentary on workers at Madame Alexander's Dolls Factory, a plant in Manhattan that employed generations of immigrant workers, most recently Dominicans. It closed in 2012 after more than a decade of shipping jobs overseas ended in a change in ownership. In its emphasis on labor and commitment, albeit with a sad ending, *The Faces behind the Dolls: Los Rostros Detrás de las Muñecas* is a welcome corrective to discussions of Dominican New Yorkers that emphasize cultural explanations for poverty. The problem of New York City's economy, the film suggests, is not a lack of a work ethic among immigrants but the lack of secure, economically sustaining jobs for immigrant workers.[58]

Literary works also revised the image of the neighborhood. In the novels of Angie Cruz, born in Washington Heights in 1972 and raised at Broadway and 165th Street, northern Manhattan becomes part of a flow of stories, people, and memories that swirl between the United States and the Dominican Republic. *Soledad* (2001) and *Let It Rain Coffee* (2005) explore a Washington Heights that is a crossroads of past and present, alive with pain, resilience, and possibilities. (*Soledad* begins with a young Dominican woman living downtown summoned home to the Heights because her mother is in ill health. Soledad gripes, "It's *always* like that: just when I think I don't give a shit about what my family thinks, they find a way to drag me back home.") In both books, readers far from northern Manhattan could discover the complexity of Dominican experiences. *Soledad*, like the writings of Junot Diaz set in northern New Jersey, suggested that as important as Washington Heights was for Dominicans, it was no longer the only plausible setting for their lives in the United States.[59]

A red carpet was rolled out to Broadway outside Coogan's. Inside nervousness mixed with joy and pride as the crowd watched a live broadcast of the 2008 Tony Awards for excellence in Broadway theater. Earlier in the evening *In the Heights*—a musical about the Latinos of northern Manhattan and the meaning of home—won prizes for its score, choreography, and orchestration. Yet the biggest prize of the night remained. "One more award—one big one," said Peter Walsh, the co-owner of Coogan's. Finally, around 11 p.m., Whoopi Goldberg announced the winner of the 2008 Tony Award for Best Musical: *In the Heights*. Coogan's erupted in cheers. Guillermo Linares, now commissioner of the Mayor's Office of Immigrant Affairs, was euphoric.

"A motorcade," he exulted, "we gotta do a motorcade. We got to bring it in the community." Onstage, producer Jill Furman accepted the award surrounded by members of the show's cast and creative team, among them Lin-Manuel Miranda—the Puerto Rican New Yorker from Inwood who conceived the musical, wrote its music and lyrics, played one of its lead roles, and had already taken the stage to wave a small Puerto Rican flag and rap out his acceptance speech for best score. At Coogan's, celebrants went home to the sound of firecrackers popping in the streets of Washington Heights.[60]

The neighborhood portrayed in the musical was a far cry from the one portrayed in the news media in the early 1990s. Gone were the stories of drug dealers and murderers. Instead, the musical fused rap, hip-hop, salsa, and merengue to paint an optimistic portrait of hard-working immigrants striving for the American dream. *In the Heights*, so far the most acclaimed work of art to emerge from northern Manhattan, was the product of a dynamic neighborhood, old and new currents in popular culture, and the genius of Lin-Manuel Miranda. Miranda, the son of one of the publishers of the *Manhattan Times*, was at once an insider and an outsider in the new New York that emerged in northern Manhattan in the late twentieth century. Miranda lived in a neighborhood with plenty of bodega owners, taxi drivers, and guys hanging out on the corner, but he went to the Upper East Side every day to study at Hunter College High School, one of the city's most academically demanding public schools. He wrote a little for the *Manhattan Times* and attended Wesleyan University, where he first wrote a play about his old neighborhood that eventually became *In the Heights*, produced off Broadway in 2007 and then on Broadway in 2008.

In the play, people could see more clearly something that had long been true about Washington Heights: it was a neighborhood of Latino immigrants, most of them Dominicans, struggling to make homes in northern Manhattan. Dominicans could finally claim a place of their own in New York City's rainbow of immigrant groups. For all the differences among them, Dominicans were as much a part of the Heights as the Irish, Jews, and Greeks. Yet, there was no guarantee that Dominicans as a group would achieve the kind of security and prosperity that their predecessors found, either in Washington Heights or in the suburbs beyond. Affirmation and anxiety both ran through *In the Heights*.

In structure, the play was a classic Broadway musical inspired by many works that came before it. (Miranda once joked that when disputes arose in rehearsals, he settled them by saying: No, that's not how they do it in *Fiddler on the Roof*.) In its book, music, and dance, however, the show was completely a part of contemporary New York. Miranda used Spanglish, hip-hop, Latin music, and hybrids of all three to create sights and sounds that emerged from Nueva York. In an age when so many musicals were revivals or British imports or corporate productions, *In the Heights* was grounded in its city of origin. It recalled the best works of Edward Harrigan and Tony Hart, whose songs and stories chronicled the immigrant communities of the Lower East Side at the end of the nineteenth century, and the best mid-twentieth-century Broadway musicals, like *On the Town*, which turned popular music and dance into memorable theater. With *In the Heights*, the sounds and soul of New York reclaimed the Broadway stage.

Miranda cast the Latino experience in northern Manhattan in universal terms. *In the Heights* was not just a musical representation of days and nights in an ethnic enclave; it was a dynamic meditation on the meaning of home. While the older Jewish and Irish communities of northern Manhattan had barely any presence in the play, Miranda said he was gratified by how many viewers told him after seeing the show that he had grasped themes common to all immigrant groups.

Like the generations before them, the people of *In the Heights* wrestle with the choice between staying in the neighborhood and leaving to make it in the wider world. There is one modestly successful businessman among them—the owner of a livery cab company—but otherwise the people of *In the Heights* are too poor to think about making money off real estate in their neighborhood. Instead, they worry about rent increases. (One subplot has gossipy hair salon owners moving to the Bronx in pursuit of cheaper rents.)

Almost all of the characters in the play are Latinos who trace their roots to the Caribbean. There are no obvious ethnic antagonists in the play, but one love affair is sharpened by the implicit point that it unites a Dominican woman and an African American man. As in *West Side Story* and *Fiddler on the Roof*, with their interethnic and interreligious love affairs, the freedom to love remains a strong theme in Broadway musicals—an inheritance from New Deal New York's opposition to bigotry and the gay men who worked the theme into many musicals. Neither does the play valorize the thug life that claimed too many lives in the Heights during the crack years. Indeed, it opens with a bodega owner who begins his day's work by chasing away a graffiti tagger.[61]

Miranda's musical closed a narrative that began in 1957, when *West Side Story* first appeared on Broadway. *West Side Story* had attempted to tell its own story of turf, ethnic conflict, and forbidden love. Its choreography was mesmerizing, its music superb, and its effort to make a musical engage social issues laudable. Its great flaw was that the Puerto Ricans depicted in the play were someone's idea of Puerto Ricans, not Puerto Ricans representing themselves. *In the Heights* was a musical by and about Latino New Yorkers. It drew deeply on Broadway traditions, but exuberantly mixed them with Latin music and hip-hop. In *West Side Story*, the Puerto Ricans are rejected newcomers who barely get to speak for themselves. The people of *In the Heights* are on their home ground, singing in their own voices. Their song is New York City's song.

In the Heights acclaims the hard work and communal feel that define the neighborhood, with all of these framed by the contrary tugs of the Caribbean and New York City, past and present, the community and the individual. Indeed, some of the sharpest conflicts in the play embroil individuals who wrestle with the weight of their family's and neighbors' expectations in work, education, and love. Like Maria in *West Side Story*, or Tevye's daughters in *Fiddler on the Roof*, it is women who aspire to live boldly in this play—overturning traditions, going away to college, or heading downtown to start a new career. Men are the ones who stay in the neighborhood—partly out of loyalty to their community, partly because their talents for running a bodega or a car service don't translate well in the wider world.

All of these conflicts and worries are resolved in the last act by a miraculous intervention. In this respect, *In the Heights* is very much part of the Broadway tradition. The ending is not entirely happy—departures from the neighborhood in the face of rent increases echo the Jewish departure from Anatevka in *Fiddler on the Roof*, but without the violence of a pogrom. You can't help but wonder whether the neighborhood scholarship girl will be satisfied with her taxi dispatcher boyfriend once she earns a degree from Stanford. Nevertheless, the final scenes of *In the Heights* are sustaining, affirming, and even cautiously optimistic about what the future will bring. In all these respects, the play is very much in tune with the real world of Washington Heights.

EPILOGUE

AT A DISCUSSION OF THE HISTORY OF NORTHERN MANHATTAN, a longtime resident asked me a sharp question: Wasn't my research focusing too much on the negative aspects of the past in Washington Heights?[1]

It was true that I identified problems in the neighborhood, I said, but I did that to illuminate the challenges that its residents faced. Every New York City neighborhood, I said, has its flaws. The strength of Washington Heights, I insisted, lay in its residents' ability to confront and—sometimes to overcome—problems that wracked cities in the late twentieth century.

Our exchange was one of many conversations I had with senior citizens from northern Manhattan under the auspices of the YM-YWHA. We met at the Y and in common rooms of local apartment buildings after lunch or dinner. My job was to deliver a short talk on the history of northern Manhattan and then run a discussion about what we might learn from its recent past. The talks were attended by an ethnically and racially mixed group of elderly people who were typically Jewish, Irish, African American, and Latino.

I discovered quickly that the past provided both islands of consensus and grounds for disagreement. Everyone shook their heads at the racist and anti-Semitic efforts to keep African Americans and Jews out of Washington Heights. People cringed when I mentioned that Kenneth Clark was directed to attend a vocational school. The Farmer case was universally seen as a tragedy. Crime was widely recognized as a blight on everyone's life. At the same time, the record of the Lindsay administration in upper Manhattan, and

Figure 14: Lin-Manuel Miranda and the cast of *In the Heights*, United Palace Theater, West 175th St. Photograph by Mike Fitelson.

the activism of Ellen Lurie, received some sharp criticism. It was especially difficult to discuss northern Manhattan's school wars. Some white residents fiercely rejected any use of the term segregation, pointing out that African American students had long attended George Washington High School. But people were awkward talking about the racially aligned gang fights outside it, the tracking practices inside it, and the different experiences of white, African American, and Latino students there. For some older residents of Washington Heights, it can be difficult to square their right to the city with that of newer African American and Latino residents. At the end of my first session, after a long debate on school politics, an elderly African American man who had kept quiet throughout the night sidled over to me. Then he leaned over and whispered in a low and friendly voice, "You can learn a lot if you're willing to listen." I like to think he spoke for all of us.

It would be wrong, however, to think that the history of Washington Heights boiled down to nothing more than differences and divisions. Even though people never achieved anything like "unity," they did find ways to work together often enough to make a significant difference in the welfare of their neighborhood. As Marshall Berman observed of many corners of New York that emerged from the "city of ruins" of the 1970s, in Washington Heights people faced disaster, carried on, and "in the midst of falling apart, found ways to rise." All of this was on display on July 24, 2008, at a celebration of the life of Stanley Michels, the former city councilman from northern Manhattan who had worked tirelessly for tenants, public parks, and environmental health. Under bright summer sunshine in Fort Tryon Park, where a glance takes in the Hudson River, the cliffs of the Palisades, and the towers of the George Washington Bridge, I wandered through a crowd of Michels's friends and family. Beneath leafy trees and a temporary canopy stood old and new generations of Washington Heights.[2]

The old Washington Heights of Irish, Jewish, and Greek residents was present, but the current officials and officeholders were mostly Dominicans and African Americans. Sick with cancer, Michels listened with his family as speakers recalled his life and extolled his work. Henry Stern, a former city councilmember and parks commissioner, reminisced about how Michels, a boxer, protected Stern from bullies when they went to public school together in Inwood. Recalling Michels's political evolution, Stern joked, "I knew him as a regular, I knew him as a reformer." He also reminded listeners that Michels, a Democrat, was a staunch advocate for tenants. "I am only sorry," Stern quipped, "that we did not achieve his goal of free rent for all." Michels loved jazz, so Marjorie Eliot and friends played tunes and backed up the singing of Jackie Rowe-Adams—a union leader, Harlem mother, and an activist against gun violence who lost two sons in shootings.

Friends from politics and government described Michels as one of the saviors of Washington Heights. He was born into the New York of Fiorello La Guardia, but when he was first elected to the city council in 1977 there was widespread fear that Washington Heights would burn like the South Bronx. In response, Michels worked to save threatened housing stock. The parks were also a mess, but over the years he allocated $50 million to green spaces in Inwood, Washington Heights, and Harlem. Remarkably, given the dire conditions of the 1980s and early 1990s, Michels had lived to see all three neighborhoods rebound.

Guillermo Linares, now a member of the Bloomberg administration, called Michels "a champion of all New Yorkers." Amid the murders of the crack years, Linares said, Michels fought not only to get a new police precinct for Washington Heights—the 33rd—but also to improve relations between the police and the community. The crime drop, Linares insisted, was one of Michels's achievements. As Linares concluded, his voice rising so that no one could miss the importance of his words, he addressed Michels directly and said that "millions of people's lives today are better for your leadership and dedication."

Michels finally rose to respond. Visibly ailing and speaking with emotion, he praised Steve Simon (his former chief of staff and a perpetual presence in efforts to improve northern Manhattan) and thanked his family for their support. "This is a neighborhood where we all worked together for the benefit of all," he said. With that, the celebrants unveiled a sign announcing that the walkway into Fort Tryon Park, with its splendid view of cultivated gardens and the Hudson River beyond, would now be known as the "Stan Michels Promenade." Marjorie Eliot and friends broke into Stevie Wonder's "I Just Called to Say I Love You." A week later, Michels died.

Michels was an important figure in northern Manhattan, but as he himself recognized there was credit to be shared in Washington Heights' passage out of its bleakest years. A network of neighborhood agencies and dedicated individuals played important parts. Dominican organizations, together with older nonprofits like the Northern Manhattan Improvement Corporation and the Washington Heights–Inwood Coalition, played a vital role in sustaining northern Manhattan and easing the stubborn persistence of poverty. Equally important were the police officers, activists, elected officials, and residents who achieved, sometimes in contentious and uneven ways, a vital measure of collective efficacy in struggles against crime.

Indeed, the decline of crime was the biggest and most influential change for the better in Washington Heights—a development shared with the rest of the city that had special resonance uptown, where the killings of the crack years drove so many people to fear and despair. In 2010 the *Manhattan Times* asked State Assemblyman Linares: "What has been the biggest change in Northern Manhattan over the last 10 years?" Linares's response was unequivocal: the crime drop. The area went from being one of the city's most dangerous areas to one of its safest. "This change," Linares told the *Manhattan Times*, "has made Northern Manhattan much more attractive as a place to live, work, visit, shop, and to start a business."[3]

The collective efficacy deployed against crime, like the collective efficacy that met the problem of housing decay in the 1970s, was not a universal solution. The poverty of Washington Heights, for example, had roots in global economic relations that could not be overturned from one New York City neighborhood. Local action could ameliorate but not end economic inequality in northern Manhattan. But local action could make a dent in problems that were, due to complex social and economic factors, open to solutions close at hand. When housing abandonment threatened Washington Heights the Community Preservation Corporation, activists, and city officials brought in sufficient resources to stem the progress of blight. Together, they saved buildings that were then populated by Dominican immigrants. Similarly, for all the profound questions raised by crime and the crack trade in Washington Heights, both problems turned out to be susceptible to local solutions applied by police, activists, and elected officials.

Once collective efficacy made its contribution to the crime drop, people in Washington Heights could begin to reclaim their right to the city. Fearfully at first, and then energetically, they recovered their streets and sidewalks. Informally on their home blocks, and then in organized events like the Arts Stroll, they emerged from fear and isolation. The newly safe streets made possible the vigorous cultural scene that contributed significantly to the revival of northern Manhattan.

Of course, crime and fear did not vanish entirely. Drug dealing remained a presence in northern Manhattan, but without the turf wars of the past. People continued to use cocaine, but the industry that supplied them moved indoors and was not what it once was in Washington Heights. Street crime, although diminished, could still set people on edge. Moreover, domestic violence was a serious problem. A municipal report issued in 2008 calculated that northern Manhattan had the highest rate of domestic violence in all of Manhattan. The problem was found in all ethnic groups. Among Dominicans, it festered in the lives of angry, patriarchal, and frustrated men who lashed out at independent women and women whose undocumented immigration status made them slow to seek help from authorities. Battering was strenuously opposed by Dominican elected officials and neighborhood organizations, but it remained a problem long after other forms of violence ceased to torment upper Manhattan.[4]

Another echo of the high crime years was the "stop and frisk" tactics of the police department. During the Bloomberg administration, the number of African American and Latino men stopped by the police surged. The practice—as four police officers (two of them from northern Manhattan) explained to me in a long conversation at Coogan's—damaged the friendly relations between police and residents that are vital to effective policing.[5] The criminal justice system could produce destabilizing effects of its own. The Rockefeller drug laws, with their stiff sentences for drug offenses, wracked Washington Heights even after the laws were reformed and New York City reduced its incarceration rate. A map tabulating the density of paroles and prison admissions by zip code showed that southern Washington Heights, according to a 2008 study, had northern Manhattan's highest rate of parolees and prison admissions. Also unsettling in the neighborhood—upsetting families, fragmenting communities, and creating mistrust between residents and authorities—has been the deportation of Dominican residents under a tightening of immigration laws that began under the Clinton administration and accelerated after the September 11 attacks. In the same years, however, there have been improvements. One of the best achievements of the crime drop years has been the decline in incarceration in New York State since the 1990s, driven largely by a reduction in felony arrests in New York City that has reduced the number of people in jail, in prison, on parole and on probation. Coming as it has alongside the crime drop, the trend shows that mass incarceration is not necessary to reduce crime. It also points to a future in New York City where the experience of imprisonment is less common.[6]

As welcome as the crime drop was, it was part of a larger set of changes that left New York City with a thinner, less generous political culture. Before the fiscal crisis, fear, and economic decay of the 1970s, Susan Fainstein argues, New York City was "possibly the most egalitarian of any American city." Since then, it has become a global city with greater inequality, diminished democracy, and—thanks to arrival of two million people from around the world—a place of continued and "extraordinary" vitality.[7]

Yet as early as 1981, when Ira Katznelson published his study of Washington Heights and Inwood, *City Trenches*, he noted a paradox. As the gulf between rich and poor grew in northern Manhattan, in New York City, and indeed in most American cities, there were no upheavals of protest. It was stretching things, he concluded, to call this a story of success.[8]

In 2012, the historian Michael B. Katz picked up the same question in his book *Why Don't American Cities Burn?* and offered three explanations for the absence of protests. First, new forms of segregation separated warring groups from each other. There were no longer gang wars between the descendants of the Jesters and the Egyptian Kings because the heirs of the Jesters were all living in white suburbs, leaving their black and Latino rivals behind in the city.[9] Second, just enough African Americans had been incorporated into the middle class to diminish the urgency of protest. The incarceration of large numbers of African American men, and militarized forms of policing, Katz also argued, had locked up or dissuaded potential protestors.[10]

The third and final factor Katz examined was immigration. Despite some anti-immigrant sentiment among some Americans, the United States is far more open to immigrants than European countries. Even though the U.S. government has deported large numbers of undocumented workers, immigrant protestors in the United States have generally sought citizenship and have largely seen government as a "potential ally," Katz argues. Their presence in cities has "irrevocably smashed" thinking about the United States in terms of blacks and whites alone.

Washington Heights displays these tensions and achievements in microcosm for an array of recent immigrant groups—not just the numerically dominant Dominicans, but also the Mexicans, Ecuadorians, Salvadorans, and Cubans of northern Manhattan. If the current social order has some legitimacy for immigrants, it is because the social peace and prosperity of New York City is in significant measure their achievement. This does not by itself compensate for massive inequalities, but it does give immigrants a reason to attach themselves to life in New York despite all countervailing pressures.

In this situation, Katz argues, the "existential dilemma" of urban studies is the challenge of telling the stories of American cities in ways that recognize the dogged energy of city dwellers, the obstacles faced by poor people and immigrants in cities, and the importance of government in creating just cities. Neither naive optimism nor paralyzing cynicism will work.[11]

All of these contradictions and challenges are abundantly on display in New York City and Washington Heights. Immigrants, as David Dyssegaard Kallick has noted, have played an important role in restoring New York City's population and economic vitality since the bleak years of the 1970s. Indeed, they are more widely scattered through the spectrum of occupations than conventional wisdom suggests. Yet the rewards of their labor are unevenly distributed. Immigrants and their children are making their way in an economy that is sharply polarized at the expense of middle income jobs. Moreover, they work in an economy where race and ethnicity influence economic outcomes. White immigrants earn more than immigrants of color, and Latino immigrants tend to earn low wages whatever their level of education.[12] Washington Heights often seems to be poised between hope and fear, between poverty and prosperity. This delicately balanced duality is closely tied to the neighborhood's Dominican community, which includes the very poor, striving immigrants, and American-born or raised residents making impressive strides into the middle class through politics, business, the arts, science, and medicine.

In 2010 Dominicans in northern Manhattan were still the majority of Hispanics in a Hispanic-majority area. Their economic, social, and political status set the basic terms for Washington Heights and Inwood. Citywide, according to a social science study, the children of Dominican immigrants were doing better than young Puerto Ricans and African Americans, but not as well as the children of other immigrant groups—West Indians, Chinese, and Russians. Dominican-born workers were also more likely to be union members than U.S.-born workers, but less unionized than other immigrant groups who were more likely to be public sector workers or longer-term residents of the United States.

Looking at the span of immigrants in white collar versus service and blue collar jobs, Dominicans were more likely to labor in blue collar or service work than immigrants overall or native-born Americans. However, they were less likely to be found in these less rewarding areas of work than immigrants from Mexico, Honduras, and Ecuador. This was a testament to Dominican determination and the fact that many Dominicans confront an unforgiving job market and an American bias against dark-colored skin. Equally significant, Dominicans who live transnational lives often wound up splitting limited financial resources between two countries, diminishing the amount of money they could devote to themselves in the expensive city of New York.[13] As in so many other measurements, Dominicans found themselves poised in a shaky middle ground: better off than the worst off, but still not fully secure and prosperous.[14] Their precarious position as an ethnic group spelled continued uncertainty for Washington Heights.

The 2010 federal census documented Dominicans' complicated position in northern Manhattan. The New York City Department of City Planning reported that the population of Washington Heights and Inwood went from 208,414 in 2000 to 190,020 in 2010. Most striking was the decline of the number of Hispanics overall in Washington Heights and Inwood and Dominicans in particular, with Dominicans moving into upper Harlem and the Bronx, presumably in pursuit of less expensive housing. The black population of upper Manhattan continued a long-term decline, especially in the southern Heights. The white population of Washington Heights grew—especially among young people. The population shift was reflected in the neighborhood's public schools, some of which had for the first time in many years more seats than they could fill.

Hispanics who had earlier moved into more prosperous parts of Washington Heights and Inwood west of Broadway maintained a presence, but their numbers fell. In 2000, census tract 273 in the western Heights along upper Fort Washington Avenue was 33 percent Hispanic; in 2010 the figure was 26 percent. In 2000 census tract 295 in western Inwood was 60 percent Hispanic; in 2010 56 percent. It is not yet clear whether these changes signal a wholesale transformation of the neighborhood or the emergence of a new but recognizable community with a larger white population, a smaller black population, and a middle class grounded in Latinos and the children of Dominican immigrants that is a strong but not growing presence.

Alongside these changes, neighborhood social service agencies that had long served the poor closed or shrank and new institutions emerged. The growth of northern Manhattan's multiethnic arts scene, the rise of the *Uptown Collective* blog, the opening of the "community bookstore and arts space" Word Up, and a strip of cafés on western Dyckman Street catering to young American-born or American-raised Latinos all suggest that the children of Latin America will be an important part of a reviving and gentrifying Washington Heights.[15]

Ironically, if there is unease in northern Manhattan today it is the consequence of better times than anyone imagined in the bad days of the crack epidemic. In the forums I conducted under the auspices of the YM-YWHA, the drop in crime was universally appreciated. Older inhabitants—African American, Latino, and white—who knew Washington Heights and Inwood in their bleakest years regaled me with stories about the changes wrought by new residents they described as "professionals," "young people," and "yuppies." Most of the changes were good, they said: better places to shop and eat. They also had some complaints about the new people's child-rearing practices. Two older women complained to me that recent residents' children were ill-mannered, showed insufficient respect for their elders, and were even seen urinating in the gutter. I listened and concluded that this was the kind of complaint that old-timers had long leveled at newcomers in Washington Heights and Inwood.

It would be easy but misleading to say that the senior citizens I spoke with objected to gentrification. They clearly liked some aspects of gentrification, in particular the neighborhood's greater commercial vitality. What they objected to was the prospect of rent increases that might price them, their children, or their grandchildren out of the neighborhood. Compared to other neighborhoods, Washington Heights and Inwood never had much publicly subsidized affordable housing to begin with, and over the years the number of these apartments has declined. Rent stabilization that limits rent increases in privately owned apartment buildings is common in northern Manhattan, but tenants can lose this protection in a number of ways. Residents and elected officials alike argue that landlords have a financial incentive to push tenants off rent stabilization, leading to evictions, housing court proceedings, and neglect of conditions in stabilized apartments. One man, an Irish American schoolteacher and longtime Heights resident, e-mailed me to explain the dilemma. Once, he said, people left Washington Heights for a better place—typically, the New Jersey suburbs. Now, they left for cheaper and less pleasant neighborhoods, like parts of the west Bronx, because they couldn't afford Washington Heights. And there was no chance that the children of today's modestly middle-class residents would take up residence in Washington Heights. It was just becoming too expensive.[16]

It is not simply gentrification, but more accurately economic inequality that threatens the different peoples of Washington Heights. In interviews and informal conversations with residents, people often expressed to me a fear of losing their apartment because a rent increase makes it unaffordable. Most troubling for senior citizens, however, was something even more specific: the thought that, having stuck it out in difficult times, they and their descendants in their neighborhood might not be able to enjoy the future. Having regained their right to their city in the face of crime and blight, they now feared losing it to inequality.

If old and new residents agree on the problems before them, it is not clear—given the vigor of the real estate market and the limits on government intervention in New York—how much they can do about it. Nor is it clear that the young people who move to northern Manhattan in search of lower rents—who are often seeking to make their own futures in New York—should have to abandon their right to the city so that older residents can enjoy theirs.

The phrase "right to the city" has origins on the left, but it can surely be interpreted in narrow and even exclusionary ways. Collective efficacy can be employed to elevate a common good or to keep out newcomers. The history of Washington Heights suggests that, for most people, the right to the city is an abstraction. They experience the city most vividly not in well-defined neighborhoods—like Washington Heights or Inwood—but in smaller enclaves, like the upper reaches of Fort Washington Avenue, where my parents' world ran no farther south than 181st Street and no farther east than Broadway.

If one of the defining urban problems of the last fifty years is the difficulty of cities making policies that adequately meet the needs of poor and working people, we cannot expect neighborhoods in isolation to do any better. Neighborhood life might be made more democratic from the bottom up, but social and economic conditions can be improved only with money and resources collected and allocated from higher levels of government. Radicals, liberals, and even moderates can make their own contributions to this cause.

The transition from La Guardia's New York to Bloomberg's New York has been described as a shift from the New Deal to the New Gilded Age. In recovering a healthier balance between economic and civic interests, and between the individual and the collective, we can still learn much from New Deal New York. Its racial exclusions were real and should never be ignored or repeated, but it offered high and inclusive ideals worth living up to: "a great democratic community where . . . millions of people may enjoy larger measures of freedom." My research convinced me that it is still too early to call Washington Heights, much less New York City, "a great democratic community." Still, after many years of studying disputes and differences, it was bracing to participate in discussions at the Y and hear many different kinds of people in Washington Heights and Inwood recognize that when it came to economic inequality, they shared common interests and a common problem.[17]

In the 2013 mayoral race, Democrat Bill de Blasio—the city's public advocate and a former member of the city council from Brooklyn—argued that New York was defined by a "tale of two cities," one increasingly rich and the other economically stagnant or poor, and vowed to reduce inequality. He also opposed "stop and frisk" policing and embraced the multiracial, multiethnic reality of the city. His opponent, the Republican Joseph J. Lhota, a deputy mayor in the Giuliani administration, distinguished himself as chairman of the Metropolitan Transit Authority by getting the city's subways running quickly after the disaster of Hurricane Sandy. Lhota ran on a narrow platform, arguing that de Blasio's strategies for policing and economic development would bring back high crime and damage the city's prosperity. De Blasio trounced Lhota and easily carried northern Manhattan.[18]

De Blasio's electoral victory and his appointments and initiatives early in his first term suggested that he had effectively made himself the beneficiary of a new common sense that had emerged over the last two decades in New York City. In campaigning against stop and frisk and appointing William J. Bratton as police commissioner, de Blasio addressed distinct but complementary goals: he sought to improve police–community relations, to change a policy that seemed to criminalize young men of color, and to maintain the low crime rates that New Yorkers valued since the early 1990s. Bratton was, after all, the police commissioner whose policies had been associated with the crime drop since his days in the Giuliani administration. Equally important, the generally enthusiastic and affectionate reaction to de Blasio's African American wife and multiracial children suggested that New York City was more at ease with ethnic and racial differences. Entrenched patterns of inequality showed that New York was by no means a "post-racial city," but the enthusiasm for de Blasio's family suggested that the city's grizzled racial and ethnic animosities had lost some of their political potency. In support for de Blasio's strong stance against economic inequality there was a loud signal that New Yorkers, whatever their differences, shared a deep concern that a squeezed middle class and a growing gap between rich and poor were bad for the city. The challenge that remained for de Blasio after inauguration day was to craft a mix of policies and political alignments that would bring a shared prosperity and a better economic future to a majority of New Yorkers.

The old Washington Heights was lifted up by the New Deal and sustained (at least for a time) by the Great Society, both of which were national efforts to reduce inequalities of power and prosperity. In a world where the wealth of nations no longer sustains individual neighborhoods and nations have limited capacities to cope with globalization, analysts look to local, metropolitan, and global solutions to urban problems.[19]

New York City is finally emerging from the political stances and mindsets of the urban crisis. In that time, too many of New York City's large public services—especially the police and the schools—were ineffective. Thrown back on their own resources, many New Yorkers embraced local activism and what Marshall Berman has called "a romance of the small." That response, for all its merits, is not by itself adequate to meet the problems wrought by globalization. The social and economic problems of the twenty-first century demand measures that are at once local and global, regional and national, participatory but sustained by larger and unavoidably impersonal structures. In effect, people will have to reconcile their localism and cosmopolitanism in constructive ways. Fortunately, there are precedents for this in the history of Washington Heights.[20]

As the years of the urban crisis recede into the past, the peoples of Washington Heights live in crosscurrents of remembering and forgetting. Each has its uses.

For the youngest residents of Washington Heights, there is little memory of the bleak years that scarred the neighborhood's reputation. Their optimism, and their elders' resolve, took public form on June 6, 2012, when residents of northern Manhattan trekked through Washington Heights and Inwood in Hike the Heights. The event was organized by northern Manhattan's community organizations, the New York City Department of Parks and Recreation, and Mindy Thompson Fullilove, MD—who had researched the depths of fear in the neighborhood as it emerged from the crack years. The reporter Sarah Rahman observed that walkers included middle-aged Dominicans, enthusiastic white gentrifiers, and African American and Latino kids. Rahman interviewed participants and was struck by two sets of responses. The middle-aged Dominicans, vocal activists, had lived through the years of crack, crime, and decay. They did not want to go back to them and opposed budget cuts proposed by Mayor Bloomberg because they feared that they would begin a return to the bad old days. The young African American and Latino kids, however, had no memory of the crack years. They liked Washington Heights and couldn't see why anyone would think badly of it. They were also confident that they were capable of handling any problems that appeared in their neighborhood.[21] Whether the future rewards those young people's convictions or shatters them will be the final verdict on the drop in crime and rise in gentrification in Washington Heights and New York City.

A year later, in a small park in the middle of Broadway at 167th Street, a gathering of Dominicans, historically minded New Yorkers, and mayoral candidates celebrated the renaming of Broadway from 159th Street to 218th Street as Juan Rodriguez Way. The event—at a location next to a monument to men from Washington Heights and Inwood who had served in World War I, across the street from New York-Presbyterian Hospital, a block from the Audubon Ballroom, and two blocks south of Coogan's—was one more layer in the dense mix of history and memory in Washington Heights. It was also testimony to the changing Dominican presence in New York City.

Research conducted by the Dominican Studies Institute at the City College of New York built a strong case that the first settler to take up residence in what we now know as New York City was Juan (or Jan) Rodríguez, a man of at least partially African ancestry from the island of Hispaniola, which would one day become the home of the Dominican Republic. From the podium in the middle of Broadway, Ramona Hernandez, director of the CUNY Dominican Studies Institute at the City College of New York, joyfully made the point in Spanish and English: the first immigrant in New York was black, a free man from the Caribbean, and Dominican.[22]

Amid the waving of Dominican flags it was possible to forget that Rodríguez came to Manhattan Island (which was not yet New York) from a place that was not yet called the Dominican Republic. As in all ethnic politics, the naming reflected a rich mixture of emotions and ideas: pride in an immigrant whose own personage brought together Africa, the Caribbean, and North America; a desire to put a Dominican imprint on a neighborhood that was becoming less Dominican; and an effort to expand our understanding of who counts in history. For those who think of the English and the Dutch when they think of colonial New York, Juan Rodriquez Way is a reminder that Gotham has long been shaped by peoples from Africa and the Caribbean. Pushing against Dominicans who reject their country's links to Haiti and Africa, Juan Rodriguez Way was an affirmation of Dominicans' multiracial heritage. Speaker after speaker applauded Rodríquez, who bolted from one merchant to another to pursue his own trading interests with the native peoples, as a man of courage, nerve, and independence—qualities long valued in street-smart New York. In naming upper Broadway Juan Rodriguez Way, Dominicans were putting their stamp on the city. They were also claiming their own place as New Yorkers.

The event was identifiably Dominican, but it was not narrow. City Councilman Ydanis Rodriguez, a left-leaning Democrat from northern Manhattan who participated in the Occupy Wall Street movement, drew applause when he spoke for Dominicans and all immigrants about the need for everyone to work together. At the same time, the presence of a succession of mayoral candidates among the speakers was a sure sign that Dominicans were a political constituency of their own to be courted for their votes. Dominicans had followed their own distinct route into the "city trenches" of urban politics, but once they occupied them their political efforts—claiming turf, working to win help from city government, and learning to appeal to both ethnic identity and high principles—had much in common with older ethnic groups. The dedication of Juan Rodriguez Way was both an ending and a beginning in the story of Washington Heights and Dominican New York.

Washington Heights, like the rest of New York City, is a place where simple predictions are confounded by relentless change. Only thirty years after troopships brought jubilant GIs home to New York in 1945, the city was in the depths of the fiscal crisis. Thirty years after the 1977 blackout that was dubbed "The Night of the Animals," the musical *In the Heights* opened off Broadway, affirming the Latino search for home in upper Manhattan and venting anxieties about gentrification. The past and present continue to rub against each other in illuminating ways in northern Manhattan. As the pace of change quickens, an afternoon stroll can bring disorienting surprises. In the fall of 2013, I toured the area with Rosemary Santos, a Dominican American college student researching the recent history of her home neighborhood of Inwood.

Santos and I each had our moments of amazement as we walked south on Broadway from Inwood to Washington Heights. Hers came when we passed a stylish new apartment building that would not look out of place in the gentrifying East Village. Change was something Santos was familiar with: her own family had made the trek from the east side of Broadway to the west. But this building was a new world come to rest in her old neighborhood.

For me, the big shocker was on the banks of the Hudson River. For decades, an old Quonset hut and marina at the foot of Dyckman Street, along with the Inwood Canoe Club to the south, had been reminders of my father's boathouse days. As recently as the summer of 2003, I had launched kayaks at the marina with my friend Frank Carvill and paddled for a happy afternoon on the Hudson. In 2013 the Quonset hut was still there, but it served as storage space for La Marina, a hot spot for riverside dining, dancing, and imbibing. The joys to be found on the banks of the Hudson River are an old theme in my family, but the pleasure ground emerging there was a long way from my dad's weather-beaten world of canoes and boathouses.[23]

On the banks of the Hudson, and in the side streets and avenues of Washington Heights, change mixes gains and losses with hopes and disappointments. In its close brushes with disaster, the history of Washington Heights shows how human action can avert terrible possibilities. Neighborhood activists, however, could not revive a neighborhood by themselves. Improvements in Washington Heights usually rested on support from larger entities of local, state, and federal government. In an era when federal support for cities is not what it was in La Guardia's time, and when New York's mayors since the 1970s generally rejected the kind of redistributive justice that contradicts the logic of the marketplace, solutions to the worst problems of Washington Heights—particularly poverty—were well beyond the reach of residents. Despite such obstacles, the residents of Washington Heights did a lot. Thanks to their efforts, northern Manhattan in the twenty-first century is no longer haunted by fears of terminal decline.

The distribution of the full fruits of neighborhood residents' victory over the many problems that formed the urban crisis and its aftermath, however, remains uncertain. No neighborhood can, by itself, overcome the economic remaking of Manhattan for the world's leisure class. Yet this much is clear: the people who saved Washington Heights in the days of crime and crack deserve more for their pains than a stiff rent increase.[24] The biggest problem people faced in northern Manhattan, which they overcame often enough to revive their neighborhood in difficult times, was the deep-seated tendency of New Yorkers to stick to their familiar turf and tribe. Digging in during hard times, by itself, was not enough. In Washington Heights, in struggles for public safety, for better schools, for adequate housing, and for healthy parks, all the people who made progress proceeded by finding allies across racial, ethnic, and geographical boundaries. Together, in the best sense, they fought for the right to the city—to revive and restore their neighborhood so that they might enjoy a better future there. They learned to work together not because they were all the same, but because they learned to find each other and pursue shared interests that they could achieve only by acting in common. In their efforts, gathering places such as church basements, the YM-YWHA, and Coogan's were as important as the public spaces, such as parks and sidewalks, that they strove to reclaim. In sustaining their neighborhood, residents of Washington Heights discovered their better selves. And they passed on to future generations a neighborhood that still has the basic ingredients of a good city life: solid housing, commercial vitality, beautiful parks, safe streets, and mass transit.

"The past, the present and the possible cannot be separated," argues Henri Lefebvre.[25] If the history of northern Manhattan contains ugly episodes we should not repeat, it also contains achievements worth building on and a lesson for the future. In Washington Heights and the rest of New York, a just, democratic, and sustaining city will be found only by working on both sides of Broadway.

ACKNOWLEDGMENTS

I BEGAN THIS BOOK WITH THE BELIEF that by writing about one neighborhood I could fit in everyone and everything that mattered. In one volume, I hoped to introduce Washington Heights to the world and both sides of Broadway to each other. Years later, I am humbled by the density of human experiences that can be unearthed in a few square blocks of Washington Heights, not to mention all of northern Manhattan.

Washington Heights is rich in residents, former residents, public servants, workers, and knowledgeable observers who shared their memories with me in interviews. Without them, this book would not exist. I offer my deepest thanks to Michael Cohn, Susan Cohn, the Rev. Dr. Barbara K. Lundblad, Al Kurland, Dave Crenshaw, John Culpepper, Manfred Kirchheimer, James Renner, Deborah Dash Moore, Noreen Walck, Sophie Heymann, Celedonia "Cal" Jones, Bob Greenfield, Frank Estrada, Jim Clarke, Gary Zaboly, Herman "Denny" Farrell, Isaiah Bing, James Berlin, Jack Boucher, Frank Hess, Maurice Murad, Leib Lurie, Al Lurie, David Rogers, Judy Baum, Sara Lurie, Samuel Kostman, Daryl West, Laura Altschuler, Helen Blumenthal, Marielys Divanne, Nelsy Aldebot, Ramona De La Cruz, Msgr. Kevin Sullivan, Jerry Travers, Martin Englisher, Msgr. Joachim Beaumont, Deborah Katznelson, John Brian Murtaugh, Franz Leichter, Tom Tedeschi, Edward I. Koch, Michael Lappin, Franz S. Leichter, Beth Rosenthal, Dana Vermilye, Ruth Messinger, Connie Sutton, Joel Rothschild, Roberta Tournour, Ed Sullivan, Milagros Batista, Mary Ely Peña-Gratereaux, anonymous officers in the 34th precinct of the NYPD, Blanca Bettino, Ira Katznelson, David N. Dinkins, Peter Walsh, David Hunt, Regina Gradess, Vivian Ducat, Ray Segal, Mike Fitelson, Elizabeth Loris Ritter, Marjorie Eliot, Steve Simon, Nicholas Estavillo, Amy Sewell, Marilyn Agrelo, Sixto Medina, Sergio Castilla, Jonathan Ullman, Jon Michaud, Demetrios Mihailidis, Led Black, Paul Mishler, Yvonne Stennett, Calvin Thomas, and Rabbi Margaret M. Wenig.

In addition to the many people who sat down with me for interviews, I have been the beneficiary of the thoughts of many individuals in Washington Heights who indulged my questions and observations on park benches and street corners, in coffee shops and on bar stools. I thank you all. If my retelling of the neighborhood's history includes any errors, the fault is mine alone. If this book neglects to tell stories that you think are worth retelling, I encourage you to tell them in your own way. The history of Washington Heights is big enough and complicated enough to deserve more than one book.

Over the years, I have been the beneficiary of fine work from many researchers. I am happy to thank Bruce Cronin, A. J. Madu, Sarah Rahman, Kate Schlott, and Karen Verlaque.

Lucia della Paolera did work as both a translator and researcher. Jesus Ron did translations in an early phase of my research. The proofreading of Aimee Sabo and Lisa DeLisle was a blessing in the final stretch.

Mike Siegel, a skilled, creative, and resourceful cartographer at the Rutgers Cartography Lab, helped me convey changes and continuities in northern Manhattan.

Vivian Ducat and Ray Segal helped me understand the history of Washington Heights and directed me to great photographs of the neighborhood. Joel Rothschild shared his memories and his collection of documents on the Grinnell and Washington Heights.

Demetrios Mihailidis shared with me his memories of Greek Washington Heights and walked me through his old neighborhood with his wife, Olga Touliatos, and their son, Anthony.

Dan Milner—musician, folklorist, and geographer—walked through Washington Heights and Inwood with me and shared his insights on their cultural geography. Jim Melchiorre—former colleague at the Media Studies Center and Inwood resident—shared with me his thoughts on life in northern Manhattan.

Without knowing it, Ron Grele got me started on this book when I took his graduate course in oral history at New York University in 1980, in which I interviewed Irish Americans about their lives in northern Manhattan; my work in oral history is richer for his advice. In the same period, Tom Bender's graduate seminars in urban history at New York University set me to thinking about city life and community in ways that I still ponder.

In the early stages of my research Dorota Socha, then of the Fort Washington Library of the New York Public Library system, gave me access to an extraordinary collection of local newspapers from northern Manhattan that she had compiled. At the CUNY Dominican Studies Institute, a great resource for researchers, I benefited immensely from the deeply informed advice of Chief Librarian Sarah Aponte. Assistant Librarian Nelson Santana and Chief Archivist Idilio Gracia Peña generously directed me to innumerable sources. At the New York City Municipal Archives I received help from Leonora Gidlund, David Ment, and Kenneth Cobb. I have also benefited from the help of the staff of the City Hall Library. In Butler Library at Columbia University, the staff of the Center for Oral History and the staff of the Rare Book and Manuscript Library have been unfailingly helpful.

Librarians at Rutgers–Newark have given me advice over the years. Among them, Roberta Tipton and Natalie Borisovets have been especially helpful in answering questions related to this book. I also want to acknowledge the assistance of librarians at the Stephen A. Schwarzman Building of the New York Public Library and the New York Society Library, where I did much of my research.

Crossing Broadway has been improved by questions and suggestions raised when I presented portions of this book at the Gotham Center for New York City History at the City University of New York Graduate Center; the New School; the Center for Jewish History; the Massachusetts Historical Society; and at meetings of the Researching New York conference at the State University of New York at Albany, the American Historical Association, the Organization of American Historians, the American Studies Association, the Urban History Association, and the Society for Architectural, City and Regional Planning History. At Yeshiva University, Barbara Blatner's invitation to speak at a freshman orientation gave me a valuable opportunity to share ideas with a new generation of students in Washington Heights. Inside and outside these events Joe Salvo, David Rosner, Robert O. Self, Jesse Hoffnung-Garskof, Michael Flamm, Marta Gutman, Jim Carey, Alexander von Hoffman, Fritz Umbach, Elliott Gorn, and Suleiman Osman offered useful comments, suggestions, and answers to my questions.

In the early stages of drafting this book, I received important and helpful advice from Steve Fraser, Anne Edelstein, and Sam Stoloff. Steve Jaffe generously read an entire draft of the book and spent the better part of a day with me discussing revisions. The book is much better for his advice.

Old friends from graduate school days in the History Department at New York University provided valuable suggestions and support. I am happy to thank, after many years of research and friendship, Suzanne Wasserman, Elaine Abelson, Andie Tucher, Lynn Johnson, Susan Yohn, Dan Soyer, Jack

Tchen, Pauline Toole, Marci Reaven, Jeanne Houck and Nancy Robertson. At Rutgers–Newark, American Studies graduate students Sheila Moreira, Rosie Uyola, Sean Singer, and Stuart Gold offered insights on both writing and the recent history of New York City. Among faculty colleagues at Rutgers–Newark, I received ideas and encouragement from Alan Sadovnik, Mark Krasovic, Mara Sidney, Ruth Feldstein, Jim Goodman, Timothy Stewart-Winter, and Jan Lewis. In the American Studies Program at Rutgers–Newark, the superior administrative work of Georgia Mellos helped me concentrate on this book amid all the challenges of life and work.

Working along the border of recent history and current affairs, I learned a great deal from journalists who have reported on Washington Heights and New York City, especially Jim Dwyer (at both *New York Newsday* and the *New York Times*) and Seth Kugel of the *Times*. Sara Rimer's reporting in the *New York Times* on Washington Heights and the George Washington High School baseball team helped me see the neighborhood's strengths in the years of crime and crack. Bill Murphy, Mickey Carroll, and Bob Liff, all formerly of *New York Newsday*, shared with me their deep knowledge of politics and government in New York City. I also learned a lot from community newspapers published across the decades in Washington Heights and Inwood, especially *Heights-Inwood* and the *Manhattan Times*.

I wrote *Crossing Broadway* at The Writers Room, a collegial writers' colony in New York City ably led by Donna Brodie, executive director. Among the many members who shared ideas with me, David Evanier was especially helpful.

Michael McGandy at Cornell University Press has been a model editor. He grasped the value of this project from the start and his sharp questions and high standards have all improved the book. In the peer review process, I was lucky to have Joshua B. Freeman and Eric Schneider, two fine historians of New York, as readers. Their suggestions and queries made *Crossing Broadway* a better book. At Cornell, Karen Hwa and Max Richman ably steered the book through the home stretch.

In many ways, this book began with family stories about Washington Heights and life in New York City. My parents, Max and Mildred Snyder, my aunts Inez Campbell and Tess Gordon, my aunt Helen Lowe, and my cousin Steve Lowe all shared important memories with me. My sister, Ellen Snyder-Grenier, who was born after our family left Washington Heights, shared with me her expertise in photo research and an interview she conducted with our father decades ago about Hudson River canoeing and boathouses.

My friend Frank Carvill was killed in action in Iraq long before I completed this book, but our conversations about politics, history, and New York City are present in every page. Week in and week out over many years, Peter Eisenstadt offered encouragement when my energy flagged as well as wise advice on historical, political, and editorial questions. Without his help I never would have finished.

My family, starting with my parents, has been my greatest source of inspiration. My wife, Clara J. Hemphill, a New Yorker by choice, brought to this project her love and support, her encyclopedic knowledge of New York City public schools, and her unique ability to meld the sharp pen of a journalist with the analytical mind of a social scientist. My son, Max, a New Yorker by birth, helped me see what our city looks like from the perspective of a young man who grows up with hip-hop, safe streets, and classmates from all over the world. My daughter, Allison, also a native New Yorker, who performed with the National Dance Institute while I was writing *Crossing Broadway*, helped me feel the rhythms of the city in its arts and the best possibilities of its culture onstage. This book is dedicated to them.

NOTES

PROLOGUE

1. Author interview with Dave Crenshaw in New York City, 2012, and comments at "A Tribute to Dave 'Coach' Crenshaw," May 2, 2012, New York City, program in possession of author. Washington Heights, according to a widely recognized definition, is northern Manhattan from West 155th Street to Dyckman Street. Inwood, to its immediate north, occupies the rest of Manhattan. Together they comprise Community District 12.

2. Author interview with Al Kurland, New York City, April 12, 2012. Kurland was honored by the Petra Foundation; see www.petrafoundation.org/fellows/Al_Kurland/index.html.

3. My interviews with elderly Irish Americans in 1990 bore fruit in the essay "The Neighborhood Changed: The Irish of Washington Heights and Inwood, 1945–1990," in *The New York Irish*, ed. Ronald Bayor and Timothy Meagher (Baltimore: Johns Hopkins University Press, 1996), 438–60. On the murder of Lena Cronenberger, for which Washington Heights teenager Ivan Mendoza was convicted, see *New York Times*, "Youth, 15, Held in Two Murders," April 19, 1982, B3, and "Editorial Notebook: Bargaining over Murder," August 19, 1983, A20. On Giuliani and D'Amato's drug buy, see photograph in *New York Times*, July 10, 1986, A1, and "New York, Day by Day," B3, in the same issue.

4. The Gannett Center for Media Studies has since closed. Its absence is a great loss for all who care about the best possibilities of journalism and its relationship to academic institutions. My thanks to Everette Dennis, then director of the Gannett Center, and my research assistant there, Bruce Cronin, for all their help.

5. Foremost among the books that have looked at Washington Heights, all of which have taught me a great deal, are Ronald H. Bayor, *Neighbors in Conflict: The Irish, Germans, Jews, and Italians of New York City, 1929–1941* (Baltimore: Johns Hopkins University Press, 1978); Ira Katznelson, *City Trenches: Urban Politics and the Patterning of Class* (Chicago: University of Chicago Press, 1981); Robert Jackall, *Wild Cowboys: Urban Marauders and the Forces of Order* (Cambridge: Harvard University Press, 2005); Stephen Lowenstein, *Frankfurt on the Hudson: The German Jewish Community of Washington Heights, 1933–1983, Its Structure and Culture* (Detroit: Wayne State University Press, 1989); Jesse Hoffnung-Garskof, *A Tale of Two Cities: Santo Domingo and New York after 1950* (Princeton: Princeton University Press, 2008); and James Renner, *Washington Heights Inwood and Marble Hill* (Charleston, SC: Arcadia Publishing, 2007). The value of looking at a small place to understand a large problem was made unforgettably clear to me as a freshman at Livingston College in John Gillis's European history survey during the spring of 1974, when I read Willam Sheridan Allen's *The Nazi Seizure of Power: The Experience of a Single German Town, 1930–1935* (Chicago: Quadrangle

Books, 1965). My understanding of New York has been endlessly enriched by Marshall Berman, *All That is Solid Melts into Air: The Experience of Modernity* (New York: Penguin, 1988).

6. On the transformations of American cities, see Michael B. Katz, *Why Don't American Cities Burn?* (Philadelphia: University of Pennsylvania Press, 2012), 20–22. On the transformation of New York City, see Susan S. Fainstein, *The Just City* (Ithaca: Cornell University Press, 2010), 111–12. My thanks to Robert Self for offering useful ideas on the politics and culture of New York City.

7. See David Harvey, "The Right to the City," *New Left Review* 53 (September–October 2008): 23; Robert E. Park, cited in Harvey, "The Right to the City," 23; and Henri Lefebvre, *Writings on Cities*, translated and edited by Eleonore Kofman and Elizabeth Lebas (Malden, MA: Blackwell, 1996), 53, 75, 140–41, 158, 173–74.

8. See David Harvey, *Rebel Cities: From the Right to the City to the Urban Revolution* (Brooklyn: Verso, 2012), xv; Park, cited in Harvey, "Right to the City," 23; and Lefebvre, *Writings on Cities*, 140–41, 157.

9. The parallel lives point was made to me by Deborah Katznelson of the Young Men's and Young Women's Hebrew Association of Washington Heights and Inwood during a ride on a downtown subway train from Washington Heights. The Y has long been both proudly Jewish and committed to the welfare of the larger community around it.

10. On "collective efficacy," see Robert Sampson, *Great American City: Chicago and the Enduring Neighborhood Effect* (Chicago: University of Chicago Press, 2012), 27, 127, 152–53, 368–69, and Thomas J. Sugrue, "Chicago and the Primacy of the Social," in *Public Books* at http://publicbooks. org/nonfiction/great-american-city#sugrue. I make no claim to matching Sampson's quantitative research or grasp of social theory, but I do believe that the ideas he has generated in *Great American City* help us understand other cities and neighborhoods in new and important ways that illuminate the social dimensions of responses to urban problems.

11. My thinking on the urban crisis and the need to understand both the successes and failures of responses to it in new ways is much influenced by Katz, *Why Don't American Cities Burn?*, especially 154–61. Equally important for my thinking about inequality and the urban poor—namely that their problem is less a culture of poverty than a shortage of economically rewarding work—is much influenced by Katherine S. Newman, *No Shame in My Game: The Working Poor in the Inner City* (New York: Russell Sage, 1999), especially 61, 298.

CHAPTER 1

1. See Anne-Marie Cantwell and Diana diZerega Wall, *Unearthing Gotham: The Archaeology of New York City* (New Haven: Yale University Press, 2001), 57–59, 93, 113–16, 119–20; Gregory Dowd quotation, 119.

2. See "exploration" in *Encyclopedia of New York City*, ed. Kenneth T. Jackson (New Haven: Yale University Press, 1995), 386, and Anthony Stevens-Acevedo, Tom Weterings, and Leonor Alvarez Francés, *Juan Rodriguez and the Beginnings of New York City* (New York: Dominican Studies Institute, 2013), 1–2, 5–6.

3. See Cantwell and Wall, *Unearthing Gotham*, 143–45, and Edwin G. Burrows and Mike Wallace, *Gotham: A History of New York City to 1898* (New York: Oxford University Press, 2000), 23–24.

4. On the geography and construction of Fort Washington, see Barnet Schechter, *The Battle for New York: The City at the Heart of the American Revolution* (New York: Walker, 2002), 117, 118, 209–10, 246, 247, 249; "Fort Tryon Park" in *Encyclopedia of New York City*, ed. Kenneth T. Jackson, 2nd ed. (New Haven: Yale University Press, 2010), 473.

5. On the military campaign for Manhattan, see Burrows and Wallace, *Gotham*, 234–35, 236–40, 243, and Steven H. Jaffe, *New York at War: Four Centuries of Combat, Fear, and Fatigue in Gotham* (New York: Basic Books, 2012), 99; on the Morris Mansion, see http://www.morrisjumel. org/timeline/1776/.

6. Schechter, *Battle for New York*, 249–55.

7. On the early history of the neighborhood, see Ira Katznelson, *City Trenches: Urban Politics and the Patterning of Class* (Chicago: University of Chicago Press, 1981), 14, 217–21, 237–43. On Bennett Park, see James Renner, *Washington Heights, Inwood, and Marble Hill* (Charleston, SC: Arcadia Publishers, 2007), 12. On the Audubon estate, see "John James Audubon" in *Encyclopedia of New York City* (2010 edition), 75–76.

8. On the Billings estate, see Renner, *Washington Heights, Inwood, and Marble Hill*, 60–61.

9. See Clifton Hood, *722 Miles: The Building of the Subways and How They Transformed New York* (New York: Simon and Schuster, 1993), 86–90.

10. Ibid., 75–77. Lee A. Lendt, "A Social History of Washington Heights, New York City," Columbia-Washington Heights Community Mental Health Project (New York, 1960), 11–13, 58–59; and "Thirty Blocks of Broadway Transformed in Three Years," *New York Times*, April 26, 1908, RE14 (real estate section).

11. On the Church of the Intercession, see *A Short History of the Church of the Intercession* at http://intercessionnyc.dioceseny.org/history.htm; on Audubon Terrace, see "Audubon Terrace," *Encyclopedia of New York City* (2010 edition), 76, and "Another Fine Museum Added to the City's List," *New York Times*, January 19, 1908, SM4. On the Audubon Park buildings, see *Audubon Park Historic District*, submitted to the New York Landmarks Preservation Commission by the Audubon Park Historic District Committee, March 2003, especially 32–35, 39–43, and 69–71.

12. See Hood, *722 Miles*, 135–36.

13. Ibid., 110–11.

14. Ibid., 75–77. Lendt, "Social History of Washington Heights, New York City," 11–13, 58–59; on housing laws that created an improved environment in northern Manhattan and the Bronx, see Richard Plunz, *A History of Housing in New York City* (New York: Columbia, 1990), 49, 85, 348 n96; and interview with Leo Shanley, New York City, 1990.

15. On state legislation that granted property tax exemptions in exchange for new housing construction, see Ronald Lawson and Mark Naison, eds., *The Tenant Movement in New York City* (New Brunswick, NJ: Rutgers University Press, 1986), 83.

16. On the George Washington Bridge, see *Encyclopedia of New York City* (2010 edition), 504–5, and, for the opening of the bridge and much more, Michael Aaron Rockland, *The George Washington Bridge: Poetry in Steel* (New Brunswick: Rutgers University Press, 2008), 65–67; on the Cloisters and Fort Tryon Park, see *Encyclopedia of New York City* (2010 edition), 272 and 473; on Columbia-Presbyterian Medical Center, see *Encyclopedia of New York City* (1995 edition), 258–59. My thanks to Mara Sidney and Jim Goodman for explaining to me the pleasures of living in an art deco building on upper Fort Washington Avenue.

17. On Callas, see Arianna Huffington, *Maria Callas: The Woman behind the Legend* (New York: Cooper Square Press, 2002), Kindle edition; "Maria Callas, 53, Is Dead of Heart Attack in Paris," *New York Times*, September 17, 1977, and a history of Saint Spyridon at www.saintspyridon.net and a short history of the Greek and Armenian communities in Washington Heights at *The Peopling of New York 2011* at http://macaulay.cuny.edu/eportfolios/berger2011/washington-heights/the-immigrants-of-washington-heights/armenian-and-greek-immigrants/.

18. On Hudson View Gardens, see Andrew Scott Dolkart, "Hudson View Gardens: A Home in the City," *SITES* 20 (1988): 34–38, 39–40.

19. On the restrictions at Hudson View Gardens, see ibid., 42. For examples of advertisements mentioning these restrictions, all of which appeared in the *New York Times*: for "restricted," see "Tudor Garden Apartments in Manhattan," March 15, 1925, RE10; for "exclusive," see "Of Course It Is Cheaper to Buy Than to Rent!," August 10, 1924, RE7; for "exclusively for 'desirable' families," see "By-laws Protect Tenant-Owners," August 31, 1924, RE7; for "approved," see "Save Half Your Rent," September 21, 1924, RE12; and for "live among the kind of people you like," see "Invest Half Your Rent in an Apartment Home in Manhattan," September 18, 1925, 41.

20. See N. Roth letter, December 10, 1927 in Papers of the National Association for the Advancement of Colored People, reel 2, part 5, NAACP Administrative File, Subject File: Segregation-Residential-Washington Heights, NY, hereafter referred to as the Washington Heights file of the NAACP Papers.

21. For correspondence on the case in the Washington Heights file of the NAACP Papers, see letter of Louis Marshall to Arthur B. Springarn of January 28, 1928; letter of James Weldon Johnson to Louis Marshall of February 3, 1928; memo of Miss Randolph to Mr. Johnson and Mr. Andrews on the tenants at 966 and 968 St. Nicholas Avenue, February 7, 1928; a memo on the tenants' legal difficulties dated February 15, 1928; and February 2, 1928 letter written by William Andrews on NAACP letterhead stationery.

22. See memo of April 4, 1928, in the Washington Heights file of the NAACP Papers. On the presence of African Americans in the southeast Heights by 1940, see *New York City Market Analysis* (1943) a joint publication of News Syndicate Co., *New York Times* Co., *Daily Mirror*, and Hearst Consolidated Publications, 23, available at www.1940snewyork.com.

23. See "Residential Security Map," prepared by Division of Research and Statistics, with the cooperation of the Appraisal Department, Home Owners' Loan Corporation, April 1, 1938, copyright Hagstrom Company, New York City, at http://www.urbanoasis.org/projects/holc-fha/digital-holc-maps/. On Home Owners' Loan Corporation policies and color coding, see Kenneth T.

Jackson, *Crabgrass Frontier: The Suburbanization of the United States* (New York: Oxford University Press, 1985), 197–98.

24. See "Fiorello La Guardia," *Encyclopedia of New York City* (2010 edition), 717–18. Also see the excellent study by Howard Zinn, *La Guardia in Congress* (Ithaca: Cornell University Press, 1958), especially chapters 6, 7, 8, and 11, Kindle edition.

25. The station identification of WNYC is from the author's personal communication with Andy Lanset, WNYC archivist, November 11, 2008. After Pearl Harbor, the phrase "in peace" was dropped.

26. Mason B. Williams, *City of Ambition: FDR, La Guardia, and the Making of Modern New York* (New York: W. W. Norton, 2013), 180–82, 225, 239–43, and Ronald H. Bayor, *Fiorello La Guardia: Ethnicity and Reform* (Wheeling, IL: Harlan Davidson, 1993), 103–10, 141–44, 158–60, 165–67.

27. See Ira Katznelson, *Fear Itself: The New Deal and the Origins of Our Time* (New York: W. W. Norton, 2013), and Williams, *City of Ambition*. For the Wortman cartoon, see James Sturm and Brandon Elston, eds., *Denys Wortman's New York: Portrait of the City in the 1930s and 1940s* (Montreal: Drawn and Quarterly, 2010), 72.

28. On La Guardia and his impact on municipal government and the relations between the city and federal government, see Charles Garrett, *The La Guardia Years: Machine and Reform Politics in New York City* (New Brunswick, NJ: Rutgers University Press, 1961), 179; Thomas Kessner, *Fiorello H. La Guardia and the Making of Modern New York* (New York: McGraw-Hill, 1989), 300–308, 339–41, and Williams, *City of Ambition*, 176–78.

29. "Text of La Guardia's Address Assailing City Government," *New York Times*, October 3, 1933, 18.

30. See "Ballad for Americans," music by Earl Robinson and words by John LaTouche, and Lisa Barg, "Paul Robeson's Ballad for Americans: Race and the Cultural Politics of 'People's Music,'" *Journal of the Society for American Music* 2, no. 1 (February 2008): 27–29, 31–32, 41–42, 44–45, 57–58. On Robeson, see Martin Duberman, *Paul Robeson: A Biography* (New York: New Press, 2005); on the politics of the Popular Front, see Michael Denning, *The Cultural Front: The Laboring of American Culture* (London: Verso, 1996).

31. These points owe much to *Swing Time: Reginald Marsh and Thirties New York*, an exhibit at the New-York Historical Society viewed July 13, 2013, and Morris Dickstein, *Dancing in the Dark: A Cultural History of the Great Depression* (New York: W. W. Norton, 2009). Also see *Babes in Arms*, 1939, at http://www.lorenzhart.org/babes.htm.

32. On the opening of the pool, see "Mayor Opens Pool in Highbridge Park," *New York Times*, July 15, 1936, 4. On the pool's setting and design, see Marta Gutman, "Highbridge Pool and Bathhouse," in *Robert Moses and the Modern City*, ed. Hillary Ballon and Kenneth T. Jackson (New York: W.W. Norton, 2007), 142–43. The Mumford quotation is from Marta Gutman, "Equipping the Public Realm," in *Robert Moses and the Modern City*, 79. Also see Williams, *City of Ambition*, 196.

33. See "Pool Opens Tomorrow," *New York Times*, July 13, 1936, 17, and "Mayor Opens Pool in Highbridge Park," *New York Times*, July 15, 1936, 4. For an excellent analysis of the New Deal and parks and recreation in New York City, see Roy Rosenzweig and Elizabeth Blackmar, *The Park and the People: A History of Central Park* (Ithaca: Cornell University Press, 1992), 447–63.

34. On conditions in Harlem during the Depression, see Cheryl Lynn Greenberg, *Or Does It Explode? Black Harlem in the Great Depression* (New York: Oxford University Press, 1991), 42–47, 69–75, 84–86, 175–78, 181–86; quotation from 183.

35. See Greenberg, *Or Does It Explode?*, 192–95, and Khalil Gibran Muhammad, *The Condemnation of Blackness: Race, Crime, and the Making of Modern Urban America* (Cambridge: Harvard University Press, 2011), 2–6, 97–117, 237–263, 272–75.

36. See Shane White, Stephen Robertson, and Stephen Garton, History Department, University of Sydney, "Year of the Riot: Harlem 1935," at http://sydney.edu.au/arts/history/research/projects/riot.shtml. On policing and the events of 1935 in Harlem, see Marilynn S. Johnson, *Street Justice: A History of Police Violence in New York City* (Boston: Beacon Press, 2003), 186–89.

37. On New Deal programs that improved life in Harlem by 1943, see Greenberg, *Or Does It Explode?*, 216, 218, 219, 223. On efforts by the La Guardia administration, see Bayor, *Fiorello La Guardia*, 165–67.

38. For the source of the phrase "at home in America" and on the Jewish populations of the Heights, see Deborah Dash Moore, *At Home in America: Second Generation New York Jews* (New York: Columbia, 1981), 82. For the calculation of three-eighths of Washington Heights being Jewish, see Stephen Lowenstein, *Frankfurt on the Hudson: The German Jewish Community of Washington Heights, 1933–1983, Its Structure and Culture* (Detroit: Wayne State University Press, 1989), 42.

39. On the Jews of Washington Heights and Inwood, see Lowenstein, *Frankfurt on the Hudson*, 47–51, 66–68, 99.

40. On the neighborhood's ethnic and class composition, see Katznelson, *City Trenches*, 79–86. On population, see Ronald H. Bayor, *Neighbors in Conflict: The Irish, Germans, Jews, and Italians of New York City, 1929–1941* (Baltimore: Johns Hopkins University Press, 1980), 152. On the Irish in the Depression and New Deal, see James R. Barrett, *The Irish Way: Becoming American in the Multiethnic City* (New York: Penguin, 2012), 227–29, 230–31. Also see Matthew J. O'Brien, "Transatlantic Connections and the Sharp Edge of the Depression," in *New Directions in Irish-American History*, ed. Kevin Kenny (Madison: University of Wisconsin Press, 2003), 79–89, 91.

41. See *New York City Market Analysis*, 23, 24. Also see Lowenstein, *Frankfurt on the Hudson*, 45.

42. Based on mayoral and presidential vote totals tabulated by assembly districts in northern Manhattan for presidential races in 1932, 1936, 1940, and 1944, and mayoral races in 1933, 1937, and 1941. Assembly district boundaries do not precisely conform to the perceived borders of Washington Heights and Inwood, but from 1917 to 1944 the 23rd Assembly District covered Manhattan north of the mid-160s. After the reapportionment of 1944, the same general area—with the exception of part of the northeast Heights—was covered by the 15th Assembly District. For presidential results, see *New York Times*, "New York City and Up State Vote for Principal National and State Offices," November 9, 1932, 4; "Tables Showing Results of Yesterday's Voting for President and Congress," November 4, 1936, 8; "Vote in State for President," November 6, 1940, 6; and "Congressional Results in the Nation; State Vote for President and Senator," November 8, 1944, 4. For mayoral results in races involving La Guardia, see "Mayors Elected in New York State," November 8, 1933, 16; "Tables Showing the Vote for City-Wide Officials and Borough and County Posts," November 3, 1937, 14; and "Tables Detailing the Division of the Votes in the New York City Election," November 5, 1941, 15. In 1945, when La Guardia did not run for mayor, the Democrat William O'Dwyer handily won northern Manhattan in the mayoral race. See "Tabulation of the Election Results in New York and New Jersey," *New York Times*, November 7, 1945, 4.

43. Lowenstein, *Frankfurt on the Hudson*, 68–69.

44. Ibid., 66–67, 74–75, 77, 79–80.

45. See Rosalyn Manowitz, *Reflections on the Holocaust* (New York: Hebrew Tabernacle Congregation, 1978), v.

46. Author interview with Michael Cohn, New York City, January 8, 1990.

47. For the anecdote about the barber, see Manowitz, *Reflections on the Holocaust*, 172. For the dachshund joke, see Lowenstein, *Frankfurt on the Hudson*, 34–35, 57.

48. See Lowenstein, *Frankfurt on the Hudson*, 100.

49. Ibid., 47–50, 52–53, 183. The Immigrant Jewish War Veterans, founded in 1938, were the American successor to the Reichsbund Judischer Frontsoldaten, founded in Germany after World War I to defend Jews against anti-Semitism and commemorate Jewish soldiers' service in the Great War in a conservative spirit of German patriotism. During World War II, the Immigrant Jewish War Veterans, who eventually changed their name to the Jewish Veterans' Association, enthusiastically supported the American war effort. They raised money in war bond drives, ran classes to prepare members for U.S. citizenship, and took great pride in an honor roll of their sons in the U.S. armed forces. See also Tim Grady, "Fighting a Lost Battle: The Reichsbund judischer Frontsoldaten and the Rise of National Socialism" in *German History* 28, no. 1 (March 2010): 1–3, 6–8, 10, 12–13, 16–17, 20.

50. Telephone interview with Frank Hess, August 28, 2009.

51. See Bayor, *Neighbors in Conflict*, 155–56, 162; also see Stephen H. Norwood, "Marauding Youth and the Christian Front: Antisemitic Violence in Boston and New York during World War II," *American Jewish History* 91, no. 2: 238, 243, 260.

52. Bayor, *Neighbors in Conflict*, 87–104, 152–55. Interviews with Michael Cohn, New York City, 1990, and Paul O'Dwyer, New York City, 1992.

53. Bayor, *Neighbors in Conflict*, 156–57, and Lendt, "Social History of Washington Heights," 75–77. For the Anti-Defamation League Report, see memo from Louis A. Novins to CRC and ADL Regional offices of January 4, 1944, and attached report, in the American Jewish Committee Papers, box 34, Community Issues folder, Center for Jewish History; quotation is from page 1.

54. See ADL report: on the desecration of synagogues and also Protestant churches, see 10, 11, 15, 18, 19, 26, and 27. The quotation is from statement VI, page 21.

55. ADL Report, 11, 19, 27, 8, 14; for the anecdote on the Jewish boy and his Catholic friend, 7.

56. See Max Frankel interview in Kirchheimer, *We Were So Beloved*, 112, and Max Frankel, *The Times of My Life and My Life with the* Times (New York: Random House, 1999), 44–47.

57. See Frankel, *Times of My Life*, 53–54.

58. Author interview with Noreen Walck, Dumont, New Jersey, 1990; and author telephone interview with Sophie Heymann, September 7, 2008.

59. On the Anti-Defamation League reports and statements, see "Anti-Semitic Acts Stir Protests Here," *New York Times*, December 30, 1943, 19; also "Police Plan Drive to End Vandalism," *New York Times*, January 3, 1944, 23. For the municipal report, see "Anti-Semitism Report By Herlands Calls for Tighter Controls by Police," *New York Times*, January 11, 1944, 1. For reactions to the report on anti-Semitism, among them Quill's call for a meeting, see "Herlands Backed on Laxity Charges," *New York Times*, January 12, 1944, 15. For Quill's biography, see *Encyclopedia of New York City* (2010 edition), 1069–70.

60. Bayor, *Neighbors in Conflict*, 156–57; and Lendt, "Social History of Washington Heights," 75–77. On "The House I Live In," see the song with words by Lewis Allan (pen name of Abel Meeropol) and music by Earl Robinson; the film *The House I Live In*, 1945; and Nancy Kovaleff Baker, "Abel Meeropol (a.k.a. Lewis Allan): Political Commentator and Social Conscience," *American Music* 20, no. 1 (Spring 2002): 55–56. On the incident in Queens, see Letter to American Jewish Committee re "Christian Front" meeting in Queens County on October 6, 1945, in "Hate Groups, New York, New York City, 46–60" folder, American Jewish Committee Papers, box 36, gen. 13.

61. *The WPA Guide to New York City: the Federal Writers' Project Guide to 1930s New York*, with an introduction by William H. Whyte (New York: Pantheon Books, 1982), 294, 296.

62. See Faith Ringgold, *Tar Beach*, 1988, Solomon R. Guggenheim Museum, New York. On the 145th–155th Street boundaries of Sugar Hill, see http://www.sugarhillmap.com/about.asp. For a definition with a more limited area, see Andrew S. Dolkart, *Hamilton Heights/Sugar Hill Northwest Historic District*, designation report (New York: Landmarks Preservation Commission, 2002), 2. For a brilliant exploration of working-class African American men and their beliefs and behavior, see Mitchell Duneier, *Slim's Table: Race, Respectability, and Masculinity* (Chicago: University of Chicago Press, 1992), 83, 123, 124.

63. Roger Wilkins, "The Legacies of Segregation: Smashing through the Generations," in *The Integration Debate: Competing Futures for American Cities*, ed. Chester Hartman and Gregory D. Squires (New York: Routledge, 2010), 255–58.

64. Harry Belafonte with Michael Shnayerson, *My Song: A Memoir* (New York: Knopf, 2011), 13–14, 24–25, 31, 41, 42, 45.

65. Dominic J. Capeci Jr., *The Harlem Riot of 1943* (Philadelphia: Temple University Press, 1977), 161.

66. On police violence and the 1943 Harlem Riot, see Johnson, *Street Justice*, 198–200. On the geography of the riot, see Capeci, *Harlem Riot of 1943*, 101.

67. Jacques d'Amboise, *I Was a Dancer* (New York: Knopf, 2011), 17, 23–26, 32–34, 60–64.

68. Ibid., 26, 29–30, 55, 60, 64–66, 85–88.

69. On changes in the southern Heights in the 1940s, see Eric C. Schneider, *Vampires, Dragons, and Egyptian Kings: Young Gangs in Postwar New York* (Princeton: Princeton University Press, 2001), 83–85. On the decline of the German Jewish population south of 155th Street in the 1940s, see Lowenstein, *Frankfurt on the Hudson*, 218.

70. Author interview with Celedonia "Cal" Jones, July 8, 2008, New York City.

71. See author interview with John Culpepper, June 6, 2005, New York City.

72. For the memories of Dorothy (Fiege) Goddard, see her recollections on the "Personal Memories of Washington Heights" website at http://home.comcast.idreos/HMem.htm.

73. Rebecca B. Rankin, ed., *New York Advancing* (New York: City of New York, 1936), 105.

74. See Geoffrey Perrett, *Days of Sadness, Years of Triumph: The American People 1939–1945* (1973; Madison: University of Wisconsin Press, 1985), 347–49. Also see "Education: New Lost Generation," *Time*, January 29, 1945, 91.

75. On the slow recognition of gangs, see Schneider, *Vampires, Dragons and Egyptian Kings*, 54–64. Also see Bradford Chambers, "Boy Gangs of New York: 500 Fighting Units," *New York Times Magazine*, December 10, 1944, SM16.

76. Kessner, *Fiorello H. La Guardia and the Making of Modern New York*, 371–76, 534–36; see 534 for Kessner's point on La Guardia preferring a safe lie on race to a dangerous truth.

77. On the New York City total for 1950, see "population" in *Encyclopedia of New York City* (1995 edition), 921. The population of northern Manhattan in 1950, from 155th Street river to river north, was calculated with U.S. Census data using Social Explorer at http://www.socialexplorer.com/tables/C1950TractDS/R10735122.

78. Racial and ethnic tensions in the southern Heights in the context of a changing neighborhood were noted as early as 1945. For a report on an effort to ease tensions between African American and Jewish students at PS 169, at Audubon Avenue and 168th Street, see "School Plan Used to Decrease Bias," *New York Times*, September 16, 1945, 42.

79. "Our Changing City: Manhattan's West Side," *New York Times*, July 4, 1955, 13.

80. "Our Changing City: Harlem Now on the Upswing," *New York Times*, July 8, 1955, 25

81. See "Our Changing City: Conflicts in the Upper Bronx," *New York Times*, July 15, 1955, 23; and for the quotation on Irish and Jewish movement in response to black and Puerto Rican arrivals, *New York Times*, "Our Changing City: New Faces in the Lower Bronx," July 11, 1955, 25.

82. See Joshua B. Freeman, *Working-Class New York: Life and Labor since World War II* (New York: New Press, 2001), 8, 9, 12, 41, 53, 66–71, 100–103, 114–17, 143–44 (quotation on "municipal social democracy," 103). On Dyckman Houses, see Nicholas Dagen Bloom, *Public Housing That Worked: New York in the Twentieth Century* (Philadelphia: University of Pennsylvania Press, 2008), 271, 161.

83. "Our Changing City: Along Manhattan's West Side," *New York Times*, July 4, 1955, 13.

84. Interview with author's mother, Mildred Snyder, New York City, December 27, 2008.

85. See "Washington Heights Project," report attached to August 16, 1957, letter from Maurice H. Greenhill, MD, to Mayor Robert F. Wagner, Wagner Subject Files, box 160, Juvenile Delinquency folder, 1957, 3, and Robert Lee, "Upper Manhattan: A Community Study of Washington Heights," a paper prepared for the Protestant Council of the City of New York, 1954, 9.

86. Lee, "Upper Manhattan," 7, 17 (quotation, 17).

87. "Juvenile Delinquency in Critical Areas," 1957, Wagner Papers, box 163, 1957 folder; "Perspectives on Delinquency Prevention," submitted by Deputy Mayor Harry Epstein, Wagner Papers, box 159, 1955 Juvenile Delinquency folder; "976,936 Added to Youth Board Appropriation; Agency to Open 4 New Areas, Extend 4 Old Ones," in *Youth Board News*, June 1955, 1, in Wagner Papers, box 48, January–June 1955 folder; "Washington Heights Project" report.

88. August 28, 2009, telephone interview with Frank Hess and telephone interview with Maurice Murad, August 28, 2009.

89. See Katznelson, *Fear Itself*, 101, 124, 131, 458, and quotation from 457; also Katznelson, *When Affirmative Action Was White: An Untold Story of Racial Inequality in America* (New York: W. W. Norton, 2005). Accounts of conduct around Highbridge Pool are based on the following interviews: author telephone interview with Herman D. "Denny" Farrell, 2010; author telephone interview with defendant who requested anonymity, December 21, 2006; author interview with Bob Greenfield and Frank Estrada, New York City, June 21, 2007. On the atmosphere inside the pool, Marta Gutman and author interview with Bob Greenfield, New York City, March 21, 2007. Also see reference to fights in the locker room at Highbridge Pool in Edwin Torres's novel *Carlito's Way* (New York: Saturday Review Press, 1975), 7.

CHAPTER 2

1. Much of this chapter is based on Robert W. Snyder, "A Useless and Terrible Death: The Michael Farmer Case, 'Hidden Violence,' and New York City in the Fifties," *Journal of Urban History* 36, no. 2 (March 2010): 226–50. I thank the editors of the journal for permission to use material from the article in this book. For an insightful account of the Farmer case that helped me understand its particularities and context, see Eric C. Schneider, *Vampires, Dragons and Egyptian Kings: Youth Gangs in Postwar New York* (Princeton: Princeton University Press, 1999), 79–91. Schneider's account of the actual killing is on 79–83. Also see *Who Killed Michael Farmer?*, April 21, 1958, CBS Radio Network (on file at the Edward R. Murrow Library at the Fletcher School of Law and Diplomacy, Tufts University). The fullest study of the Farmer case written in the era of the murder and trial is Irwin D. Davidson and Richard Gehman, *The Jury Is Still Out* (New York: Harper, 1959); it provides a figure of eighteen members of the Dragons' and Kings' raiding party and calls it the best available estimate (p. 1). However, other books from the period explore the case or the issues that framed it. See David Wilkerson, with John and Elizabeth Sherrill, *The Cross and the Switchblade* (New York: Pyramid Books, 1962); Lewis Yablonsky, *The Violent Gang* (New York: Macmillan, 1962); William M. Kunstler, *First Degree* (New York: Oceana Publications, 1960); and Harrison E. Salisbury, *The Shook-Up Generation* (New York: Harper, 1958).

2. For accounts of the background of the assault, see Martin Sullivan memorandum of testimony, "Martin Sullivan" folder, box 2–42348, People versus Leroy Birch et al. (hereafter referred

to as Farmer case), case number 2630–57, Municipal Archives of New York City. All testimony and related documents cited hereafter are from the New York City Municipal Archives records for this case. Also see interview with James Ricks in "James Ricks" folder, box 2–42348, and Francis McCosh memorandum of testimony, "Jesters" folder, box 2–42348. On some of the Dragons and Egyptian Kings drinking the night of the killing, see Louis Alvarez testimony, 4274–77, 4307–09. On the use of a garrison belt in a fight, see Schneider, *Vampires, Dragons, and Egyptian Kings*, 148. On the assault, see testimony of Leoncio DeLeon, 3333–34 and 3340–42; also testimony of Louis Alvarez, 4267–68. On the actions of the Dragons and Egyptian Kings on the night of the killing, see DeLeon testimony, 3330–33, 3342–47, and 3350–51; also see testimony of Richard Hills, 3907.

3. On McShane and Farmer's evening prior to the assault, see Roger McShane memorandum of testimony, "Roger McShane" folder, box 2–42348; John Boucher memorandum of testimony, "Jesters" folder, box 2–42348; Raymond Farmer testimony, trial transcript, 1342–43; and McShane trial testimony, 1346–56 and 1357 on the boys' plan to swim. Members of the Dragons and Egyptian Kings later said that they asked Farmer if he was a Jester; in their version, Farmer said that he was. However, other sources in the neighborhood did not identify Farmer as a Jester. Martin Sullivan told the prosecutor that Farmer was not a member of the Jesters, see "Memorandum of Testimony," Martin Sullivan folder, box 2–42347; DeLeon testified that he had first met Farmer among groups of boys from the Heights who had confronted him and that Farmer had swung a pipe at him; see 3341–42. According to an interview with John McCarthy in the "John McCarthy" folder, box 2–42347, Farmer was friendly with the Jesters but not a member while McShane was a member but would deny it. For different accounts of the assault, also see statements made to an assistant district attorney on July 31, 1957, by Charles Horton, Louis Alvarez, and Edward Valderrama in box 2–42347. Valderrama revised his story in trial testimony, 4180–91, as did Jose Garcia, who said that he admitted to stabbing Farmer only to avoid a beating by police, 2739. Horton also said that he initially testified falsely to avoid a beating by police, 3659–95. Fifty years after the incident, Farmer's exact status with the Jesters was the subject of disagreement. Jack Boucher, former captain and member of the Jesters, describes Farmer as a member. Farmer's brother Raymond, however, says that he and Michael were friends of the gang without being members. See author's interview with Jack Boucher, May 22, 2007, in New York City, and his telephone interview with Raymond Farmer, June 18, 2007.

4. See McShane memorandum of testimony; also statement by McShane in Murrow, *Who Killed Michael Farmer?*, 9–14. In a different retelling of the opening exchange between the two groups, Leoncio DeLeon testified that Farmer grabbed him, after which he, DeLeon, hit Farmer with a stick and the incident was under way, 3391. A defendant interviewed by the author over the telephone on December 21, 2006, who wished to remain anonymous, said he overheard the boys exchange words before the assault erupted but did not actually witness the opening of the attack. For the initial summary of the prosecution's version of the case, which remains persuasive in its general outline of the incident, see M. G. Guerreiro, "Original Case Report," July 31, 1957, "Original Case Reports and Memo" folder, box 2–42348.

5. On the wounds, see report of Dominick D. Di Maio, MD, in "Autopsy" folder, box 2–42348. Also see McShane memorandum of testimony. My thanks to Kami Kim, MD, Albert Einstein College of Medicine of Yeshiva University, for helping me understand the autopsy report.

6. On Farmer's words, see December 23, 1957, statement of police officer John Collich in "Ptl. John Collich" folder, box 2–42349. Also see John Boucher memorandum of testimony in "Jesters" folder, box 2–42348, and Davidson and Gehman, *Jury Is Still Out*, 26.

7. On race, crime, and conservative ethnic politics in the mayoral election of 1965, and the dynamics of the Civilian Complaint Review Board debate, see Vincent J. Cannato, *The Ungovernable City: John Lindsay and His Struggle to Save New York* (New York: Basic Books, 2001), 37–38, 44–45, 52–55, 56–63, and 183–88.

8. See Jeff Wiltse, *Contested Waters: A Social History of Swimming Pools in America* (Chapel Hill: University of North Carolina Press, 2007), 121, 123, 140–41. On integration and segregation in New York City pools, see Marta Gutman, "Highbridge Pool and Bathhouse," in *Robert Moses and the Modern City: The Transformation of New York*, ed. Hillary Ballon and Kenneth T. Jackson (New York: W. W. Norton, 2007), 81–83. I thank Brad Parks, formerly of the *Star-Ledger*, for pointing out that journalists tell the stories that people are ready to hear.

9. On the attractions of pools and amusement parks, see Victoria W. Wolcott, "Recreation and Race in the Postwar City: Buffalo's 1956 Crystal Beach Riot," *Journal of American History* 93, no. 1 (June 2006), 63–90. On sex and the volatility of pools, see Wiltse, *Contested Waters*. On integration and segregation in the use of New York City pools, see Gutman, "Highbridge Pool and Bathhouse."

On the Palisades Park struggle in the context of New York City's civil rights movement, see Martha Biondi, *To Stand and Fight: The Struggles for Civil Rights in Postwar New York City* (Cambridge, MA: Harvard University Press, 2003), 82–84.

10. On "hidden violence," see Arnold R. Hirsch, *Making the Second Ghetto: Race and Housing in Chicago, 1940–1969* (Chicago: University of Chicago Press, 1998), 40.

11. Thomas Sugrue, *Origins of the Urban Crisis: Race and Inequality in Postwar Detroit* (Princeton: Princeton University Press, 2005), 13, 210–11, 213–15, 235–37, 246–55; Nelson Lichtenstein, *State of the Union: A Century of American Labor* (Princeton: Princeton University Press, 2002), 75; Stephen Grant Meyer, "As Long as They Don't Move Next Door: Segregation and Racial Conflict in American Neighborhoods" (PhD diss., University of Alabama, 1996); and Kevin Kruse, *White Flight: Atlanta and the Making of Modern Conservatism* (Princeton: Princeton University Press, 2005). The phrase "hidden violence" is from the title of the second chapter of Hirsch, *Making the Second Ghetto*, 40. Hirsch offers valuable analysis of "hidden violence" and communal violence in postwar Chicago on 53–67, 68–69, 74–75, 81–87, 90, 99.

12. On Highbridge Pool, see Gutman, "Highbridge Pool and Bathhouse," 142–43; on the larger story of Moses and public recreation also see, in the same volume, Marta Gutman, "Equipping the Public Realm: Rethinking Robert Moses and Recreation," in Ballon and Jackson, *Robert Moses and the Modern* City, 72–85. For Farmer's address, see his autopsy report in "Autopsy" folder, box 2–42348.

13. On film footage of pool use, see Gutman, "Highbridge Pool and Bathhouse," 143; also see author's telephone interview with Herman D. Farrell, New York state assemblyman, 2007.

14. On the East Harlem episode, see Robert Moses, *Theory and Practice in Politics: The Godkin Lectures, 1939* (Cambridge: Harvard University Press, 1939), 17–18. On the struggle to integrate a pool at Palisades Park, just across the Hudson from Washington Heights in New Jersey, see Biondi, *To Stand and Fight*, 82–84; for an illuminating discussion of ethnic rivalries and the Thomas Jefferson Park Pool in East Harlem, see Elena Martinez and Marci Reaven, "Thomas Jefferson Park Pool," in *Hidden New York: A Guide to Places That Matter*, ed. Marci Reaven and Steve Zeitlin (New Brunswick, NJ: Rivergate Books, an imprint of Rutgers University Press, 2006), 95–105, especially 102–5 on Puerto Rican efforts to overcome Italian opposition to their use of the pool. On police violence and the 1943 Harlem Riot, see Marilynn S. Johnson, *Street Justice: A History of Police Violence in New York City* (Boston: Beacon Press, 2003), 198–200. On the geography of the riot, see Dominic J. Capeci Jr., *The Harlem Riot of 1943* (Philadelphia: Temple University Press, 1977), 101.

15. On changes in the southern Heights in the 1940s, see Schneider, *Vampires, Dragons, and Egyptian Kings*, 83–85. On the decline of the German Jewish population south of 155th Street in the 1940s, see Stephen Lowenstein, *Frankfurt on the Hudson: The German Jewish Community of Washington Heights, 1933–1983, Its Structure and Culture* (Detroit: Wayne State University Press, 1989), 218. On changes in northern Manhattan's Irish community, see Robert Snyder, "The Neighborhood Changed: The Irish of Washington Heights and Inwood, 1945–1990," in *The New York Irish*, ed. Ronald Bayor and Timothy Meagher (Baltimore: Johns Hopkins University Press, 1996), 444–46.

16. See Ira Rosenwaike, *Population History of New York City* (Syracuse: Syracuse University Press, 1972), 174.

17. Robert Lee, "Upper Manhattan: A Community Study of Washington Heights," a paper prepared for the Protestant Council of the City of New York, 1954, 7, 17 (quotation). For an insightful analysis of the changing demography of the southern Heights and gang conflict (which is not indicated by the article's headline), see "No Racial Bias Seen in Teen Warfare," *Amsterdam News*, August 10, 1957, 1. On blockbusting, see Ira Katznelson, *City Trenches: Urban Politics and the Patterning of Class* (Chicago: University of Chicago Press, 1981), 86.

18. Marta Gutman and author interview with Robert Greenfield, March 21, 2007, New York City; also author interview with Greenfield and Frank Estrada, June 21, 2007, New York City.

19. See Maureen Murphy Nutting, "Choices," in *Becoming Historians*, ed. James M. Banner and John R. Gillis (Chicago: University of Chicago Press, 2009), 122–25.

20. Author telephone interview with Jim Clarke, June 19, 2012.

21. See "Frankie Lymon and the Teenagers Biography," http://rockhall.com/inductees/frankie-lymon-and-the-teenagers/bio/.

22. On delinquency, see Schneider, *Vampires, Dragons, and Egyptian Kings*, 50; also Grace Palladino, *Teenagers: An American History* (New York: Basic Books, 1996), and James B. Gilbert, *A Cycle of Outrage: America's Reaction to the Juvenile Delinquent in the 1950s* (New York: Oxford University Press, 1986). On the shift in perspective in the late 1950s, see Michael W. Flamm, *Law and Order:*

Street Crime, Civil Unrest, and the Crisis of Liberalism in the 1960s (New York: Columbia University Press, 2005), 16. On the bitterness of the linkage of crime and race in the 1965 mayoral election, see Cannato, *Ungovernable City,* 59–63.

23. Clarke interview, December 22, 2012; author telephone interview with Gary Zaboly, 2012; and Zaboly letter to the author of September 15, 2012.

24. "Juvenile Delinquency in Critical Areas," 1957, Wagner Papers, box 163, 1957 folder; "Perspectives on Delinquency Prevention," submitted by Deputy Mayor Harry Epstein, Wagner Papers, box 159, 1955 juvenile delinquency folder; "$976,936 Added to Youth Board Appropriation; Agency to Open 4 New Areas, Extend 4 Old Ones," *Youth Board News,* June 1955, 1, in Wagner Papers, box 48, January–June 1955 folder; "Washington Heights Project" report. Also see Ralph Whelan memorandum, "Explanation of Proposed Expansion of Youth Board Program for 1955/56," June 13, 1955, Wagner Papers, box 48, "Community Activities" folder for January–June 1955. The report of Maurice H. Greenhill, MD, compiled after the Farmer murder, found evidence of widespread dissatisfaction with the policing of Washington Heights. See "Washington Heights Inquiry" memo in "Juvenile Delinquency—Manhattan Health Board" folder, box 165, Wagner Subject Files, New York City Municipal Archives.

25. This description of the atmosphere around the pool is based on the following interviews: Farrell interview; author telephone interview with Isaiah Bing, 2007; author telephone interview with defendant who requested anonymity, December 21, 2006; author interview with Bob Greenfield and Frank Estrada, June 21, 2007. On the atmosphere inside the pool, see Marta Gutman and Robert Snyder interview with Bob Greenfield, March 21, 2007. For a reference to fights in the locker room at Highbridge Pool, see Edwin Torres's novel, *Carlito's Way* (New York: Saturday Review Press, 1975), 7.

26. Author interview with Boucher.

27. On race in the neighborhood, see Boucher interview; author's telephone interview with Farmer case defendant, December 21, 2006; and author and Marta Gutman interview with Robert Greenfield. On gang composition, see Boucher, memorandum of testimony. Also see McShane trial testimony, 1353–54. For the mention of "a colored boy" in the Jesters, see "Memo of Interview with James Ricks by Det. Griffin," "James Ricks" folder, box 2–42348. For an analysis of how a mostly white group of young men in a housing project can accept a black member and yet still maintain deep feelings of racism, see Jay MacLeod, *Ain't No Makin' It: Aspirations and Attainment in a Low-Income Neighborhood,* 2nd ed. (Boulder: Westview Press, 1995), 36–38; for MacLeod's points on how these white men's respect for individual African Americans in a mostly black rival group does not diminish their hostility to the black group overall, see 40–44. For Schneider's analysis of gang composition, which first alerted me to the complexity of the situation, see *Vampires, Dragons, and Egyptian Kings,* 86–88.

28. For stories that broke the story of Farmers' murder in the *Times* and *Post,* see "Youth, 15, Killed in Park Stabbing," *New York Times,* July 31, 1957, 46; and "Polio-Crippled Boy Slain . . . ," *New York Post,* July 31, 1957, 2. The *Post* quoted the policeman who found the mortally wounded Farmer saying that "the boy told him that 'lots' of Negroes had attacked the two boys." For different explanations of the origin of the incident, see "Grill 9 Youths in Gang Killing," *Daily News,* August 1, 1957, 3; "4 Youths Held Here . . . ," *New York Times,* August 1, 1957, 17; "Cops Guard Gang-War District . . . ," *New York Post,* August 1, 1957, 3; "Book 12 Gang Youths . . . ," *World-Telegram and Sun,* August 1, 1957, 1; and "Youths Tell of Slaying," *Journal-American,* August 1, 1957, 1; and "No Racial Bias Seen In Teen Warfare," *Amsterdam News,* August 10, 1957, 1. See also Benjamin Luke Marcus, "Last One In: Community, Conflict, and the Preservation of McCarren Park Pool" (MS thesis, Columbia University, May 2006), 41, 42, 74–75; also Gutman, "Equipping the Public Realm," 82–83.

29. In Oakland, California, in 1944 city officials claimed that a race riot between blacks and whites was a "spontaneous outburst" with no link to previous racial conflicts or police harassment of blacks. See Marilynn S. Johnson, *The Second Gold Rush: Oakland and the East Bay in World War II* (Berkeley: University of California Press, 1993), 167–69. Also see Capeci, *Harlem Riot of 1943,* 119–20.

30. For the quotation from the Youth Board source on the Wadsworth Avenue precinct in Washington Heights, see "Cops Guard Gang War District," *New York Post,* August 1, 1957, 29.

31. For explanations of the origin of the incident, see "Grill 9 Youths in Gang Killing," *Daily News,* August 1, 1957, 3; and "4 Youths Held Here in Fatal Gang Fight; Police Patrol Scene," *New York Times,* August 1, 1957, 17. Also see "12 Youths Held in Gang Slaying of Polio Boy, 15," *Herald*

Tribune, August 1, 1957, 1; "Cops Guard Gang-War District, 17 Booked in Death of Heights Boy," *New York Post*, August 1, 1957, 3.

32. For the *El Diario* photograph and caption referring to racial questions, see *El Diario de Nueva York*, August 1, 1957, 1. For the August 2 "Crimen de Michael Farmer" headline in *El Diario*, see *El Diario de Nueva York*, August 2, 1957, 3. On *El Diario*, see Joseph P. Fitzpatrick, "The Puerto Rican Press," in *The Ethnic Press in the United States: A Historical Analysis and Handbook*, ed. Sally Miller (Westport, CT: Greenwood Press, 1987), 307–9.

33. See "No Racial Bias in Teen Warfare," *Amsterdam News*, August 10, 1957, 1; also Capeci, *Harlem Riot of 1943*, 119–20.

34. See "Teen-Age Burst of Brutality," *Life*, August 12, 1957, 34–35.

35. On the role of the Communist Party and African American activists in creating a New York civil rights movement, see Biondi, *To Stand and Fight*, especially 221–22 on the limitations of the Wagner administration on civil rights. On the Old Left's ability to outlast McCarthyism and remain vital in New York, see Joshua B. Freeman, *Working-Class New York: Life and Labor since World War II* (New York: New Press, 2000), 90–95. For an analysis of Wagner, see Fred J. Cook and Gene Gleason, "Wagner: The Man Out Front," in "The Shame of New York," a special issue of the *Nation*, October 31, 1959, 274–78. The quotation is from 275.

36. For the quotation "sick with crime," see "City Crime Scored by G.O.P. Nominee," *New York Times*, August 6, 1957, 1. For other examples of Republican attacks on Wagner emphasizing crime, see, "Crime Is Stressed by Christenberry," *New York Times*, October 22, 1957, 1, and "Teen Crime Issue Taking Spotlight in City Hall Race," August 19, 1957, 1. On Wagner's responses, for the "irresponsible" quotation, see "Wagner Attacks Critics on Crime," *New York Times*, September 17, 1957, 26; for the "hard" and "soft approaches," see "Wagner Depicts Tactics on Crime," *New York Times*, October 10, 1957, 25.

37. On the evolution of the investigation and its findings, see August 16, 1957, letter of Maurice H. Greenhill, MD, to Mayor Wagner and the attached report, "Washington Heights Project," in "Juvenile Delinquency, 1957" folder, box 165, Wagner Subject Files, New York Municipal Archives. See description of Velez family in "SUMMARIES: Inventory of Children's Reactions," in "Juvenile Delinquency—Mental Health Board" folder, box 165, Wagner Subject Files, New York Municipal Archives.

38. For Greenhill's public statement on the research, see "Washington Heights Inquiry," a press release dated August 15, 1957, Wagner Subject Files, box 165, juvenile delinquency-Mental Health Board folder. The Greenhill quotation is in "Wagner Summons Meeting Tuesday on Gang Violence," *New York Times*, August 17, 1992, 1. Also see "Crime Data Plea by G.O.P Is Denied," *New York Times*, September 19, 1957, 1.

39. I am grateful to Michael Flamm of Ohio Wesleyan University for sharing his insights on Wagner's mayoralty. For an account of the town meeting and indictments in the *Times*, see "14 Boys Indicted in Two Killings, City Parley Held," *New York Times*, August 21, 1957, 1. On Wagner's leadership as mayor, see Ruth Cowan, "The New York City Civilian Review Board Referendum of November 1966: A Case Study of Mass Politics" (PhD diss., New York University, 1970), 434–35; on Wagner getting elected mayor with African American votes won with a promise to appoint blacks to important positions, see Biondi, *To Stand and Fight*, 221–22. Also see "Robert F. Wagner," in *Encyclopedia of New York City*, ed. Kenneth T. Jackson, 2nd ed. (New Haven: Yale University Press, 2010), 1371.

40. For an account of the town meeting and indictments, see "14 Boys Indicted in Two Killings, City Parley Held," *New York Times*, August 21, 1957, 1; for the *Post* story, see *New York Post*, August 21, 1967, 46. For the poem see "Verses for a Slain Boy," *New York Mirror*, October 3, 1957, 4.

41. On the crowded courtroom and court-appointed counsel, see "Court Is Jammed at Murder Trial," *New York Times*, January 14, 1958, 28. For further details on the hearing and court-appointed counsel, see Davidson and Gehman, *Jury Is Still Out*, 7–8. On Davidson's biography, see "Irwin D. Davidson, 75, Legislator and Jurist Who Served 40 Years," *New York Times*, August 2, 1981, 28.

42. On the selection of the jury, see Davidson and Gehman, *Jury Is Still Out*, 10–16.

43. On Reynolds, see Davidson and Gehman, *Jury Is Still Out*, 18. On the opening of the trial, see "7 Boys Go On Trial in Killing of Youth," *New York Times*, February 2, 1958, 55, and "Ask Death for 7 Teeners on Trial in Gang Slaying," *New York Post*, February 6, 1958, 6.

44. On Murray Kempton's life, see "One of a Kind," *Newsday*, May 6, 1997, A5. For "The Evidence," see *New York Post*, February 7, 1958, M4.

45. On the absence of the quotation from the public record during the trial, see Schneider, *Vampires, Dragons, and Egyptian Kings*, 280 n11. For the quotation from the judge, see Davidson, *Jury Is Still Out*, 27, and, for his further thoughts on race, ethnicity, and the gangs' conflict, 64.

46. All quotations from "The Evidence" are from the *New York Post*, February 7, 1958, M4.

47. "Race Issue Ruled Out in Trial of 7," *Amsterdam News*, February 22, 1958, 1.

48. For examples of clashes between the defense and prosecution, see trial transcript, 1720–22, 2187, 2305, 2424, 2934–36, 3691, and 4439; also see Davidson and Gehman, *Jury Is Still Out*, 43, 192–94. On charges of police brutality, see trial testimony of Charles Horton, 3659–65; Vincent Pardon, 2270–74; Jose Garcia, 2750, 2755; Richard Hills, 4024–27; Louis Alvarez, 4287–93, 4459; Leoncio DeLeon, 3395–97, 3448; and Vincent Carrasquillo, 2609–10, 2611, 2616, 2618–19. For police testimony claiming that there were no beatings at the station, see Detective Edward J. Griffin, 4631–32; Deputy Inspector Edward F. Carey, 4691–95; Detective Joseph Brady, 4676, 4688, 4771, 4690–91; Detective John Vickers, 4808–9; Detective John Weber, 4866; Detective James Mackin, 4929; Deputy Inspector John J. Green, 4703, 4705, 4706, 4725–27, 4745–55. Assistant District Attorney Manuel Guerreiro testified that the defendants did not complain of brutality when he interrogated them, 2954–56. On the brutality question, also see Davidson and Gehman, *Jury Is Still Out*, 61–62, 75, 84–85, 124–25. On defense attorney Emil Schlesinger clashing with prosecutor Robert Reynolds, see Davidson and Gehman, *Jury Is Still Out*, 219. On the defendant who still maintains that defendants were beaten into confessions, see author interview with defendant, who wishes to remain anonymous.

49. Davidson and Gehman, *Jury Is Still Out*, 33–34, 128–29, 135, 145, 163. On the black-jacketed spectators, see 17. On the angry, name-calling letters to Davidson himself, see 128. On the letter to *El Diario* threatening the police, see 146. Also see Wilkerson, *Cross and the Switchblade*, 18.

50. See Davidson and Gehman, *Jury Is Still Out*, 63–64.

51. See trial testimony, 3610–11.

52. On firearms, see Ralph Lago testimony on pages 1620, 1621–25, 1659–58; for objections lodged by defense attorney Emil Schlesinger charging the irrelevance of testimony about the Dragons and Kings having access to a rifle, see 1168–71; see testimony of Leoncio DeLeon charging that the Jesters threatened him and Lago and others with a rifle, 3333, 3340. For Alvarez on his efforts to get reinforcements, see his testimony on 4268–70. For an account of the night of June 30, see Davidson and Gehman, *Jury Is Still Out*, 56–57.

53. On the summaries, see, in the *New York Times*, "Summaries Begin in Murder Trial," April 8, 1958, 23; "Boy Called 'Sick' in Murder Trial," April 9, 1958, 18; "Hysteria Decried in Trial of 7 Boys," April 10, 1958, 30; and "7 Youths' Defense Hit by Prosecutor," April 12, 1958, 40. For examples of defense attorneys raising the issue of brutality, see 4772–73, 4745–55, 4779, 4812–13, 4824–25, 4867–69, 5073–74, and 5120–21. For differences in defense lawyers' strategies, see 1856–57, 2241–42, 5077–82, 5184, 5186, 5190, 5273, 5345–46, 5348, 5302.

54. "Trial of 7 Youths Goes to the Jury," *New York Times*, April 15, 1958, 36. Also see Davidson and Gehman, *Jury Is Still Out*, 286–88, 292.

55. See "4 Teens Guilty . . . ," *Daily News*, April 16, 1956, 2; "4 Youths Convicted . . . ," *New York Times*, April 16, 1958, 1; Davidson and Gehman, *Jury Is Still Out*, 295; and "Lawyers Plan Appeals for Pair Facing Life in Farmer Slaying," *New York Post*, April 16, 1958, 3.

56. See "Farmer's Dad . . . ," *World-Telegram and Sun*, April 16, 1958, 1; "Teens Guilty . . . ," *Daily News*, April 16, 1958, 1; "Mozalbetes se Salvan de la Silla Electrica," *El Diario*, April 16, 1958, 1; "Map Appeal in Teen Killing," *New York Post*, April 16, 1958, 1; "Four Youths Convicted . . . ," *New York Times*, April 16, 1958, 1.

57. See "The Jury's Verdict," *World-Telegram and Sun*, April 17, 1958, 26; and "The Farmer Verdict," *Daily News*, April 17, 1958, 37.

58. See "Question Verdict in Murder Trial," *Amsterdam News*, April 26, 1958, 26. My thanks to Stanley Nelson, whose documentary *Soldier without Swords* explores the history of the African American press, for discussing the *Amsterdam News* with me.

59. See "The Verdict," *New York Post*, April 17, 1958, M4.

60. "4 Slayers of Boy Get Stiff Terms; Judge Indicts Public for Apathy," *New York Times*, May 29, 1958, 1.

61. See *Who Killed Michael Farmer?*, April 21, 1958, CBS Radio Network transcript on file at the Edward R. Murrow Library at the Fletcher School of Law and Diplomacy, Tufts University). The deleted narration is on 16; the points on intimidation on 46–47; the concluding lines are on 60.

62. See Yablonsky, *Violent Gang*, vii, xi, 195, and 193.

63. Davidson and Gehman, *Jury Is Still Out*, 299–308.

64. See Salisbury, *Shook-Up Generation*, 12, 17, and 116. For an analysis of the complex and not always benign consequences of the narrowed focus on individual and family, see Nikolas Rose, *Governing the Soul: The Shaping of the Private Self* (London: Routledge, 1990), 123, 131, 155–57, 174, 176–77.

65. For an illuminating discussion of the efforts of black leaders and white liberals to blame a racial clash on juvenile delinquency in order to avoid viewing the confrontation as a sign of deteriorating race relations, segregationists' linkage of integration and delinquency, and the difficulties of Buffalo civil rights activists trying to identify increasing segregation and declining race relations, see Wolcott, "Recreation and Race in the Postwar City: Buffalo's 1956 Crystal Beach Riot," www.history cooperative.org.proxy.libraries.rutgers.edu/journals/jah/93.1/wolcott.html, paragraphs 2, 23, 48, 51.

66. On depictions of delinquents in films, see Flamm, *Law and Order*, 17–19. On *West Side Story*, see the clipping file in the theater collection of the Lincoln Center branch of the New York Public Library: John Chapman, "Brilliant, Daring Musical," *Sunday News*, October 6, 1957, Section 2, 1; Richard Coe, "West Side Has That Beat," *Washington Post and Times Herald*, August 20, 1957, B2; Milton Berliner, "West Side (Success) Story," August 20, 1957, 2; Marya Mannes, "Black and White in New York," *Listener*, January 9, 1958, 59–60; Gerald Fay, "Musical with a Message," *Guardian*, n.d.; Herbert Whittaker, "Exciting, Dazzling . . . ," *Globe and Mail* (Toronto), November 16, 1957.

67. See Schneider, *Vampires, Dragons, and Egyptian Kings*, 88.

68. For the quotation, see ibid., 13.

69. Kempton, "The Verdict," *New York Post*, April 17, 1958, M4. On the murder of Julio Ramos in Jefferson Park, whose similarities to the Farmer case were noted in the *New York Times*, see "Four Youths Held in Harlem Killing," June 2, 1958, 45; "Seven Boys Go on Trial as Gang Slayers," March 31, 1959, 21; and "Five Teen-Agers Found Guilty in Slaying of Ramos in Harlem," May 29, 1959, 9. The cry of "spic in the park" was reported in court by Assistant District Attorney Robert Reynolds, who also prosecuted the Farmer case. See "Decision to Kill Laid to 7 Youths," *New York Times*, April 8, 1959, 50. On convictions on the case, see "Five Teen-Agers Found Guilty In Slaying of Ramos in Harlem," *New York Times*, May 29, 1959, 9. On sentencing, see "3 Teen-Agers Get 5 to 20 Years For Fatal Beating in Park Here," *New York Times*, July 10, 1959, 5, and "Youth Sentenced in Park Slaying," *New York Times*, July 24, 1959, 26.

70. Jerome Robbins and Robert Wise, directors, *West Side Story*, 1961.

71. See lyrics to "Tonight" in the film version of *West Side Story*, at http://www.westsidestory.com/site/level2/lyrics/tonight.html.

CHAPTER 3

1. See notebook in Ellen Lurie Papers, box 2, Archives of the Puerto Rican Diaspora, Centro de Estudios Puertoriquenos, Hunter College, CUNY (hereafter referred to as Lurie Papers); and author telephone interview with Leib Lurie, September 26, 2010.

2. Author telephone interview with Leib Lurie, September 26, 2010.

3. In her letter to Miss Melamed of February 12, 1964, Lurie says her son and daughter will be leaving PS 187 "immediately"; her thoughts in her spiral bound notebook on choosing PS 161 and the letter are in Lurie Papers, box 2.

4. See Lurie resumés in boxes 5 and 12, Lurie Papers. On the traffic light and tree planting, see Lurie's diaries in a blue loose-leaf binder, box 10, Lurie Papers. Her thoughts on "apartness" are in an entry for March 1961.

5. Samuel Zipp, *Manhattan Projects: The Rise and Fall of Urban Renewal in Cold War New York* (New York: Oxford, 2010), 255, 258, 298, 303, 304, 319. The phrase "untrained social worker" comes from a draft of a paper, "Community Action in East Harlem," that Lurie prepared to deliver to the 39th annual meeting of the American Orthopsychiatric Association; a copy of the paper is in box 9, Lurie Papers.

6. See Jerald E. Podair, *The Strike That Changed New York: Blacks, Whites, and the Ocean Hill-Brownsville Crisis* (New Haven: Yale University Press, 2002), 14–15, and, on the system in 1940, Diane Ravitch, *The Great School Wars: New York City, 1805–1973: A History of the Public Schools as Battlefield of Social Change* (New York: Basic Books, 1974), 239.

7. Podair, *Strike That Changed New York*, 14.

8. Ibid., 14–15; Deborah Dash Moore, *At Home in America: Second-Generation New York Jews* (New York: Columbia University Press, 1981), 91, 95, 96, 100.

9. Moore, *At Home in America*, 119, and Joshua M. Zeitz, *White Ethnic New York: Jews, Catholics, and the Shaping of Postwar Politics* (Chapel Hill: University of North Carolina Press, 2007), 26. Also see Ruth Jacknow Markowitz, *My Daughter, the Teacher: Jewish Teachers in the New York City Schools* (New Brunswick, NJ: Rutgers University Press, 1993).

10. Gerald Markowitz and David Rosner, *Children, Race, and Power: Kenneth and Mamie Clarke's Northside Center* (New York: Routledge, 2000), 25–26. On Lucienne Bloch and the mural *The Evolution of Music*, see luciennebloch.com/biographies/lucienne_bloch.htm and schools.nyc. gov/community/facilities/PublicArt/Art/artitem.htm?an=21231. On the school's nickname, see author interview with Samuel Kostman, June 14, 2010, Englewood, NJ.

11. Podair, *Strike That Changed New York*, 17.

12. Cheryl Lynn Greenberg, *Or Does It Explode? Black Harlem in the Great Depression* (New York: Oxford University Press, 1997), 189–90.

13. Ibid.; Ben Keppel, *The World of Democracy: Ralph Bunche, Kenneth B. Clark, Lorraine Hansberry, and the Cultural Politics of Race* (Cambridge: Harvard University Press, 1995), 17; Markowitz and Rosner, *Children, Race, and Power*, 24–25, and the Kenneth Clark interview, Columbia Oral History Research Office, www.columbia.edu/cu/lweb/digital/collections/nny/clarkk/transcripts/ clarkk, 1, 4, 10–13, 21.

14. Clark interview, 6–7, 21–24.

15. Keppel, *World of Democracy*, 18, and Clark interview, 24–27, 33.

16. On the episode with the guidance counselor, see Markowitz and Rosner, *Children, Race, and Power*, 93–94. On Fast, and Clark's pain over the economics prize, see Clark interview, 25. For biographical details, see Harold Takooshian, "Kenneth Bancroft Clark," in William L. O'Neill and Kenneth T. Jackson, *Scribner Encyclopedia of American Lives, Thematic Series: The 1960s*, vol. 1 (New York: Charles Scribner's Sons, 2003), 178–80.

17. Markowitz and Rosner, *Children, Race, and Power*, 18–19, 26–30, 32–33, 34–35; also Keppel, *World of Democracy*, 7, 19.

18. Markowitz and Rosner, *Children, Race, and Power*, 90–92, 94.

19. Ibid., 94–95.

20. Ibid., 90.

21. Ibid., 95–96, and Public Education Association, assisted by the New York University Research Center for Human Relations, *The Status of the Public School Education of Negro and Puerto Rican Children in New York City* (1955), 3.

22. *Status of the Public School Education of Negro and Puerto Rican Children in New York City*, 7, 8, 11, 14, 17–18, 20, 21, 22.

23. See Martha Biondi, *To Stand and Fight: The Struggles for Civil Rights in Postwar New York City* (Cambridge, MA: Harvard University Press, 2003), 247, and Markowitz and Rosner, *Children, Race, and Power*, 98–99, 101–2.

24. Markowitz and Rosner, *Children, Race and Power*, 102–3; also "Parents Visit JHS 136, 139," *Amsterdam News*, February 1, 1958, 9.

25. On the Skipwith case, the boycott, and Callender, see Adina Back, "Exposing the 'Whole Segregation Myth': The Harlem Nine and New York City's School Desegregation Battles" in *Freedom North: Black Freedom Struggles Outside the South 1940–1980*, ed. Jeanne F. Theoharris, Komozi Woodward, and Matthew Countryman (New York: Palgrave Macmillan, 2003), 73. On Zuber, see Thomas J. Sugrue, *Sweet Land of Liberty: The Forgotten Struggle for Civil Rights in the North* (New York: Random House, 2008), 192–93. Also see "School Boycott Rests with Theobald," *Amsterdam News*, October 11, 1958, 6.

26. For a biography of Polier, see http://jwa.org/encyclopedia/article/polier-justine-wise.

27. See Polier decision in *In Re Charlene Skipwith*, ruling of Justine Wise Polier, December 15, 1958, Domestic Relations Court of the City of New York, Children's Court Division, New York County, 870, 872–73. Also see the Skipwith case file in Gerald E. Markowitz and David Rosner Papers, box 12, folders 42–43, Rare Book and Manuscript Library, Columbia University Libraries.

28. Markowitz and Rosner, *Children, Race, and Power*, 103–4; James L. Hicks, "Wasting Time," *Amsterdam News*, January 3, 1959, 7, and reprints of excerpts of the decision that ran on January 17, 4; January 31, 10; and February 7, 10; Carrie E. Haynes quotation is from "Harlem Salutes Justice Polier," *Amsterdam News*, March 7, 1959, 24.

29. "Local School Board Clams Up on Issue," *Amsterdam News*, March 21, 1959, 3.

30. On the difficulties of integration, see Ellen Lurie, "A Study of George Washington Houses," conducted by the Union Settlement Association, 1955–56, in Union Settlement Association Series I–

Administration box 11, folder 13, Rare Book and Manuscript Library, Columbia University Library. On Benjamin Franklin High School, see Ellen Lurie, "A Proposal to Accentuate the Positive," submitted to the Lavanburg Foundation, September 1959, and Lurie Papers, box 5. On housing reform and organic order, see Lurie, "A Study of George Washington Houses," V–5, III–8, III–16, and, on "Planned Integration," V–7, Lurie Papers, box 5.

31. See Ellen Lurie letter of April 16, 1963, written in response to a query about residential neighborhoods from the New York City chapter of the American Institute of Architects, box 5, Lurie Papers.

32. See Ellen Lurie, "The Neighborhood Concept and Integration—Is There A Conflict?", presented at the New York City chapter of Housing and Redevelopment Officials, December 13, 1963, 8, 7, 11, in box 5, Lurie Papers.

33. March 1961 entry, blue loose-leaf binder, box 10, Lurie Papers.

34. See Truda T. Weill, *Community in Action: A Report on a Social Integration Project in School Districts 12, 13 and 14, Manhattan, 1951–1958* (New York: Board of Education, City of New York, n.d.), 1–2, 6, 7, 16, 17, 18–27. For the dimensions of districts 12, 13 and 14, see 2.

35. Ibid., foreword.

36. See undated rough draft of a letter or report, which begins "I am finding this much harder to write than I had anticipated," box 5, Lurie Papers.

37. See ibid.

38. These thoughts are from a letter Ellen Lurie wrote to David Freeman of the Rockefeller Brothers Fund on July 13, 1962, seeking a grant to work in Washington Heights. The letter to the foundation incorporated elements of the thoughts Lurie wrote down in June from the vantage point of Fort Tryon Park. See box 5, Lurie Papers.

39. Lurie letter of July 13, 1962, to Freeman, box 5, Lurie Papers.

40. On the crisis of confidence, see Ravitch, *Great School Wars*, 263. On the school board policy and members of the board that would represent districts 12–13–14, see Board of Education press release for August 20–21, 1962, Max J. Rubin Files, box 15, folder 105, Board of Education Records, NYC Department of Records/Municipal Archives (hereafter Rubin Files). Also see David Rogers, *110 Livingston Street: Politics and Bureaucracy in the New York City Schools* (New York: Random House, 1968), 370.

41. See "Minutes of Open Meeting, Local School Board, Districts 12, 13, 14," October 30, 1962, Rubin Files, box 15, folder 105.

42. See Dan W. Dodson, "A Progress Report on Integration of Negroes in Secondary Schools in New York City," June 3, 1946, William O'Dwyer Papers, box 43 NYC Department of Records/Municipal Archives; and Dodson, "Integration in High Schools," December 27, 1946, Mayor's Committee on Unity Papers, box 1605, both cited in Biondi, *To Stand and Fight*, 242. On Dodson and his work with Branch Rickey to integrate baseball, see Jules Tygiel, *Baseball's Great Experiment: Jackie Robinson and His Legacy* (New York: Oxford University Press, 1997), 57–58.

43. See Rogers, *110 Livingston Street*, 381–84, and "Summary of and Brief Comments on the Work of Local School Board, Districts 12, 13 and 14," Rubin Files, box 15, folder 402.

44. My analysis of the letters is based on letters in the Rubin Files, box 13, folders 354, 358, and 359.

45. See August 23, 1963, letter from the Parents' Association of PS 98 in Rubin Files, folder 358.

46. See "New Group Fights Mass Pupil Shifts," *New York Times*, October 3, 1963, 20.

47. See "New Parent Unit Organized Here," *New York Times*, October 4, 1963, 24, and Steven Gregory, *Black Corona: Race and the Politics of Place in an Urban Community* (Princeton: Princeton University Press, 1998), 78.

48. See Rogers, *110 Livingston Street*, 158–60; Podair, *Strike That Changed New York*, 30–33. The statement on integration and quality education is from an EQUAL advertisement in the *New York Times*, June 19, 1964, 15.

49. See Clarence Taylor, *Knocking at Our Own Door: Milton A. Galamison and the Struggle to Integrate New York City Schools* (New York: Columbia University Press, 1997), 131, 132, 134, 137, 138, 140.

50. Taylor, *Knocking at Our Own Door*, 141–42. On Lurie, see "Headquarters of Harlem Boycott," *Amsterdam News*, February 8, 1964, 1. Also see "Boycott Cripples City Schools, *New York Times*, February 4, 1964, 1.

51. "Oppose Shifting of Pupils," *New York Times*, March 13, 1964, 1.

52. "School Boycott Is Half as Large as the First One," *New York Times*, March 17, 1964, 1; also Taylor, *Knocking at Our Own Door*, 147–49, 150, 154–56, 159, 162.

53. See, in the *New York Times*, "Rights Rally at City Hall Today," May 18, 1964, 23, and "Rights Turnout," May 19, 1964, 1. On the Allen Report, see Ravitch, *Great School Wars*, 280–86.

54. See "Last Call," in Murray Kempton, *Rebellions, Perversities, and Main Events* (New York: Times Books, 1994), 30–34, quotation from 34.

55. Author telephone interview with Leib Lurie, September 26, 2010, and interview with Sara Lurie, June 23, 2010, in New York City.

56. Sara Lurie interview.

57. Leib Lurie interview.

58. See Lurie's spiral-bound diary in Lurie Papers, box 2.

59. Author telephone interview with Daryl West, July 6, 2010, and a Daryl West e-mail in the author's possession.

60. For the descriptions of Lindsay and Beame on the campaign trail, see "This Tuesday's Winner—and Loser," *New York Times Magazine*, October 31, 1965, 46.

61. For the text of his campaign advertisement, see "Lindsay for Mayor," in Sam Roberts, ed., *America's Mayor: John V. Lindsay and the Reinvention of New York* (New York: Museum of the City of New York/Columbia University Press, 2010), 30. Ellen Lurie's support for Lindsay is discussed in author's interview with Al Lurie, May 14, 2010, New York City.

62. See Vincent J. Cannato, *The Ungovernable City: John V. Lindsay and the Struggle to Save New York* (New York: Basic Books, 2001), 1–4, 7, 10, 29–30.

63. In the *New York Times*, see "Javits Headquarters Opens," August 24, 1946, 26, and "Sketches of Winners for Congress in City Races," November 6, 1946, 6; "Ryan, in Manhattan 20th, Is Opposed by Robinson," October 31, 1962, 28.

64. On Zaretsky, see "Joseph Zaretsky, Former Albany Leader, Dies," *New York Times*, December 21, 1981, D11, and Ira Katznelson, *City Trenches: Urban Politics and the Patterning of Class* (Chicago: University of Chicago Press, 1981), 127–28. The 1965 Democratic primary results confirmed the strength of the Wagner tendency in northern Manhattan. Paul Screvane, city council president and Wagner ally, easily outpolled his rivals—including Comptroller Abraham Beame and the liberal Democrats Paul O'Dwyer and Rep. Ryan. See "Tabulations of the Vote," *New York Times*, September 16, 1965, 50.

65. See "Mission Statement" and "The Magazine's Credenda," at www.nationalreview.com/articles/223549/our-mission-statement/william-f-buckley-jr. On the founding of *National Review*, see John Judis Jr., *William F. Buckley, Jr.: Patron Saint of Conservatives* (New York: Simon and Schuster, 1988), 133–34 and 138–39. Also see Vincent J. Cannato, *The Ungovernable City: John Lindsay and His Struggle to Save New York* (New York: Basic Books, 2001), 38–40.

66. "Results of Citywide and Local Races," *New York Times*, November 4, 1965, 52.

67. For Lindsay's inaugural speech, see "Text of Lindsay's Inaugural Address at City Hall," *New York Times*, January 2, 1966, 56. On IS 201, see Podair, *Strike That Changed New York*, 34–35.

68. Rogers, *110 Livingston Street*, 374–75, and "Mrs. Lurie Reappointed to School Board," *H-I Highlights*, December 1966, in Lurie Papers, white box 23/red box 1. See box 7, Lurie Papers for material on the denial of her five-year reappointment; an EQUAL press release; Lurie's letter of July 25, 1966, to Lloyd K. Garrison, president of the Board of Education; and her letter of September 1, 1966, on her reappointment for one year with the concluding sentences, "I shall not keep my eyes closed or my ears covered or my mouth shut. I have only one year, but you know and I know that others will take my place. The twentieth century will not be kept waiting much longer."

69. Podair, *Strike That Changed New York*, 79, 81–83, and Joshua B. Freeman, *Working-Class New York: Life and Labor since World War II* (New York: New Press, 2001), 204–5, 223–24.

70. Wendell E. Pritchett, *Brownsville, Brooklyn: Blacks, Jews, and the Changing Face of the Ghetto* (Chicago: University of Chicago Press, 2002), 230–231.

71. See Peter R. Eisenstadt, *Rochdale Village: Robert Moses, 6,000 Families, and New York City's Great Experiment in Integrated Housing* (Ithaca, NY: Cornell University Press, 2010), 193–95, 204, 205; Podair, *Strike That Changed New York*, 14–15, 28, 39, 41, 52–53, 54–57, 69–70, and Freeman, *Working-Class New York*, 223–25. Also useful for understanding the strike and the issues around it are Daniel H. Perlstein, *Justice, Justice: School Politics and the Eclipse of Liberalism* (New York: Peter Lang, 2004), and Christina Collins, *"Ethnically Qualified": Race, Merit, and the Selection of Urban Teachers, 1920–1980* (New York: Teachers College Press, 2011).

72. Pritchett, *Brownsville, Brooklyn*, 235–36.

73. Ibid.

74. For log of calls dated October 17, 1968, see box 11, folder 8, Executive Deputy Superintendent Nathan Brown Files, Board of Education Records, NYC Department of Records/Municipal Archives.

75. See, in the *New York Times*, "Local Board Dismissed," October 5, 1968, 24; "Pupils Here Bored," October 25, 1968, 50; and "Pupil Attendance Up," October 17, 1968, 42. On Haas's efforts to keep the schools open, see Katznelson, *City Trenches*, 156–57.

76. See Pritchett, *Brownsville, Brooklyn*, 235–36; Ravitch, *School Wars*, 386–87; Taylor, *Knocking at Our Own Door*, 205, and "Public Schools," in *Encyclopedia of New York City*, ed. Kenneth T. Jackson, 2nd ed. (New Haven: Yale University Press, 2010), 1056.

77. See Eisenstadt, *Rochdale Village*, 195.

78. For letters on the redrawing of the district boundaries, see in the Isaiah Robinson Papers, Board of Education Collection: letter from the principal of PS 187, box 21, folder 23; an announcement of April 6, 1970, criticizing the new boundaries and encouraging parents to protest in box 21, folder 17, and a letter from the Parents' Association of PS 123 advocating no changes in district boundaries, dated October 10, 1969, in box 21, folder 21.

79. Katznelson, *City Trenches*, 157–62.

80. See "Board of Education" in *The Encyclopedia of New York City*, ed. Kenneth T. Jackson (New Haven: Yale University Press, 1995), 121–22.

81. For election results, see "Complete Results of Balloting . . . ," *New York Times*, November 6, 1969, 40.

82. Katznelson, *City Trenches*, xiii–xiv, and interview with author, New York City, June 26, 2012.

83. Ibid., 18–19, quotation from 6.

84. Quotation from ibid., 18.

85. Ibid., 178–89.

86. Ibid., 160–62, 168–69. Laura Altschuler, a Heights resident who was active around education issues, in an interview emphasized to me the value of school board meetings, however contentious they may have been, as public forums in a divided and heterogeneous neighborhood. Author telephone interview with Laura Altschuler, 2012.

87. Katznelson, *City Trenches*, 118–21, 176–79, 181, 186–89. Also see Thomas Bender, "Space, Time, and Politics," *Reviews in American History* 10, no. 3 (September 1982): 325–29, and a review of *City Trenches* by David A. Gerber, *Journal of Social History* 16, no. 3 (Spring 1983): 161–62.

88. The mismatch between demands, needs, and resources at the local level anticipates the inequalities of neoliberalism, which as David Harvey argues can be redressed only by higher levels of government, which are starved of revenues under neoliberal policies. See David Harvey, *Rebel Cities: From the Right to the City to the Urban Revolution* (New York: Verso, 2012), 82–83. Homer R. Wade's letter of January 20, 1971, is in the Harvey Scribner Files, series 1101, subseries 2, box 10, folder 6, Board of Education Records, NYC Department of Records/Municipal Archives.

89. See "Bitter Dispute . . . ," *New York Times*, April 1, 1974, 33.

90. Katznelson, *City Trenches*, 156, 172–75.

91. For correspondence on the issue see Office of the Secretary/Appeals papers, folders 19–20, box 2, subseries 1, Board of Education Records, NYC Department of Records/Municipal Archives.

92. On the PS 187 controversy, see Katznelson, *City Trenches*, 173–74, and "Bitter Dispute . . . ," *New York Times*, April 1, 1974, 33.

93. On the PS 187 controversy, see Katznelson, *City Trenches*, 173–74, and "Parents and Anker Aides Clash . . . ," *New York Times*, June 27, 1974, 49.

94. See "Parents and Anker Aides Clash . . . ," *New York Times*, June 27, 1974, 49, and "Parents Claim Victory in Clash with Anker Men," *Heights-Inwood*, July 4, 1974, 2.

95. Katznelson, *City Trenches*, 174.

96. Author interview with Marielys Divanne, New York City, 2012.

97. Katznelson, *City Trenches*, 189.

98. See Pedro Mir, "There Is a Country in the World: A Poem, Sad on More Than One Occasion," reprinted in *Callaloo* 23, no. 3 (Summer 2000): 850–57; and "Countersong to Walt Whitman," translated from the Spanish by Jonathan Cohen, http://www.uhmc.sunysb.edu/surgery/mir.html.

99. See Frank Moya Pons, *The Dominican Republic: A National History* (New Rochelle, NY: Hispaniola Books, 1995), 10, 323–29, 336–39, 341; Allan M. Klein, *Sugarball: The American Game, the Dominican Dream* (New Haven: Yale University Press, 1991), 9–12; and Jesse Hoffnung-Garskof, *A Tale of Two Cities: Santo Domingo and New York after 1950* (Princeton: Princeton University Press,

2008), 25–28. On the U.S. occupation of the Dominican Republic, see Bruce J. Calder, *The Impact of Intervention: The Dominican Republic during the U.S. Occupation of 1916–1924* (Austin: University of Texas Press, 1984). For a summary of U.S.-Dominican relations leading up to and during the 1965 U.S. intervention, see Alan L. McPherson, *Yankee No! Anti-Americanism in U.S.–Latin American Relations* (Cambridge: Harvard University Press, 2003), 117–62.

100. On the massacre, see Richard Lee Turits, "A World Destroyed, a Nation Imposed: The 1937 Haitian Massacre in the Dominican Republic," *Hispanic American Historical Review* 82, no. 3 (August 2002); Pons, *Dominican Republic*, 357–68, 370–90; and Hoffnung-Garskof, *Tale of Two Cities*, 28–36. For examples of the use of term "genocide," which is sometimes used alongside terms such as massacre and slaughter that carry a less systematic connotation, see Eric Paul Roorda, "Genocide Next Door: The Good Neighbor Policy, the Trujillo Regime, and the Haitian Massacre of 1937," *Diplomatic History* 2, no. 3 (Summer 1996), and Mark Memmott, "Remembering to Never Forget: Dominican Republic's 'Parsley Massacre,'" October 1, 2012, National Public Radio, http://www.npr.org/blogs/thetwo-way/2012/10/01/162092252/remembering-to-never-forget-dominican-republics-parsley-massacre.

101. See McPherson, *Yankee No!*, 117–62.

102. See Hoffnung-Garskof, *Tale of Two Cities*, 70–80, 90–93. Also see Aristide Zolberg, "Immigration Control Policy: Law and Implementation," in *The New Americans: A Guide to Immigration since 1965*, ed. Mary C. Waters and Reed Ueda, with Helen B. Marrow (Cambridge, MA: Harvard University Press, 2009), 30–32.

103. See Hoffnung-Garskof, *Tale of Two Cities*, 94–96. The story behind "Yankee go home and take me with you," credited to the Dominican historian Frank Moya Pons, is on 95.

104. On problems at the school as early as 1966, see James Tierney letters of October 22, November 4, and November 11, 1966, UFT Papers, box 127, folder 6. For an insightful report on the situation at George Washington High School, see Richard J. Margolis, "The George Washington Story: The Agony of an Urban High School," *New Leader*, June 14, 1971, 11–17. For biographical details, see "Richard J. Margolis, Writer for Children and Columnist, 61," *New York Times*, April 23, 1991. Margolis reports, on page 12, that the school was redistricted in the mid-1960s to take in students from a section of Harlem as far south as 145th Street, but that the redistricting also cut off George Washington from the whiter Riverdale section of the Bronx. For a UFT perspective on the episode, see Irving Witkin, *Diary of a Teacher: The Crisis at George Washington High School* (New York: United Federation of Teachers, 1970).

105. *Cherry Tree*, student newspaper of George Washington High School, March 26, 1970, in UFT Papers, box 127, folder 8.

106. Hoffnung-Garskof, *Tale of Two Cities*, 133–35.

107. Author interview with Nelsy Aldebot, Bronx, NY, 2013.

108. Sara Lurie interview with author.

109. Author telephone interview with Ramona De La Cruz, 2013.

110. Hoffnung-Garskof, *Tale of Two Cities*, 139–45. Also see author interview with Sara Lurie, June 23, 2010, New York City; and author interview with Aldebot.

111. This paragraph and the immediately following paragraphs are based on the author's interview with Aldebot.

112. See "Politics: Procaccino Gives School Policy," *New York Times*, October 30, 1969, 40. For earlier complaints about George Washington and its students, see letter of Mrs. Charles Trummer to Mayor Lindsay of March 14, 1967, Bernard Donovan Papers, box 32, folder 1; and "City Schools Act to Halt Drug Abuse," *New York Times*, February 8, 1968, 21. For a complaint on a student dismissal there, see "Dismissal of Principal Is Demanded," *New York Times*, October 20, 1967, 39.

113. See *Report on George Washington High School*, New York Civil Liberties Union, May 1970. For the leaflet, see UFT Papers, box 127, folder 6. On the birth of the table idea in February 1970, see *G. W. Free Press* in Robinson Papers, box 17, folder 28.

114. See Margolis, "The George Washington Story," 11–17, especially 13–16, for a discussion of the table issue. Critics of Lurie shared reminiscences with me at YM-YWHA forums.

115. Margolis, "George Washington Story," 12–14.

116. Sara Lurie interview; table group leaflet of March 13, 1970, UFT Papers, box 127, folder 7; March 11, 1970, letter of the Upper Manhattan Clergy Association, box 17, Lurie Papers; and the rabbis' letter of March 19, 1970, UFT Papers, box 127, folder 7.

117. See parents' letter to John Lindsay of April 16, 1970, and copy of April 22, 1970, telegram to Irving Anker in UFT Papers, box 127, folder 7. Also see May 11, 1970, letter to the president

of the Board of Education from David Hess and seven other teachers, Robinson Papers, box 17, folder 28.

118. See Strauss letters of March 16, 1970, and October 16, 1970, in UFT Papers, box 127, folder 7.

119. See, in box 17, Lurie Papers: Lurie letter to Nat Hentoff; letters from parents and teachers supporting students who faced transfer out of the school; and *Report on George Washington High School*, New York Civil Liberties Union, May 1970.

120. Margolis, "George Washington Story," 15–16.

121. See Louis Simon letter of December 2, 1970, Robinson Papers, box 17, folder 28; Lurie letter to Hentoff, box 17, Lurie Papers. On the injuries and arrests, see "2 Hurt, 3 Seized in School Melee," *New York Times*, December 2, 1970, 23.

122. Biographical details on Samuel Kostman are from author interview with Samuel Kostman, June 14, 2010, Englewood, NJ, and a personal copy of Kostman's curriculum vitae.

123. On Wingate and East Flatbush, see, in the *New York Times*, "Fire and Disturbances Clear Washington and Wingate Highs," May 8, 1969, 39, and " 'Blockbusting': Dilemma in East Flatbush Area," December 9, 1969, 57.

124. "Washington High Gets Fourth Principal This Year," *New York Times*, December 3, 1970, 75.

125. On discharges, see December 16, 1970, letter of Alfred Gutman to Isaiah Robinson; on the table, see December 8, 1970, letter of James Boffman to Irving Anker in Robinson Papers, box 17, folder 28.

126. On transfers, see January 7, 1971, letter of Samuel Kostman to Isaiah Robinson Jr. in Robinson Papers, box 17, folder 28, and "School Rescinds Transfer Orders," *New York Times*, January 15, 1971, 39; and, on the table, "High School Loses Its Complaint Table," *New York Times*, January 21, 1971, 30. On the Glick assault, see "Teacher Beaten Unconscious, Washington High Student Held," *New York Times*, December 18, 1970, 46. On the consultative council, see February 3, 1971, letter of Harriet Mannheim, Jimmy Pelton, Sara Lurie, and Verna Kein to Dr. Scribner and the Board of Education in Robinson Papers, box 17, folder 28. On the fighting, see "Five Seized and Five Hurt . . . ," *New York Times*, February 20, 1971, 31; "Cops Stand By . . . ," *New York Post*, February 23, 1971, 21; and "GW Students Blame Drug Traffic . . . ," *Amsterdam News*, February 27, 1971, 1.

127. For the Kostman announcement, see Council of School Supervisors and Administrators Records, Tamiment Collection, box 13, folder 15.

128. On the ESL classes, see a December 2, 1971, letter from Kathryn O'D. Griffith to Kostman and his reply of December 7, 1971, in the papers of the Council of Supervisors and Administrators, Tamiment Library and Robert F. Wagner Labor Archives, New York University, Wagner 269, box 13, folder 15. On the wide range of initiatives undertaken by Kostman, including the academy that Ellen Lurie praised, see "Washington High: From Riot to Hope," *New York Times*, June 1, 1971, 41. On the weekend in Netcong, see "Weekend in Country Calms Washington H.S. Tempers," *New York Times*, January 11, 1972, 39.

129. Kostman interview.

130. See "Washington High: From Riot to Hope," 41, and Margolis, "George Washington Story," 17. For the Shanker column, see "George Washington High School: The Climate One Year Later," *New York Times*, June 13, 1971, E9.

131. On the gay rights group, see *Growing Up Gay: A Youth Liberation Pamphlet* (New York: Youth Liberation Press, 1976) at http://aurora.barnard.edu/crow/archive/lesbian/.

132. Kostman interview.

133. Aldebot interview.

134. De La Cruz interview.

135. See, in the *New York Times*, "Many Schools Crowded on First Day," September 9, 1986, B3; "As Class-Cutting Rises, 'Snowball Effect' Is Feared," June 27, 1988, B1; "Albany Issues List of Schools in Trouble," December 19, 1989, B1; and "In New York City High Schools, Paths to Diploma Grow Longer for Many," June 3, 1996, 1. Also see Ira J. Singer, "George Washington High School Registration Review Report," November 15–16, 1989, in UFT Papers, box 183, folder 21. For a valuable study set in a school much like George Washington High School in the 1990s, see Nancy López, "Unraveling the Race-Gender Gap in Education: Second-Generation Men's High School Experiences," in *Becoming New Yorkers: Ethnographies of the New Second Generation*, ed. Philip Kasinitz, John H. Mollenkopf, and Mary C. Waters (New York: Russell Sage Foundation, 2004), 28–56.

136. Joshua Freeman makes this last point in *Working-Class New York*, 219.

137. See Ellen Lurie, *How to Change the Schools: A Parents' Action Handbook on How to Fight the System* (New York: Random House, 1970), 251–52, 267.

138. Clipping of op-ed column by Hope Irvine, *Heights-Inwood*, January 6, 1997, box 10, Lurie Papers.

139. "Ellen Lurie, 47, a Rights Activist and School Integration Leader," *New York Times*, June 22, 1978, D19.

CHAPTER 4

1. On the Y meetings, see author interview with Martin Englisher, YM-YWHA of Washington Heights and Inwood, New York City, 2008; also "Big Shots . . ." and "Koch Unveils," *Heights-Inwood*, August 9, 1978, 1. On the fear in the Heights in the 1970s that the neighborhood's future would be similar to that of the South Bronx, see author interviews with Monsignor Kevin Sullivan, John Brian Murtaugh, Franz Leichter, and Tom Tedeschi, New York City, 2012.

2. My thinking here is influenced by Albert O. Hirschman, *Exit, Voice, and Loyalty: Responses to Decline in Firms, Organizations, and States* (Cambridge: Harvard University Press, 1970), 3, 4, and William Julius Wilson and Richard P. Taub, *There Goes the Neighborhood: Racial, Ethnic, and Class Tensions in Four Chicago Neighborhoods and Their Meaning for America* (New York: Vintage, 2007), 7, 181.

3. Monsignor Sullivan and Michael Lappin, interviewed separately October 1, 2010, New York City, were the first to alert me to the combination of housing-stock preservation and Dominican arrivals in saving Washington Heights from devastating decay.

4. See Jim Carroll, *The Basketball Diaries* (New York: Penguin Books, 1987), 17, 18, 11–12, 48–50, 99–100, 104, 126–27, 145–46. Quotations are from 17.

5. Author interview with Jerome Travers, New York City, June 28, 2011.

6. "Old and New of Washington Heights," *New York Times*, April 2, 1969, 49. The population was done in Social Explorer using U.S. Census data from 1960 and 1970. See http://www.social explorer.com/tables/C1960TractDS/R10735124 and http://www.socialexplorer.com/tables/C1970/R10735125. Also see *Community Information: Manhattan Community Planning District 12* (New York: Department of City Planning, n.d.), 2, 3, 7a–7b; and Nathalie Friedman and Naomi Golding, *Neighborhood Variation: The Implications for Administrative Decentralization: An Analysis of Sub-communities in Manhattan Community Planning District 12* (New York: Bureau of Applied Social Research, Columbia University, 1974), 4, 7–10.

7. *A Community Profile of Manhattan Community Planning District 12*, prepared by the Bureau of Applied Social Research, Columbia University (New York, 1973), 6–9.

8. Nathalie Friedman and Naomi Golding, *Urban Residents and Neighborhood Government: A Profile of the Public in Seven Urban Neighborhoods of New York City*, prepared for the NYC Neighborhood Study for the Charter Revision Commission (New York, 1973), 15, 17, 31, 36.

9. *A Community Profile*, quotation from 8, 10–11.

10. See Joshua B. Freeman, *Working-Class New York: Life and Labor since World War II* (New York: New Press, 2001), 6–14.

11. Miriam Greenberg, *Branding New York: How a City in Crisis Was Sold to the World* (New York: Routledge, 2008), 100–102. For references to the "billion dollar mile," see, in the *New York Times*, "Jersey Education," February 5, 1975, 80; "Quietly, Land on the Palisades Goes on Sale," May 7, 1978, R1; and "Englewood Cliffs Adding CNBC to Corporate Logos," August 27, 2000, RE9.

12. Nathalie Friedman and Theresa F. Rogers, *Administrative Decentralization and the Public* (New York: Bureau of Applied Social Research, Columbia University, 1974), 12, 27, 14, 10, 9, 22, 15–16, 27–29.

13. Freeman, *Working-Class New York*, 256–57.

14. Ibid., 270–71.

15. "New York Parks Cope with Growing Decay . . . ," *New York Times*, May 26, 1977, 25.

16. "Washington Heights—Top of the Island," *New York Times*, September 16, 1977, 77.

17. See *Goodbye to Glocca Morra* (Radharc, 1968) and author interview with Travers.

18. *Goodbye to Glocca Morra*.

19. "Fear of Violence, Locked Doors Mark Inwood Bar Scene," *Heights-Inwood*, July 25, 1974, 2. Author interview with Buddy McGee, 1990, New York City.

20. On the Irish in the suburbs of metropolitan New York, see Morton D. Winsberg, "The Suburbanization of the Irish in Boston, Chicago and New York," in *Eire-Ireland* 21, no. 3 (Fall 1986): 97–98, 101–2. For a summary of the Jewish suburban experience, see Deborah Dash Moore, "Suburbanization in the United States," in *Jewish Women: A Comprehensive Historical Encyclopedia*, at http://jwa.org/encyclopedia/article/suburbanization-in-united-states.

21. Dash Moore, "Suburbanization in the United States."

22. Author interview with Helen Walck, Dumont, New Jersey, 1990. For an example of a bitter departure from Inwood, see "Goodbye and Good Riddance to Inwood," *Daily News*, December 7, 1989, 47.

23. Max Frankel, *The Times of My Life and My Life with the* Times (New York: Random House, 1999), 47.

24. See "Point of View," *Tabernacle Bulletin*, May 1, 1973.

25. Rabbi Lehman delivered the sermon February 3, 1974. It was reprinted in the *Tabernacle Bulletin* issues of April 15, 1974, and May 1, 1974.

26. On the expanding boundaries of the South Bronx, see Evelyn Gonzalez, *The Bronx* (New York: Columbia University Press, 2004), 7, 109; also "South Bronx" and "Highbridge," in *Encyclopedia of New York City*, ed. Kenneth T. Jackson, 2nd ed. (New Haven: Yale University Press, 2010), 1213 and 594–95.

27. See Gonzalez, *The Bronx*, 2.

28. *CBS Reports: The Fire Next Door*, CBS News, March 22, 1977.

29. *The Police Tapes*, PBS, January 3, 1977.

30. On Taki, see "'Taki 183' Spawns Pen Pals," *New York Times*, July 21, 1971, 37, and http://taki183.net. For films that look at graffiti with interest and appreciation produced by a German Jew who grew up in Washington Heights, see Manfred Kirchheimer's *Stations of the Elevated* (1980) and *SprayMasters* (2007).

31. "Empty Shops Worry 207th Street Residents," *New York Times*, January 9, 1977, 43.

32. On the blackout in northern Manhattan, see *Heights-Inwood*, July 20, 1977, 1, 7, and July 27, 1977, 1. See *New York Times*, "New York's Power Restored Slowly; Looting Widespread, 2,700 Arrested; Blackout Results in Heavy Losses," July 15, 1977, 42; "When Poverty's Part of Life, Looting Is Not Condemned," July 15, 1977, 4; and "'Disaster' Status Given New York and Westchester to Speed Loans; Services Resume after Blackout," July 16, 1977, 48. For more responses to the blackout, see James Goodman, *Blackout* (New York: Farrar, Straus and Giroux, 2003), 25–35, 38–50, 51–74, and Jonathan Mahler, *Ladies and Gentlemen, the Bronx Is Burning: 1977, Baseball, Politics, and the Battle for the Soul of a City* (New York: Farrar, Straus and Giroux, 2005), 190–95, 197–217.

33. For the headline "Por Que?" see *El Diario*, July 15, 1977, 1. For two examples of very different reactions, see Pete Hamill, "Black Night of Our Soul," *Daily News*, July 15, 1977, 2, and William Safire, "Christmas in July," *New York Times*, July 18, 1977, L27. For more on debates over the significance of the blackouts, see Mahler, *Ladies and Gentlemen*, 223–27, and Goodman, *Blackout*, 75–77, 82–83, 113, 119–21, 132–36, 151–54, 157–60, 169–71, 201–6, 218–21, 224–28.

34. See Reminiscences of Edward I. Koch, 1976, 55–57, 71–72, 75, 77–92, 106, 108–22, 139–42, 143–49, 149–51, 192–96, 197–202, 203–9, 216–20, 247–253 in the Oral History Research Office Collection of the Columbia University Libraries. Also see Jonathan Soffer, *Ed Koch and the Rebuilding of New York City* (New York: Columbia University Press, 2012), 123–24, 125–27, 128, 129–30, 133, 138–40, 141.

35. On the election, see Soffer, *Ed Koch and the Rebuilding of New York City*, 142. For an insightful discussion of the Koch coalition, see John Mollenkopf, *A Phoenix in the Ashes: The Rise and Fall of the Koch Coalition in New York City Politics* (Princeton: Princeton University Press, 1994), 6–7, 103–5. On Bess Myerson, see "Bess Myerson" at http://jwa.org/encyclopedia/article/myerson-bess. For election results, see "Results in the Primary Election Voting in the Contests Held Here Thursday," *New York Times*, September 10, 1977, 16; *New York Post*, September 20, 1977, 31; and "Results of Voting in Elections Tuesday in New York City and Rockland County," *New York Times*, November 10, 1977, 89. On efforts to reach out to Koch in the fall of 1977, see author interviews with Sullivan and Tedeschi. On early overtures from the Koch administration to neighborhood activists grounded in churches and synagogues in Washington Heights and Inwood, see "Wagner at Bat," *Heights-Inwood*, February 22, 1978, 9.

36. On the appeal of Koch's reform roots in northern Manhattan during the period of reform ascendancy there, see Tedeschi interview.

37. For the "make it like it was" anecdote, see Arthur Browne, Dan Collins, and Michael Goodwin, *I, Koch: A Decidedly Unauthorized Biography of the Mayor of New York City* (New York: Dodd, Mead, 1985), 161.

38. On Koch's inaugural address, see "Text of Address . . . ," *New York Times*, January 2, 1978, 13, and Soffer, *Ed Koch and the Rebuilding of New York City*, 146–47. On early overtures from the Koch administration to neighborhood activists grounded in churches and synagogues in Washington Heights and Inwood, see "Wagner at Bat," *Heights-Inwood*, February 22, 1978, 9.

39. My thanks to William Massey for sharing with me the findings of his undergraduate thesis research at Columbia University.

40. See Ira Katznelson, *City Trenches: Urban Politics and the Patterning of Class* (Chicago: University of Chicago Press, 1981), 127–28, and *New York Times*, "Recanvass Names Walsh Victor By 99 Votes in Assembly Race," November 10, 1970, 38, and "Freshman in Albany: An 'Exhilarating' Process," April 16, 1973, 41.

41. Tedeschi and Leichter interviews; also "Leichter, the Senate's Minority of One, Finds an Audience Beyond Albany," *New York Times*, May 30, 1993, A35, and biography at http://www.franzleichter.com/.

42. Tedeschi interview; *Daily News*, "RIP Stanley Michels," August 1, 2008, http://www.nydailynews.com/blogs/dailypolitics/2008/08/rip-stanley-michaels.html; "Stanley E. Michels, 75, Longtime Councilman," *New York Times*, August 2, 2008, C10.

43. Author interview with John Brian Murtaugh, New York City, April 20, 2012, and biography at www.newyorkstatepolitics.com/Bios.aspx.

44. On the housing crisis and its urgency, see Jacqueline Leavitt and Susan Saegert, *From Abandonment to Hope: Community-Households in Harlem* (New York: Columbia University Press, 1990), 3; Nathan Leventhal interview, Edward I. Koch Administration Oral History Project, Columbia University Oral History Research Office, 1993; Ronald Lawson, with the assistance of Reuben B. Johnson III, "Tenant Responses to the Urban Housing Crisis, 1970–1984, " in *The Tenant Movement in New York City, 1904–1984*, ed. Ronald Lawson, with the assistance of Mark Naison (New Brunswick, NJ: Rutgers University Press, 1986), 209; and Soffer, *Ed Koch and the Rebuilding of New York City*, 178–79.

45. See *Report of Washington Heights–Inwood Task Force*, August 1, 1978, 7–9.

46. "Housing Gets Big Lift in Washington Heights," *New York Times*, July 20, 1980, R1, and author interview with Lappin.

47. Lappin interview. On redlining in northern Manhattan, see personal copy of Franz S. Leichter and Glenn F. von Nostitz, *Don't Bank on Us: Mortgage Lending Practices of Banks in Northern Manhattan, July 1979*, 1–3. My thanks to Glenn F. von Nostitz for providing me with this report.

48. Leichter and von Nostitz, *Don't Bank on Us*, 5–6, 32–33.

49. See ibid., 33–34; Lappin interview; also Alexander von Hoffman, *House by House, Block by Block: The Rebirth of America's Urban Neighborhoods* (New York: Oxford University Press, 2003), 51–54. On tenant complaints, see "CPC Scored," *Heights-Inwood*, March 25, 1981, 3; also "Little Consortium of Big Banks Is Aiding Inwood," *New York Times*, June 4, 1988, 29. On the CPC, see New York City Preservation Corporation, www.communityp.com/about/about-us. Also see Murtaugh interview on wariness of Lappin's work for fear of being associated with a rent increase.

50. Sullivan interview. On the Breuer community, see Stephen Lowenstein, *Frankfurt on the Hudson: The German Jewish Community of Washington Heights, 1933–1983, Its Structure and Culture* (Detroit: Wayne State University Press, 1989), 64–65, 114–18, 168–69.

51. "Politicians Must Bear the Burden," *Heights-Inwood*, September 28, 1977.

52. See, in *Heights-Inwood*, "The Grand Alliance," January 25, 1978, and "Robert Wagner at Bat," February 22, 1978, 9.

53. Author interview with Beth Rosenthal, New York City, 2012, and www.saintspyridon.net.

54. Rosenthal interview.

55. Rosenthal interview and Rosenthal letter to author of June 27, 2013; also author's telephone interview with Dana Vermilye, August 10, 2013.

56. See Leichter interview; *Northern Manhattan Improvement Corporation: 30 Years*, published by the Northern Manhattan Improvement Corporation, in author's possession; and Rosenthal letter of June 27, 2013.

57. See "Big Shots . . ." and "Koch Unveils," *Heights-Inwood*, August 9, 1978, 1.

58. See *Washington Heights-Inwood Task Force Update*, March 13, 1979.

59. See Soffer, *Ed Koch and the Rebuilding of New York City*, 292–93, 303; Leavitt and Saegert, *From Abandonment to Hope*, 4–5; and Lawson and Johnson, "Tenant Responses," in Lawson and Naison, *Tenant Movement in New York City*, 221–28; and Gerald Sazama, *A Brief History of Affordable Housing Cooperatives in the United States*, Department of Economics Working Paper 1996–09, University of Connecticut, Storrs, January 1996, 9.

60. Neil F. Carlson, *UHAB Comes of Age* (New York: Urban Homesteading Assistance Board, 2004), 2, 5, 6. Also, author interviews with Joel Rothschild, February-March 2009, New York City. The contradictions of housing redevelopment and brownstoning in Harlem, which illuminate the

complexities of the situation around the Grinnell, are insightfully explored in Brian Goldstein's doctoral dissertation, "A City within a City: Community Development and the Struggle over Harlem, 1961–2001" (PhD diss., Harvard University, 2013).

61. On the Grinnell and its early history, see Matthew Spady and Jacqueline Thaw, *The Grinnell at 100: Celebrating Community, History, and an Architectural Gem* (Raleigh, NC: Lulu Enterprises, 2011), 33–36, 39–41. Also see Audubon Park Historic District Committee, *Request for Evaluation for Historic District Status Submitted to the New York Landmark Preservation Committee* (March 2003), 10–14, 17–21, 70. For the description of the Grinnell's design and more, see New York City Landmarks Preservation Commission, *Audubon Park Historic District Designation Report* (May 12, 2009), 39–43, quoted material from 39.

62. Author interview with Connie Sutton, June 26, 2008, New York City; interview with Matthew Spady, New York City, 2010; Spady and Thaw, *Grinnell at 100*, 41–43.

63. Rothschild interviews.

64. Sutton and Rothschild interviews; Spady and Thaw, *Grinnell at 100*, 42–44; and comments of Wayne Benjamin, Gwen Gilyard, Richard James, Connie Sutton, and Joel Rothschild at the *Voices of the Grinnell* public oral history session, January 30, 2008, New York City.

65. Sutton and Rothschild interviews; Spady and Thaw, *Grinnell at 100*, 45; and comments of Benjamin, Gilyard, James, Sutton, and Rothschild at the *Voices of the Grinnell* public oral history session, January 30, 2008, New York City. On the wider context of the rent strike strategy, see Lawson and Johnson, "Tenant Responses," in Lawson and Naison, *Tenant Movement in New York City*, 228–29.

66. Rothschild interview; Lawson and Johnson, "Tenant Responses," in Lawson and Naison, *Tenant Movement in New York City*, 234–35; Carlson, *UHAB Comes of Age*, 5–9, and "7A Management" at http://www.nyc.gov/html/hpd/html/owners/supporting-7a.shtml.

67. Rothschild interview; on the angry divisions among Grinnell tenants in this era, see Benjamin and James at the *Voices of the Grinnell* event and Spady and Thaw, *Grinnell at 100*, 45.

68. See Leavitt and Saegert, *From Abandonment to Hope*, 4–6, 248; Spady and Thaw, *Grinnell at 100*, 47–48. Also see New York Private Housing Finance—Article 11, also known as the "Housing Development Fund Companies Law," Section 576, at http://law.onecle.com/new-york/private-housing-finance/PVH0576_576.html. The $250,000 deed of sale between the City of New York and the Grinnell Housing Fund Development Corporation, in author's possession, is dated November 3, 1982.

69. In my research on cooperatives Andrew Reicher, executive director of the Urban Homesteading Assistance Board, has been a great source of advice. Also see author's personal communication with Ann Henderson, Urban Homesteading Assistance Board, August 15, 2012 and January 12, 2014.

70. On the conflicts and contradictions of the Grinnell in its early years as a cooperative, see Rothschild interview; Spady and Thaw, *Grinnell at 100*, 47–48; Benjamin and James comments at *Voices of the Grinnell*. On the origins and long-term situations of HDFC cooperatives, see Bill Morris, "Co-ops: The Last Gasp of Affordable Housing," www.habitatmag.com/layout/set/print/Publication-Content/2008-June.

71. On this problem, see Henderson e-mail to author; also, on the different perspectives of cooperative residents, see Leavitt and Saegert, *From Abandonment to Hope*, 46, 50, 262 n1, 263 n1; and Susan Saegert and Lymari Benitez, "Limited Equity Housing Cooperatives: Defining a Niche in the Low-Income Housing Market," *Journal of Planning Literature* 19, no. 4 (May 2005): 430–31.

72. On the sales price dilemma, see Rothschild interview; Henderson, Urban Homesteading Assistance Board; and Morris, "Co-ops."

73. See Soffer, *Ed Koch and the Rebuilding of New York City*, 290–304.

74. On Koch administration housing policies, see author interview with Edward I. Koch, July 16, 2010, New York City. Also see Soffer, *Ed Koch and the Rebuilding of New York City*, 304. For an early account of the gulf between the housing for the rich and poor that was evident by the 1980s, see Richard Plunz and Marta Gutman, "The New York Ring," *Eupalino*, no. 1 (Winter 1983–84): 32.

75. See, for example, "A Renaissance in a Forgotten Neighborhood," *New York Times*, October 9, 1981, B1. On the record of the CPC in northern Manhattan, see "Little Consortium of Big Banks Is Aiding Inwood," *New York Times*, June 4, 1988, 29. Kathleen Dunn, director of the Washington Heights Neighborhood Preservation Program at the New York City Department of Housing Preservation and Development (HPD) who eventually became a deputy commissioner of HPD and executive vice president and director of development at the CPC, explained the contributions of the CPC,

the HPD, and city and federal funds in restoring 18 percent of the housing in northern Manhattan in a telephone interview with the author March 13, 2014.

76. The calculation of population loss in northern Manhattan north of 155th Street is based on U.S. Census data in Social Explorer. The 1950 calculation is available at http://www.socialexplorer.com/tables/C1950TractDS/R10735122, while the 1980 calculation is at http://www.socialexplorer.com/tables/C1980/R10735127. The figure of a total population of 179,919 in Community District 12 is from *Statement of Community District Needs: Fiscal Year 1984* (New York, October 1982), 139. While municipal figures and census data calculated with Social Explorer can differ in details, over-all they confirm a pattern of population loss in northern Manhattan from 1950 through 1980. On Soviet Jews, see Jennifer Barber, "The Soviet Jews of Washington Heights," *New York Affairs* 10, no. 1 (Winter 1987): 34, 36–39; author interview with Victoria Neznansky, New York City, 2013; and Annelise Orleck, "Soviet Jews: The Continuing Russification of Jewish New York," in *One Out of Three: Immigrant New York in the Twenty-First Century*, ed. Nancy Foner (New York: Columbia University Press, 2013), 91–92, 101–2, 109–12.

77. The population calculation is based on U.S. Census data in Social Explorer at http://www.socialexplorer.com/tables/C1970/R10735125 and http://www.socialexplorer.com/tables/C1980/R10735127. Also see *Community Information: Manhattan Community Planning District 12*, 2, 3, 7a–7b.

78. Daniel Matthew Bore, "Hospital Restructuring in the Inner City during the 1980s: Its Impact on Health Care Delivery, Utilization, and Community Health Status" (PhD diss., Columbia University, 1992), vol. I, 3–4, 34–38, 81, 94, 106–7, 111–15.

79. See Robert A. McCaughey, *Stand Columbia: A History of Columbia University in the City of New York* (New York: Columbia University Press, 2003), 577. On the Wood murder, see "Surgeon's Slaying Stuns Upper West Side," *New York Times*, November 4, 1981, B1.

80. See McCaughey, *Stand Columbia*, 577.

81. See Franz S. Leichter and Glenn F. von Nostitz, *The Return of the Sweatshop: A Call for State Action*, October 1979, 1–2. On Alex Rose, see *Encyclopedia of New York City* (2010 edition), 1123. Also see Marlene Zurich, *Academic Health Centers in Distressed City Neighborhoods: Toward a Good Neighbor Policy* (MS thesis, Columbia University, 1987).

82. See Leichter and von Nostitz, *Return of the Sweatshop*, 3–5, 15–16, appendix. Leichter and von Nostitz issued subsequent reports on the role of organized crime in sweatshop work around the city. Led Black described how his parents eagerly went to work in garment shops in the area described in the Leichter report in an author interview, July 23, 2012, New York City.

83. See Jesse Hoffnung-Garskof, *A Tale of Two Cities: Santo Domingo and New York after 1950* (Princeton: Princeton University Press, 2008), 68, 80, 93–96. The quotation is from Eugenia Georges, *The Making of a Transnational Community: Migration, Development, and Cultural Change in the Dominican Republic* (New York: Columbia University Press, 1990), 196. Also see author interview with Led Black.

84. Author interview with Sixto Medina, 2012, New York City.

85. See Patricia Pessar, *A Visa for a Dream: Dominicans in the United States* (Boston: Allyn and Bacon, 1996), 4–5; and Silvio Torres-Saillant and Ramona Hernandez, *The Dominican Americans* (Westport, CT: Greenwood, 1998), 34–35, 59.

86. On the PRD and the Dominican left in Washington Heights, see Hoffnung-Garskof, *Tale of Two Cities*, 119–25.

87. See Robert Jackall, *Wild Cowboys: Urban Marauders and the Forces of Moral Order* (Cambridge: Harvard University Press, 1997), 75; Jorge Duany, *Quisqueya on the Hudson: The Transnational Community of Dominicans in Washington Heights* (New York: Dominican Studies Institute, 1994), 5, 41–44; and Pessar, *Visa for a Dream*, 69–70.

88. On the assassination, see Ben Alexander, "Contested Memories, Divided Diaspora: Armenian-Americans, the Thousand-Day Republic, and the Polarized Response to an Archbishop's Murder," *Journal of American Ethnic History* 27, no. 1 (Fall 2007): 32–33. On the Irish Northern Aid Committee office in Inwood, see "Inwood Is Losing Its Brogue," *New York Times*, August 18, 1984, 25.

89. See Rudy Anthony Sainz, "Dominican Ethnic Associations: Classification and Service Delivery Roles in Washington Heights" (DSW thesis, Columbia University, 1990), 146–47, 161–70, 179; and Milagros Ricourt, *Dominicans in New York City: Power from the Margins* (New York: Routledge, 2002), 96–98.

90. On the general subject of Dominican women's organizations in northern Manhattan, see Pilar Monreal Requena, "Resistencia y Acomodacion en las Asociaciones de Mujeres Dominicanas de Nueva York," in *Genero y Sociedad* 4, no. 1 (May–August 1996), translated for the author by Lucia

della Paolera. On the Dominican Women's Development Center, see http://www.dwdc.org/index.php/about-us/history/.

91. "Maria Luna, 70 . . . ," *Daily News*, May 19, 2011; and "Albert Blumberg, 91, Philosopher and Communist," *New York Times*, October 13, 1997. Also see Eugenia Georges, *Dominican Self-Help Organizations in Washington Heights: Integration of a New Immigrant Population in a Multiethnic Neighborhood* (New York: Inter-University Program for Latino Research and the Social Science Research Council, 1988), 7–8. On Albert Blumberg, see author telephone interview with Peter Klein, December 4, 2012.

92. On Alianza Dominicana, see author interview with Milagros Batista, New York City, 2012; Moises Pérez, Jacqueline Martinez, and Laura Frye, "Community Health Workers: A Successful Strategy for Restoring the Health of a Community," in Allan J. Formicola and Lourdes Hernandez-Cordero, *Mobilizing the Community for Better Health: What the Rest of America can Learn from Northern Manhattan* (New York: Columbia University Press, 2011), 43, 45; and Hoffnung-Garskof, *Tale of Two Cities*, 214. For a biography of Dr. Lantigua, see http://www.cumc.columbia.edu/dept/medicine/generalmed/profile_pages/aim_lantigua2011.html. On the political significance of community-based organizations, see Nicole P. Marwell, *Bargaining for Brooklyn: Community Organizations in the Entrepreneurial City* (Chicago: University of Chicago Press, 2007), 23–24, 110–11, 112, 113, 231–32.

93. See Batista interview; Led Black interview and the research of Ramona Hernandez discussed in "Dominicans Scrabbling for Hope," *New York Times*, December 16, 1997, B1. For an analysis of Dominican families that illuminates both the centrality of women to Dominican families in changing transnational circumstances and the tension between women's agency and social and economic inequality, see Ramona Hernandez, "The Dominican American Family" in Roosevelt Wright Jr., Chalres H. Mindel, Thanh Van Tran and Robert W. Hubenstein, *Ethnic Families in America: Patterns and Variation*, 5th ed. (New York: Pearson, 2012), 149, 152–53, 165–66, 169–71.

94. See Miriam Mejia, "Reasons," in *Voices of the Diaspora: Stories and Testimonies of Dominican Immigrant Women*, compiled by Mary Ely Peña-Gratereaux (New York: Cayena Publications, 2008), 187–88.

95. See Peggy Levitt, "Dominican Republic," in *The New Americans: A Guide to Immigration since 1965*, edited by Mary C. Waters and Reed Ueda with Helen B. Marrow (Cambridge: Harvard University Press, 2007), 400–401; see "Introduction" in *Dominican Migration: Transnational Perspectives*, by Ernesto Sagas and Sintia E. Molina (Gainesville: University of Florida Press, 2004), 13–14; and Hoffnung-Garskof, *Tale of Two Cities*, 119–25, 206–10; and Diego Graglia, "Forty-Two Aprils Later" (MA thesis, New York University, 2007), 52.

96. See Fernando Lescaille, *Dominican Political Empowerment* (New York: Dominican Public Policy Project, 1992), 2; Graglia, "Forty-Two Aprils Later," 44, 45, 46–47, 50–55. On Medina's political loyalties, see author interview.

97. Quoted in Graglia, "Forty-Two Aprils Later," 55.

98. On the founding of the ACDP and its roots in Linea Roja, see Ana Aparicio, *Dominican-Americans and the Politics of Empowerment* (Gainesville: University of Florida Press, 2006), 61, 66, 70. On Guillermo Linares's biography, see "Washington Heights Councilman 'One of Us,'" *New York Newsday*, July 8, 1992, 26; "Dreaming Local," in *TC People*, July 5, 2012; *Manhattan Times*, June 8, 2011, 16; and Linares's official biography at http://assembly.state.ny.us/mem/Guillermo-Linares/. Linares's life and political career are also discussed in Michele Wucker, *Why the Cocks Fight: Dominicans, Haitians, and the Struggle for Hispaniola* (New York: Hill and Wang, 1999), 211–16, 224, 226, 227. For the anecdote on the picture of Trujillo in the home of the Linares family, see "Fifty Years after His Death, Does Trujillo Still Matter?," *Manhattan Times*, June 8, 2011, 16.

99. See Aparicio, *Dominican-Americans*, 77, 79, and Guillermo Linares, "Dominicans in New York: The Struggle for Community Control in District 6," *Centro Journal* 2, no. 5 (Spring 1989): 79–81.

100. For statistics and complaints on crowding, see letters in Alvarado Collection, Board of Education Papers, New York City Municipal Archive, box 41, folder 39. For coping strategies and problems, see, in *New York Times*, "Some Schools Are Jammed as Others Beg for Students," September 27, 1984, B1; "S.A.T. Scores Rise in City's Schools," October 7, 1984, 51; and "Crowded City Schools Using Halls for Classrooms," November 18, 1985, B1. On reading tests, see "Reading Scores Fall in City for the First Time in 5 Years," May 3, 1984, B1.

101. For the Rivera quotation, see "Some Schools Are Jammed as Others Beg for Students," *New York Times*, September 27, 1984, B1; for Michels, see "Board, to Lessen Crowding, Urges Busing

More Students," *New York Times*, September 19, 1984, B4; and Luis Rivera letter to the editor, "Re-zone Schools, But Keep Decentralization," *New York Times*, November 15, 1984, A30.

102. "Some Schools Are Jammed as Others Beg for Students," *New York Times*, September 27, 1984, B1.

103. On the difficulties of school siting debates in general, see author telephone interview with Ruth Messinger, New York, 2012.

104. On the history of the siting of PS 48, see *Uptown Dispatch*, October 31–November 14, 1986, 5; and "School Days, School Bus Maze," *Newsday*, September 12, 1989, 3. On resistance to integration in the western Heights, author telephone interview with Ramona De La Cruz, 2013; author interview with Robert Jackson, New York City, 2012; and author interview with a Greek American resident of the neighborhood who wishes to remain anonymous, 2012. For letters about the dire need for the school, see letter from M. Finkelstein and attached memo, Assistant to the Chancellor Arlene Pedone Files, "District 6" folder, box 37, Board of Education Records, NYC Department of Records/Municipal Archives; also letters in folder 389, box 41, Chancellor Anthony J. Alvarado Central Files, Series 1120 Papers, Board of Education Records, NYC Department of Records/Municipal Archives.

105. On the Breuer community and its place in Washington Heights, see Lowenstein, *Frankfurt on the Hudson*, 78, 114–15, 116–18, 122, 129–31, 141–42. On the debates around PS 148, see Murtaugh, Sullivan, and Miranda interviews.

106. On Wurzberger, see Lowenstein, *Frankfurt on the Hudson*, 95–96. On the presence of Jews on all sides of the issue, see Murtaugh interview and "There Are No Winners in the Battle over P.S. 48," *Uptown Dispatch*, October 31–November 14, 1986, 5. In the early 1990s, while doing social action work for Beth Am, more than once I heard the dispute described as a confrontation that pitted "the Jewish community" against Dominicans.

107. See "There Are No Winners in the Battle over P.S. 48," *Uptown Dispatch*, October 31–November 14, 1986, 5.

108. See "Neo-Nazis Running in School Board Elections," *Uptown Dispatch*, April 20–May 3, 1983, 1. For a description of the contest in 1983, see "LaRouche Slate Is Fought in Races for School Board," *New York Times*, April 22, 1983, B3; for the atmosphere at the vote tally in 1983, see "A Long Vote Count Begins," *New York Times*, May 13, 1983, B1. For a description of the strategy employed to defeat the LaRouche candidates, written by Stanley Michels and Franz Leichter, see "School Voting: A Long Vote Count Begins," *New York Times*, April 3, 1986, A27. For letters on the bitter disputes over the board and the district, see box 59, folder 482, Chancellor Richard R. Green Central Files, Board of Education Records, NYC Department of Records/Municipal Archives. For descriptions of the disputes on and around school politics, also see Medina and Miranda interviews.

109. See Medina and Altschuler interviews.

110. See, in *New York Times*, "Quinones Sends a Team to Study Problem District: Upper Manhattan Unit Is Subject of Inquiry," January 21, 1987, B3; "Removal of School Board Members in District Seen," February 1, 1987, 32; "Citing Disarray, Quinones Ousts a School Board," March 21, 1987, A27; "3 of Principals in District Lose Their Positions" July 16, 1987, B2; and "Voters Re-elect 6 to 2 Boards under Inquiry," May 18, 1989, B1. Also see Board of Education letter of July 7, 1987, on the suspension in box 7, folder 16, Chancellor Nathan Quinones Central Files, Board of Education Records, NYC Department of Records/Municipal Archives (hereafter called Quiniones Files); a confidential memo of May 18, 1987, in box 256, folder 2438, Quinones Files; "Management Review of Community School District Six" in box 256, folder 2437, Quinonones Files; and Thomas Sabol letter of March 1, 1988, in Green Files, box 59, folder 482. A letter of March 25, 1987, to Chancellor Quinones expressing "distress" at the situation in District 6 from Rep. Charles B. Rangel, Rep. Theodore Weiss, Manhattan Borough President David Dinkins, State Senator Franz Leichter, State Senator Olga Mendez, Councilman Stanley Michels, State Assemblyman Herman D. Farrell and State Assemblyman John Brian Murtaugh is in box 183, folder 1762, Chancellor Nathan Quinones Subject Files Series 1125, Board of Education Records, NYC Department of Records/Municipal Archives.

111. Urban poverty is often studied by analyzing the character traits of the poor. The significance of the absence of economically sound jobs for poor people who work is emphasized usefully in Katherine S. Newman, *No Shame in My Game: The Working Poor in the Inner City* (New York: Russell Sage, 1999).

112. See "Between 2 Worlds: Dominicans in New York," *New York Times*, September 16, 1991, A1.

113. Ricourt, *Dominicans in New York City*, 68–71.

114. On the charter, see Kenneth T. Jackson, ed., *Encyclopedia of New York City* (New Haven: Yale University Press, 1995), 203–8, and 2010 edition, 230–33; on the city council, see *Encyclopedia of New York City* (2010 edition), 256–57. On the reforms of 1989, see Frank J. Mauro and Gerald Benjamin, eds., *Restructuring the New York City Government: The Reemergence of Municipal Reform*, vol. 37, no. 3 (New York: Academy of Political Science, 1989), especially Joseph P. Viteritti, "The Tradition of Municipal Reform: Charter Revision in Historical Context," 29, and Frank J. Mauro, "Voting Rights and the Board of Estimate: The Emergence of an Issue," 67.

115. *Section Five of the Voting Rights Act: Hearings Before the New York City Districting Commission* (November 27, 1990), filed at the City Hall Library, New York City, testimony of Maria Luna, 84–88, quotation from 88, and Rafael Lantigua, 77–82, quotations from 81, 82.

116. Ibid., testimony of Adriano Espaillat, 88–98, quotations from 88–89, 90.

117. Ibid., testimony of Guillermo Linares, 124–128, quotations from 125, 125–26, 127–28.

118. Ibid., testimony of Stanley Michels, 132–40; also testimony of Sixto Medina, 140–48, and appendix containing a statement from the North Manhattan Committee for Fair Representation.

119. On Linares and school politics in northern Manhattan, see Hoffnung-Garskof, *Tale of Two Cities*, 119, 214–15. Also see Nicole P. Marwell, "Ethnic and Postethnic Politics in New York City: The Dominican Second Generation," in *Becoming New Yorkers: Ethnographies of the New Second Generation*, ed. Philip Kasinitz, John H. Mollenkopf, and Mary C. Waters (New York: Russell Sage Foundation, 2004), 231, 234–35, and Fernando Lescaille, *Dominican Political Empowerment* (New York: Dominican Public Policy Project, 1992), 4. On Linares's primary and general election victories in the 1991 council race, see, in the *New York Times*, "New Voices . . . ," September 13, 1991, B5, and "New York City Council Results . . . ," November 6, 1991, B1.

120. On this duality in the Koch administration, see Soffer, *Ed Koch and the Rebuilding of New York City*, 304.

121. Sullivan interview.

122. On the drug buy, see photograph and article, "New York Day by Day," *New York Times*, July 10, 1986, A1 and B3. On the debate that followed, also see the *New York Times*, "Morgenthau Calls U.S. Bid to Fight Cocaine 'Minimal,'" July 11, 1986, B1.

CHAPTER 5

1. Author's observations, winter 1990, on a foot patrol with an officer from the 34th Precinct. My thanks to the precinct command for arranging a week of patrolling with officers on foot and in sector cars, which contributed enormously to what I learned about police work and life in Washington Heights during the crack years. Also useful for understanding the world of drug dealing in Washington Heights was Terry Williams, *The Cocaine Kids: The Inside Story of a Teenage Drug Ring* (Reading, Massachusetts: Addison-Wesley, 1991), 22–26.

2. Community Research Group of the New York State Psychiatric Institute and Columbia School of Public Health, Mindy Thompson Fullilove, principal investigator, *Towards a Comprehensive Understanding of Violence in Washington Heights: A Report on Violence in Washington Heights*, July 1996, 44.

3. This question is taken up in Robert Jackall, *Wild Cowboys: Urban Marauders and the Forces of Order* (Cambridge: Harvard University Press, 1997).

4. On the complexity of the fear of crime, which related to many things—including anxiety about social change—see Stephen Farrall, Jonathan Jackson, and Emily Gray, *Social Order and the Fear of Crime in Contemporary Times* (Oxford: Oxford University Press, 2009), 236, 238–40, 258–59. The essays collected in Jason Ditton and Stephen Farrall, eds., *The Fear of Crime* (Aldershot, UK: Ashgate/Dartmouth, 2000) are also valuable.

5. See "'Death in Family' Shuts Manhattan Candy Store," *New York Times*, November 19, 1966, 34; "Neighbors March on Station House," *New York Times*, November 20, 1966, 83; and "Uptown Residents Seek More Police," *Amsterdam News*, November 20, 1966, 3. The *Amsterdam News* report credits the organization of the march to the Riverside-Edgecombe Neighborhood Association.

6. For examples of residents of what might be called either the southern Heights or upper Harlem expressing concern about crime and policing in their neighborhoods, see "Who IS Responsible for Harlem's Crime?," *Amsterdam News*, February 15, 1964, 44. On police violence and crime, see Marilynn S. Johnson, *Street Justice: A History of Police Violence in New York City* (Boston: Beacon Press, 2003), 234–40, 245–48, 253–54; on the death of Charles Bivins, see "Middle Class Leaders in

Harlem Ask Crackdown on Crime," *New York Times*, December 24, 1968, 25, and, in the *Amsterdam News*, "Charles Bivins Slain Last November 18," November 22, 1969, 2, and "The Bivins Fund Is Still Growing," April 5, 1969, 2. On the NAACP campaign, see, in the *Amsterdam News*, "NAACP Board Upholds Dismissal of Atty. Steel," December 14, 1968, 1; "Fighting Crime," February 22, 1969, 14; and "Crime Fight Moving," March 8, 1969, 1; also "N.A.A.C.P. Deplores Harlem 'Terror'," *New York Times*, December 13, 1968, 1. On Ellison, see Arnold Rampersad, *Ralph Ellison: A Biography* (New York: Knopf, 2007), 474–75.

7. "Profile of a Mugging," *Heights-Inwood*, June 27, 1974, 8; July 4, 1974, 8; July 11, 1974, 8.

8. See Farrall, Jackson, and Gray, *Social Order and the Fear of Crime*, 238–40, 258–59.

9. Vincent J. Cannato, *The Ungovernable City: John Lindsay and His Struggle to Save New York* (New York: Basic Books, 2001), 44, 167–69, 171–76. The phrase "oxygen of publicity" is credited to Margaret Thatcher in a speech to the American Bar Association delivered in 1985. Thatcher was talking about news coverage of terrorism, but I think the phrase also applies to the way issues that simmered at the local level erupted into metropolitan consciousness through the media during the years of the urban crisis. For Thatcher's speech, see http://www.margaretthatcher.org/document/106096.

10. On the general issues of police brutality and campaigns against it in the 1960s in New York City, see Johnson, *Street Justice*, chapter 7. On the 1966 referendum, see Edward T. Rogowsky, Louis H. Gold, and David W. Abbott, "Police: The Civilian Review Board Controversy," in *Race and Politics in New York City: Five Studies in Policy-Making*, ed. Jewell Bellush and Stephen M. David (New York: Praeger, 1971), 69–75; Michael W. Flamm, *Law and Order: Street Crime, Civil Unrest, and the Crisis of Liberalism in the 1960s* (Philadelphia: University of Pennsylvania Press, 2005), 219 n67.

11. On the vote tally by assembly districts, see *Annual Report of the Board of Elections in the City of New York for the Year 1966*, 119. New York electoral records, which for 1966 offer results only according to relatively large assembly districts, preclude a fine-grained analysis of voter behavior. Nevertheless, in general in 1966, the further uptown you went the more likely you were to be in an area of lower crime and a whiter populace. In Assembly District 71, which covered the western part of Hamilton Heights and all of Washington Heights from 155th Street north to 181st Street, from the Hudson River to the Harlem River, citizens voted to retain the civilian review board by a margin of 14,228 to 11,317. Yet in Assembly District 73, from 181st Street north through all of Inwood, voters favored abolishing civilian review by a margin of 23,447 to 13,276.

12. During the pretrial hearings for what became known as the trial of the Panther 21, three firebombs exploded at the home of the presiding judge John Murtagh. On the firebombing of the Murtagh home, see John M. Murtagh, "Fire in the Night," *City Journal*, April 30, 2008, www.city-journal.org/2008/eon0430jm.html. On the verdict, see "13 Panthers Here Held Not Guilty on All 12 Counts," *New York Times*, May 14, 1971, 1. For accounts of the slaying of police officers Jones and Piagentini, see "2 Policemen Slain by Shots in Back; 2 Men Are Sought," *New York Times*, May 22, 1971, 1; "The New York Ten," *New York Times*, December 12, 1971; and Fritz Umbach, *The Last Neighborhood Cops: The Rise and Fall of Community Policing in New York Public Housing* (New Brunswick, NJ: Rutgers University Press, 2011), 95–96.

13. See "Knapp Commission," in *The Encyclopedia of New York City*, ed. Kenneth T. Jackson (New Haven: Yale University Press, 2010), 703, and *The Knapp Commission Report on Police Corruption* (New York: George Braziller, 1972), especially a summary of the commission's findings on 1–13. The commission described corruption as "widespread" on page 1.

14. See, in the *New York Times*: "Patrolman Slain by Partner's Gun in Scuffle with a Robbery Suspect," July 16, 1977, 25; "The 34th Precinct Mourns Colleague," July 17, 1977, 31; and "5,000 Police Attend Slain Officer's Rites," July 19, 1977, 39.

15. See "Crime," *Encyclopedia of New York City* (2010 edition), 329–30. Tweed's New York in the early 1870s had a murder rate of 6.5 per 100,000, and in the late days of Prohibition, from 1931–35, the city's murder rate was 7.4 per 100,000, but these were aberrations surrounded by periods of lower murder rates. For an illuminating analysis of the brutal reality of the upsurge in murder in New York from the 1960s to the 1990s and more, see Eric H. Monkkonen's *Murder in New York City* (Cambridge: Harvard University Press, 2001), 7–25, 151–62, and 170–79. For a national perspective on crime in American society and American culture, see Lawrence M. Friedman, *Crime and Punishment in American History* (New York: Basic Books, 1993), 453–65. For a police detective's perspective on working in upper Manhattan during the crack years, see Austin Francis Muldoon III, "Washington Heights, New York City," *Global Crime* 6, no. 2 (May 2004): 222–29.

16. Author interview with Led Black, New York, 2012. Also see http://www.uptowncollective.com.

17. Author interview with Led Black.

18. On neighborhood ties in the drug trade, see Philippe Bourgois, *In Search of Respect: Selling Crack in El Barrio*, 2nd ed. (New York: Cambridge University Press, 2003), 22–24, 18; Moisés Pérez, Jacqueline Martinez, and Laura Frye, "Community Health Workers: A Successful Strategy for Restoring the Health of a Community," in *Mobilizing the Community for Better Health: What the Rest of America can Learn from Northern Manhattan*, ed. Allan J. Formicola and Lourdes Hernandez-Cordero (New York: Columbia University Press, 2011), 41–42; Williams, *Cocaine Kids*, 48–51, 56, 103–5; and "The Rise and Fall of El Feo," *New York Times*, September 15, 1996, CY1.

19. See Pérez, Martinez, and Frye, "Community Health Workers," 42; also Williams, *Cocaine Kids*, 8–9, 86–87, 132.

20. For a discussion of the relationship between crime and neighborhood environments, see Jeffrey Fagan and Garth Davies, "The Natural History of Neighborhood Violence," *Journal of Contemporary Crime and Criminal Justice* 20, no. 2 (May 2004): 127–47, quotation from 132. For a discussion of the violence of the crack trade, and its tendency to flourish in socially fragmented areas, see Jeffrey Fagan and Ko-lin Chin, "Violence as Regulation and Social Control in the Distribution of Crack," in *Drugs and Violence: Causes, Correlates and Consequences*, ed. Mario De La Rosa, Elizabeth Y. Lambert, and Bernard Gropper, National Institute on Drug Abuse Research Monograph 103 (1990), 28, 30, 32, 35–37. Also, on the impact of the crack trade on the Dominican community, see Jesse Hoffnung-Garskof, *A Tale of Two Cities: Santo Domingo and New York after 1950* (Princeton: Princeton University Press, 2008), 224–25. Also see Pérez, Martinez, and Frye, "Community Health Workers," 43, and Williams, *Cocaine Kids*, 8–9, 86–7, 132.

21. See Jorge Duany, *Quisqueya on the Hudson: The Transnational Identity of Dominican Immigrants* (New York: CUNY Dominican Studies Institute, 1994), 22–23, and author interview with Radhames Morales, New York City, March 1, 1990.

22. Author interview with Manuel Peña, July 13, 2012, New York City.

23. See Lotte E. Feinberg, "Integrity and Corruption Control in the NYPD: 1970–2000," in *Crime and Justice in New York City*, vol. 2, ed. Andrew Karmen (Mason, OH: Thomson Learning Custom Publishing, 2004), 58–59, 61–63. For a summary of police corruption in the 30th Precinct, immediately south of the Heights, see "Stories of Courage and Sacrifice, Corruption and Betrayal in Blue," *New York Times*, April 25, 1994, A1. For the rumors of corruption in 1986, see August 5, 1986, memo from Hershey, Hawkins, and Magnum to Charles J. Hynes in the Mollen Commission Report Appendix, Exhibit 8. Also see "Ex-Sergeant Is Sentenced," *New York Times*, June 17, 1997, B3, and "Talk in Washington Heights: Fear, Drugs, and Now Corruption," *New York Times*, June 22, 1992, B1. For a detailed report on the scope of the drug trade and the sense of futility that pervaded police responses to it, see "A City Deluged," *New York Newsday*, December 17, 1989, 13–16.

24. On the peaceable side of drug dealers, see author interview with Evan Hess, New York City, 2013 and comments at the *Voices of the Grinnell* history session, January 30, 2008, New York City. For a spirited but insightful portrait of gentrifiers living alongside drug dealers in Hamilton Heights, see Judith Matloff, *Home Girl: Building a Dream House on a Lawless Block* (New York: Random House, 2008). On the importance of violence and intimidation in running a crack crew, and the impact of this on the community around the crew, see Bourgois, *In Search of Respect*, 9–11, 24, 34, 53–4, and Williams, *Cocaine Kids*, 33.

25. Jackall, *Wild Cowboys*, 74–79.

26. See ibid., 73–81, and, in the *New York Times*, "A Dominican Suspect Indicted," April 5, 1989, B3; "Suspect in Officer's Killing Dies," July 1, 1989, 27; and "Suspect in Officer's Death Is Buried," July 3, 1989, 24. On the conviction of two more men in the Buczek killing years later, see "Two Convicted of Murdering Police Officer," *New York Times*, May 29, 2003, B3. On extradition, see Joshua H. Warmund, "Removing Drug Lords and Street Pushers: The Extradition of Nationals in Columbia and the Dominican Republic," *Fordham International Law Journal* 22, no. 5 (1998): 2390, 2391, 2398, 2413, 2416–18, 2422–24.

27. For different accounts of the Occhipinti case that draw different conclusions, see Jackall, *Wild Cowboys*, 81–88; Hoffnung-Garskof, *Tale of Two Cities*, 226–27; and Edward Conlon, "The Pols, the Police, and the Gerry Curls," *American Spectator* 27, no. 11 (November 1994): 36. On the raids while they were taking place, see "I.N.S. Raids Strike a Nerve in Washington Heights," *New York Times*, April 10, 1990, B1. On the trial, see in the *New York Times*, "I.N.S. Official Accused," May 26, 1991, 41, and "Immigration Agent Guilty of Violating Rights," June 29, 1991, 26. Also see author interview with Nicholas Estavillo, New York City, 2012.

28. On reactions to the commuted sentence, see, in the *New York Times*, "Bush Frees Ex-U.S. Agent . . . ," January 16, 1993, 23, and "Freed Agent Vows to Seek Vindication," January 17, 1993, 31. For a nuanced account of the case in the context of the career of Manuel de Dios Unanue, who

was murdered while covering the drug trade, see Bill Berkeley, "Dead Right," *Columbia Journalism Review* (March–April 1993): 40–41, 42–43. For a general discussion of the case and allegations that surrounded it, see Wayne Barrett, *Rudy! An Investigative Biography of Rudolph Giuliani (New York: Basic, 2000)*, 256–60. For an example of the endurance of the Occhipinti case on the Web, see http://www.thesocialcontract.com/artman2/publish/tsc0901/article_778.shtml.

29. My following account of the Highbridge incident is based on the following: from the *New York Times*, "Tension and Violence at a Swimming Pool," August 7, 1989, A1; "Killing Prompts Added Security at Swimming Pools," August 8, 1989, B3; "Suspect Sought in Shooting of Girl at Highbridge Pool," August 9, 1989, B1; and "Suspect is Extradited in '89 Pool Shooting," September 7, 1998, B2. The gunman was convicted in *The People of the State of New York v. Domingo Espiritu*, 1599/99, tried in the Supreme Court of New York, New York County. The conviction was upheld despite repeated appeals.

30. Breslin's account is from "Cool Water Sparkles as a City Is Maimed," *Newsday*, August 10, 1989, 2.

31. On the mayoral results in 1989, see "The Vote for New York City Mayor," *New York Times*, November 8, 1989, B8. On Dinkins's friendships, see Wilbur C. Rich, *David Dinkins and New York City Politics: Race, Images, and the Media* (Albany: State University of New York Press, 2007), 27–28; "Paul O'Dwyer, New York's Liberal Battler for Underdogs and Outsiders, Dies at 90," *New York Times*, June 25, 1998, B9, and author interviews with O'Dwyer. Also see John H. Mollenkopf, *A Phoenix in the Ashes: The Rise and Fall of the Koch Coalition in New York City Politics* (Princeton: Princeton University Press, 1992), 89–91, 175. For a shrewd analysis of the tendency to understand African American politics through false binaries of universalism versus particularism, or "Malcolm versus Martin," that was destructively common in the news media, especially in New York City, see Thomas J. Sugrue, *Not Even Past: Barack Obama and the Burden of Race* (Princeton: Princeton University Press, 2010), 6–7, 35–37. My thanks to Pauline Toole for pointing out Dinkins's tendency to be both a party regular and a progressive Democrat.

32. See author interview with Maria Laurino, New York City, 2012.

33. "Mr. Dinkins' Neighborhood," *7 Days*, January 31, 1990, 17–20. On *7 Days* and its editor, Adam Moss, see "Paper Boy," *New York* magazine, January 21, 2002, http://nymag.com/nymetro/news/media/columns/medialife/5617/.

34. On Dinkins balancing interests, see J. Philip Thompson, *Double Trouble: Black Mayors, Black Communities, and the Call for a Deep Democracy* (New York: Oxford University Press, 2006), 199.

35. See Rich, *David Dinkins and New York City Politics*, 148–49.

36. On Dinkins's plans for policing, see "The Plan," *New York Newsday*, October 2, 1990, 3; "Dinkins Proposes . . . ," *New York Times*, October 3, 1990, 1; "Liberties Union . . . ," New York Times, June 15, 1990, B3. Also see a collection of op-ed pieces debating the merits of hiring five thousand more police in the *New York Times*, September 22, 1990, 23.

37. Descriptions of local responses to the drug trade in this paragraph and the next are drawn from Perez, Martinez, and Frye, "Community Health Workers," 46–49; Hoffnung-Garskof, *Tale of Two Cities*, 223–25; and, in the *Uptown Dispatch*, "Anti-Drug March Stages," February 7–21, 1986, 1; "Rally Would Target Drugs" and "Crack Expelled from School," August 8–22, 1986, 1; and "Local Youths Take on Drugs and Dirt," August 10–17, 1987, 3. The account of the march conducted by Msgr. Joachim Beaumont is drawn from the author's interview with the monsignor conducted in the Bronx, NY, 2012 and his interview with John Brian Murtaugh, New York City, April 20, 2012. Al Kurland shared with me his memories of local efforts to fight the drug trade and improve police protection in an interview in New York City, April 12, 2012.

38. Noreen Walck interview with author, Dumont, New Jersey, 1990. Also see William Julius Wilson and Richard P. Taub, *There Goes the Neighborhood: Racial, Ethnic, and Class Tensions in Four Chicago Neighborhoods and their Meaning for America* (New York: Alfred A. Knopf, 2006), 8.

39. Douglas Massey and Nancy A. Denton, *American Apartheid: Segregation and the Making of the Underclass* (Cambridge: Harvard University Press, 1998) 64, 68, 70–72, 76, 83–88, 98–109, 114, 221. Also see Llana Barber, "Latino Migration and the New Global Cities: Transnationalism, Race, and Urban Crisis in Lawrence, Massachusetts, 1945–2000" (PhD diss., Boston College, 2010).

40. See Hoffnung-Garskof, *Tale of Two Cities*, 167–68.

41. For the deeply humane story of a Brooklyn janitor, his wife and children, and their home under construction in the Dominican Republic, see the film *My American Girls: A Dominican Story* (2001). On the Dominican vulnerability to the worst in two countries, see Roberto Suro, *Strangers among Us: Latino Lives in a Changing America* (New York: Vintage, 1999), 198. For the Levitt

quotation, see Peggy Levitt, *The Transnational Villagers* (Berkeley: University of California Press, 2001), 200.

42. *Nueba Yol*, 1995.

43. See "Neighbors of Narcotics," *Washington Heights Citizen and the Inwood News*, February 13–26, 1990, 9; author interview with Barbara K. Lundblad, New York City, February 8, 1990; author interview with Deborah Dash Moore, New York City, 2009; "In 26 Tongues, Common Complaints," *New York Times*, August 20, 1989, 34. Bruce Cronin's interviews, conducted in the spring of 1990 under the auspices of the Media Studies Center and in the author's possession, are a valuable source of insight on the perspectives of elderly residents in northern Manhattan. On Yeshiva University and its mall on Amsterdam Avenue, see "Yeshiva Shootings Believed Linked to 2 Others," *New York Times*, June 24, 1983, 6; "Yeshiva U. Told to Take Back Its Mall," *Newsday*, September 14, 1987, 31; and "Yeshiva Student Robbed, Stabbed Seen as Bias-Related," *Newsday*, November 5, 1988, 5. On the complexities of leaving and staying, see Albert O. Hirschman, *Exit, Voice, and Loyalty: Responses to Decline in Firms, Organizations, and States* (Cambridge: Harvard University Press, 1970), 43.

44. Author interview with Moore.

45. Author interview with Margaret Moers Wenig, New York City, August 22, 2013, and Hirschman, *Exit, Voice and Loyalty*, 43.

46. On the early history of Beth Am, see *History of the Beginning of Beth Am, The People's Temple*, and Albert L. Sussman, *Historical Report on Beth Am, The People's Temple, April 1950 thru January 1955*, in author's possession.

47. Wenig interview and Margaret Moers Wenig, *The Fifteen Year Sermon*, 2009.

48. See Wenig interview; Wenig, *Fifteen Year Sermon*; and, for an example of interfaith learning at Beth Am, Rev. Barbara K. Lundblad, *God's Word On the Doorpost: Deuteronomy, 6:4–9* (Lutheran Series of the Protestant Hour, June 2, 1988), in author's possession.

49. See Wenig interview and *Fifteen Year Sermon*.

50. Author interview with Milagros Batista, New York City, 2012. Perez, Martinez, and Frye, "Community Health Workers," 46–49; Hoffnung-Garskof, *Tale of Two Cities*, 224–225, and, in the *Uptown Dispatch*, "Anti-Drug March Stages," February 7–21, 1986, 1; "Rally Would Target Drugs" and "Crack Expelled from School," August 8–22, 1986, 1; and "Local Youths Take on Drugs and Dirt," August 10–17, 1987, 3.

51. Kurland interview and June 27, 2013, letter from Kurland in author's possession.

52. Author interview with Dave Crenshaw, New York City, 2012; comments at dinner in honor of Crenshaw; author interviews with Calvin Thomas, New York City, 2012, and June 27, 2013 letter from Kurland in author's possession.

53. Author telephone interview with Blanca Battino, May 16, 2012, and http://mlb.mlb.com/players/jeter_derek/turn2/lifestyle.jsp.

54. See, in Bob Grant column, *Washington Heights Citizen and the Inwood News*, April 24–May 7, 1990, 9, and Michael Cohn letter, *Washington Heights Citizen and the Inwood News*, May 8–20, 1990, 7–8.

55. Author interview with Susan Cohn, New York City, 2012.

56. "The *Manhattan Times* Profile: Peter Walsh," *Manhattan Times*, March 29, 2001, 7; "Neutral Territory," *New York Times*, October 5, 1997, CY4; "PSST—Wanna Really Get to Know New York," in "NY '92 Guide," *Newsday*, July 12, 1992, 15.

57. My account of the Jheri Curls and the death of Jose Reyes is based primarily on a trial transcript from case *People of the State of New York v. Rafael Martinez*, et al., indictment number 12131-91, hereafter referred to as Martinez transcript. On Reyes's disposition, see in Martinez transcript Nellie Reyes, 1575–76; also author's interviews with Pauline Turner and Gus Pappas, New York City, 2006; also see Edward Conlon, "The Pols, the Police and the Gerry Curls," 46, and Felix Gillette, "The Gang That Couldn't Wear Its Hair Straight," *Village Voice*, June 6, 2006, at http://www.villagevoice.com/2006-05-30/news/the-gang-that-couldn-t-wear-its-hair-straight/full/.

58. On the move, see Martinez transcript, 47; on the changed routine on the streets, see in the Martinez transcript the testimony of Detective Ricardo Cobeo, 2270–71, and Gilmore, 1365–67, 1373.

59. On learning "to see and not see," see Cassandra Lewis in Gillette, "The Gang That Couldn't Wear Its Hair Straight." Researching Washington Heights in the winter of 1990, I repeatedly heard suspicions that with all the drug money flowing through the neighborhood, at least some police officers must have become corrupt. For a memo that reviews precincts around the city for corruption allegations involving police and drug dealers from January to June 1986, which identifies the 34th Precinct as one of those with a significant number of allegations, see memo of Hershey, Hawkins,

and Magnum to Charles J. Hynes of August 5, 1986, Mollen Commission Report Appendix, Exhibit A. For news stories that raise the issue of corruption among police in the 34th Precinct in the early nineties, see "U.S. Is Investigating Reports of Corrupt New York Police," *New York Times*, June 19, 1992, A1; also "Thoughts in the Face of Corruption," *New York Times*, June 23, 1992, B1.

60. On avoiding dealers, see author's interview with Pauline Turner and Cassandra Lewis in Gillette, "The Gang"; on treating dealers with respect, see in the Martinez transcript the testimony of Adelin Johnson during jury selection, 226.

61. On the confrontation between the gang and Reyes, see Conlon, "The Pols . . . ," 46. On the signs, see in the Martinez transcript the testimony of Edwin Matos, 8773–74, and Nellie Reyes, 1577–88; also Santiago testimony, 2709–11.

62. On Gilmore's visit see Martinez transcript, 1373–81; on Hilbert's visits and padlock strategy, see Martinez transcript, 5299–06. Also see in the Martinez transcript the testimony of Irah Vinas, 4334, and Julian Martinez, 6636–39.

63. For the fullest available account of the shooting, see the following from the Martinez transcript: the testimony of Robert Reyes, 7952–54; also see the testimony of Daniel Colon, who witnessed events before and after the shooting, on 5834, 5480, and 5750–53. Crucial for the outcome of the Martinez case was the fact that both witnesses—while identifying Roberto Gonzalez as the gunman—described his clothing in entirely different ways. Gonzalez was ultimately acquitted in the shooting.

64. On the money left in Reyes's pockets, see Martinez transcript, Camacho summation, 11380–84.

65. See Martinez transcript, Paul Bailey testimony, 4791–94.

66. See in the Martinez transcript the testimony of Nellie Reyes, 1581. Eventually police did find witnesses, implicated in drug and weapons charges, who testified with the obvious hope of receiving favorable treatment in exchange.

67. For early accounts of the shooting and reactions, see "Upper Manhattan Block Erupts," *New York Times*, July 5, 1992, 20, and "Rage as Cop Kills Suspect," *Daily News*, July 5, 1992, 5. For a detailed account of Garcia's death, and also the later death of Dagoberto Pichardo, see September 10, 1992, report of Robert M. Morgenthau, district attorney of New York County, to Raymond W. Kelly, acting police commissioner, in author's possession, hereafter referred to as Morgenthau report. On O'Keefe's record and reputation among police officers, see Jackall, *Wild Cowboys*, 274.

68. "HE BEGGED FOR LIFE," *Daily News*, July 6, 1992, 1, and "NAPALM THE HOOD," *New York Post*, July 6, 1992, 1.

69. See "Grim Specter of L.A. Nears," *Daily News*, July 7, 1992, 2. Also see "In Unrest, a Dominican Leader Steps Into Spotlight," *New York Times*, July 9, 1992, B6.

70. See, in *Daily News*, July 7, 1992: "Grim Specter of L.A. Nears," "Protestors in Rage . . ." and "Dave Visits . . . ," 2; "March Turns Ugly . . . ," *New York Post*, July 7, 1992, 4; "Angered by Police," *New York Times*, July 7, 1992, A1; and Morgenthau report, 28–29.

71. See "Remarks by Mayor David N. Dinkins [on] Situation in Washington Heights," July 7, 1992, Dinkins Papers, Box 6, location 18143, 7/92 binder.

72. See "Appeal for Calm," *Newsday*, July 8, 1992, 5, and "Heights of Frustration," *Newsday*, July 8, 1992, 18.

73. "Feeling Betrayed . . . ," *New York Times*, July 8, 1992, B2.

74. Author interviews with Batista and Murtaugh and Thomas 2012 interview. Also see "New Leadership Forms in a Crucible of Violence: Washington Heights Turns to Its Own," *New York Times*, July 11, 1992, 123.

75. See "Appeal for Calm," *Newsday*, July 8, 1992, 5; in the July 9, 1992 *Daily News*, "Hts. Rises from Depths," 5, and "Chats and Congrats," 4; "Dinkins and Brown Walk . . . ," *New York Times*, July 9, 1992, B6.

76. See August 19, 1992, memo and clippings from John Beckman to Lee Jones on the mayor's visit to the 34th Precinct on July 24, Dinkins Papers, Box 1. Also see, in the Municipal Reference Library, Lee P. Brown, 34th Precinct Initiatives, July 1992, and "34th Precinct Is Expanding," *New York Times*, August 5, 1992, B6.

77. See "City Hall Must Do Right by Washington Heights," *Daily News*, August 5, 1992, 35; "Rumor and Justice," *New York Times*, August 7, 1992, A27; and "Peace and Provocation," *New York Times*, August 12, 1992, A19.

78. See "Statement of Robert M. Morgenthau, District Attorney, New York County," September 10, 1992, especially 1–3, 8–9, and Morgenthau letter of September 10, 1992, to Police Commissioner Raymond W. Kelly, both in author's possession.

79. For a copy of Barnett's letter in the *Uptown Dispatch*, written with Thomas Kennedy, see Dinkins Papers, Box 17, "NYC Police Dept." Folder; "In Washington Heights," *New York Times*, September 11, 1992, B2; and "Angry Dave," *New York Post*, September 11, 1992, 2.

80. Dennis Duggan made the point that the silence of the NYPD on the matter of the tapes was devastating to public perception in "Wake Up Call for the Mayor," *New York Newsday*, September 17, 1992, 24. For a strong work of media criticism on the case in the context of then-emerging reality television on the police, see Jon Katz, "Covering the Cops," *Columbia Journalism Review* (January–February 1993). For a critique of coverage in the New York City press emphasizing the flaws in reporting in *Newsday* and the *Times*, see William McGowan, "Race and Reporting," *City Journal* (Summer 1993). For a good critique of crime reporting, see David J. Krajicek, *SCOOPED: Media Miss Real Story on Crime While Chasing Sex, Sleaze and Celebrities* (New York: Columbia University Press, 1998).

81. "The Impossibility of the Rule of Law," *New York Newsday*, September 11, 1992, 6.

82. On the Los Angeles riots and their death toll, see "The L.A. Riots: 20 Years Later" at http://www.latimes.com/news/local/1992riots.

83. For general descriptions of the rally, used to support the following section, see, in the *New York Times*: "Officers Rally," September 17, 1992, A1, and "Rally . . . ," September 27, 1992, 35; from *New York Newsday*: September 17, 1992, "Cops Rally," 4, 5, and "Cops Show True Colors," 2; on September 18, 1992: "Dinkins Slams . . . ," 5, and "Creatures of Chaos," 5, and "Councilwoman . . . ," 4; and in September 19, 1992, "Rudy Defends," 2.

84. For the quotations, see "Police Department Report Assails Officers in New York Rally," *New York Times*, September 29, 1992, A1, and "Commissioner's Report Cites Series of Failures," *New York Times*, September 29, 1992, B3.

85. See "Dinkins . . . ," *New York Times*, October 3, 1992, 1; "Council Backs . . . ," *New York Times*, December 18, 1992, B3; Dinkins' remarks to precinct commanders at Gracie Mansion, October 3, 1992, Dinkins Papers, Box 7, 10/92 folder, and June 25, 1993, memo from Deputy Mayor Alexander to Mayor Dinkins in Dinkins Papers, Box 17, "NYC Police Dept." folder. Also see "Police Corruption Panel . . . ," *New York Times*, September 26, 1993, 40; James Lardner and Thomas Repetto, *NYPD: A City and its Police* (New York: Henry Holt, 2000), 272–73; and "Shhh!," *New York Newsday*, November 28, 1993, 4. For testimony, see, in the Mollen Commission Transcripts, Michael Dowd, 43–46, 58–59, 103–27, 121, 127–28; Bernard Cawley, 104–6, 108–11, 114–15, 124; Joseph Trimboli, 35–36, 89–92, 95–98, 99, 103–7, and 118–26.

86. On the firebombing episode, see, in the *New York Times*: "Officials Move . . . ," July 11, 1993, 27; "Suspect in Firebombing . . . ," August 9, 1993, B3; "Man Admits Firebombing . . . ," March 15, 1994, B3. For accounts of the Williamson murder and its immediate aftermath, see, in the *New York Times*: "Officer Is Struck . . . ," October 9, 1993, 27; "Investigators Hunt for the Killer," October 10, 1993, 34; and "In Wake of Officer's Slaying . . . ," October 11, 1993, B1.

87. On the arrest, trial, and sentencing of Gil, see, in the *New York Times*: "Suspect Arrested . . . ," October 12, 1993, A1; "Tainting Tragedy," October 13, 1993, A25; "Generosity of Officer . . . ," October 13, 1995, B2; "Car Towing . . . ," October 14, 1993, B1; "Telling of Hurled Bucket . . . ," November 3, 1993, B10; "Manslaughter Conviction . . . ," February 4, 1995, 21; and "5-to-15 Year Prison Term . . . ," May 27, 1995, 23. On the general mood of the Heights, with special attention to violence and social problems, see "Unmasking Roots of Washington Heights Violence," *New York Times*, October 17, 1993, 29.

88. See "Tainting Tragedy," *New York Times*, October 13, 1993, A25.

89. See Jim Dwyer, "A Crossroads . . . ," *New York Newsday*, November 3, 1993, 11E; on fears of voter fraud, see "Two Sides . . . ," *New York Times*, November 1, 1993, B5; "Blame or Credit," *New York Newsday*, November 4, 1993, 132; and "A Rudy Makeover," *New York Newsday*, November 4, 1993, 131.

90. See "Way . . . ," *New York Newsday*, November 7, 1993, 38; "Blame or Credit," *New York Newsday*, November 4, 1993, 132. For vote tallies, see "The Vote for Mayor and Comptroller by Assembly District," *New York Times*, November 3, 1993, B4.

91. Thompson, *Double Trouble*, 238–39, and Rich, *David Dinkins and New York City Politics*, 194–95. For an analysis of racially coded language in the 1993 race, see "Rudolph Giuliani . . . ," *New York Times Magazine*, July 25, 1993, 24.

92. See edited transcript of speech in *New York Newsday*, January 3, 1994, 31.

93. See Mollen Commission, "Chapter One: An Overview and Summary of the Commission's Findings," 1–3, 4, 6–7.

94. See George L. Kelling and James Q. Wilson, "Broken Windows: The Police and Neighborhood Safety," *Atlantic*, March 1982, http://theatlantic.com/magazine/archive/1982/03/broken-

windows/304465. For a discussion of how the NYPD produced a variant on "broken windows" thinking, see Jeffrey Fagan and Garth Davies, "Street Stops and Broken Windows: Terry, Race, and Disorder in New York City," *Fordham Urban Law Journal*, 28 no. 2 (December 2000): 457–504.

95. For an admiring portrait of the Giuliani administration and its policing strategies, see Fred Siegel, *The Prince of the City: Giuliani, New York, and the Genius of American Life* (San Francisco: Encounter Books, 2005), 146–50. For a solid summary of the differences among schools of policing, see Fritz Umbach, *The Last Neighborhood Cops: The Rise and Fall of Community Policing in New York Public Housing* (New Brunswick, NJ: Rutgers University Press, 2011), 13–18. For Bratton's description of his own work, see the interview "Victory in the Subways," *City Journal* (Summer 1992), http://www.city-journal.org/article01.php?aid=1533.

96. On the two visits to the 30th Precinct, see "Bratton Harnesses Power of Symbolism," *Newsday*, April 18, 1994, A8; and "At 30th Precinct, 2 Supervisors' Rise and Fall," *New York Times*, September 30, 1994, B1.

97. For a summary of Bratton's strategies and tenure, see Andrea R. Nagy and Joel Podolny, *William Bratton and the NYPD: Crime Control through Middle Management Reform*, Yale School of Management, Yale Case 07–015, revised February 12, 2008.

98. On threats against Leslie Crocker Snyder, see "Testifying in Killing Plot Trial, Judge Describes Other Threats," *New York Times*, December 13, 2000, B3. The judge is not related to the author. On the conviction of the Jheri Curls, see Gillette, "The Gang That Couldn't Wear Its Hair Straight," and "Drug Gangs Putting Witnesses at Risk," *New York Times*, November 22, 1993, B1.

99. See "Neighborhood Report," *New York Times*, October 9, 1994, 6.

100. For number of killings in northern Manhattan in 1990 and 1998, see NYPD CompStat Report, vol. 19, no. 31, for the 33rd and 34th precincts. The 34th Precinct covered all of northern Manhattan above 155th Street during the crack epidemic, but in 1994 the southern part of the precinct was broken off to form the 33rd Precinct in order to improve and concentrate policing in the southern Heights. Guillermo Linares, a longtime Dominican American community activist and elected official in northern Manhattan, in 2010 identified the crime drop as the biggest change in Washington Heights and Inwood in the previous decade. See "The Community," *Manhattan Times*, December 8, 2010, 8. For additional statistics on the long-term decline of crime in northern Manhattan, see "Crime and Safety Report" at http://www.dnainfo.com/new-york/crime-safety-report/manhattan/washington-heights.

101. See James Traub, "New York Story," *New Republic*, January 27, 1997, 12, 14, 15.

102. See Peter Noel, *Why Blacks Fear "America's Mayor": Reporting Police Brutality and Black Activist Politics under Rudy Giuliani* (Lincoln, NE: iUniverse, 2007), 103, 107, 108–9.

103. The account of the evening, the melee, and shooting that followed is based on a grand jury investigation and report and news reports: "No Indictment for Officer in Shooting," *New York Times*, July 2, 1997, B1; "Teen's Death Opens Old Wounds," *Bridge-Leader*, April 9, 1997, 1; "1 Big Knife, 1 Police Bullet," *Daily News*, April 7, 1997, 5.

104. For early reactions to the shooting and Cedeno's death, see "Cedeno Family Seeks Independent Autopsy," *Newsday*, April 10, 1997, A32; "Hundreds Mourn Teen Shot by Cop," *Newsday*, April 16, 1997, A8; "In Cedeno Shooting, Don't Rush to Judgments," *Newsday*, April 18, 1997, A46; and "Calling for Indictment of Officer, Marchers Protest Fatal Shooting," *New York Times*, April 11, 1997, A29; "Questions and Anger at Funeral of Youth Shot by Police," *New York Times*, April 16, 1997, A8; "Ferrer Calls Youth's Death an 'Execution,'" *New York Times*, April 17, 1997, B1. On the invitation to Sharpton and his work with young people before leading protests, see author interview with Yvonne Stennett, Community League of the Heights, New York City, 2012. On Crenshaw's session, see June 27, 2013 letter from Kurland in author's possession.

105. For the "Meditative Militant" column, see *Bridge-Leader*, April 23, 1997, 2. On reactions to Cedeno's death, see author interview with Al Kurland, April 12, 2012, New York City. On Kurland's decision to identify himself as the "Meditative Militant," see Kurland letter to author of June 27, 2013.

106. On the award for Pellegrini, see "Officer Who Shot a Youth Is Honored by His Peers," *New York Times*, May 28, 1997, B1. On the protest, see "Crowd of 100 Protests Award to Officer," *New York Times*, May 29, 1997, B8.

107. On the New York County grand jury, see "No Indictment for Officer in Shooting," *New York Times*, July 2, 1997, B1. On the U.S. attorney's decision, see "U.S. Ends Rights Case in Police Killing of Youth," *New York Times*, December 12, 1997, B6. For examples of lingering discomfort with the Cedeno case, see author interviews in New York City with Stennett; Dave Crenshaw, New

York City, April 3, 2012; and Elizabeth Lorris Ritter, New York City, April 18, 2012; and Kurland letter of June 27, 2013.

108. See, in the *New York Times*: "Siege of 163rd Street: Police Take Over Drug-Ridden Block to Save It," September 21, 1997, 41; "New Captain behind Aggressive Policing in 33rd Precinct," September 28, 1997, CY6; "To the Barricades! Tale of 163rd Street," December 28, 1997, 8; and "A Drug Ran Its Course Then Hid with Its Users," September 19, 1999, 11.

109. Author interview with Stennett.

110. On the limitations of "broken windows" policing, and how it could be used to justify policing practices that harmed police-community relations, see Fagan and Davies, "Street Stops and Broken Windows," 1, 4–7, 14–15; Franklin E. Zimring, *The City That Became Safe: New York's Lessons for Urban Crime and Its Control* ((New York: Oxford University Press, 2012), 130–31, 146–47. For a skeptical view on the crime drop and its political implications, see Andrew Karmen, *New York Murder Mystery: The True Story behind the Crime Crash of the 1990s* (New York: New York University Press, 2000).

111. See Franklin E. Zimring, *The Great American Crime Decline* (New York: Oxford University Press, 2007) 11–15, 20–24, 146–56, 164–68.

112. Franklin E. Zimring, *The City That Became Safe*, 197–98, 202–6, 216–17; and A. Karpati, X. Lu, F. Mostashari, L. Thorpe, T. R. Frieden, *The Health of Inwood and Washington Heights*, NYC Community Health Profiles, vol. 1, no. 24 (New York: New York City Department of Health and Mental Hygiene, 2003), 11.

113. "A Neighborhood Gives Peace a Wary Look," *New York Times*, May 18, 1998, A1.

CHAPTER 6

1. See Mindy Thompson Fullilove; Veronique Heon, Walkiria Jimenez, Caroline Parsons, Lesley L. Green, and Robert E. Fullilove, "Injury and Anomie: Effects of Violence on an Inner-City Community," *American Journal of Public Health* 8, no. 6 (June 1998): 924–25.

2. Fullilove and the Community Research Group, *Towards a Comprehensive Understanding of Violence in Washington Heights: A Report on Violence in Washington Heights*, July 1996, 9–10, 8, 37–39.

3. Ibid., 40–41, 42, 43.

4. Ibid., 44. On Fullilove's life and education, see www.brynmawr.edu/sandt/2004_october/place.html. Also see her book, *Root Shock: How Tearing Up City Neighborhoods Hurts America and What We Can Do about It* (New York: Ballantine, 2004).

5. Fullilove and the Community Research Group, *Towards a Comprehensive Understanding of Violence in Washington Heights*, 45.

6. On John Burnside, see "From a World Lost, Ephemeral Notes Bear Witness to the Unspeakable," *New York Times*, September 25, 2001, B9.

7. "Sonuvagun, if It Isn't Dominion," *New York Times Magazine*, November 11, 2001, 83.

8. See ibid., "Requiem for Brian Patrick Monaghan," *Manhattan Times*, September 27, 2001, 5, and "Missing: A Streetscape of a City in Mourning" at www.citylore.org/urban-cultural-exhibits/.

9. See "Requiem for Brian Patrick Monaghan," "207th Street Shrine Moves to NY Historical Society," *Manhattan Times*, January 10, 2002, 5, and "Sonuvagun, if It Isn't Dominion." Also see the online version of "Missing: A Streetscape of a City in Mourning" at www.citylore.org/urban-cultural-exhibits/.

10. On Bruce Reynolds, see "New Daffodils for Garden That Outlived a Creator," *New York Times*, November 30, 2001, B1; on the Bruce Reynolds Garden, see www.nycgovparks.org/parks/ishampark/highlights/14066, and http://myinwood.net/tag/bruce-reynolds-garden/.

11. "Now Boarding, Dreams," *New York Times*, November 18, 2001, SM83.

12. "El Avion" (The Airplane), portion of lyrics by Kinito Mendez, sung by Mendez and Johnny Ventura, translated by Robert Dominguez, *Daily News*, November 14, 2001, 28.

13. Descriptions of the flight and its crash are taken from "The Crash of Flight 587: New Setback for an Industry," *New York Times*, November 13, 2001, and *Aircraft Accident Report: American Airlines Flight 587*, National Transportation Safety Board, November 26, 2004. On Papi Lafontaine, "Kinito Mendez's Tragic Note," *Entertainment Weekly*, November 23, 2001, http://www.ew.com/ew/article/0,,253273,00.html. See also Gary Younger, "Flight to the Death," *Guardian*, November 10, 2006, at http://www.theguardian.com/lifeandstyle/2006/nov/11/weekend.garyyounge; and "Sorrow Mixed with Some Nagging Doubt in Santo Domingo," *Daily News*, November 14, 2001, 116.

14. On the Alianza Dominicana and Flight 587, see "A Time of Mourning, and a Rare Time in the Sun," *New York Times*, November 16, 2001, D2; "Data Shows Jet Shook after Hitting Wake of 747," *New York Times*, December 11, 2001, D1.

15. See "Coming Home to Sorrow: In Native Land, 'Immense' Grief for Families of Flight 587 Dead," *Newsday*, November 26, 2001, A2, and "Grief Replaces Festivity in Village That Lost 43," *Daily News*, November 16, 2001, 7.

16. See "A Special Report: Who They Were, the Victims of American Flight 587," *Newsday*, September 27, 2001, B6

17. See *Newsday* for Angie Cruz, "Death of the Invisibles," November 17, 2001, B4, and for the Ray Sanchez column, "In the Subways: NY Dominicans Face Sad Reality," November 19, 2001, A2.

18. See "Egan Speaks to Dominicans at Mass for Crash Victims," *New York Times*, November 16, 2001, D10, and "Where Death Fell from Sky, Lives Intersect," *New York Times*, November 18, 2001, 31. On losses, funeral masses, and Saint Elizabeth's, see "Dedication Planned for New Saint Elizabeth's Peace Garden," October 2002, http://www.steliznyc.org/newsstories/s1002peace.asp.

19. Ramona Hernández and Francisco Rivera-Batiz, *Dominicans in the United States: A Socioeconomic Profile, 2000* (New York: CUNY Dominican Studies Institute, 2003), 3–6.

20. E. C. Olson, G. Van Wye, B. Kerker, L. Thorpe and T. R. Frieden, *Take Care: Inwood and Washington Heights*, NYC Community Health Profiles, 2nd ed., vol. 19, no. 42 (New York: New York City Department of Health and Mental Hygiene, 2006), 2.

21. A. Karpati, X. Lu, F. Mostashari, L. Thorpe, T. R. Frieden, *The Health of Inwood and Washington Heights*, NYC Community Health Profiles, vol. 1, no. 24 (New York: New York City Department of Health and Mental Hygiene, 2003), 11.

22. Hernandez and Rivera-Batiz, *Dominicans in the United States*, 3–6.

23. Analysis of U.S. Census tracts 273 (the western Heights) and 295 (northwest Inwood) performed in Social Explorer for 1990 at http://www.socialexplorer.com/tables/C1990/R10726592 and for 2000 at http://www.socialexplorer.com/tables/C2000/R10726597.

24. See Philip Kasinitz, Mary C. Waters, John H. Mollenkopf, and Jennifer Holdaway, *Inheriting the City: The Children of Immigrants Come of Age* (New York: Russell Sage, 2009), 170.

25. For citywide stories of revival and gentrification in northern Manhattan, see "A Renaissance in a Forgotten Neighborhood," *New York Times*, October 9, 1981, B1; "If You're Thinking of Living In: Washington Heights," September 16, 1984, R9; and "A Haven for the Rent-Crazed," *Daily News*, July 13, 1981. For articles on gentrification in Washington Heights and Inwood community newspapers, see "Apartment Hunting in Upper Manhattan," *Uptown Dispatch*, January 17–30, 1985, 5, and "There Goes the Neighborhood: The Co-opting of Upper Manhattan," *Uptown Dispatch*, March 14–27, 1985, 5, and, for the Perkins quotation, "Moving Up: The great wall of gentrification," *Uptown Dispatch*, November 22–December 5, 1995, 12.

26. See Deborah Dash Moore interview, New York City, 2009.

27. See http://cooperator.com/articles/668/1/Washington-Heights-is-at-its-Height/Page1.html.

28. On the phenomenon of Hudson Heights, for an early use of the term in the press, see "An Aerie Straight out of the Deco Era," *New York Times*, October 18, 2009, 7. For the founding statement of the Hudson Heights Owners Coalition, see www.hhoc.org, and http://ny.curbed.com/archives/2011/04/08/how_to_gentrify_a_neighborhood_just_study_hudson_heights.php. For an example of wide-ranging community activism conducted by a member of the Hudson Heights Owners Coalition, see author interview with Elizabeth Loris Ritter, New York City, 2012.

29. Author interview with Luis Miranda, New York City, July 31, 2012, and author interview with Mike Fitelson, New York City, 2012.

30. For a reprint of the front page of the first issue of the *Manhattan Times*, which appeared February 24, 2000, and was headlined "From Quisqueya to the Heights: The Dominicans of Northern Manhattan," see http://www.manhattantimesnews.com/10-Year-Anniversary/. For more on the paper and its history, see Luis Miranda interview. For MirRam, see http://www.mirramgroup.com/index.html. For an editorial criticizing the Bloomberg mayoralty and its impact on northern Manhattan, see "Mayor: Fernando Ferrer," *Manhattan Times*, November 3, 2005, 6. On Bloomberg, see "Mayor Crossed Ethnic Barriers for Big Victory," *New York Times*, November 10, 2005, 1.

31. "Mayor: Fernando Ferrer," *Manhattan Times*.

32. See "On Building Bridges," *Manhattan Times*, May 18–24, 2006, 1; "A Bridge to Raise the Community's Spirits," *Manhattan Times*, May 25–31, 2006, 20; and author interview with Mike Fitelson, New York City, 2012.

33. See http://www.washington-heights.us/, http://www.dnainfo.com, and http://www.uptowncollective.com/.

34. See Ken Auletta, "After Bloomberg," *The New Yorker*, August 26, 2013, http://www.new yorker.com/reporting/2013/08/26/130826fa_fact_auletta?currentPage=all, and Joyce Purnick, *Mike Bloomberg: Money, Power, Politics* (New York: Public Affairs, 2009). On New York City's economy in Bloomberg's last year in office, its strengths relative to the rest of the state, and inequality within the city, see Fiscal Policy Institute, *The State of Working New York 2013: Workers Are Paying a High Price for Persistent Unemployment*, New York City, August 28, 2013, available at http://fiscalpolicy.org/wp-con tent/uploads/2013/08/SWNY-2013.pdf, and James A. Parrott, Fiscal Policy Institute, "Patterns of Income Polarization in New York City," presented at the annual meeting of the American Sociological Association, New York City, August 13, 2013, available at http://fiscalpolicy.org/wp-content/uploads/2013/10/Patterns-of-Income-Polarization-NYC-American-Sociological-Assoc-Aug-2013.pdf.

35. Author interview with Fitelson.

36. Author notes from artists' talk on the NoMAA exhibit "Northern Manhattan as Muse," January 18, 2012, New York City.

37. On Natasha Beshenovsky, see Mike Fitelson, *Northern Manhattan as Muse* (New York: Mike Fitelson, 2011), 8–9. See author interview with Fitelson and author notes from artists' talk on the NoMAA exhibit "Northern Manhattan as Muse." See Peralta's artwork and biography at http://www.mtonyperalta.com and his T-shirts at http://www.theperaltaproject.com/.

38. On the medieval festival see, in the *New York Times*, "Medieval Festival Today at Cloisters," September 4, 1971, 13; "Jousters and Jugglers Gather at Cloisters," August 5, 1977, 56; "Medieval Festival: Fort and Cloisters Bedecked," September 30, 1985, C10; "Fort Tryon Park Joins the Medieval World," September 22, 1989, C14. Also see www.whidc.org/home; author's observations; and author's telephone interview with Jim Clarke, June 19, 2012.

39. Author interview with Peter Walsh, New York City, 2012; author's observations at 2012 race; and www.nyrr.org/races-and-events/coogan's-salsa-blues-and-shamrocks-5k-kids'-races/race-recap and www.dnainfo.com/new-york/20120305/washington-heights-inwood/coogans-salsa-blues-shamrocks-5k-fills-washington-heights-with-green.

40. City of New York Parks and Recreation, Henry J. Stern, commissioner, *Northern Manhattan Parks: A Study* (New York: 1990), 28, 48–49, 59, 66–68, 71–74, 75–76.

41. See *New York Times*, "Answers about New York's Parks," May 19, 2010, A6; "Parks Even the Parks Dept. Won't Claim," July 6, 2005, B1; "For Parks, It's Not Easy Getting Green," May 21, 2004, B1; "Will Streeters' Generosity Bloom?" May 16, 1999, BU2; "Bette Midler Was Here: A Park Gets a Second Act," May 28, 1999, E36; "Always Divine, Now Garbage Has Made Her a Saint," November 17, 1999, H10; and "Unsavory Visitors, Creeping Back after a 10-Year Hiatus," October 30, 2005, 133, and www.forttryontrust.org. Also see "Highbridge Parks Projects," City of New York Parks and Recreation, February 11, 2010. On David Rockefeller's gift, see http://www.nycgovparks.org/news/daily-plant?id=22206. My thanks to Steve Simon for helping me understand the subtle points of upper Manhattan's parks and their support systems.

42. Author's telephone interview with Tom van Buren on Quisqueya en el Hudson, April 28, 2014. Also see Phillip Lopate, *Waterfront: A Journey around Manhattan* (New York: Crown, 2004), 385–95, quotation from 391. For Sara M.'s comment, see www.yelp.com/biz/highbridge-park-new-york. Jon Pareles' observation is in "Dominican Rarities, Abundant In Energy," *New York Times*, July 2, 1997, C17.

43. See Jim Carroll, *The Basketball Diaries* (New York: Penguin Books, 1987), 17, 18, 11–12, 48–50, 99–100, 104, 126–27, 145–46. Also see Jim Carroll, "Catholic Boy," and descriptions of his memorial services, at http://www.catholicboy.com. Also see, in the *New York Times*, "Jim Carroll, 60, Poet and Punk Rocker Who Wrote 'The Basketball Diaries'," September 14, 2009, A19, and "Jim Carroll's Long Way Home," September 25, 2009, and John F. McMullen, *The Inwood Book: Poems, Short Stories and a Novel* (New York: John F. McMullen, 2010). Author interview with Manfred Kirchheimer, New York City, April 5, 2012, and *We Were So Beloved* (1986).

44. Author interview with Kirchheimer, and *We Were So Beloved*.

45. On the Audubon Theatre and Ballroom, see Kenneth T. Jackson, ed. *Encyclopedia of New York City*, 2nd ed. (New Haven: Yale University Press, 2010), 76; and www.nypap.org/content/audubon-ballroom.

46. On Marjorie Eliot, see author interview with Eliot, May 2011, New York City. For articles on her in the *New York Times*, see "Sweet Sounds Ease the Pain, Then and Now," November 1, 2003, B1, and "Holding Out Hope for a Missing Son," February 19, 2011, A7. On Eliot's honors from City Lore, see citylore.org/urban-culture/peoples-hall-of-fame/2000-honorees/. On 555 Edgecombe Avenue, see Andrew S. Dolkart, *555 Edgecombe Avenue Apartments*, Landmarks Preservation Commission, June 15, 1993.

47. Leaflet for the concert, presented May 8, 2009, in the author's possession, and author's notes.

48. See *The Evolution of an Ethnic Community: Dominican-Americans in Upper Manhattan*, curated by Sarah Aponte, Rob Laurich, Julio Rosario, and Sydney Van Nort (2001). The text and panels for the exhibit are stored in the archives of the City College Library of the City University of New York.

49. On the 2008 exhibit, *Sosúa: A Refuge for Jews in the Dominican Republic*, at the Museum of Jewish Heritage—A Living Memorial to the Holocaust, see http://www.mjhnyc.org/sosua/index.htm. Also see Marion A. Kaplan, *Dominican Haven: The Jewish Refugee Settlement in Sosua, 1940–1945* (New York: Museum of Jewish Heritage—A Living Memorial to the Holocaust, 2008).

50. Author interview with Victoria Neznansky, New York City, 2013.

51. On the massacres, see Richard Lee Turits, "A World Destroyed, a Nation Imposed: The 1937 Haitian Massacre in the Dominican Republic," *Hispanic American Historical Review* 82, no. 3 (August 2003): 589–94.

52. Author's notes, performance at New York-Presbyterian, June 5, 2011, New York City, and the film *Sosúa: Make a Better World* (2012).

53. See "The New Metropolitanism" in Thomas Bender, *The Unfinished City: New York and the Metropolitan Idea* (New York: New Press, 2002), 228–30.

54. On *El Circulo Vicioso*, see http://movies.nytimes.com/movie/258269/El-Circulo-Vicioso/overview; also see the coverage of community debate on the film in "El Circulo Vicioso," *Manhattan Times*, October 19, 2000, 6. Also see *Washington Heights*, 2002, http://www.imdb.com/title/tt0314871/ and *Manito*, 2002, http://www.imdb.com/title/tt0298050/.

55. *Mad Hot Ballroom*, 2005, http://www.imdb.com/title/tt0438205/; author interviews with Amy Sewell and Marilyn Agrelo at screening of *Mad Hot Ballroom*, Columbia University, New York City, December 10, 2010; "Where the Rumba Is as Much a Part of the School as Recess," *New York Times*, May 13, 2005, E20.

56. My conclusions are based on my private screenings of *Take the Bridge* and *GWB* and my interviews with Sergio Castilla and Jonathan Ullman, New York City, 2012. Also see www.gwbthemovie.com/, and takethebridge-movie.com/.

57. For Led Black's review of the film, see www.uptowncollective.com/2011/08/19/gwb-the-review/. On getting out of the Bronx, see Marshall Berman, *All That Is Solid Melts Into Air: The Experience of Modernity* (New York: Penguin Books, 1988), 326–7.

58. See *The Faces behind the Dolls: Los Rostros Detrás de las Muñecas* [A Dominican Labor Experience] (2011) and Sintia Molina, Mary Ely Pena-Gratereaux, and Anneris Goris, *The Faces behind Madame Alexander's Dolls: A Dominican Labor Experience* (New York: Cayena Publications, 2010). On the closing of the plant, see "Iconic Doll Company Madame Alexander Quietly Shutters Harlem Headquarters," *DNAinfo New York*, December 21, 2012, at http://www.dnainfo.com/new-york/20121221/west-harlem/iconic-doll-company-madame-alexander-quietly-shutters-harlem-headquarters. On the Jewish businesswoman who founded the enterprise, see "The Woman Behind the Dolls," *Tablet*, May 7, 2013, at http://www.tabletmag.com/jewish-life-and-religion/131508/the-woman-behind-the-doll.

59. See "Writing Has to Be Generous: An Interview with Angie Cruz" by Silvio Torres-Saillant, *Calabash* 2, no. 2 (Summer–Fall 2003): 108–9, 121, 123. Also see Angie Cruz, *Soledad* (New York: Simon and Schuster, 2001) and *Let It Rain Coffee* (New York: Simon and Schuster, 2005). For novels about Dominicans beyond Washington Heights, see, for example, Junot Diaz, *The Brief Wondrous Life of Oscar Wao* (New York: Riverhead, 2007) and Jon Michaud, *When Tito Loved Clara* (Chapel Hill, NC: Algonquin, 2011). *When Tito Loved Clara*, set in Inwood and the New Jersey suburbs, explores both places in light of Dominican mobility, the lack of it, race, ethnicity, and gender relations.

60. For the events of the evening, see "Local Boy," *Manhattan Times*, June 19, 2008, 19; for the list of Tony Awards for *In the Heights*, see http://www.tonyawards.com/p/tonys_search; for acceptance speeches by Lin-Manuel Miranda and Jill Furman, see http://www.youtube.com/watch?v=PYeMCgPT5HQ and http://www.youtube.com/watch?v=0fq5LwiMvgg.

61. The point about the freedom to love was made in a panel on *West Side Story* at the 2012 meeting of the American Studies Association in San Juan, Puerto Rico.

EPILOGUE

1. Author's notes on discussions with senior citizens that I conducted at events organized by the YM-YWHA in 2011 and 2012. I thank Francesca Di Mauro and Mira Myteberi for their help in organizing these programs.

2. Account of the event based on author observations of July 24, 2008; program from the Stan Michels Promenade Dedication Ceremony; and author telephone interview with Marjorie Eliot, November 9, 2012. The quotation from Marshall Berman is from Berman's "Emerging from the Ruins," *Dissent*, winter 2014, 64.

3. See "The Community," *Manhattan Times*, December 8, 2010, 8.

4. On the causes and consequences of changes in drug markets, and the role of policing in this effort, see Preeti Chauhan and Loren Kois, *Homicide by Neighborhood: Mapping New York City's Crime Drop*, Research and Evaluation Center, John Jay College of Criminal Justice, City University of New York, July 2012, 9, 13, 18. For a federal report of 2004 on continued use of cocaine in the New York metropolitan area based on drug treatment admissons in Newark, New Jersey, and on Washington Heights as a source of drug distribution, see *New Jersey Drug Threat Assessment Update* (April 2004) at http://www.usdoj.gov/ndic/pubs6/6380/cocaine.htm. For a federal report based on data collected in 2008 that showed use of smoked cocaine enduring but lagging behind that of alcohol, heroin, and marijuana in patients admitted for substance abuse treatment in New YorkCity, see *Metro Brief*, 2, at http://www.samhsa.gov/data/StatesInBrief/2k9/CityReports/NewYorkCity_NY_ BHSIS.pdf. On domestic violence see New York City Department of Health and Mental Hygiene, *Intimate Partner Violence against Women in New York City* (New York, 2008), 8. Also see *Strategic Plan: Northern Manhattan Collaborates* (January 1995), 24, 77, and Community Research Group of the New York State Psychiatric Institute and Columbia School of Public Health, Mindy Thompson Fullilove, principal investigator, *Towards a Comprehensive Understanding of Violence in Washington Heights: A Report on Violence in Washington Heights*, July 1996, 29–36. Also Milagros Ricourt, *Nombrando la esperanza: Mujeres Dominicanas hablan de violencia doméstica* (Washington Heights, New York City: Centro de Desarrollo de la Mujer Dominicana, 2006). Also see http://theuptowner. org/2011/11/18/more-immigrants-reporting-domestic-violence-in-washington-heights-inwood-3/.

5. See "Judge Rejects New York Stop and Frisk Policy," *New York Times*, August 12, 2013, and, for a collection of statistics and survey data on stop and frisk, http://topics.nytimes.com/top/reference/ timestopics/subjects/s/stop_and_frisk/. See also Report of Jeffrey Fagan, PhD, submitted in *David Floyd, et al., vs. City of New York*, United States District Court, Southern District of New York, 08 Civ 01034 (SAS). On Community Board 12 in northern Manhattan in 2012 calling for scrutiny and changes in the procedure, see http://www.dnainfo.com/new-york/20120308/washington-heights-inwood/ reform-of-nypd-stop-and-frisk-policy-gains-support-upper-manhattan.

6. See Northern Manhattan Coalition for Immigrant Rights, in cooperation with the Immigration Rights Clinic of New York University Law School, *Deportado, Dominicano, y Humano: Dominican Deportations and Related Police Recommendations* (New York, 2009), and David C. Brotherton and Luis Barrios, *Banished to the Homeland: Dominican Deportees and Their Stories of Exile* (New York: Columbia University Press, 2011). On the impact of incarceration on communities, see Bruce Western and Becky Pettit, "Incarceration and Social Inequality," and Todd R. Clear, "Death by a Thousand Little Cuts: Studies of the Impact of Incarceration," in *Blind Goddess: A Reader on Race and Justice*, ed. Alexander Papachristou (New York: New Press, 2011). On the density of parolees and prison admissions by zip code in 2008, see www.justiceatlas.org. On the Rockefeller drug laws, see http://criminaljustice.state.ny.us/drug-law-reform/index.html. On the decline of incarceration in New York State, see James Austin and Michael P. Jacobson, *How New York City Reduced Mass Incarceration: A Model for Change?* (New York: Vera Institute of Justice, Brennan Center for Justice and JFA Institute, 2013), 8–9, 12–16, 18–25.

7. Susan Fainstein, *The Just City* (Ithaca: Cornell University Press, 2010), 111–12.

8. Ira Katznelson, *City Trenches: Urban Politics and the Patterning of Class* (Chicago: University of Chicago Press, 1981), 189.

9. Michael B. Katz, *Why Don't American Cities Burn?* (Philadelphia: University of Pennsylvania Press, 2012), 83–86.

10. Ibid., 86–97.

11. Ibid., 58, 97–100.

12. See David Dyssegaard Kallick, "Immigration and Economic Growth in New York City," in *One out of Three: Immigrant New York in the Twenty-First Century*, ed. Nancy Foner (New York: Columbia University Press, 2013), 65, 69–70, 75, 77, 82

13. See Silvio Torries-Saillant and Ramona Hernandez, "Dominicans: Community, Culture and Collective Identity" in Foner, *One Out of Three*, 223–25, 229–30, and 230–33; and Philip Kasinitz, Mary C. Waters, John H. Mollenkopf, and Jennifer Holdaway, *Inheriting the City: The Children of Immigrants Come of Age* (New York: Russell Sage, 2009), 170. Also see Kallick, "Immigration and

Economic Growth in New York City," in Foner, *One out of Three*, 82. On the numbers and percentages of Hispanics and Dominicans in Washington Heights and Inwood according to the 2010 U.S. Census, see, from the New York City Department of City Planning, *Manhattan Community District 12*, 47, and *NYC 2010: Results from the 2010 Census: Components of Change by Race and Hispanic Origin for New York City Neighborhoods*, 36–38, 43, 46.

14. See Ruth Milkman and Laura Braslow, *The State of the Unions 2012: A Profile of Organized Labor in New York City, New York State, and the United States* (New York: Joseph S. Murphy Institute for Worker Education and Labor Studies and the Center for Urban Research, CUNY, 2012).

15. For summaries of census data and main trends in northern Manhattan, see www.nyc.gov/html/dcp/html/census/dynamics_pop.shtml; for summaries of Community Board 12, which covers Washington Heights and Inwood, see www.nyc.gov/html/dcp/html/neigh_info/mn12_info.shtml. On U.S. Census tracts 273 and 295, see Social Explorer calculations for 2000 at http://www.socialexplorer.com/tables/C2000/R10735130 and for 2010 at http://www.socialexplorer.com/tables/C2010/R10735131. Enrollment in District 6 schools declined from 29,829 in 2003–4 to 17,799 in 2013–14, according to the Department of Education's Periodic Attendance Reporting Statistical Summaries; see https://reports.nycenet.edu/Cognos84sdk/cgi-bin/cognosisapi.dll. On the closing or consolidation of social service agencies in northern Manhattan, see "What Happened to Alianza Dominicana?" at http://theuptowner.org/what-happened-to-alianza-dominicana-the-mysterious-fall-of-an-iconic-dominican-institution and "Latinos Lose Another Nonprofit," at http://www.voicesofny.org/2013/11/latinos-lose-another-community-agency.

16. On the problem of affordable housing in northern Manhattan, see author interview with Evan Hess, New York City, 2013; Assemblyman Adriano Espaillat, *Project Remain/Nos Quedamos: Will Washington Heights-Inwood be Displaced?*, a report to New York State Division of Housing and Community Renewal Commissioner Deborah VanAmerongen (June, 2007), 1, 3–7; "Housing" section in *Community District 12–Manhattan FY 2013 Statement of District Needs and Priorities*; and letter of April 28, 2014, to the author from Max Weselcouch, director, Moelis Institute for Affordable Housing Policy, Furman Center for Real Estate and Urban Policy, New York University. The message from a teacher and Heights resident was a personal communication with author.

17. Gentrification, and how it had wrought the biggest changes in the neighborhood since Dominicans arrived, was a major theme in discussions with senior citizens that I conducted at events organized by the YM-YWHA in 2011 and 2012. For the quotation, see Rebecca B. Rankin, ed., *New York Advancing* (New York: City of New York, 1936), 105.

18. On the election, see "De Blasio is Elected New York City Mayor in Landslide," *New York Times*, November 5, 2013, http://www.nytimes.com/2013/11/06/nyregion/de-blasio-is-elected-new-york-city-mayor.html.

19. Benjamin R. Barber, *If Mayors Ruled the World: Dysfunctional Nations, Rising Cities* (New Haven: Yale University Press, 2013), 5, 340. Also see Bruce J. Katz and Jennifer Bradley, *The Metropolitan Revolution: How Cities and Metros Are Fixing Our Broken Politics and Fragile Economy* (Washington, DC: Brookings Institution Press, 2013), 171–72, 174, 176, 178. On progressive urban insurgencies, see Harold Meyerson, "The Revolt of the Cities," *The American Prospect* (2014), http://prospect.org/article/revolt-cities. For a collection of essays on progressive policy-making for New York City compiled by John Mollenkopf and Brad Lander, see *Toward a 21st Century City for All* at http://www.21cforall.org. For a skeptical analysis of the prospects for reducing urban inequality, see Richard Florida and Stephanie Garlock, "Why It's So Incredibly Difficult to Fight Urban Inequality," http://www.theatlanticcities.com/neighborhoods/2013/11/why-it-so-incredibly-difficult-fight-urban-inequality/7519/. For a survey of liberal urban politics in 2014, see Thomas B. Edsall, "Will Liberal Cities Leave the Rest of America Behind?" *New York Times*, April 29, 2014, at http://www.nytimes.com/2014/04/30/opinion/edsall-will-liberal-cities-leave-the-rest-of-america-behind.html. For an argument on why local organs of government, like community boards, need to gain the power to work to reduced the disorder caused by globalization, see Alex S. Vitale, *City of Disorder: How the Quality of Life Campaign Transformed New York Politics* (New York: New York University Press, 2008), 183–94.

20. Berman, "Emerging from the Ruins," 61.

21. On Hike the Heights 2012, see https://sites.google.com/site/hiketheheights/home, and report by Sarah Rahman in author's possession.

22. All details on the event are from author notes from ceremonies at the naming of Juan Rodriguez Way, May 15, 2013. Juan Rodríguez was also the subject of a panel discussion at the Dominican Studies Institute and a monograph by Anthony Stevens-Acevedo, Tom Weterings, and Leonor

Alvarez Frances, *Juan Rodriguez and the Beginnings of New York City* (New York: Dominican Studies Institute, 2013).

23. Before the advent of La Marina, the riverfront stretch that I cherished as a link to my dad's youth turned out to be the setting of a drug-dealing operation. On the bust at the Tubby Hook Café, see "New York City Special Narcotics Prosecutor Bridget G. Brennan Announces the Break Up of Gang Selling Drugs out of the Dyckman Street Marina," press release, Office of the Special Narcotics Prosecutor of the City of New York, December 15, 2006. On the transition from the Tubby Hook Café to La Marina, see "Barren Marina . . . ," at http://www.dnainfo.com/new-york/20091105/washington-heights-inwood/barren-marina-once-den-of-drugs-garbage-gets-new-life-inwood. The claim in the article that little happened on the site from the 1930s to the 1960s ignores the boathouse scene, which was dominated by working-class people and which came apart in the 1960s as men like my father turned toward suburban family life and a hurricane devastated his old boathouse. On La Marina and the controversies around it, see "La Marina Owners Address Traffic and Overcrowding Concerns" at http://www.dnainfo.com/new-york/20121018/washington-heights/la-marina-owners-address-traffic-overcrowding-concerns.

24. On this general point, see David Harvey, *Rebel Cities: From the Right to the City to the Urban Revolution* (Brooklyn: Verso, 2012), xvi. On the aftermath of the crime drop in northern Manhattan, see an editorial in the *Manhattan Times*, November 3, 2005, 6. My thanks to Eric Schneider for the point on the remaking of Manhattan for the world's leisure class.

25. Henri Lefebvre, *Writings on Cities*, translated and edited by Eleonore Kofman and Elizabeth Lebas (Malden, MA: Blackwell, 1996), 148.

INDEX

Coughlin, Charles E., 30
"Countersong to Walt Whitman," 97
crack cocaine, 157; community mobilizations against, 169–70, 173–75, 193; corruption and, 162–63; crime, violence, and, 162–65, 179; Dominicans and, 162–64, 194–96; impact of on Washington Heights, 1, 7, 157–59, 162–66, 171–72, 177–79, 192–95; landlords and, 193; police and, 164–65, 178–79, 184–85; revulsion at, 189; suburban customers and, 158–59, 162
Crenshaw, Dave, 1, 7, 174–75, 191
Crenshaw, Gwen, 152, 175
Crenshaw, Richard, 155, 175
crime, 1–2, 162, 175–76, 223; community responses to, 1, 7, 160, 169, 173–75, 178–79; drop in, 10, 188–90, 193–95, 208, 226–27; fear and, 114–15, 118–19, 159–62, 195, 197; in George Washington High School, 104–6; incarceration and, 228; media and, 162; as political issue, 32–33, 51, 55–56, 160–61, 166–68, 187–88, 193–95, 233–34; victims of, 46, 66, 119, 139, 160, 164–65, 179. See also crack cocaine; domestic violence; incarceration; police, New York City
Cruz, Angie, 202, 219
Cruz, Gustavo, 175
Cubans, 6, 125, 130, 229
Culpepper, John, 37

D'Amato, Alfonse, 2, 157
d'Amboise, Jacques (Joseph Ahearn), 35–36
Davidson, Irwin D., 48, 57–60, 63
de Blasio, Bill, 233–34
De La Cruz, Ramona, 100–101, 108–9
De Leon, Leoncio, 53, 58, 61
delinquency, juvenile, 38, 43, 51, 62–67. See also Farmer case
Democrats, 41, 157; dominance of liberal Democrats in northern Manhattan, 127–28; in New Deal era, 20–23, 27; as reformers and regulars, 123–24, 126–27
demonstrations: against drug dealing, 169–70; over policing, 160, 180–83; over schools, 95–96, 103–4
deportations, 228
Depression, 20–26
Devaney, John, 131
Diaz, Junot, 219
Dinkins, David, 135, 166; crime, policing, and, 160, 166–68, 185–87; riots of 1992 and, 181–85
Divanne, Marielys, 96
DNAinfo.com, 207
domestic violence, 146, 227–28
Dominican Republic: relations with United States, 96–99

Dominican Studies Institute of the City University of New York at City College, 214–15, 235
Dominican Women's Development Center, 144, 170
Dominicans: African Americans and, 100–101, 104–6, 221; drug trade and, 162–66, 170–71, 184–85, 196; ethnic identity and, 101, 142; families of, 145–46, 162–64; as immigrants, 98–99, 138, 141–43, 201–3, 230–31; Jews and, 149–52, 172–73, 215–16; New York City and, 141–42, 146–47, 152, 154–57, 201–3, 214–19, 235–36; organizations of, 144–47, 231; politics of, 142–47, 152–56; social and economic mobility of, 202–4, 229–31; suburbs and, 170; women among, 144–46, 203, 221–22; work and, 140–42, 152–53, 229–30. See also collective efficacy; poverty; transnationalism
drug dealers, attitudes toward, 164, 174–75, 179, 217, 273n24; fall of, 189–90; operations of, 1, 158–59, 162–63, 192–93, 227; violence and, 162, 178–79. See also crack cocaine
drugs, 227. See also crack cocaine
Dubnau, Dave, 152
Ducat, Vivian, 213–14
Dunleavey, Barry, 160
Dyckman Houses, 41, 113
Dyckman Street (boundary of Washington Heights and Inwood), 206

East Harlem, 26, 49, 66, 70, 77–78
economic conditions: New York City, 38–42, 112, 115–17, 152–53, 202–3, 229–30; northern Manhattan, 26, 112, 122–23, 230–32
Egan, Edward, 202
Eisenstadt, Peter, 91
El Diario de Nueva York, Farmer case and, 54, 61, 64
elections, mayoral in New York City: 1933, 20; 1957, 55–56; 1965, 86–88; 1977, 123–26; 1989, 166; 1993, 187; 2005, 206; 2013, 233–34
Eliot, Marjorie, 213–14, 225–26
Ellison, Ralph, 160
enclaves, life in, 6, 27, 31, 37, 122. See also neighborhoods; turf
EQUAL, 82
Espaillat, Adriano, 132, 155, 192
estates in northern Manhattan, 13–14
Estavillo, Nicholas, 165
ethnic and racial conflict: between Dominicans and African Americans, 100–101, 104–6, 191, 221; Irish and Jews, 30–33; Jews and Dominicans, 149–52. See also bridge building
exclusion, 5, 8, 18–20, 35–37, 40, 43–44, 47–49, 52, 59, 134, 149–51, 223

Faces Behind the Dolls/Los Rostros Detrás de las Muñecas (book, film), 218–19
Farmer, Michael, 46, 48, 58; murder of, 46, 59; press depictions of, 46, 51